PROPORTIONALITY IN INTERNATIONAL LAW

Proportionality in International Law

Michael Newton
VANDERBILT UNIVERSITY

Larry May
VANDERBILT UNIVERSITY

OXFORD
UNIVERSITY PRESS

OXFORD
UNIVERSITY PRESS

*Oxford University Press is a department of the University of Oxford. It furthers the University's objective of
excellence in research, scholarship, and education by publishing worldwide.*

Oxford   New York
Auckland   Cape Town   Dar es Salaam   Hong Kong   Karachi   Kuala Lumpur   Madrid
Melbourne   Mexico City   Nairobi   New Delhi   Shanghai   Taipei   Toronto

With offices in
Argentina   Austria   Brazil   Chile   Czech Republic   France   Greece   Guatemala   Hungary
Italy   Japan   Poland   Portugal   Singapore   South Korea   Switzerland   Thailand   Turkey
Ukraine   Vietnam

Oxford is a registered trademark of Oxford University Press in the UK and certain other countries.

Published in the United States of America by
Oxford University Press
198 Madison Avenue, New York, NY 10016

First issued as an Oxford University Press paperback, 2014.
ISBN 978-0-19-935505-1 (paperback : alk. paper)

Library of Congress Cataloging-in-Publication Data

Newton, Michael A., 1962- author.
  Proportionality in international law / Michael Newton, Larry May.
    pages cm
  Includes bibliographical references and index.
  ISBN 978-0-19-935503-7 (hardback : alk. paper)
1. Proportionality in law. I. May, Larry, author. II. Title.
  K247.N49 2014
  341.01—dc23

                                                                        2013039939

*To those who serve in harm's way
with honor and commitment to humanity*

Contents

1

INTRODUCTION

PROPORTIONALITY, ALONG WITH distinction, necessity, and humanity, make up the chief principles that have been thought to govern armed conflict for hundreds of years. There has been a close relationship between the work of philosophers writing in the Just War tradition and lawyers who work in international law, especially today in international criminal law. Proportionality is debated in these two domains but also, very importantly, in military academies and in boot camps where those who are assigned the task of fighting armed conflicts are told that if they act disproportionately they will face legal proceedings afterwards. Conduct later seen to be *disproportionate* also raises a host of political and operational complications that commanders know are best avoided if at all possible. It is our goal to provide a comprehensive and also understandable analysis of proportionality that is useful for those who often must make tragic choices during armed conflict.

The authors of this book bring diverse expertise to the topic of proportionality in international law. The book seeks to meld abstract philosophical and legal analysis with very specific and highly emotive contemporary combat cases. The cases are discussed largely from the perspective of those who must make decisions, often in the midst of armed conflict. We hope to bring to the proportionality debate both analytic rigor and also sensitivity to facts on the ground. We will succeed to the extent that we impart more clarity to our readers about what proportionality has meant and what it could mean going forward as well as encouraging our readers to appreciate the very difficult task of making proportionality assessments, often while bullets whiz overhead.

This book seeks to analyze the modern usages of proportionality in order to achieve a more complete understanding of the values that proportionality preserves.

The most widespread references to proportionality come in the *jus ad bellum* and *jus in bello* debates linked respectively to the initiation and conduct of armed conflicts. Proportionality is thus intimately linked to overarching concepts of self-defense, lawful force, and the controlled application of violence. Proportionality also has a distinctive usage in post-conflict settings, so called *jus post bellum*.[1] As we will document, the concepts of proportionality are also central tenets in the formation of the European Union (EU) and are thus important to the decision-making of constitutional courts. The same term occurs in such fields as human rights analysis, criminal sentencing decisions and other law enforcement scenarios, election disputes and how to secure representation, the regulation of international financial markets, and of course in the decisions about whether to wage war and how to do so lawfully.

In this introductory chapter, we will set the stage for our much more elaborate discussions later in the book. We will first briefly set out some of the central ideas of the book in section I. We will explain our overall orientation in this study as well as a sense of why proportionality calculations are so important and so contentious. Then in section II, we will give a detailed example, drawn from Afghanistan, of how proportionality is relevant today. In the third section, we will provide a preliminary sense of the kind of guidance for soldiers and commanders that we will offer in much greater detail by the end of the book.

I. A PRELIMINARY UNDERSTANDING OF *JUS IN BELLO* PROPORTIONALITY

Proportionality is the most controversial and arguably the most important when discussed in the context of armed conflict. The Latin phrase, *jus in bello*, has historically captured the rules and laws of war that concern the stage where a war has already been initiated and is now being fought. There are several well-recognized rules of armed conflict that set reasonable limits on how this fighting is to take place, such as that civilians should not be directly targeted. Proportionality is the rule that limits the severity of lethal force so that it only is properly employed in a way that is commensurate with the goal to be achieved.

The term proportionality recurs across an array of disciplines and usages; each conveys legally distinct meanings and applications as a technical matter. Chapters 4 and 5 contrast the applications of proportionality in both *jus ad bellum* (the law and morality of resort to force) and within *jus in bello* (the normative doctrines

---

[1] Melissa Labonte, *Jus Post Bellum, Peacebuilding, and Non-State Actors: Lessons from Afghanistan*, in ETHICS, AUTHORITY, AND WAR: NON-STATE ACTORS AND THE JUST WAR TRADITION 221–225 (2009), eds. Eric A. Heinze and Brent J. Steele. *Also see* LARRY MAY, AFTER WAR ENDS: A PHILOSOPHICAL PERSPECTIVE (2012).

applicable for using force in the midst of conflicts). The same term has very different meanings with often profound and context specific implications. One of the primary goals of this book is to clarify the boundaries of the proportionality concept. We hope that such clarity will in turn prevent reflexive acceptance that the term conveys common obligations, whatever the legal and philosophical context.

In the realm of mathematics and architecture, proportionality has rather objectively ascertainable implications. The frequentist interpretation of Bayes's theorem, for example, specifies that if "various alternatives are equally likely, and then some event is observed, the updated probabilities for the alternatives are proportional to the probabilities that the observed event would have occurred under those alternatives."[2] Thus, if a quantity x is proportional (directly) to another quantity y, then x is written as $x = ky$, where k is called the Constant of Proportionality.[3] By contrast, proportionality as applied within moral and legal discussions is inherently complex because it is not simply matter of mathematical expectancy or extrapolation of a known premise.

Proportionality limits the use of lethal force within the war-fighting domain by reference to a relatively fixed standard: The costs of the use of lethal force must be outweighed by the value of what the lethal force is meant to accomplish, the military objectives of the use of force. As we will often characterize it, proportionality involves the application of a fixed standard by individuals who must subjectively consider context and circumstance in assessing the relative weights of the military objectives they pursue. Proportionality sets limits on what commanders and soldiers can do—they are not free to act in their own discretion. The thresholds of proportionality we will discuss, especially in the final chapter, permit greater or lesser permissibility, but that permissibility is relative to the fixed, rather stringent sets of restrictions (what we will call thresholds within which the principle of proportionality functions as a default governing constraint).

Some have said that in war commanders must be given deference to take those actions that will win wars. To a certain extent, *jus in bello* proportionality is both somewhat consistent with this view and also somewhat opposed to it. At the moment of decision, the commander has to assess whether the use of lethal force is appropriate, given what the commander judges to be necessary to accomplish the mission he or she has been given. But in another sense, this discretion is limited in that the commander is supposed to act only on the basis of what a reasonable person would do in these circumstances, and the thresholds of proportionality we will set

---

[2] Bayes's Theorem Principle of Proportionality, available at http://www.cut-the-knot.org/Probability/Proportionality.shtml

[3] Constant of Proportionality, available at http://www.icoachmath.com/math_dictionary/Constant_of_Proportionality.html

out are fixed in the sense of reflecting what any reasonable commander should find acceptable.

Reasonableness means, at a minimum, that in judging the values of the means against the goal to be achieved, the decision is not fully up to the discretion of the commander—since if the commander acts unreasonably he or she has gone beyond the bounds of this discretion. At the moment of decision, the commander is the one who is best placed to weigh whether the use of lethal force is appropriate. But even in that pressure-cooker environment, proportionality sets the following limit: Act only in ways that are reasonable, that someone in the shoes of the commander would view as appropriate.

The shorthand phrase *reasonable commander* or *average actor* hardly captures the complexity of these interrelated factors, and the subjective valuations at the center of even the most elemental proportionality calculation. Yet, in deciding what is proportionate and what is disproportionate, especially during war or armed conflict, what is a reasonable assessment is about the best that can be hoped for. Nonetheless, as this book proceeds we will give advice to decision-makers about better and worse ways to make these assessments.

In this book, we will spend considerable time setting out the historical sources of *jus in bello* proportionality as well as the myriad legal frameworks today that define what proportionality means as a matter of international law. Our contention is that there is a core of *jus in bello* proportionality that has remained fixed for generations. A major goal of our book is to set out that core as clearly and comprehensively as possible. Here we aim to clear up confusion.

But another major goal of our book is critically to assess the current law of proportionality in normative terms. A distinction drawn in law is important here. The actual state of law at any given moment is called *lex lata* whereas what that law should be, from a given normative perspective, is called *lex ferenda*. We are interested in both of these projects: the description of the current state of international law especially concerning *jus in bello* proportionality (lex lata), and the normative assessment, often drawn in human rights terms, of what that law should be (lex ferenda).

At the moment, the long-standing rules of *jus in bello* proportionality as articulated in international humanitarian law are being challenged by those who are strongly influenced by human rights norms. As one example, traditional proportionality assessment was focused almost exclusively on weighing the likely collateral damage (the indirect damage to civilians) against the military objective. The lives of soldiers on both sides of the armed conflict were not weighed in the calculation of whether the lethal use of force was disproportionate in a given case. This was and still is the current state of the law (*lex lata*) of proportionality.

But many people are asking why the lives of soldiers should not be added into the *jus in bello* proportionality calculation. One reason, of course, is that if the lives of soldiers were given very great weight, lethal force would rarely if ever be proportionate. Wars could not be fought and won if a given commander could lawfully use lethal force against lawful targets only in strict proportion to the casualties anticipated or suffered by friendly forces. In this book, we will not seriously consider revised proportionality rules that would make all lethal action during war disproportionate. Instead, we are primarily interested in giving advice to soldiers and commanders who have already entered into combat situations. In this sense, we take an explicitly soldier-oriented perspective in seeking to understand and map the contours of proportionality

Nonetheless, we will ask why it is, from the standpoint of what the law should be (*lex ferenda*), that the lives of soldiers should not be part of the proportionality calculation. And in fact today, commanders are raising just this question: Should not the lives of the soldiers under my command matter in assessing whether a given strategy or tactic is proportionate or disproportionate? And should we not also ask about the lives of "enemy" soldiers? Taking a soldier-centered perspective in our book will also cause us to wonder, as a matter of what the law should be, if the current state of law should not be changed so as better to support the lives of soldiers.

The human rights concerns just voiced will give a distinctive flavor to our analysis in this book. It is important though to notice two uses of human rights in what follows. The first use of human rights is as a normative perspective, in which every person's life and liberty is to be respected and given equal weight. But there is another use of human rights, namely, as a currently recognized legal regime governing non-international hostile situations. We will sometimes refer to a human rights perspective as a normative framework (*lex ferenda*), and sometimes refer to human rights as a matter of accepted law (*lex lata*). In Chapter 5, these two uses are brought together, but only partially.

Before setting out an elaborate example, let us briefly indicate the framework of proportionality if armed force is at issue. In our view, there are five distinct thresholds for *jus in bello* proportionality that we envision: (1) for war or armed conflict; (2) for the special case of self-defense during war and in other contexts; (3) for emergency situations, such as terrorist attacks, and for other hostile acts committed by non-State actors against States; (4) for the preemption of hostilities and the accompanying erosion of human rights and safety; and (5) for areas where states exercise a very high degree of control over the population, such as during occupation or relief operations in the wake of natural disasters. These thresholds establish increasingly stringent proportionality conditions, ending with a situation that is almost entirely governed by human rights considerations rather than war-fighting norms. As we will show, the human rights situations are the most stringent and the situations governed by the laws and customs of war, especially involving self-defense, are the most permissive threshold restraints that govern what are proportionate responses. These threshold considerations are what we earlier referred to as the fixed component of proportionality assessments. The subjective component involves how these are interpreted and applied to concrete cases in very specific contexts. We will next provide an elaborate example of the issues and problems that arise today when commanders try to decide when it is reasonable to use lethal force. Here three issues are most important: self-defense, context, and comparable weights.

II. AN EXAMPLE OF FRIENDLY FIRE BETWEEN THE UNITED STATES AND PAKISTAN

We now will raise an example to illustrate the importance of the proportionality debate and focus attention on what we regard as the imperative need for a more precise understanding of its components and normative import, especially concerning context and comparability. For more than ten years after September 11, 2001, the United States and its allies waged war in Afghanistan against the Taliban, who were believed to be harboring the perpetrators of the attacks on the World Trade Towers in New York City. Much of the war was fought in the tribally controlled, semi-autonomous, regions of Afghanistan on its border with Pakistan. As Taliban fighters sought sanctuary outside the borders of Afghanistan, Operation Enduring Freedom often spilled over into the mountainous regions of Pakistan due to the tenuous authority exercised by the Pakistani government.

On the night of November 26 and the morning of November 27, 2011, 24 Pakistani troops were killed by the US just inside of the Pakistan border. American forces had been sent to the village of Maya several miles from the Afghanistan-Pakistan border in order to engage and clear Taliban fighters from the village. Soon after arriving at Maya, US soldiers reported that they were fired upon first by machine gun fire and then by increasingly accurate mortar fire that seemed to originate from a position on the ridgeline very near the Pakistan border.

The Pakistanis claimed that the firing was not directed at the U.S. troops. To their credit, Pakistani officials had established the two outposts some 1,000 feet apart in an effort to help seal the notoriously porous border which would have had the salutary benefits of preventing the enemy from seeking safe haven on Pakistani soil and protecting Pakistani tribes from cross-border attacks. The response by the United States to the perceived attack against their troops was to launch helicopter and gunship attacks for between one and two hours against the Pakistani positions, resulting in death of 24 Pakistani troops and destruction of the Pakistani military base.

The outcry from Pakistan was immediate and fierce, and the military effect on North Atlantic Treaty Organization (NATO) operations was equally immediate and nearly disabling. The Pakistanis termed the sustained attacks as a "grave infringement" of national sovereignty, and closed the Torkham border crossing causing trucks full of needed supplies to sit idly at the border. Thousands of Pakistani citizens protested in the streets, and the military funerals were the centerpiece of profound national unity and grief. Labeling the American response as "unprovoked" the Pakistani Prime Minister Yousef Rasa Gilani announced that the US would be required to vacate the Shamsi Air Base located in southwestern Baluchistan province.

Neither side, Pakistan or the United States denied that Pakistani military casualties resulted from US helicopter attacks. In fact, this incident was the most important friendly-fire incident of the entire decade of war. There is dispute about whether Pakistani forces intentionally fired on the US ground forces in Maya village. There is also dispute about the length and intensity of the US attack, particularly in view of the Pakistani claim to have informed "US/ISAF about the incident at multiple levels within minutes of initiation of US/ISAF fire." The Pakistani response bluntly concluded, "The US Investigative Report, is structured around the argument of 'self-defense' and 'proportional use of force,' an argument 'which is contrary to the facts and therefore self serving.'"

The Pakistani claim that the US response was disproportionate turns on three issues. First, was the US response one of self-defense? Second, even if in self-defense, was the response excessive for initial self-defense given the context? Third, did the response that lasted perhaps as long as two hours, and was by all accounts overwhelming, risk much more in terms of casualties than what was to be gained? We will examine each of these issues in light of our preliminary suggestions about proportionality concerning weighing and context that we develop more fully in the next chapter. Notice, initially, that the proportionality considerations were not here about collateral damage to civilians but to combatants.

Self-defense often is a threshold consideration for justifying armed attacks. In terms of proportionality, self-defense is a threshold consideration in that armed action would not normally be justified at all unless it satisfied this, or a few other possible, threshold considerations that made the armed action prima facie justified. Yet even if armed action is completely warranted on the basis of soldiers defending themselves, proportionality poses a set of secondary limitations, such as whether or not the type of lethal force, and its extent, was warranted to overcome the self-defense threat. But if one cannot make a case for self-defense at all, then proportionality issues would be very different and would have to satisfy a much more restrictive assessment. This is because the response would not even be prima facie justified as self-defense in the absence of positive identification of an enemy as required by the

Central Command Rules of Engagement (ROE) or the declaration of an enemy as a hostile force that would authorize deliberate targeting based on the status of that enemy force.

Apart from the self-defense debate, the second consideration concerns context. Here we should first think about whether the US lethal response against Pakistani soldiers was accidental or intentional. Of course, the response was meant to be lethal, but from the US perspective, the context was a response aimed at countering an enemy attack by Taliban insurgents. But was that a reasonable interpretation of the context? The Pakistanis claimed that it was not reasonable since the US knew that there were Pakistani soldiers in the area. And was it the case that the killing of Pakistani troops, as opposed to killing of Taliban fighters, was intentional?

These matters of context are very important for determining whether the US response was proportionate since it might be argued that stopping an attack by enemies takes much more fire-power than stopping an attack by supposed allies who were mistakenly shelling US troops. Indeed, it could be argued that the only way to be sure that enemy insurgents would stop attacking US troops, who claimed to be tied down and unable to retreat, would have been to kill all of them. There is one other important contextual matter: the US and Afghan operations were conducted in that particular region at that time without prior notice to the Pakistanis because previous operations had been compromised by intelligence leaks to the Taliban operating in the border region.

It is interesting to consider how a past history of interaction can affect proportionality in such cases. The Pakistanis claim that there had been four similar incidents in which Pakistani border troops were killed, supposedly accidentally, and where US officials promised to make sure it did not happen again. Assuming this is true, since the United States did not deny it, the question is whether this contextual history of interaction should affect the assessment of proportionality of the November 26, 2011, incident. Furthermore, Pakistani officials vigorously asserted that they had given NATO a map with the marked location of the two outposts. The context of this incident certainly does change when considering the past history of interaction. It could explain why the Pakistanis continued to fire, perhaps fearing that the US forces would again kill them, as indeed they did. It could also make it less likely that these killings could be simply written off as non-culpable accidents.

The third consideration concerns how to weigh the expected losses. This is the core consideration of most proportionality assessments. On one side of the balance is the concern for the lives of the US troops under fire and seemingly unable to retreat. The competing considerations involve the relative military worth of the lives of those firing on the US troops. And here is a key, highly contentious, matter: Do we weigh the lives of enemies as less than lives of allies? Today, many philosophers have argued that the lives of those who act unjustly during war should be treated differently than those who act justly. We do not share this view. But even if we could tell whether it was the United States or Pakistani forces that were in the right that is not the only issue. Regardless of which side one fights for, in our view self-defense can arise nonetheless. We take up this issue in much more detail in Chapter 6.

One more context specific consideration here is that the U.S. forces dispatched an F-15 fighter and an AC-130 gunship to shoot flares in a show of force to demonstrate that NATO forces were clearly on the receiving end of the shelling due to the fact that the Taliban have no air assets. Yet from the perspective of the US commanders on the ground, the fact that the Pakistani fire continued following the show of airpower seemed to confirm the source of the fire as coming from an enemy and the reality that force was the only method for eliminating the threat posed to American lives. This illustrates the operational reality that, although the proportionality principle is important, and often paramount, it is by no means independent of other principles and considerations. As we will illustrate in subsequent chapters, proportionality is only one of an array of other applicable norms, *inter alia* those of distinction, humanity, and military necessity.

Every combat operation functions within the larger fabric of the laws and customs of warfare, to include the interrelated backdrop of other legal tenets. As one last illustration of this interconnected set of legal imperatives, consider the duty imposed upon an attacking force by Article 57(2)(c) of Additional Protocol I to the Geneva Conventions, to provide "effective advance warning" of any attacks "which may affect the civilian population, unless circumstances do not permit."

The correlative duty of the commander is to "take all feasible precautions in the choice of means and methods of attack with a view to avoiding, and in any event to minimizing, incidental loss of civilian life, injury to civilians and damage to civilian objects."[4] From the perspective of coalition forces, the fire emanated from a remote region with no known civilian structures or population, and did not abate following a show of force. Thus, the proportionality principle was a secondary concern to the immediate and overwhelming self-defense need to end the threat.

In hindsight, and from the comfort and safety of western offices, we must ask whether the risk to the Pakistani soldiers was offset by the risk to US soldiers. At least in this proportionality calculation we have lives on the one side and lives on the other, so a seemingly simpler proportionality calculation could be made than if the two things to be weighed are seemingly incommensurable. But the calculation is more complex than that. For the other thing to be added into the mix in the broader

---

[4] Protocol Additional to the Geneva Conventions of August 12, 1949, and relating to the Protection of Victims of International Armed Conflicts (Protocol I), June 8, 1977, Article 51(2)(a)(ii).)

sense is the strategic objectives of the US military mission, which indeed saved civilian lives and was intended in the larger sense to build an Afghan society that is free of the depredations and human rights abuses suffered at the hands of the Taliban. As a matter of intellectual fairness, how can the larger salutary purposes for the use of force be considered as part of the proportionality analysis, while the circumstances of a controversial and aggressive war are discounted when evaluating the appropriate and proportionate response of forces in the midst of such conflicts?

Finally, the relative value placed on the military objectives is sometimes highly contested. From the US perspective, defeating the Taliban in this border area was valued very highly, while such defeat would prove crippling from the Taliban perspective. From the Pakistani perspective, such a defeat may have been seen as a decidedly mixed value. As a result, context will again intrude into our other considerations, such as weight, and make the overall proportionality assessment very difficult.

III. SOME PRELIMINARY DIRECTIONS

What is clear from the various accounts of what went wrong in Maya village is that though they invoked proportionality as the dispositive measure, neither the Americans nor the Pakistanis were precise in their assessments of its dimensions. They also did not have shared criteria for assessing its threshold inquiries. This is the aspect of the controversy that is of concern to us, and which is highly illustrative of the costs of indeterminacy in the international debates over proportionality.

Proportionality is integral to military professionalism. If there can be safe harbor for war-fighters accused of disproportionate acts because there is no shared consensus on the criteria for evaluating the conduct in question, then proportionality becomes a hollow constraint. Noncombatant lives and property would be further endangered if proportionality becomes the property of the adversary with the most compliant media and the most well-tuned propaganda machine. Unless there is a refocused international clarity and common understanding of its parameters in international dialogue, war-fighters may well begin simply to discount proportionality in practice.

The Pakistanis admit that they fired in a nearly random fashion, hardly taking into account what were the likely consequences of such firing. US/ISAF authorities admitted that various protocols were not followed that could have allowed them to identify who was shooting at their troops in Maya. Could the incident, and ensuing loss of life, have been averted if proper proportionality assessments had been made, even when the adrenaline of incoming fire affected decision-making? With the benefit of hindsight it seems probable that the incident could have been averted—since in the abstract, the US had no reason to fire on Pakistanis sitting on their side of the Afghanistan and Pakistan border. Even if both sides had engaged in the same kind of proportionality assessment, unless they were both using the same metric, using common assumptions, and had the same sense of what was valuable and how it was to be valued, the tragedy might still have occurred due to the inherent frictions of war.

Many of the objections to the use of proportionality focus on how hard it is for commanders to make such calculations when they are in battle or in other situations where quick decisions need to be made and where there is no time for elaborate calculations. As in the debates in ethical theory about utilitarianism, we will respond to this objection by offering rules of thumb as aids to commanders who must make very quick decisions in certain situations. Since we do not think that proportionality turns on what is merely extensive, we do not find it as difficult for commanders to make proportionality judgments as do some critics. In any event, modern targeting principles operate on a very rigid computerized analysis that is conducted with the full participation of a battle staff, and frequently subject to competing considerations in political channels. Commanders and others who make proportionality judgments must only determine whether their projected conduct is on the positive side of the threshold separating proportionate from disproportionate behavior. And such assessments, we believe, in light of the rules of thumb and threshold considerations we will propose, are not nearly as difficult as critics often claim.

We will discuss several such rules of thumb and operational principles as the book develops. Let us here mention one principle that partially responds to the weighing problem. The principle could be called the *civilian precautionary principle*: "whenever civilian lives are greatly risked incidental to a tactic, very clear and weighty military objectives have to be enunciated for the tactic to be prima facie proportionate." This principle indicates a special context and an appropriate level of review and action but will have to be refined in order to be usable in concrete cases. For example, there is one very common ROE that prohibits unobserved indirect artillery fire into built-up civilian areas in the absence of express authority from a more senior level of command. Our position is that such a rule of thumb should be accepted as an aspect of proportionality and common sense even absent express articulation in the ROE unless imminent circumstances of self-defense warrant exception. To be clear, commanders are certainly free to insist upon such a constraint as the default principle for the use of artillery fire as a matter of unit discipline, though the circumstances of imminent individual self-defense or defense of others may warrant exceptions.

As another variation on this theme, consider the plight of an American infantry unit in the early spring of 2012. A Q37 radar positioned at a remote combat outpost in eastern Afghanistan consistently acquired and tracked the flight of enemy 107mm rockets that were landing in a remote portion of the province, far from coalition troops. The remote location, use of the same point of origin, and roughly the same point of impact led U.S. forces to conclude that insurgents were using the position to train new rocket teams and improve their accuracy. Intercepted radio communications verified that a Russian-speaking individual was leading this training. This rocket training was followed by an overall increase in the accuracy of indirect fire aimed at US forward operating bases and combat outposts.

Using terrain analysis and unmanned aerial vehicles to identify patterns of life of combatants in the area, US forces planned an operation to disrupt insurgent training efforts. This operation centered on a heavy barrage of artillery fire aimed at the most frequently used point of origin as well as likely locations for insurgent observers. Due to the unique nature of the mission—firing artillery at individuals who were training insurgents rather than directly engaging US forces—the operation was sent to higher headquarters for approval. To the disappointment of company and battalion-level leaders, the mission was disapproved due to concerns that engaging enemies under these conditions would not be consistent with the standing rules of engagement at that time. Here the problem was not of a built-up area, but an unverified concern that someone other than an enemy insurgent might have a chance of being injured. The higher headquarters thus, perhaps unwisely, weighted a statistical chance of injury to civilians or foreign trainers above the certainty of added risk to US forces from well-directed incoming indirect fire.

The principles and guidelines we will develop will largely be of the following sort: principles that guide behavior in a class of common cases in which proportionality considerations arise. We have already seen another rule of thumb in what was discussed earlier: "try to find a common denominator so that the weighing can be done between things that are similar not dissimilar." This principle will have to be further refined given the evident problems with dealing with weighing and context.

Proportionality is at its core intended to be applied by war-fighters as an extension of disciplined professionalism even in the midst of mind-numbing fatigue, adrenalin, and soul felt fear. However, there is widespread anecdotal evidence that because proportionality is so frequently invoked as a form of political posturing, and so frequently misunderstood in application, listeners are prone to discount the need for discriminating analysis and application of its precise meaning due to its very familiarity. Because proportionality is such a textured concept that is prone to inconsistent application and occasionally paralyzing debate, its imprecision carries the risk that it will be honored in name only, and discarded by war-fighters when it is most important in practice. The persistent problem is that the omnipresence of the concept of proportionality, both in the context of *jus ad bellum* and *jus in bello* debates, is nearly matched by the misunderstandings, misapplications, and misstatements associated with its use. Recurring debates over the application of proportionality inspired this work.

Proportionality may well be the most controversial imperative in modern conflicts from the legal, moral, and political perspectives. This is particularly problematic from the perspective of the war-fighter given the emergence of a globalized system of international accountability and post-conflict justice mechanisms. Nevertheless, the gap between the internationally accepted articulations of proportionality and its applications in practice cannot be permitted to widen. The mere invocation of proportionality cannot become an effective extension of combat power by serving to cripple combatant capabilities artificially. This, then, is the goal of this work, and we shall spend the next eleven chapters explicating our views for preserving, and also evaluating, the proportionality principle. In Chapter 2, we will begin this task by providing a detailed analysis of what proportionality means, at its most basic before, in Chapter 3, then surveying the many ways that proportionality is used, especially in very diverse legal contexts, with a goal to understanding the way proportionality might be different in the context of international law.

2

WHAT IS PROPORTIONALITY?

IN ITS SIMPLEST formulation, *proportionality* means that a response or action must be commensurate with the anticipated goal to be achieved. War and armed conflict, the primary subject of this book, must be initiated and conducted, as well as ended, proportionately. At its simplest, to act disproportionately in war or armed conflict is to use clearly excessive force given the goals to be accomplished.[1] Proportionality allows the assessment of otherwise competing, or even seemingly incompatible, operational imperatives. Despite its seeming simplicity, and contrary to much writing in this domain, we will argue that proportionality places severe restraints in these areas of war and armed conflict. Proportionality is the key principle that requires the use of violence to be in some sense measured and also humane. Soldiers and other combatants have rights, and these rights carry commensurate correlative duties that require that the loss of lives must be offset by equally serious matters if the initiation, conduct, or ending of war is to be justified.

Ours is the "era of proportionality" in the sense that one encounters proportionality as an integral aspect of legal and moral discourse in virtually every effective legal system.[2] Proportionality occupies a central position between military efficiency and moral fairness. Military commanders see proportionality as an element of the professional ethos that provides the latitude needed to accomplish their strategic and tactical mandates. Public perceptions may see precisely the same actions from a distance and conclude that the doctrine permits commanders more latitude than needed. It often does not help that the details of the debate are hidden from public

---

[1] Here it is important not to confuse "clearly excessive" with "merely extensive," as we argue in Chapter 6.
[2] AHARON BARAK, PROPORTIONALITY: CONSTITUTIONAL RIGHTS AND THEIR LIMITATIONS (2012).

view; nor is there precise popular agreement on the interface between competing bodies of law and moral principles.

In this chapter, we will discuss some of the conceptual difficulties in understanding and grounding a concept of proportionality in war and armed conflict in a way that is useful for scholars. But as in the rest of the book, our primary intention is to address those commanders and soldiers who must be the practitioners of proportionality. In the first section, we will address the question of what proportionality is at its most basic. In the second section, we will address the most difficult components of proportionality, how comparisons are to be made and why context is so important. In the third section, we will examine how proportionality is understood at the International Criminal Court (ICC). In the fourth section, we provide a few more examples. And in the fifth section, we address the overriding problem of how a fixed standard of proportionality can be understood within the context of decisions, for instance by commanders, that are subjective. Proper proportionality analysis employs a fixed standard understood in terms of thresholds that, when crossed, requires certain behavior, but the processes of weighing the behavior and the determination of context and circumstance involved in that weighing are both subjective. With this chapter, we will set the stage for more detailed analysis to follow in later chapters.

I. WHAT IS PROPORTIONALITY AT ITS MOST BASIC?

At its most basic level, proportionality requires a subjective weighing of two fixed values. The Oxford English Dictionary (OED) echoes the way fixed standards are part of proportionality by describing proportion as the "relation between one thing and another in terms of size, quantity, number, or the like; comparative relation, ratio." However, the OED also frames "proportion" in a more useful, yet subjective manner: the appropriate, fitting, or pleasing relation (of size, etc.) between things or parts of a thing; the due relation of one part to another; balance, symmetry, and harmony.

According to Black's *Law Dictionary*, the term *proportionate* in law means "Adjusted to something else according to a certain rate of comparative relation." The plain legal dictionary definition then refers the reader to the explanation of *pro rata*. At its simplest, proportionality requires the decision maker to reach two or more evaluative judgments and assess those judgments against each other. The definition of pro rata helps us understand proportionality by employing the following example:

> If a corporation has ten shareholders, each of whom has 10 percent of the stock, a pro rata dividend distribution of $1,000 would mean that each shareholder would receive $100.

This is seemingly a very easy case. Each of the ten shareholder's proportionate dividend is 10 percent of the $1,000 total dividend, or $100. But the simplicity is somewhat misleading, since the values have been fixed to start with. We are adjusting dividends to shares of stock. And both of these can be given a numeric measure so that it is relatively easy to figure out what each shareholder's proportionate share should be.

The great challenge in practice lies in balancing subjective and often shifting relationships in a manner that sustains a relationship of "balance, symmetry, harmony" envisioned by the OED. And so the first thing to discuss is how to get seeming incommensurables to be such that they can be weighed and measured against each other. To do so, a common denominator must be found. Finding such a common denominator is difficult. The difficulty can be illustrated by comparing civilian lives on the one hand and military objectives on the other, as is true in the traditional proportionality assessment in international humanitarian law.

In many aspects of life, proportionality assessments are relatively easy. But then we come up against cases in which there are apples on the one side and oranges on the other, and no clear common denominator for fruits. We seem to be blocked by our inability to translate the values of these fruits in terms of some third factor, or even to translate the value of one, the apple, in terms of the value of the other, the orange. About proportionality in war, Michael Walzer has said "proportionality turns out to be a hard criterion to apply, for there is no ready way to establish an independent or stable view of the values against which the destruction of war is to be measured."[3] Wartime proportionality assessments involve weighing military objectives against the loss of civilians or soldiers likely to occur from securing the military objective. And Walzer is right to say that *military objectives* and *lives* do not have an easy common denominator. What Walzer and others have not so clearly understood is the way that context also matters.

Because of the importance of context, proportionality is what philosophers sometimes call a *three-place predicate.* Proportionality is a weighing of what is likely to be lost, say, lives (x), compared to what is likely to be gained, say, a given military objective (y), in a specific context (z), say, if all other ways to achieve y have been exhausted. The contexts can include those in which other alternatives have been, or have not been exhausted; one State is significantly stronger, or weaker, than another State; one State is clearly defending, or aggressing, against another State; or a State, or non-State actor, is opposed by another State, or non-State actor. In each of these contexts, there will be at least slightly different assessments about how to compare lives lost and military objectives gained.

---

[3] MICHAEL WALZER, JUST AND UNJUST WARS 129 (1977).

II. COMPARABILITY AND CONTEXT

What is a proportionate response even in a two-person case often seems like an easy concept to understand, but it often turns out to be highly complex in application. Think about a case of two children, one of whom has just hit the other on the arm. If the second responds by hitting the first similarly on the arm, we may have an example of proportionate response. But it may be that the second child is entitled to do more than this—we may be a situation in which the threshold of self-defense is relevant. Yet without special considerations obtaining, such as a history of such aggressive behavior on the part of the first child, during which a similar response has not deterred future attacks, the proportionate response is the maximal response that can reasonably be justified as a response to the first attack. On this construal, proportionality of response sets a limit. And though it is sometimes justifiable to go beyond this limit, as in some cases of self-defense, to do so requires reference to special considerations.

Consider the problem of assessing weights. One standard proportionality question is whether a specific tactic is proportionate to its goal. Assume that the goal is achieving a particular military objective, such as securing a road so that military vehicles can proceed to their destinations. What is thrown into the balance is the loss of lives or damage to protected property as collateral damage from the road-securing operation. We are in the predicament of trying to ascertain how to weigh civilian lives risked against getting military vehicles moved expeditiously to legitimate military destinations.

But how is this weighing to be done? As we said, one typically looks for a common denominator. Perhaps the military objective can be reconceptualized in terms of lives as well. If so, perhaps proportionality will indeed be a simple matter. But military objectives rarely can be so readily translated into lives saved that they can be easily weighed against lives likely to be lost as a matter of collateral damage. In almost any conceivable tactical situation, there will also be relevant second- and third-order considerations that might well affect the proportionality balance in either direction. This thorny calculus is complicated by larger considerations over the most expeditious or advisable way to end the hostilities. The cessation of conflict is indeed often the only sure way to end the suffering and tremendous carnage caused by modern armed conflicts.

One of the most interesting recent debates about this topic concerns the context of whether or not the war to be fought is defensive or aggressive. Some within the Just War tradition have claimed that if one fights in an aggressive war, then whatever military advantages one anticipates from the use of a given tactic or weapon, those advantages must be heavily discounted because they are themselves in the service of a larger war that is unjustified. If one accepts this argument, then the larger *jus ad bellum* context can make more of a difference in *jus in bello* proportionality assessments than any other factor. We will offer our reasons to doubt this destabilizing proposition, even as we recognize the pull it has on many people's intuitions about these issues.

To be clear, the term *proportionality* has legally distinct meanings and applications as a technical matter in both *jus ad bellum* (the law of resort to force) and within *jus in bello* (the legal doctrine applicable for using force in the midst of conflicts)—these involve the threshold considerations such as self-defense. Yet, the same term has very different meanings with very different and often profound implications. It is not a simple matter of mathematical or the unthinking extrapolation of a known premise, but not everything is up for grabs either. We will discuss these matters at length in our book.

We are concerned with proportionality in international law, especially in armed conflict. The example of the two children is apt in some ways, but also problematic in several other respects, if used as a complete guide to wartime situations. In war or armed conflict, we need to ask why retaliatory violence is indeed justified at all, and why it is that proportionate retaliation has a prima facie claim to be acceptable. To think from the perspective of the historical Jesus, one might well ask why the proper response to being hit is not merely "to turn the other cheek." Hugo Grotius asked this question in the context of war at the beginning of his seminal 1625 book, *De Jure Belli ac Pacis*, seemingly because whether lethal violence can ever be an appropriate and justifiable response is a question that needs to be addressed before considerations such as proportionality can be broached.[4] In his classic work published in 1758, Emer de Vattel cautioned that "Whoever knows what war really is, whoever will reflect upon its terrible effects and disastrous consequences, will readily agree that it should not be undertaken without the most urgent reasons for doing so."[5] Proportionality considerations, hence, are ones that arise in the middle of a discussion, as it were. Even in the seemingly simple case of the two children, we need to know whether one child is much bigger, stronger, or older than the other child. We also should have some knowledge of the relevant history of interactions between these children. Proportionality can only occur at

[4] HUGO GROTIUS, THE LAW OF WAR AND PEACE, at ch. 2 (Francis W. Kelsey trans., Oxford Clarendon Press 1925) (1625).

[5] EMER DE VATTEL, LE DROIT DES GENS, OU PRINCIPES DE LA LOI NATURELLE, APPLIQUÉ À LA CONDUITE ET AUX AFFAIRES DES NATIONS ET DES SOUVERAINS (THE LAW OF NATIONS, OR PRINCIPLES OF THE LAW OF NATURE, APPLIED TO THE CONDUCT AND AFFAIRS OF NATIONS AND SOVEREIGNS), Bk. III. Ch. III §24 243 (1758) (trans. Charles G. Fenwick 1916).

the beginning, rather than the middle, of a conversation if little is known or at least, given what is known, there do not appear to be any special considerations. If there are no special considerations, proportionality is thought to be very important because it is seemingly a clear and uncontroversial way quickly to decide what responses are justified and what responses are unjustified.

Consider again the case of the two children. Assume that the children have been acting out roles in a play and the first child was supposed to hit the other child on the arm as a signal that the second child was to get up and sing. Given this context, it is not appropriate for the second child to hit the first at all, never mind in a way similar to how the first child hit her. Here is how context and special considerations matter even in very simple cases. In the complexity of warfare and shifting strategy, proportionality considerations may well warrant restraint that seems appropriate in the specific context, but seems utterly out of place in light of larger strategic considerations. Conversely, as we shall see in Chapter 12, some limitations articulated in terms of proportionality may well be undesirable from the standpoint of the actors under fire, but mandated by the larger political or strategic goals of the operation. This is especially problematic in the age of new media in which every incident will be reported, spun, and dissected across cultures and continents.

Inter-State relations are much more complex than interpersonal ones, but we can see another analogy between individuals and States that should give us pause. The expression "saber-rattling" is ages old and refers to the actions of States that seem seriously menacing but are really best seen as if they were scripted actions in a stage-play. The proper response to saber-rattling is either to ignore it or engage in similar saber-rattling. It is not appropriate to attack, even though that might be appropriate if a real threat had been initiated or is deemed to be imminent. Of course, trying to discern whether the context is one of saber-rattling, a prelude to aggressive war, or a genuine and completely lawful effort to deter an attack and thus preserve peace, is often very difficult.

Another matter to think about initially is that proportionality is often dependent on roles. Imagine that one party is a professional boxer, and the other party is not. The boxer may be trained to retaliate "blow-for-blow" against other boxers. But if one is outside the ring, the boxer's retaliatory response to non-boxers must be muted compared with the retaliatory response appropriate to other professional boxers in the ring. Similarly, professional soldiers are trained to respond "blow-for-blow" against other professional soldiers while on the battlefield. But proportionate response will be very different for the professional soldier, as also for the professional boxer, when encountering people who do not have similar, and often lethal, retaliatory skills.

So, there might be two quite different conceptions of proportionate response here based on the roles the actors play.

The idea that *jus in bello* proportionality means that the commander must employ forces or fire in a "like for like" manner that allows the enemy to dictate the terms of battle and cedes the tactical initiative is deeply flawed. On the other hand, as we will discuss in detail in Chapter 6, the technical application of proportionality as a matter of *jus in bello* may well be complicated in practice by the application of human rights principles that derive from this role-based discrepancy.

On one level, it may be that nearly anything that a boxer does to a non-boxer in terms of the use of violent force is disproportionate. And, similarly, it could be argued that nearly any violent force used by soldiers against civilians is also disproportionate. If this is true, then proportionality can set very severe limits on what can be done in armed conflict. In any event, we can say that proportionality is about limits set when considering context.

An important difficulty, when faced with issues concerning war and armed conflict, is that the values often appear incommensurable. Chapter 5 provides the detailed historical evolution of this familiar dimension of the *jus in bello* practice. In order subjectively to assess the values, then, one must to a certain extent defer to the perspective of the reasonable decision maker, or at least acknowledge the reality that decisions are often made under suboptimal conditions with often imperfect or inaccurate information. And in order to do such weighing or comparing, context matters to the extent that the values we place on these two factors will vary considerably from situation to situation. Nonetheless, the framework is meant to be fixed and consistent.

In the modern era of accountability, it can be reasonably forecast that a court or arbitral panel may well engage in a post hoc reassessment of the initial valuation. This fact raises a series of complex decisions regarding the information available to the actor at the time, the discernible intent, the role of bias or preconceptions, and perhaps most importantly of all, the appropriate degree of deference due to those who had to decide after the fact. To consider this matter in more detail we turn to the way an important tribunal, the ICC, in light of Protocol I of the Geneva conventions, has come to understand proportionality.

III. PROPORTIONALITY AT THE INTERNATIONAL CRIMINAL COURT AND PROTOCOL I

In his seminal work *War and Law Since 1945,* Geoffrey Best pointed out that "proportionality is certainly an awkward word. It is a pity that such indispensable and noble words as proportionality and humanitarian(ism) are in themselves so lumbering, unattractive and inexpressive."[6] Proportionality is, nevertheless, a deeply embedded and indispensable aspect of decision-making during war or armed conflict. Although proportionality might once have been an arcane concept embedded in military practice far removed from public awareness or debate, its modern application is anything but disconnected from public (and often politicized) critiques. The modern use of drones in geographic areas removed from immediate hostilities on the ground has exacerbated the political and legal sensitivity associated with proportionality determinations, as we will see in Chapter 10.

By some measures, proportionality should rarely be a major factor since it is so difficult to calculate it. According to the Rome Statute of the ICC, the war crime of disproportionate strikes is committed by

> Intentionally launching an attack in the knowledge that such attack will cause incidental loss of life or injury to civilians or damage to civilian objects or widespread, long-term and severe damage to the natural environment which would be *clearly* excessive in relation to the concrete and direct *overall* military advantage anticipated.[7] (italics not in the treaty text)

Chapter 5 will describe the history of this accepted and uncontroversial articulation of *jus in bello* proportionality. For the moment, it should be noted that this treaty based criminal definition was intended to provide the comprehensive and modern articulation of the proportionality principle (at least as understood in the context of armed conflicts).

Perhaps more tellingly, all States Party to the ICC joined with the major non-Party States, including the United States, India, and China, to provide a consensus on the

---

[6] GEOFFREY BEST, WAR AND LAW SINCE 1945 324 (1994).

[7] Rome Statute of the International Criminal Court art. 8(2)(b)(iv), July 1, 2002, 2187 U.N.T.S. 90 (emphasis added). Early in the history of the ICC, the extension of potentially unchecked international power over actors representing sovereign States was cited as one of the primary reasons the United States was originally unwilling to go forward with the Rome Statute "in its present form." D. J. Scheffer, *The United States and the International Criminal Court*, 93 AM. J. INT'L L. 14, 21 (1999). On December 31, 2000 which was the last day permitted by the treaty, Ambassador Scheffer signed the Rome Statute at the direction of President Clinton. *See* Rome Statute art. 125(1) (stipulating that states may accede to the Statute at a later time, but that signature was permissible only until December 31, 2000). The White House statement clarified that President Clinton ordered the signature because the United States seeks to "remain engaged in making the ICC an instrument of impartial and effective justice in the years to come," and reaffirmed America's "strong support for international accountability." President William J. Clinton, *Statement on the Rome Treaty on the International Criminal Court*, Dec. 31, 2000, 37 WEEKLY COMP. PRES. DOC. 4 (Jan. 8, 2001), *reprinted in* S. D. MURPHY, UNITED STATES PRACTICE IN INTERNATIONAL LAW, vol. 1, 1999–2001, at 384 (2002). Nevertheless, the President's statement made clear that he would "not recommend that my successor submit the treaty to the Senate for ratification until our fundamental concerns are satisfied." *Id.*

Elements of Crimes of the ICC. Hence, the treaty based crimes are buttressed by detailed definition and clarification of the constituent details that must be proven beyond a reasonable doubt to warrant conviction for the war crime of engaging in a disproportionate attack. This is important because the elements provide a detailed composite of the acts and mental requirements needed to prove every crime found in the Rome Statute.

The very certainty of the legal formulation nevertheless contains the seeds of highly controversial evaluations. Indeed, the most modern articulation added the words "clearly" and "overall" that are emphasized above. As we will develop in Chapter 5, the formulation in the Rome Statute accords perfectly with the developed state of customary international usage of the term proportionality in the *jus in bello* context. Some seem to believe that very little if any damage or loss is "clearly excessive" given the difficulties of comparing seeming incommensurables. This challenge is even more sharply raised by those who would advocate an automatic deference to the subjective evaluations of the military or paramilitary commander in all, or almost all, circumstances.

During the negotiations that led to the Protocol I formulations of proportionality in 1977, some delegations warned that the rule should be clear enough to preclude giving military commanders a practically unlimited right to launch any attack based on their subjective assessment of military advantage.[8] Others argued that the clear treaty prohibitions are important in the quest to express proportionality as a valuable tool for humanitarian protection that does not create an unrealistic ban on attacks and that can be followed by combatants.[9]

The problem in practice is not just with the need to show that a projected loss of civilian life, for instance, is excessive, but that it is "clearly" so. The problem of seeming incommensurability is not a complete bar to engaging in the comparisons needed to be made in proportionality calculation. Instead, the problem is that it seems to be rare indeed that such calculations will be "clear" in the sense that they are beyond controversy, and in a criminal law setting "beyond a reasonable doubt."

This calculus is further clouded by the lack of any agreement, and little discussion of the nexus between moral and legal considerations. The very high bar to establishing the crime of disproportionate use of force is completely uncontroversial as a matter of international criminal law. Does that settle the matter? Does the accepted international criminal law articulation of proportionality provide the appropriate framework for all proportionality calculations or is there a set of overriding moral

---

[8] Int'l Comm. of the Red Cross, 14 Official Records of the Diplomatic Conference on the Reaffirmation and Development of International Humanitarian Law Applicable in Armed Conflicts, Geneva (1974–1977), at 61 (para. 13) (1978) (referencing concerns raised by the Polish delegation among others).

[9] *Id.* at 64 (para. 48).

values that is relevant? If so, how does one decide the relevant evaluative standards? Can child soldiers even think in these terms? Should an uneasy and largely uninformed public set the terms of debate? Is it more appropriate to channel these issues through the prism of legislative process or anxious political dialogue? What is the connection between acceptability of proportionate strikes as a popular matter and the fact that the relevant criminal bar is rarely reached?

Instead of merely focusing on what is clearly excessive in the criminal sense, we will develop a different language, namely, that of thresholds. And in establishing thresholds, we will be mindful of the fact that proportionality assessments are always somewhat unclear in that they involve probability factors as well as the seeming incommensurables to which we have already alluded. Probabilities are an integral part of proportionality since, as one can see in the ICC Rome Statute text reprinted above, the factors to be considered are ones that can be anticipated, albeit imperfectly. In most situations, proportionality assessments are made "before the fact" and in almost every context, proportionality assessments are made on the basis of imperfect information and often with too much stress and too little time from the perspective of the decision-maker.

Hence, the word in the accepted ICC definition "anticipated" may be both controversial in hindsight yet completely conventional in the sense that it reflects well established customary international law and military practice. Even if proportionality assessments are made in judgment of past events, what is being judged is whether one has in the past engaged in reasonable assessments of what was predicted to occur if a war was initiated, or a certain tactic was employed, or a postwar strategy was adopted.

Accepting the premise that humanity will not celebrate the end of armed hostilities in our lifetimes, the essential goals of constraining the adverse effects of those conflicts to the smallest subset of humankind over the shortest period of time must remain a key legal and moral objective. We will discuss specific tactical problems, such as counterinsurgency (in Chapter 8), the use of human shields (in Chapter 9), targeted killings by drones (in Chapter 10), or cyber war (in Chapter 11), in which a clearer understanding of the parameters of *jus in bello* proportionality is well in order. In the longer scope of history and jurisprudential development, the very reasons for proportionality and the rule of law, even in the midst of conflict, cannot be overlooked or overcome by the press of expediency.

To that end, we will develop a theory of thresholds. Thresholds of proportionality establish a range of reasonable behavior that counts as satisfying the probability requirement, and a corresponding range of unreasonable behavior that fails to satisfy the proportionality requirement (and is thus disproportionate). Within the range, some behavior will be more, and other behavior less, *clearly* proportionate. At the point at which one has crossed the threshold and is about to cross a higher threshold will be those cases of excessively disproportionate behavior; and at the point at which one has simply crossed the threshold will be those cases of clearly not excessively disproportionate behavior. But those cases are not the only ones that should concern military commanders and others who must make proportionality judgments. The cases that barely fall on one or the other side of the threshold are also matters of importance. If, for instance, one is very likely to cause, on balance, more harm than good, then this is an example of disproportionate behavior, even in those cases in which it is not strictly excessive.

Phrased another way, even lawful conduct as defined by the *jus in bello* standard of international criminal law may well be inadvisable, unethical, counterproductive, or ineffective if used as the standard for the battlefield conduct. Commanders and their lawyers have long recognized this implicit reality. This is the reason that Rules of Engagement (ROE) are so commonly more restrictive than the technical parameters of the law might require.

From the perspective of those at the lowest rungs of command authority, looking up, the distinction is immaterial. The ROE are promulgated with the force of law as the lawful orders of superior commanders. Nevertheless, when lives hang in the balance, an immediate and uncontroversial assessment is in order. One might well argue that the strongest degree of deference is due to those whose life and liberty is most immediately endangered by the presence of combat. Experience shows, however, that the immediacy of a decision will seldom, if ever, be completely uncontroversial. At least in part, this is because proportionality is about probabilities that cannot be portrayed precisely.

IV. SOME ADDITIONAL EXAMPLES

Despite the difficulty in applying a highly technical term that comes loaded with ideological and historical baggage, it is of utmost importance when the stakes are the highest. For example, during the early phases of the war in both Iraq and Afghanistan, ROE applicable to US forces required that certain targets could only be attacked with prior approval of certain levels of command authority. ROE commonly place a higher premium on minimizing collateral damage than the obligations strictly derived from the laws and customs of war. In modern military practice, it is well accepted that "nothing stops a commander from placing a high[er] premium on minimizing collateral damage [than that required by the law of armed conflict]."[10]

---

[10] For the distinction between the obligations of the laws and customs of war and the scope of the Rules of Engagement promulgated by the higher level commanders in the context of Operation ALLIED FORCE, the Kosovo air war, see CENTER FOR LAW AND MILITARY OPERATIONS, LAW AND MILITARY OPERATIONS

One of the more visible applications of this so-called "restrictive" ROE measure was the high-level decision not to target Taliban leader Mullah Omar during the early days of Operation Enduring Freedom. In a controversial magazine article, Seymour Hersh reported that General Tommy Franks, the CENTCOM Commander, decided not to authorize, as a matter of restrictive ROE, an immediate strike on a convoy that intelligence sources indicated was carrying Mullah Omar to safety on the first night of the war because of reservations expressed by the CENTCOM Staff Judge Advocate.[11] Though this narrative was later disputed in other reporting,[12] the decision not to target Mullah Omar because of concerns about collateral damage provides an important illustration of the critical importance of a clear understanding and application of proportionality.

In another example from Iraq, the American envoy, Paul Bremer, decided not to authorize an operation that was already underway to arrest the fiery Shiite militia leader Moqtada Sadr, because of a concern for the reactions by the population that supported Sadr. US officials worried that the arrest might not be proportionate to the objectives of the military operation, since Sadr's arrest could spark an increase in sectarian killing of civilians. In April 2004, Sadr was charged by an Iraqi judge under Iraqi law for the murder of a political opponent, Shia leader Abdul Majid al-Khoei, yet Bremer's decision forced American forces already in place to watch the cleric drive by in his convoy. Bremer's decision nullified the hard and unpopular decision by the judge who represented perhaps the best hope for delegitimizing Sadr and for undermining his growing influence.

The so-called Mahdi Army led by Sadr was later responsible for thousands of killings and human rights abuses in both Baghdad and Najaf, and Sadr was a divisive force that helped to exacerbate ethnic tensions and harden the resistance to coalition forces. As these examples illustrate, the seemingly esoteric considerations of proportionality, such as the minimization of collateral damage, often generate collateral consequences that are monumental in terms of lives and property.

As with so much about war and armed conflict, context will often drive decisions and inclinations, yet there will often be disputes over even what counts as relevant contexts. During armed conflicts, decision-makers may be influenced by the larger strategic and operational context and yet articulate guidance in terms of proportionality. At the same time, other actors will justifiably use the tactical, or micro-context, as an affirmative justification for a particular decision.

IN KOSOVO, 1999–2001: LESSONS LEARNED FOR JUDGE ADVOCATES 50–51 (stating that "nothing stops a commander from placing a high[er] premium on minimizing collateral damage [than that required by the law of armed conflict]").

[11] Seymour M. Hersh, *King's Ransom: How Vulnerable Are the Saudi Royals*, NEW YORKER, Oct. 22, 2001.

[12] *See*, e.g., John L. Miller, *Sly Sly: A Journalist's Latest Tricks*, NAT'L REV., Dec. 3, 2001.

There were some strikes within the city of Baghdad conducted using the area weapon Multiple Launched Rocket System (called MLRS) as American forces approached Baghdad in the spring of 2003, even as commanders turned down requests for other strikes from subordinate units. The micro-analysis of each proposed target varied according to the situation and evolving tactics of Iraqi defenders. Proportionality makes a difference in these cases in which the lives of soldiers as well as civilians are at stake.

To recall our first example, though General Franks decided not to authorize the strike against Mullah Omar we just described, he ordered Operation RHINO, a strike by Army Rangers and other Special Operations elements on the residence of Taliban leader Mullah Omar in the middle of Kandahar, center of the Taliban movement, on October 19, 2001. Mullah Omar's escape from Kandahar on December 7, 2001, marked the end of the Taliban regime, and the beginning of more than a decade of insurgency that still afflicts Afghanistan even as we write.[13] By all accounts, the Mullah has been a key leader and source of the Taliban inspired atrocities and human rights abuses that plague rural Afghans.

In May 2008, British papers derided German forces in Afghanistan as "bridge builders" for permitting an important Taliban leader with links to the killers of British soldiers to escape unharmed from a wedding party despite having him in their targeting sights. The German approach to waging war in Afghanistan generated friction with coalition partners due in part to differing views on acceptable proportionality considerations and ROE that strictly forbid the use of lethal force unless narrowly based on a clear self-defense rationale. The German approach places proportionality squarely into the narrowest tactical context which as we shall see almost mirrors the human rights domain. British papers trumpeted such headlines as "Taliban Chief Escapes the Shot-Shy Germans."[14]

Commenting on the assemblage of more than 100 Taliban fighters for a graveside gathering in July 2005, the US Central Command issued a statement that "a decision was made not to strike the group of insurgents at that specific location and time"[15] because of a worry about how the civilian population would react. Here again, collateral damage to civilian populations was given overriding weight in the proportionality assessment. The incident provides another example in which proportionality

---

[13] Frontline Chronology, http://www.pbs.org/wgbh/pages/frontline/shows/campaign/etc/cron.html [last visited March 9, 2012].

[14] Allan Hall & Matthew Hickley, *Taliban chief escapes the shot-shy Germans*, THE DAILY MAIL (London), May 20, 2008, at 25.

[15] A New York Post op-ed observed that the "The Taliban, as savage a foe as American forces have ever encountered, follow no rules at all. A failure to fire on an assemblage that size, simply to protect the cultural sensitivities of a cold-blooded foe, borders on insanity." *Insanity*, N.Y. POST, Sept. 14, 2006, at 40.

was the pretext for a decision labeled as "insane" by many American media outlets. Proportionality assessments are seldom greeted with universal applause.

Another consideration here is that there are civilians and then there are civilians. Some civilians have as much training in the lethal use of force as soldiers. Unfortunately, in the modern forms of asymmetric warfare, it is often very difficult to tell whether a person is a true civilian as opposed to what is euphemistically called "an insurgent." One relevant example that can be recalled is, perhaps surprisingly, the My Lai massacre in the midst of the Vietnam War. Massacres are normally unjustified mass killings of civilians by soldiers. In My Lai, members of C Company, 1st Battalion, 20th Infantry Regiment of the US Army killed old men, women, and children and dumped their bodies into a mass grave. The killing is sometimes described as a textbook case of disproportionate use of violent force.

Yet, even though the killings took place as the members of the My Lai hamlet were eating breakfast, the defense counsel at the ensuing court martial raised significant questions about whether these civilians were civilians. Defense counsel argued that during the week before the massacre, several members of C Company had been killed during an ambush staged by civilians including children. Indeed, just the day before, members of C Company were warned that children and old people in the area around My Lai were really insurgent warriors.

Of course, that the soldiers did not do anything to try to ascertain the status of these villagers, but merely "mowed them down," is likely to signal that C Company's use of force violated the principle of distinction (the principle that forbids combatants from ever internationally targeting civilians as such) and was also disproportionate, though not as straightforwardly as the popular imagination ascribed. Similarly, at the time of this writing, no member of the team of Marines that murdered unarmed Iraqi civilians in the village of Haditha has faced jail time despite the flurry of legal maneuvers and charges. This apparent discrepancy has outraged Iraqi politicians and the larger population, yet conflicting contextual applications of proportionality are at the heart of the debate.

V. PROPORTIONALITY'S PARADOX: FIXED STANDARDS ASSESSMENTS REACHED SUBJECTIVELY

Proportionality in war or armed conflict has often meant that whatever are the advantages of waging war, they must not involve even greater burdens, especially on innocent others. Traditionally, the main class of burdens to be weighed against military advantage is the loss of civilian life or property. We will later discuss, in Chapter 6, the more recent expansion of the proportionality principle to include the burdens that occur due to the death or disability of soldiers as well. In both the traditional and contemporary variations, the proportionality principle in war or armed conflict requires a weighing in advance of initiating war or combat mission that shows that what is gained by military force is greater than what is lost.

In its most common association with conflicts, the term *proportionality* has deep historical roots that color our modern interpretations. This is because the historical notion of proportionality is founded on the cornerstone precept that war should spare innocents to the greatest extent possible. In this context, to use violence disproportionately meant that the use of force in war unjustly affected innocent civilians. The moral imperative for minimizing harm to persons who are not participating in conflict cuts across the world's major religions. Its Medieval Christian roots are obvious and germinated into the Just War tradition that will be discussed at length in Chapter 4.

One of the earliest Jewish philosophers wrote from Alexandria that the Jewish concept of warfare "distinguishes between those whose life is one of hostility and the reverse. For to breathe slaughter against all, even those who have done very little or nothing amiss, shows what we should call a savage and brutal soul."[16] Early Muslim thought similarly opined that "Umar wrote to the commanders to fight in the way of Allah and to fight only those who fight against them, and not to kill women or minors, nor to kill those who do not use a razor."[17]

The legal articulations of the proportionality principle at the very core of the laws and customs of war developed as a logical extension of this shared moral consensus. Yet the very familiarity has often obscured proportionality's precise content and normative implications. Proportionality is an inherently subjective concept, in that the weighing involves a placing of value on the various factors in war, which was systematically developed to be applied from the perspective of the actor (normally a military commander) in a manner that preserves inarguable fixed standards such as humaneness and the sparing of the innocent. As we have already indicated though, there is already an additional quasi-objective component in the subjective judgment in that the perspective is supposed to be a reasonable commander, not the actual person who may have all sorts of biases and failings.

The confluence of subjective and quasi-objective motivations and criteria partially helps to explain the unresolved debates over the term. No one disputes the importance of proportionality as perhaps the preeminent measure for evaluating the efficacy of particular actions during conflicts. Even as the principle of proportionality is regularly invoked as an overarching moral and legal imperative, its rhetorical power

---

[16] Philo, The Special Laws, 4:224–225.
[17] Ella Landau-Tasseron, *"Non-Combatants" in Muslim Legal Thought* (Washington: Hudson Institute, Center on Islam, Democracy, and the Future of the Muslim World, 2006), at 21.

is commonly co-opted in public discourse as a vehicle for opposing a particular conflict or for framing a debate over acceptable means versus ends.

This book is intended to provide a synthesis of the doctrine of proportionality as it has evolved in international law and practice, as well as a normative evaluation of where the development of the principle of proportionality should go from here. Proportionality is at the very heart of modern operations as embedded in the laws and customs of war and applicable ROE, the rules that States have formulated to guide the behavior of soldiers and official actors. One of the relevant questions that spurs us in the next chapter to catalogue and analyze the various meanings of proportionality as comprehensively as possible is the initial query whether the *jus in bello* usage of proportionality is unique in contrast to its other uses in other disciplines.

Assuming that proportionality is in some sense unique in the practice of military and paramilitary forces, should the *jus in bello* usages and understandings transcend the understandings derived from other fields, or is there a discernible drift of tenets that can be documented? If there is such a drift or evolution, what does that portend for the conduct of hostilities? The concept of proportionality grew out of deeply intertwined philosophical foundations, and is applied in the midst of the inherent uncertainties and moral challenges of modern conflicts.

Part of our motivation for undertaking this comprehensive and multidisciplinary collation and analysis of concepts is to help bridge a yawning gap between the legal and moral imperatives linked to proportionality and their applications in practice. At the outset, we recognize that this is an ambitious goal, perhaps overly so. There are many examples of conduct during armed conflicts that falls far short by any objective measure of the normative aspirations that impelled proportionality from ancient times.

Lieutenant General William R. Peers reported that one of the causes of the crimes committed at My Lai was that "[n]either units nor individual members of Task Force Barker and the 11th Brigade received the proper training in the Law of War (Hague and Geneva conventions), the safeguarding of noncombatants, or the Rules of Engagement."[18] Soldiers at My Lai, and in many other instances of illegality, have carried ROE cards in their pockets requiring them to "use force proportionately" or, in some cases, to "apply the proportionality principle at all times against enemy and civilian targets."[19] Lackadaisical and legalistic classroom training that is often viewed

---

[18] WILLIAM R. PEERS, THE MY LAI INQUIRY 230 (1979). To be sure, General Peers correctly observed that "even accepting these training deficiencies...there were some things a soldier did not have to be told were wrong—such as rounding up women and children and then mowing them down, shooting babies out of mothers' arms and raping." *Id.*

[19] CENTER FOR LAW AND MILITARY OPERATIONS, RULES OF ENGAGEMENT (ROE) HANDBOOK FOR JUDGE ADVOCATES, App. C (2000)(containing a host of examples of pocket cards given to military person-nel in a wide range of missions, multinational operations, and peacetime missions as well as those intended for use at the onset of hostilities).

as an inconvenient formality cannot in isolation prevent the commission of war crimes. The killers at My Lai, for example, operated under an abundance of orders requiring that war crimes be promptly reported and investigated, along with extensive training requirements.[20] But often soldiers do not understand what precisely they are to do to conform to this principle, particularly when life and limb are in imminent peril.

To take only one of dozens more possible examples that span conflicts and military cultures, the US Marines that killed 24 unarmed Iraqi civilians at Haditha carried ROE cards with the specific requirement that *"Positive Identification (PiD) is required prior to engagement.* PiD is reasonable certainty that your target is a legitimate military target."* (emphasis in original). The same ROE card carried by US Marines also contained the quite logical correlative duty to "minimize collateral damage." Yet, in the Haditha massacre, those killed included a 76-year-old man in a wheelchair as well as women and children. These deaths came in the context of, and as a reaction to, a complex operational environment where a Marine commander described finding "20 bodies, throats slit, 20 bodies, you know beheaded, 20 bodies here, 20 bodies there," at the hands of Iraqi insurgents.[21] When presented with demands from the Haditha City Council for an investigation into the civilian deaths, the Battalion Commander denied responsibility and blamed insurgents for the deaths and the city for giving them shelter. When his own Executive Officer and Operations Officer later recommended an investigation, the commander declared, "My men are not murderers," and declined to investigate.[22]

The Marine Major General in command of Anbar Province at the time later stated in sworn testimony during pretrial investigations for one of the noncommissioned officers charged with murder that, "I guess maybe if we was sitting here at Quantico and heard that 15 civilians were killed, we would have been surprised and shocked and gone—done more to look into it. But at that point in time, we felt that that was—had been, for whatever reason, part of that engagement and felt that it was just a cost of doing business on that particular engagement."[23] The attacks at Haditha

---

[20] Military Advisory Command Directive (MACV) Directive 20-4 mandated in no uncertain terms the "responsibility of all military personnel having knowledge or receiving a report of an incident or of an act thought to be a war crime to make such a report known to his commanding officer as soon as practicable." Major General George S. Prugh, Law at War: Vietnam 1964–1973 74 (Washington: Dept of the Army, 1975).

[21] Michael A. Schmidt, *Junkyard Gives up Secret Accounts of Massacre in Iraq*, N.Y. Times, Dec. 14, 2011, at A1.

[22] Defense Legal Policy Board Report of the SubCommittee on Military Justice in Combat Zones 161 (May 30 2013)(the court martial charges against the battalion commander were later subject to extended appellate litigation prior to trial based on allegations of unlawful command influence that purportedly tainted the proceedings. The charges were eventually dismissed and the commander involuntarily retired from the Marine Corps).

[23] Selected Testimony from the Haditha Investigation: Interview of Maj. Gen. Steve Johnson, N.Y. Times, Dec. 14, 2011, *available at* http://www.nytimes.com/interactive/2011/12/15/world/middleeast/haditha-selected-documents.html?ref=middleeast#document/p18/a41205.

were the first significant combat action for the company commander of the Marine squad. The context of seeing so much destruction of innocent life can help explain, although not necessarily justify, why the US Marines acted as they did.

The Haditha massacres had enormous long-term strategic consequences and were reportedly a primary factor that led to the failed negotiations for a permanent Status of Forces agreement in Iraq that would have permitted US combat forces to remain in the country and to secure its stabilization. The claimed misapplication of proportionality in the heat of the moment and under the emotional strain of intense urban combat was at the very heart of the Haditha tragedy, irrespective of the precise scope of the subsequent criminal charges or the ultimate resolution of those cases.

In one of the most significant treatments on proportionality in recent years, Judith Gardham begins her book, *Necessity, Proportionality and the Use of Force by States*, by saying that "Proportionality is a familiar idea and is designed to ensure that the ends justify the means."[24] This is right on one level and terribly misleading on another level. Gardham is right in that proportionality is about trying to justify tactics by considering what those tactics are aimed to accomplish. But Gardham's analysis is misleading in that there is much more at stake in proportionality assessments, most importantly what happens to the parties upon whom the tactic is employed, and most especially of all in *jus in bello* contexts, what happens as a result of collateral damage that is not part of the aim of those using the tactic or weapon.

The invocation of proportionality as a term of art in legal debates carries an undercurrent of moral and philosophical values and assumptions. At the same time, the increasingly common references to the same term in very different disciplines means that there is a tendency among inattentive listeners to accept its invocation uncritically. The term is so commonly used in modern parlance that popular audiences do not discriminate between the varying strands of its correct usage in each particular field. The paradox of proportionality, of trying to apply fixed standards to situations in which subjective judgments are crucial, is what makes this topic so challenging.

---

[24] JUDITH GARDHAM, NECESSITY, PROPORTIONALITY, AND THE USE OF FORCE BY STATES xv (2004).

3

PROPORTIONALITY: A MULTIPLICITY OF MEANINGS

THIS CHAPTER SUMMARIZES the proportionality principle as it functions within a variety of contexts, mainly those not involving war or armed conflict. Proportionality is an umbrella concept that captures two seemingly incompatible but equally important aspects. First, proportionality limits the exercise of governmental power by insisting that such power be well tailored to certain acceptable goals. This recurring means–ends testing cuts across legal and moral domains. Second, proportionality legitimizes power itself by authorizing its exercise, provided it meets the requirements of the doctrine. In other words, proportionality is both power limiting and power enhancing. In practice, proportionality serves as an external principle of limited government that defines the optimal relationship between States and citizens independent of specific situational applications.[1]

This chapter seeks to provide an illustrative cross-section of the modern usages of the term proportionality as it is commonly encountered in diverse legal and moral domains. Proportionality functions as a tool for contemporaneous decision-making as well as an evaluative framework for the *post hoc* assessment of often-controversial decisions. It also provides a consistent formula for the careful consideration of larger normative goals rather than giving priority to specific convenience. Properly understanding the interdisciplinary pronouncements related to the proportionality principle provides a basis for lawfully protecting the compelling yet occasionally conflicting moral and legal imperatives it seeks to protect. Our hope is that by comparing the various assumptions and usages that are imbued in the same term, we can

---

[1] Alice Ristroph, *Proportionality as a Principle of Limited Government*, 55 DUKE L. J. 263 (2005).

understand the relationship of the *jus in bello* proportionality definition as related to but distinctive from other formulations.

In this chapter, we will examine six non-armed conflict domains in which proportionality is crucial. In Section I, we will examine how proportionality is used to limit the extent of lawful governance. Here, we shall be especially interested in the use of proportionality in the European Union (EU or Union). In Section II, we examine the use of proportionality as a limit on punishment by the State. In Section III, we look at proportionality as used in international investment law. In Section IV, we look at maritime law to see some further uses of proportionality analysis. In Section V, we have a short section on the use of proportionality in discussions of countermeasures in international trade. And, finally, in Section VI, we end this survey with treaty-based human rights regimes in which, once again, proportionality has played a key role. In all these cases, there is a strong similarity in how proportionality is understood. But in later chapters, we will show that *jus in bello* proportionality is unique in several crucial respects.

I. THE LIMITS OF LAWFUL GOVERNANCE

Aristotle is credited as the first to conceive of proportionality as a form of societal justice in his work Nicomachean Ethics.[2] Aristotle postulated that among other uses, proportionality is the right relationship between the citizen and the State. Thus, in his thinking, "We allow only reason, not a human being, to be ruler," otherwise, we have tyranny.[3] This formulation, as it came to be understood in the Middle Ages, and especially by Thomas Aquinas, implies belief in an objective order that threads across centuries and societies; a kind of *jus universum* derived from common sense. This vision of proportionality in turn both warrants and limits the positive law proclamations that emanate from legislatures, kings, and public referendums. Justice, then, in this Medieval Aristotelian view, is determined by the establishment and maintenance of a proper ratio of power exercised upon people in relation to the natural rights they possess as persons. The field of human rights developed long after Aristotle's insights but is deeply indebted to Aristotle. We will return to demonstrate the effect of these intuitions within the human rights jurisprudence in Chapter 6. But the point we wish to begin with is that, as far back as ancient Greece, proportionality was seen as a limit on what government can do to the people.

---

[2] Eric Engle, *History of the General Principle of Proportionality: An Overview*, X DARTMOUTH LAW JOURNAL 1 (Winter 2012).
[3] ARISTOTLE, THE NICOMACHEAN ETHICS, Bk. 5, Ch. 6, 1134a35 (translated by Terrence Irwin, 1999), p. 77.

For now, the key point of this first section is that proportionality review has become deeply intertwined with the central nervous system of the EU as the key limit of lawful governmental authority. Article 5 of the Maastricht Treaty, as it is known throughout the world, established the EU and stated that "any action of the Community shall not go beyond what is necessary to achieve the objectives of this Treaty." In one of its earliest pronouncements, the European Court of Justice (ECJ) made clear that EU authority is limited to those measures deemed necessary to accomplish a legitimate purpose.[4] Article 2, paragraph 6 of the Lisbon Treaty, which amended the original Maastricht Treaty as the organizing norm for the EU, accordingly requires that, "The Union shall pursue its objectives by appropriate means commensurate with the competences which are conferred upon it…"[5]

For our purposes, the key provision of the Lisbon Treaty is Article 3(b), which replaced Article 5 of the original treaty. It reads in its entirety as follows:

1. The limits of Union competences are governed by the principle of conferral. The use of Union competences is governed by the principles of subsidiarity and proportionality.
2. Under the principle of conferral, the Union shall act only within the limits of the competences conferred upon it by the Member States in the Treaties to attain the objectives set out therein. Competences not conferred upon the Union in the Treaties remain with the Member States.
3. Under the principle of subsidiarity, in areas which do not fall within its exclusive competence, the Union shall act only if and insofar as the objectives of the proposed action cannot be sufficiently achieved by the Member States, either at central level or at regional and local level, but can rather, by reason of the scale or effects of the proposed action, be better achieved at Union level.

    The institutions of the Union shall apply the principle of subsidiarity as laid down in the Protocol on the application of the principles of subsidiarity and proportionality. National Parliaments ensure compliance with the principle of subsidiarity in accordance with the procedure set out in that Protocol.

---

[4] Case 6/54, *Kingdom of the Netherlands v. High Authority of the European Coal and Steel Community* (1955) ECR 103.

[5] http://eur-lex.europa.eu/LexUriServ/LexUriServ.do?uri=OJ:C:2007:306:0010:0041:EN:PDF

4. Under the principle of proportionality, the content and form of Union action shall not exceed what is necessary to achieve the objectives of the Treaties.[6] The institutions of the Union shall apply the principle of proportionality as laid down in the Protocol on the application of the principles of subsidiarity and proportionality.

The Protocol on the Application of the Principles of Subsidiarity and Proportionality in turn requires the institutions of the EU "to ensure constant respect" for its two cornerstone principles.[7] In its simplest terms, then, proportionality in the EU requires a balancing of means versus desired ends. This, of course, functions in tight nexus to the subsidiarity principle by which power not delegated to the EU is retained at the national level. Subsidiarity in the EU thus mirrors the core values enshrined in the Tenth Amendment of the US Constitution, by which the "powers not delegated to the United States by the Constitution, nor prohibited by it to the States, are reserved to the States respectively, or to the people."[8]

In the jurisprudence of the EU, proportionality has been an oft-cited and much debated norm. Indeed, the principle of proportionality "applies both to Community and to national measures and covers both legislative and administrative action."[9] It recurs in every European domestic jurisdiction in essentially the same form and has become one of the most prominent drivers of constitutional debate in every legal system.[10] German law, for example, implements a three-pronged test of constitutionality by which a statute or administrative determination must

(1) be appropriate (or suitable) (German: geeignet) for attaining its objective. This first criterion is sometimes described as evaluating the relationship between the means employed and the ends that will be accomplished, while others describe it as the measure's ability to accomplish its aim;

(2) be necessary (German: erforderlich) to achieve its intended purposes. In other words, this prong asks whether some other measure could accomplish the same permissible purpose. This is sometimes formulated as asking whether there is a less restrictive alternative available; and

---

[6] Notice here that, under one reading, the EU's principle of proportionality is not significantly different from that of necessity. We discuss the connection between necessity and proportionality in several later chapters but especially at the end of Chapter 5.

[7] http://eur-lex.europa.eu/en/treaties/dat/12007L/htm/C2007306EN.01015001.htm

[8] U.S. CONST. amend. X.

[9] Takis Tridimas, *The Principle of Proportionality in Community Law: From the Rule of Law to Market Integration*, 31 IRISH JURIST 83, 84 (1996).

[10] Alec Stone Sweet and Jud Mathews, *Proportionality Balancing and Global Constitutionalism*, 47 COLUMBIA J. TRANSNAT'L L. 72, 160 (2008).

(3) be proportionate to the objective (sometimes identified as "proportionate stricto sensu"[11]). Hence, "the burden must not be excessive relative to the objective (Zumutbarkeit)."[12]

A complex jurisprudential tangle has evolved within the EU, by which the proportionality principle requires some articulated relationship between means and ends. Put another way, subsidiarity provides the threshold needed to sustain administrative or regulatory state action, while proportionality provides the actual standard of review for assessing the action. Though the ECJ has on occasion applied a three-pronged test similar to that found in German law,[13] it has generally adopted a simpler means–end analysis of proportionality that asks only whether the means chosen to effect EU policy is suitable or appropriate, and whether it is no more restrictive than necessary to achieve a lawful end.

It is settled case-law that the principle of proportionality, which is one of the general principles of Community law, requires that measures adopted do not exceed the limits of what is appropriate and necessary in order to attain the objectives legitimately pursued by the legislation in question; when there is a choice between several appropriate measures, recourse must be had to the least onerous, and the disadvantages caused must not be disproportionate to the aims pursued.[14]

In effect, packaging proportionality as a means–end analysis reiterates the first test of the German conception and commingles the second two prongs.[15] According to the ECJ, interference with a basic right in the treaty

is warranted only if [1] it pursues a legitimate objective compatible with the Treaty and is justified by [2] overriding reasons of public interest [justifiable means]; if this is the case, it must be [3] suitable for securing the attainment

---

[11] *See e.g.* Case C-169/91, Stoke-on-Trent v. B&Q, 1992 E.C.R. I-6625, I-6658, para. 15. (applying the *stricto sensu* proportionality test, the court stated, "Appraising the proportionality of national rules which pursue a legitimate aim under Community law involves weighing the national interest in attaining that aim against the Community interest in ensuring the free movement of goods.")

[12] Jeremy Gunn, *Deconstructing Proportionality in Limitations Analysis*, 19 EMORY INT'L L. REV. 465, 467 (2005).

[13] Scholars point out that the ECJ denies direct emulation of domestic laws and at best has admitted only their influence as the "substratum" shared by Member States. Margit Cohn, *Legal Chronicles: The Evolution of Unreasonableness and Proportionality Review of the Administration in the United Kingdom*, 58 AM. J. COMP. L. 583, 612 (2010).

[14] Joined Cases C-963 & C-97/03, Tempelman v. Directeur van de Rijksdienst [2005] E.C.R. I-1895, para. 47 (describing the full proportionality test in EU caselaw).

[15] *Id.*

of the objective which it pursues and [4] not go beyond what is necessary in order to attain it."[16]

This four-pronged test is found in many cases and divides the consideration of overall necessity in prongs one and two from prongs three and four, representing a reframed proportionality within the regulatory structures of the EU. We should note, in passing, that the relationship between necessity and proportionality within the EU does not create a static dynamic. As originally understood, proportionality helped to preserve State sovereignty and flexibility within the context of a looser supranational union. Over the past decade, as the bonds between States have become ever stronger, and the regulatory thicket ever tighter, the principle of proportionality review has shifted; the premium is on preservation of the union rather than to uphold a strict precept of supranational limitation.

As a limitation on State power *vis-à-vis* national entities proportionality has nevertheless become the "universal criterion of constitutionality."[17] A compelling, example is that, even in the midst of the financial crisis that threatens its very existence, the recently enacted EU regulation designed to "reduce the risk and severity of future financial crises" mandates that supervisory measures must account for "the nature and seriousness of the infringement and should respect the principle of proportionality."

Before taking a decision on supervisory measures, "ESMA [The European Securities and Markets Authority] should give the persons subject to the proceedings the opportunity to be heard in order to respect their rights of defense"[18] Regulation 513 specifically embeds the requisite justification for such a proportionate regulation by declaring that

> Since the objectives of this Regulation, namely setting up an efficient and effective supervisory framework for credit rating agencies by entrusting a single supervisory authority with the supervision of credit rating activities in the Union, providing a single point of contact for credit rating agencies and ensuring the consistent application of the rules for credit rating agencies, cannot be sufficiently achieved at the Member State level and can therefore, by reason of

---

[16] *See*, e.g., International Transport Workers' Federation and Finnish Seamen's Union v. Viking Line ABP and OÜ Viking Line Eesti, Case C-438/05, 2007 E.C.R. I-10779 ¶ 75; Case C-341/05, Laval un Partneri Ltd v. Svenska Byggnadsarbetareförbundet and Others, 2007 E.C.R. I-11767 ¶101.

[17] DAVID BEATTY, THE ULTIMATE RULE OF LAW 162 (2004).

[18] Regulation (EU) No. 513/2011 of the European Parliament and of the Council of 11 May 2011 amending Regulation (EC) No. 1060/2009 on credit rating agencies, para. 25, Official Journal of the European Union, L 145/30 (May 31, 2011), *available at* http://eur-lex.europa.eu/LexUriServ/LexUriServ.do?uri=OJ:L:2011:14 5:0030:0056:EN:PDF.

the pan-Union structure and impact of the credit rating activities to be supervised, be better achieved at the Union level, the Union may adopt measures, in accordance with the principle of subsidiarity as set out in Article 5 of the Treaty on European Union. In accordance with the principle of proportionality, as set out in that Article, this Regulation does not go beyond what is necessary in order to achieve those objectives.[19]

The seeming conflation of proportionality and necessity portends a widening cycle whereby proportionality becomes far less powerful as a check on supranational power because it is subordinated to increasingly important, but "necessary" goals. In other words, almost any EU action becomes "proportionate" because it is deemed necessary to achieve increasingly important Union objectives.

One might well say that proportionality and necessity are inversely related as the determinant of legality, despite the Lisbon Treaty formulations. In Chapter 6, we will argue that the proper relationship between necessity and proportionality is not the one indicated in the ESMA regulations. Necessity, in some respects, takes priority over proportionality, but only in the sense that the threshold for necessity has to be crossed before proportionality becomes a relevant concern. But it is quite conceivable that something could be militarily necessary and yet not proportionate.

The spread of proportionality across legal cultures as a distinct doctrine of constitutional limitation around the world has led some to describe it as the "most successful legal transplant of the twentieth century."[20] The International Law Commission described *jus cogens* as "an overriding rule depriving any actor or situation which is in conflict with it of its legality."[21] The uniform recognition of proportionality as a limit to the appropriate exercise of state authority has even led some scholars to accept it as a peremptory norm (i.e., a *jus cogens* norm) of international law.[22] Accepting this premise would elevate proportionality to the apex of international law alongside the prohibitions against genocide and torture as a universally recognized principle from which no derogation is possible in either practice or treaty.[23] This would, of course, assume that proportionality has a sufficiently homogenous

---

[19] *Id.* para. 35.

[20] Mattias Kumm, *Constitutional Rights as Principles: On the Structure and Domain of Constitutional Justice*, 2 INT'L J.OF CONSTITUTIONAL LAW (I-CON) 574, 595 (2003).

[21] II Y.B. INT'L L. COMMISSION 262, para. 1 (1966).

[22] *See* ALEXANDER ORAKHELASHVILI, PEREMPTORY NORMS IN INTERNATIONAL LAW (Oxford University Press, 2006); Ralph G. Steinhardt, Book Review, *European Administrative Law*, 28 GEO. WASH. J. INT'L L. & ECON. 225, 231–232 (1994).

[23] Any treaty provision that contravenes a *jus cogens* norm becomes invalid to the extent of the conflict. Annalisa Ciampi, *Invalidity and Termination of Treaties and Rules of Procedure*, in THE LAW OF TREATIES BEYOND THE VIENNA CONVENTION, 360 (Enzo Cannizaro, ed. 2011).

meaning to be recognized and applied in all areas of international law. As we have seen, proportionality, as a strand of constitutional law, is neither inalterable nor completely uncontroversial, and we accordingly remain skeptical of elevating it to the exalted *jus cogens* status even as we now move to document its widespread use in a variety of other domains.

II. THE LIMITS OF LAWFUL STATE PUNISHMENT

The linkage between the power of the state to enforce its criminal laws and the essential rights of the individual represents one aspect of proportionality that is unquestionably discernible in all legal systems. Indeed, a means–end approach to proportionality as applied *in foro domestico* is almost the paradigmatic example of a recurring aspect of municipal law applied around the world that subsequently finds form in international law[24] as one of the core "general principles of law recognized by civilized nations."[25]

Even our children recognize the injustice imposed for a punishment that is altogether too harsh in light of the offense. Our youngest citizens know that such parenting is generally motivated by anger or shame or peer pressure rather than seeking sound measures to correct and teach. What is true for our families is true for our societies—a proper ratio between a wrong committed and the penalty to be expected is a foundational principle of justice and human decency that spans cultures.

Proportionality as a governing principle of punitive law is a deeply felt normative goal. The Confucian philosopher, Xun Zi (or Hsün Tzu) ca. 312–230 BCE, is credited with coining the third-century BCE imperial Chinese axiom: Let the punishment fit the crime (*xing dang zui ze wei, bu dang zui ze wu*).[26] Little if any empirical evidence shows that punishment is an effective means of deterrence, despite claims to the contrary made by Chinese legalists over two millennia ago, as well as by some contemporary criminologists.

The need for relative parity between the severity of punishment and the wrong it seeks to address has correspondingly deep roots in the common law that run at least to the Magna Carta. The desire for proportionality in sentencing runs deep in the

---

[24] *See* THE STATUTE OF THE INTERNATIONAL COURT OF JUSTICE: A COMMENTARY ¶¶ 250–264 (Andreas Zimmerman, Christian Tomushat, Karin Oellers-Frahm, eds. 2006)(recounting the process and practice of the ICJ toward applying the textual tenets of domestic law in an international context as binding legal rules rather than moral principles).

[25] Article 38(1)(c), Statute of the International Court of Justice.

[26] John O. Haley, *Introduction—Beyond Retribution: An Integrated Approach to Restorative Justice*, 36 WASHINGTON UNIVERSITY JOURNAL OF LAW AND POLICY 1,9 (2011). *See also* 3 JOHN KNOBLOCK, XUNZI: A TRANSLATION AND STUDY OF THE COMPLETE WORKS 166 (1988).

human psyche and is imbued in our sense of justice. For precisely these reasons, the aspiration for a limiting precept appeared in the text of the Magna Carta and many domestic legal codes as the era of positivism emerged during the Enlightenment. The Magna Carta held forth the promise that no man should be denied justice or "mercy" but rather adjudged "in accordance with the degree of the offense." Chapter 20 of the Great Charter prohibited the monarch from imposing a fine "unless according to the measure of the offense." It further provided that "for a great offense [a free man] shall be [punished] in accordance with the gravity of the offense."[27]

Echoing the spirit of Magna Carta, the Supreme Court of the United States (Supreme Court or the Court) has held that the Eighth Amendment prohibition on "cruel and unusual punishments" commands proportional punishments. In *Solem v. Helm* (which addressed the permissible length of sentences),[28] Justice Powell traced the history of the Cruel and Unusual Punishments Clause back to the Magna Carta as well as to the English Bill of Rights of 1689, which he found to have embodied a strong principle of proportional punishment. In *Harmelin v. Michigan*,[29] the Supreme Court specifically pointed to the Magna Carta as an early source of its Eighth Amendment proportionality analysis.

Proportionality analysis in the criminal context requires a right relationship between the penalty and offense in order to comport with basic notions of due process, fairness, reasonableness, and justice.[30] In the United States, the proportionality principle took perhaps its most prominent form in the line of death penalty jurisprudence.[31] In *Furman v. Ga.*, the US Supreme Court noted that "no matter how infrequently those convicted of rape or murder are executed, the penalty so imposed is *not disproportionate* to the crime and those executed may deserve exactly what they received."(emphasis added).[32]

In *Roper v. Simmons*[33] (which forbade the imposition of capital sentences for perpetrators who were not of legal age at the time they committed their crimes),

[27] William Sharp McKechne, Magna Carta: A Commentary on the Great Charter of King John, 1914, Ch. 20, p. 284; *Hodges v. Humkin*, 2 Bulst. 139, 80 Eng. Rep. 1015 (K.B. 1615). "By the seventeenth century, England had extended this principle to punishments that called for incarceration. In one case, the King's Court ruled that "imprisonment ought always to be according to the quality of the offence." *See also The Eighth Amendment, Proportionality, and the Changing Meaning Of Punishments*, 122 HARV. L. REV. 960 (2009).
[28] Solem v. Helm, 463 U.S. 277, 284 (1983).
[29] 501 U.S. 957, 111 S. Ct. 2680, 115 L. Ed. 2d 836 (1991).
[30] Headley, *Proportionality Between Crimes, Offenses, and Punishments*, 17 ST. THOMAS L. REV. 247, 260 (2004).
[31] Coker v. Georgia, 433 U.S. 584, 97 S. Ct. 2861, 53 L. Ed. 2d 982 (1977); Eberheart v. Georgia, 433 U.S. 917, 97 S. Ct. 2994, 53 L. Ed. 2d 1104 (1977); Enmund v. Florida, 458 U.S. 782, 801, 102 S.Ct. 3368, 73 L.Ed.2d 1140 (1982); Tison v. Arizona, 481 U.S. 137, 149, 107 S.Ct. 1676, 95 L.Ed.2d 127 (1987); Eddings v. Oklahoma, 455 U.S. 104, 111–112, 102 S.Ct. 869, 71 L.Ed.2d 1 (1982).
[32] 408 U.S. 238, 311 (1972).
[33] 543 U.S. 551, 125 S.Ct. 1183 (2005).

Justice Sandra Day O'Connor noted that the "precept of justice that punishment for crime should be…proportioned to [the] offense,"[34] applies with special force to the death penalty. The Eighth Amendment prohibition is subject to no caveat and bars inherently barbaric punishments as well as those deemed to be "'excessive' in relation to the crime committed."[35] A sanction is said to be beyond the State's authority to inflict if it makes "no measurable contribution" to acceptable penal goals or is "grossly out of proportion to the severity of the crime."[36]

In capital cases, the US Constitution demands that the punishment be tailored both to the nature of the crime itself and to the defendant's personal responsibility and moral guilt. Justice O'Connor's formulation creates a dual-pronged approach by which the necessity of the punishment as a measure of achieving relevant societal goals and its proportionality with respect to the actual crime are combined to determine what is deemed "excessive" as a matter of constitutional imperative. Disproportionately harsh punishments represent an impermissible extension of government's otherwise laudable power to punish wrongdoers in defense of the common good. In addition to *Solem*, in which the Court overturned a sentence of life without possibility of parole given under a state recidivism statute, the Court held that two Georgia statutes that prescribed the death penalty for rape and kidnapping were invalid manifestations of state power because they were disproportionally harsh.[37]

Every punishment imposed by the government must be commensurate with the offense committed by the defendant. As noted above, this is really nothing more than an assessment of whether the means employed are appropriate to achieve the desired and demonstrable ends. To quote the Canadian Supreme Court:[38]

[W]here a murder is committed by someone already abusing his power by illegally dominating another, the murder should be treated as an exceptionally serious crime. [… The] decision to treat more seriously murders that have been committed while the offender is exploiting a position of power through illegal domination of the victim accords with the principle that there must be a proportionality between a sentence and the moral blameworthiness of the offender and other considerations such as deterrence and societal condemnation of the acts of the offender.

---

[34] *Id.*, at 589 citing Weems v. United States, 217 U.S. 349, 367, 30 S.Ct. 544, 54 L.Ed. 793 (1910).
[35] Coker v. Georgia, 433 U.S. 584, 592, 97 S.Ct. 2861, 53 L.Ed.2d 982 (1977) (plurality opinion).
[36] Roper *supra*, at 589.
[37] *Id.* (State death penalty for rape and kidnapping unconstitutional as disproportionate.)
[38] R. v. Arkell, 2 S.C.R. 695, 704 (1990).

By contrast, the US Supreme Court in *Solem v. Helm* (noted above) focused not on larger theories of punishment and justice but chose to specify objective criteria that should guide the proportionality analysis: "1] the gravity of the offense and the harshness of the penalty; 2] the sentences imposed on other criminals in the same jurisdiction; and 3] the sentences imposed for commission of the same crime in other jurisdictions."[39]

In the jurisprudence of the international criminal tribunals, the comparison of sentences imposed for similar offenses and a detailed comparison of mitigating and aggravating factors between perpetrators and cases is likewise permissible.[40] The International Criminal Tribunal for the former Yugoslavia (ICTY) has noted that "the fundamental principle of proportionality must be taken into account."[41] Many Tribunal opinions accordingly dedicate great length and care to a recitation of the detailed factors in aggravation and mitigation needed to fix an individualized sentence on the basis of the applicable facts and law. The *Deronjić* Trial Chamber noted that

> The Statute explicitly vests the judges with discretion to determine the appropriate punishment for each accused and each act charged. Thus, when the Trial Chamber evaluates the different sentencing factors, it does so in the interest of the nature and gravity of the crimes committed, the circumstances surrounding the acts themselves, the degree of responsibility of an accused for the act, and the personality of the accused.[42]

We recognize the recurring resort to proportionality analysis as a key factor in assessing just punishments with one important caveat. When applied to criminal sentencing norms, it may be conceptually possible to conflate proportionality with the well-established prohibitions against laws that are constitutionally infirm as overbroad restrictions on individual liberties. This is related to the problem of conflation between proportionality and necessity that we noted previously. The

---

[39] Solem, *supra* at 292.

[40] *See, e.g.* Prosecutor v. Momir Nikolić, Case No. IT-02-60/1-A, Judgment on Sentencing Appeal, ¶¶ 40-47 (Int'l Crim. Trib. For the Former Yugoslavia Mar. 8, 2006)(The similarities to the *Obrenović* case are striking (both cases are related to the crimes committed after the fall of the Srebrenica enclave, and both accused pleaded guilty to the crime of persecutions). Therefore, the Appeals Chamber scrutinised in detail the differences with respect to the number and type of crimes, the level of participation, as well as the aggravating and mitigating circumstances (paras 42-46). It held that the difference between the sentence of Momir Nikolić and Obrenović is justified (para. 47).)

[41] Prosecutor v. Miroslav Deronjic, Case No. IT-02-61-S, Sentencing Judgment, ¶ 139 (Int'l Crim. Trib. For the Former Yugoslavia Mar. 30, 2004), *available at* http://www.unhcr.org/refworld/docid/4146efc94.html [accessed 30 January 2013].

[42] Id., ¶ 138.

Canadian Supreme Court explored this connection in upholding the life sentence adjudged against Momin Khawaja[43] for violating the Anti-Terrorism Act of 2001.

In explaining the connection between these "interrelated" doctrines, the Canadian Supreme Court wrote that overbreadth "occurs when the means selected by the legislator are broader than necessary to achieve the state objective, and gross disproportionality occurs when state actions or legislative responses to a problem are "so extreme as to be disproportionate to any legitimate government interest."[44] Avoiding a lengthy separate analysis of the two doctrines, Chief Justice McLachlin rested the majority analysis upon the foundational purpose of the Canadian statute "to provide means by which terrorism may be prosecuted and prevented" rather than imputing a broader purpose to "punish individuals for innocent, socially useful or casual acts which, absent any intent, indirectly contribute to a terrorist activity."[45]

To be convicted under the Canadian domestic terrorism statute, a perpetrator must knowingly participate in or contribute to such criminal activity but the *actus reus* must also be undertaken for the higher purpose of enhancing the ability of a terrorist group or to facilitate an act of terrorism. Thus, the higher *mens rea* requirement narrowed the band of prohibited conduct sufficiently to make the law itself sustainable, and the punishment flowing from its enforcement suitable.

For our purposes, the most salient aspect of Khawaja is the deliberate use of the means–ends test in assessing proportionality (hence the constitutionality of both the statute and the sentence):

> I return to the central question: is s. 83.18 broader than necessary or does it have a grossly disproportionate impact, considering that the state objective is the prevention and prosecution of terrorism? It is true that s. 83.18 captures a wide range of conduct. However, as we have seen, the scope of that conduct is reduced by the requirement of specific intent and the exclusion of conduct that a reasonable person would not view as capable of materially enhancing the abilities of a terrorist group to facilitate or carry out a terrorist activity. On the other side of the scale lies the objective of preventing the devastating harm that may result from terrorist activity. When the tailored reach of the section

---

[43] *See* Her Majesty the Queen v. Mohammed Momin Khawaja [2008] Ontario Superior Court of Justice, Court File 04-G30282, *reprinted in*, I Terrorism International Case Law Reporter 319 (Michael Newton, ed. 2008)(assessing a sentence of 10.5 years for support to terrorism, which was subsequently extended to life imprisonment upon the cross appeal of the Prosecutor).

[44] R. v. Khawaja, 2012 SCC 69, ¶ 40(decided Dec. 14, 2012)(*citing* Canada (Attorney General) v. PHS Services, at para, 133).

[45] *Id.* at para. 44, *citing* Application under s. 83.28 of the Criminal Code (Re), at para. 39.

is weighed against the objective, it cannot be said that the selected means are broader than necessary or that the impact of the section is disproportionate.

Though couched in the language of the comparative balancing of competing objectives, this deliberate use of a careful means–ends analysis is repeated in other applications and contexts.

By extension, the sense of justice and moral rightness embedded in the proportionality review of criminal punishments also applies to the fit between the harm caused and the appropriate civil damages to be imposed for such harm. The US Supreme Court has accordingly held that proportionality prohibits the imposition of grossly excessive or arbitrary punishments on a tortfeasor; "[i]n sum, courts must ensure that the measure of punishment is both reasonable and proportionate to the amount of harm to the plaintiff and to the general damages recovered. In the context of this case, we have no doubt that there is a presumption against an award that has a 145-to-1 ratio."[46]

Conversely, in the ICTY case of *Prosecutor v. Deronjić,* the presiding judge, Judge Schomberg penned a separate opinion dissenting from the ten-year sentence imposed by his colleagues after the perpetrator pled guilty to a single count of persecution as a crime against humanity. Judge Schomberg said that the "sentence is not proportional to the crimes it is based on and amounts to a singing from the wrong hymn sheet. The Accused deserves a sentence of no less than twenty years of imprisonment."[47]

Finally, the requirement of a proportionate linkage between the harm imposed and the larger objective is also frequently enforced in maritime law. The International Tribunal for the Law of the Sea has applied proportionality review as the evaluative criterion for what constitutes a "reasonable bond or other financial security" within the meaning of the Law of the Sea Convention.[48] States Party do not have unlimited punitive power to detain vessels flagged in other states but must "comply promptly with the decision of the court or tribunal" that imposes such a "reasonable bond or other financial security" as a condition precedent to prompt release of the ship and its cargo.[49] In *Honshinmaru,* for example, the judgment was clear that "The Tribunal is of the view that the amount of a bond should be proportionate to the gravity of the alleged offences. Article 292 of the Law of the Sea Convention is designed to ensure that the coastal State, when fixing the bond, adheres to the requirement

---

[46] State Farm Mutual Auto. Ins. Co. v. Campbell, 538 U.S. 408 (2003).

[47] Prosecutor v. Deronjic, Judgment on Sentencing Appeal Case No. IT-02-61-S, ICTY Trial Chamber 30 March 2004, Dissenting Opinion of Judge Schomburg, para. 2.

[48] United Nations Convention on the Law of the Sea, Dec. 10, 1982, 1833 U.N.T.S. 397, art. 292(1). *available at* http://www.un.org/depts/los/convention_agreements/texts/unclos/UNCLOS-TOC.htm.

[49] *Id.* art. 292(4).

stipulated in article 73, paragraph 2, of the convention, namely, that the bond it fixes is reasonable in light of the assessment of relevant factors."[50] Thus, the law of the sea mirrors the punishment norms across other areas of law because

> [i]t is by reference to the penalties imposed or imposable under the law of the detaining State that the tribunal may evaluate the gravity of the alleged offences, taking into account the circumstances of the case and the *need to avoid disproportion* between the gravity of the alleged offences and the amount of the bond.[51] (emphasis added)

We will return to maritime law later in this chapter to discuss proportionality assessments that are not related to penal sanctions.

III. THE REGULATION OF INVESTOR–STATE INTERESTS

One need make only a short conceptual leap from the use of proportionality as a limitation on State power in imposing punishments against private citizens to understand its increasing importance in the field of international investment law. Transnational trade has become the hallmark of a global economy and the corresponding necessity for promoting sustainable development within emerging economies is obvious. The countervailing interests, of course, lie in the private economic incentives of the investors, who assume the risks of development in unstable areas and who bear the pecuniary risks of business failure. Those who provide capital and economic expertise across borders often do so in the context of volatile political winds and an unpredictable or perhaps poorly trained labor force. Though there are many examples, the Al Qa'ida-inspired seizure of the In Amenas oil refinery complex in Algeria (that is in the news at the time of this writing) reminds us of the grave risks, both human and financial, that corporations and investors must make to fuel the global economy.[52] One knowledgeable insider observed that "[a]n event like this really shakes the foundations of the investment climate."[53]

---

[50] The Honsinmaru Case (Japan v. Russian Federation Application for Prompt Release), Case No. 14, Judgment, ¶ 88 (Int'l Trib. For the Law of the Sea Aug 6, 2007), *available at* http://www.itlos.org/fileadmin/itlos/documents/cases/case_no_14/Judgment_Honshinmaru_No._14_E.pdf.

[51] The Juno Trader Case (Saint Vincent and the Grenadines v. Guinea-Bissau) Application for Prompt Release, Case No. 13, Judgment, ¶ 89 (Int'l Trib. For the Law of the Sea Dec. 18, 2004), *available at* http://www.itlos.org/fileadmin/itlos/documents/cases/case_no_13/judgment_181204_eng.pdf.

[52] Adam Nossiter and Scott Sayare, *Americans Held Hostage In Algeria Gas-Field Raid*, N.Y.TIMES, Jan. 17, 2013, at A1.

[53] Clifford Krauss, *At Algerian Oil and Gas Fields Once Thought Safe, New Fears and Precautions*, N.Y. TIMES, Jan. 18, 2013, at A10.

Some commentators have noted that the principle of proportionality is a facially neutral notion. In World Trade Organization (WTO) law, one view is that there is no comprehensive principle of proportionality that can be divorced from the specific provisions of the relevant agreements such as Art. XX GATT.[54] Yet the rise of proportionality as a frequently invoked tenet within the jurisprudence of the WTO Dispute Settlement mechanism[55] and various arbitral bodies has the potential to encroach upon the regulatory discretion of the host nation by providing a blanket rationale for strengthening private property rights against otherwise legitimate state functions.[56] Nevertheless, the sovereign right of states to regulate commercial activities within their borders and to ensure the public safety, environmental health, and general public weal is overarching and undeniable. Proportionality thus becomes a crucial fulcrum to resolve one of the most important tensions in the arena of international investment. This role is subtle but vitally important as transnational trade and investment relies upon stability in the markets and the expectations of investors.

Apart from the inherent risk in providing investment capital across national boundaries, economically feasible entrepreneurships require a delicate synergy between the property rights of investors and the sovereign prerogatives of the host nation. There has been an explosion of bilateral investment treaties over the past two decades, and virtually every one of the thousands of current international investment agreements provide language to protect foreign investors from arbitrary or uncompensated seizure of their property at the hands of the host nation. The terminology in agreements related to the regulation of property rights varies considerably, but such terms as expropriation, taking, nationalization, deprivation, and dispossession are often encountered.

An overwhelming majority of international investment agreements permit states to expropriate investments as long as the taking is undertaken to implement a legitimate public purpose, in a nondiscriminatory manner, under due process of law, and against the payment of compensation.[57] Though there have been a number of cases in recent years to provide depth and context to these requirements related to direct takings at the hands of state authority, there has also been increasing debate about

---

[54] Axel Desmedt, *Proportionality in WTO Law*, 4 J INT. ECONOMIC L. 441–480 (2001).

[55] Proportionality is a prominent, well-nigh pervasive feature of litigation under the WTO Dispute Settlement Understanding because the WTO Agreement on Subsidies and Countervailing Measures requires that any countermeasure that might serve to restrict free trade be "equivalent" to "the nullification or impairment" caused by the initial trade violation. Andrew D. Mitchell, *Proportionality and Remedies in WTO Disputes* 17 EUR. J. INT'L L. 985 (2006).

[56] Han Xiuli, *The Application of the Principle of Proportionality in Tecmed v. Mexico*, 6 CHINESE J. INT'L L. 635 (2007).

[57] EXPROPRIATION: UNCTAD SERIES ON ISSUES IN INTERNATIONAL INVESTMENT AGREEMENTS, A SEQUEL 27–51 (2012), *available at* http://unctad.org/en/Docs/unctaddiaeia2011d7_en.pdf.

the appropriate balance between the State's prerogative to regulate commerce and the use of such regulatory structures to effect an indirect, or so-called "creeping" expropriation. In sum, the distinction lies between an impermissible and compensable indirect taking of private property and the use of a legitimate scope of regulatory authority that is noncompensable even if the property rights of the investors are undermined or extinguished, in extreme cases.

Over the past decade, the use of the proportionality principle as the dispositive test for deciding such issues has become a common dimension of trade regulation. Investment treaty tribunals considering disputes between States and private investors increasingly develop proportionality analysis where investment treaties frame the duties of the States in relation to investors and investments without establishing binding standards for permitted departures from or limits to these duties for public regulatory purposes to protect other important interests.[58] The ECJ described just such a proportionality analysis as follows:

Appraising the proportionality of national rules which pursue a legitimate aim under [European] Community law involves weighing the national interest in attaining that aim against the Community interest in ensuring the free movement of goods.[59]

In the context of restricting individual liberties, the European Court of Human Rights (ECHR) has examined the permissible scope of state takings that supersede private property rights as follows:[60]

Not only must a measure depriving a person of his property pursue, on the facts as well as in principle, a legitimate aim "in the public interest," but there must also be a reasonable relationship of proportionality between the means employed and the aim sought to be realized...[...]. The requisite balance will not be found if the person concerned has had to bear "an individual and excessive burden" [...] The Court considers that a measure must be both appropriate for achieving its aim and not disproportionate thereto.

---

[58] *See generally* Benedict Kingsbury and Stephan Schill, *Investor-State Arbitration as Governance: Fair and Equitable Treatment, Proportionality and the Emerging Global Administrative Law in* Albert Jan van den Berg 50 Years of the New York Convention 5 (2009), *available at* http://papers.ssrn.com/sol3/papers. cfm?abstract_id=1466980.

[59] Stoke-on-Trent, Case C-169/91 [1992] ECR I-6625, para 15.

[60] In the case of James and Others, ECtHR, Application Number 8793/79 Judgment of February 21, 1986, para. 50 (Para. 75 of the Judgment goes on to clarify that a difference of treatment is discriminatory if it has no objective and reasonable justification, that is, if it does not pursue a legitimate aim or if there is not a reasonable relationship of proportionality between the means employed and the aim sought to be realized).

Within the International Center for Settlement of Investment Disputes (ICSID), the *Tecmed v. Mexico* case[61] was the first one where the tribunal explicitly relied on the proportionality analysis to evaluate infringements on commercial rights. The *Tecmed* dispute arose out of the decision of the environmental authority to deny renewal of a permit to the Mexican subsidiary of a Spanish company to operate a landfill of hazardous waste. After finding that the deprivation had been total, the tribunal wrote the following (emphasis added to highlight the proposed evaluative criteria):

> After establishing that regulatory actions and measures will not be initially excluded from the definition of expropriatory acts, in addition to the negative financial impact of such actions or measures, the Arbitral Tribunal will consider, in order to determine if they are to be characterized as expropriatory, whether such actions or measures are proportional to the public interest presumably protected thereby and to the protection legally granted to investments, taking into account that the significance of such impact has a key role upon deciding the proportionality. Although the analysis starts at the due deference owing to the State when defining the issues that affect its public policy or the interests of society as a whole, as well as the actions that will be implemented to protect such values, such situation does not prevent the Arbitral Tribunal, without thereby questioning such due deference, from examining the actions of the State in light of Article 5(1) of the Agreement *to determine whether such measures are reasonable with respect to their goals, the deprivation of economic rights and the legitimate expectations of who suffered such deprivation. There must be a reasonable relationship of proportionality between the charge or weight imposed to the foreign investor and the aim sought to be realized by any expropriatory measure.* To value such charge or weight, it is very important to measure the size of the ownership deprivation caused by the actions of the state and whether such deprivation was compensated or not. (emphasis added)

The tribunal attributed the government's decision to deny the renewal of the permit to the pressures felt by municipal and state authorities due to social or political circumstances caused by controversy over the landfill. The tribunal established a contextual test whereby the overarching reasons asserted to support a State decision must be assessed "as a whole" in order to establish whether the resulting negative

---

[61] ICSID case no. ARB(AF)/00/2, Award (29 May 2003), 43 I.L.M. 134 (2004)[Arbitrators: Horacio A. Grigera Naoń (Argentine), President; Joseé Carlos Fernańdez Rozas (Spanish) and Carlos Bernal Verea (Mexican)], *available at* http://www.worldbank.org/icsid/cases/laudo-051903%20-English.pdf.

economic effects were proportionate.[62] The political context was deemed to be dispositive only in the exceptional circumstances in which political officials engaged in the functional equivalent of outright expropriation as a necessary step in avoiding "a serious emergency situation, social crisis or public unrest, in addition to the economic impact of such a government action, which in this case deprived the foreign investor of its investment with no compensation whatsoever."[63] This would obviously be a very rare instance.

In the language of the ICSID tribunal "[t]hese factors must be weighed when trying to assess the proportionality of the action adopted with respect to the purpose pursued." Thus, proportionality became the vocabulary for importing an implicit element in trade agreements as a means of measuring whether a decision purportedly "necessary" for achieving the nontrade policy objective pursued (such as the environment or human health) is also the least trade-restrictive alternative available. Again, importing a strict means–ends analysis under the rubric of proportionality, the total deprivation of the investment's value was deemed to be disproportionate to the demonstrable benefits accrued from the decision, and therefore found to be an impermissible indirect expropriation in *Tecmed*. To foreshadow our analysis in Chapter 7, we will argue that in *jus in bello* proportionality analysis, more is involved than these simple means–ends ways to assess proportionality.

The proportionality principle has been followed in subsequent ICSID cases, though not without some controversy.[64] The *Azurix v. Argentina* tribunal referred to the practice of the ECHR and the *Tecmed* decision and noted that proportionality provides "useful guidance for purposes of determining whether regulatory actions would be expropriatory and give rise to compensation."[65] In *LG&E v. Argentina*, the tribunal noted that "it can generally be said that the State has the right to adopt measures having a social or general welfare purpose."[66] From this uncontroversial baseline, the tribunal extrapolated what we will term, for the sake of convenience, the principle of prescriptive proportionality by asserting that "[i]n such a case, the measure must be accepted without any imposition of liability, except in cases where the state action is obviously disproportionate to the need being addressed."

On one level, the *LG&E* tribunal could be said to have engaged in the same reasoning as *Tecmed* by subsuming the very high necessity prong into its evaluation of

---

[62] *Id.* at para. 132.

[63] *Id.* at para. 133. For deeper analysis of these considerations, see Stephan Schill, *Revisiting a Landmark: Indirect Expropriation and Fair and Equitable Treatment in the ICSID Case Tecmed*, 3 TRANSNAT'L DISP MGT. 1, 7–14 (Nov. 2006).

[64] *See* ANTONIO R. PARRA THE HISTORY OF ICSID (2012).

[65] *Azurix v. Argentina*, Award, 14 July 2006, para. 312.

[66] *LG&E v. Argentina*, Decision on Liability, 3 October 2006, para. 195.

"social or general welfare," and thus, although this threshold is seldom met, regulations of that nature "must be accepted." On the other hand, *LG&E* superimposed a proportionality requirement even in light of a valid regulatory purpose and a stringent finding of necessity. It is worth noting that these cases involve ad hoc tribunals rather than established institutions like the ECHR or the ECJ. Furthermore, the expropriation claim was dismissed in each, suggesting a result-oriented approach. There is no explanation for invoking proportionality as the rule of decision beyond reference to its common usage in other contexts.

The ECHR utilizes a somewhat different logic than ICSID when it comes to the principle of proportionality within investment litigation by using it not only to determine whether or not there has been an expropriation but also to estimate the amount of compensation. Hence, compensation for what has been deemed a lawful expropriation of property must be "reasonably related to its value," even though "legitimate objectives of 'public interest' may call for less than reimbursement of the full market value."[67] In the milieu of international investment, this is presumed to be governed by the contractual provisions requiring what the United Nations (UN) General Assembly termed "appropriate" compensation for more than half a century.[68] This is of course a context specific equitable principle, which is explicitly referenced in a number of investment agreements.

Equitable compensation, which in some contexts seems to be synonymous with proportionate compensation, is subsumed within the following types of provisions that arguably give more latitude for assessing private versus public interests (e.g., "just" compensation in the Chile-Tunisia BIT (1998), "fair and equitable" compensation in the India-United Kingdom BIT (1994), or "just and equitable" compensation in the Mozambique-Netherlands BIT (2001)).[69] Many BITs now prescribe "prompt, adequate and effective" compensation (known as the "Hull formula") that seeks to guarantee fair market value compensation.

The test for necessity under the human rights regime is much more stringent as we will see in Chapter 6. The scope of permissible limitation between individual right holders and investment entities surely cannot be presumed to be identical. The ECJ hinted at just such a discrepancy in applying proportionality only after a careful comparative analysis:

---

[67] *Pincova and Pinc v. the Czech Republic,* European Court of Human Rights, Judgment, 5 November 2002, para. 53.

[68] Resolution 1803 (XVII), 14 December 1962, Declaration on Permanent Sovereignty over Natural Resources, para. 4; Resolution 3281 (XXIX), 12 December 1974, The Charter of Economic Rights and Duties of States (A/RES/29/3281), Article 2(c).

[69] EXPROPRIATION: UNCTAD SERIES ON ISSUES IN INTERNATIONAL INVESTMENT AGREEMENTS, A SEQUEL 41(2012), *available at* http://unctad.org/en/Docs/unctaddiaeia2011d7_en.pdf.

[T]he principle of proportionality...requires that measures adopted by Community institutions should not exceed the limits of what is appropriate and necessary in order to attain the legitimate objectives pursued by the legislation in question, and where there is a choice between several appropriate measures, recourse must be had to the least onerous, and the disadvantages caused must not be disproportionate to the aims pursued...[70]

Thus, at the time of this writing, the premise that property rights may be curtailed to further a legitimate purpose when state action imposes regulations that are nondiscriminatory and proportionate appears to be well established. This is true despite a lack of textual support in investment treaties or multilateral trade agreements for importing proportionality from other contexts, and notwithstanding the discrepancies noted above in the precise formulations for assessing proportionality. Proportionality in the trade context appears to replicate a means–ends approach whereby the exercise of state power must be directed at legitimate ends while employing measures that more or less maintain a rough balance between property rights and the larger public interest.

IV. MARITIME DELIMITATION

Proportionality is a cornerstone principle of maritime law, though its properties in that discipline find a dual usage that seems to commingle equity and mere extrapolation. As a principle of coastline delimitation, proportionality is best seen as a mathematical projection designed to achieve an equitable solution to disputes between States. Proportionality thus serves as the test to compare the coastal and areal ratios of adjacent maritime States. From this perspective, the proportionality test compares the ratios of space in the maritime areas allocated to the contesting States by a proposed delimitation as contrasted to the respective coastal lengths.[71] These relationships may be expressed in terms of mathematical ratios, though the caselaw demonstrates that maritime delimitations are often charged with controversy and high stakes implications. Thus, there cannot be a simple mathematical formula for fairness given the conflicting claims to resources, maritime access, historical claims, and differing societal expectations.

---

[70] Case T-13/99, *Pfizer* [2002] ECR II-3305, paras 411-13. In many instances, the ECJ delegates the decision whether domestic measure is disproportionate to the national courts. *See*, in this respect, Case C-67/98 *Zenatti* [1999] ECR I-07289, para 37.

[71] YUCEL ACER, THE AEGEAN MARITIME DISPUTES AND INTERNATIONAL LAW, 178 (2003); see also Leonard Legault, Blair Hankey, *Method, Oppositeness and Adjacency, and Proportionality in Maritime Boundary Delimitation*, in I INTERNATIONAL MARITIME BOUNDARIES 217 (Jonathan I. Charney, ed. 1993).

In its secondary role, proportionality serves as an after the fact tool to evaluate the relative lengths of the coastlines. This duality of function was endorsed by the ICJ in *Libya v. Malta*:[72]

> It is…one thing to employ proportionality calculations to check a result; it is another thing to take note, in the course of the delimitation process, of the existence of a very marked difference in coastal lengths, and to attribute the appropriate significance to that coastal relationship, without seeking to define it in quantitative terms which are only suited to the ex post assessment of relationships of coast to area. The two operations are neither mutually exclusive, nor so closely identified with each other that the one would necessarily render the other supererogatory. Consideration of the comparability or otherwise of the coastal lengths is part of the process of determining an equitable boundary on the basis of an initial median line; the test of a reasonable degree of proportionality, on the other hand, is one which can be applied to check the equitableness of any line, whatever the method used to arrive at that line.

In its November 2012 *Nicaragua v. Colombia* opinion, the ICJ further noted that jurists must avoid "applying a principle of strict proportionality" because maritime delimitation is not a mathematical process designed merely to "produce a correlation between the lengths of the Parties' relevant coasts and their respective shares of the relevant area."[73] Indeed, the ICJ quoted its own jurisprudence for support in rejecting a formulaic mathematical test because if "such a use of proportionality were right, it is difficult to see what room would be left for any other consideration; for it would be at once the principle of entitlement to continental shelf rights and also the method of putting that principle into operation."[74] Such an approach accords with that of the Arbitral Tribunal in *Barbados v. Trinidad and Tobago*, which noted that proportionality

> does not require the drawing of a delimitation line in a manner that is mathematically determined by the exact ratio of the lengths of the relevant coastlines. Although mathematically certain, this would in many cases lead to an inequitable result. Delimitation rather requires the consideration of the relative lengths of coastal frontages as one element in the process of delimitation taken as a whole. The degree of adjustment called for by any given disparity in coastal

---

[72] 1985 I.C.J. Rep. 49, para. 66.

[73] Territorial and Maritime Dispute (Nicarauga v. Colombia), Judgment, (Int'l Court of Justice Nov. 19, 2012), *available at* http://www.icj-cij.org/docket/files/124/17164.pdf.

[74] Continental Shelf (Libyan Arab Jamahiriya/Malta), Judgment, 1985 I.C.J. Reports 45, para. 58.

lengths is a matter for the Tribunal's judgment in the light of all the circumstances of the case.[75]

For our purposes, the most notable aspect of the application of proportionality to maritime disputes is the phraseology of its threshold utility. The *Barbados v. Trinidad and Tobago* tribunal specified that proportionality functions as "a final check upon the equity of a tentative delimitation to ensure that the result is not tainted by some form of *gross disproportion*" (emphasis added). The International Tribunal for the Law of the Sea has sought to avoid a "significant disproportion" of results.[76] The ICJ added the final word for the moment on this score in *Nicaragua v. Colombia*:

> The Court thus considers that its task, at this third stage, is not to attempt to achieve even an approximate correlation between the ratio of the lengths of the Parties' relevant coasts and the ratio of their respective shares of the relevant area. It is, rather, to ensure that there is not a disproportion so gross as to "taint" the result and render it inequitable. Whether any disproportion is so great as to have that effect is not a question capable of being answered by reference to any mathematical formula but is a matter which can be answered only in the light of all the circumstances of the particular case.[77]

Proportionality therefore serves as a rough proxy for a showing that there is an equitable division of resources, as for example not to put the fisherman of one State at a grossly inequitable disadvantage nor distribute minerals or oil and gas riches on the continental shelf in a grossly unfair manner. In this manner, proportionality helps to ensure a lasting and sustainable peace following the determination of a maritime boundary by an appropriately empowered tribunal. Just as in the investment context, it also serves as a useful proxy principle for seeking equitable resolution of otherwise persistent interstate disputes.

---

[75] Award, 11 April 2006, 139 INT. L. REP. 449, 547.

[76] Dispute Concerning Delimitation of the Maritime Boundary Between Bangladesh and Myanmar in the Bay of Bengal (Bangladesh/Myanmar), Case No. 16, Judgment, ¶ 499 (Int'l Trib. For the Law of the Sea Mar. 14, 2012), *available at* http://www.itlos.org/fileadmin/itlos/documents/cases/case_no_16/1-C16_Judgment_14_02_2012.pdf.

[77] Territorial and Maritime Dispute (Nicarauga v. Colombia), Judgment, ¶ 242 (Int'l Court of Justice Nov. 19, 2012), *available at* http://www.icj-cij.org/docket/files/124/17164.pdf.

to their authority. We will address many of the implications for the juxtaposition of proportionality as an interdisciplinary concept in Chapter 7, and expand on the themes introduced below. With these purposes in mind, we simply wish to introduce some of the key dimensions of the proportionality principle as applied in the human rights domain.

Within the treaty-based human rights regime, the proportionality principle has at least three specific roles: 1] As a benchmark to establish the legality of derogations; 2] With the aim to establish the legality of interferences by States with covenant rights; 3] To determine scope of application of some of the rights established by the convention. Proportionality represents one of the primary principles that serves to limit governmental intrusion into otherwise protected rights. Applying this precept, the UN Human Rights Council held that detention (i.e., the deprivation of the human right to liberty) in a national context may be necessary to prevent what it termed *abscondment*, provided that such detention is "not disproportionate to the end sought, and it was not unpredictable, given that the relevant detention provisions had been in force for some time and were published."[87]

All of the relevant human rights treaties provide that in some specific contexts, States may lawfully modify the scope of human rights protections, i.e., derogations, which would be afforded during normal conditions. The right to derogate is subject to procedural requirements and to additional subjective qualifiers. Certain rights are nonderogable such as the prohibition on arbitrary killings or torture under the International Covenant on Civil and Political Rights (ICCPR), as well as the American and European Human Rights Conventions. In Chapter 6, we will see that the nonderogable right to life from the human rights perspective is limited by narrow exceptions in extreme circumstances of self-defense and, more generally, by the principles arising from the laws and customs of war. As we shall see, the taking of life represents the precise point of friction between the broad application of human rights principles and the permissive regime of humanitarian law applicable to the conduct of war; if applied too broadly in the context of armed conflicts, the human rights prohibitions would seemingly make such armed conflict disproportionate in nearly every case.

Yet, even potentially derogable rights may have a nonderogable core.[88] For example, sitting as the High Court of Justice, the Supreme Court of Israel ruled in favor of Palestinian farmers who had been denied access to their land by the military commander ostensibly for their own protection on the grounds that "it is not rational

---

[87] C. v. Australia, Comm. 900/1999, U.N. Doc. A/58/40, Vol. II, at 188, 4.28 (HRC 2002).

[88] *See generally* U.N. Human Rights Committee, *General Comment No. 29*, U.N. Doc. CCPR/C/21/Rev.1/Add.11 on Art. 4 ICCPR, ¶ 16 (2001).

that this policy should be the sole solution to the situation in the area, since it violates the rights of the Palestinian farmers to freedom of movement and their property rights disproportionately."[89] Though the High Court of Justice based its reasoning on the implications of occupation law, the logical basis for this decision flows from the fact that when any state that is a party to the ICCPR "invokes a legitimate ground for restriction of freedom of expression, it must demonstrate in specific and individualized fashion the precise nature of the threat, and the necessity and proportionality of the specific action taken, in particular by establishing a direct and immediate connection between the expression and the threat."[90] The means–ends linkage inherent in the law of derogations incorporates proportionality by requiring that limitations on ICCPR rights must be "only to the extent strictly required."[91] This makes the necessity prong subject to the narrowest and most restrictive interpretation.

Of particular note, the fissure between *jus in bello* proportionality and the application of that same term in the field of human rights remains one of the most difficult dilemmas of the modern legal era.[92] In the *Nuclear Weapons* case, the ICJ laid out the overlapping standards for determining the applicability of legal norms in the use or threat to use nuclear weapons:

[t]he protection of the International Covenant on Civil and Political Rights does not cease in times of war, except by operation of Article 4 of the Covenant whereby certain provisions may be derogated from in a time of national

---

[89] Morar v. IDF Commander in Judaea and Samaria, HCJ 9593/04, 2 Is. L. Rep. 56, para. 30 (2006)(Article 43 "sets out the duty and power of the military commander to maintain order and security in the territory under his control. There is no doubt that one of the main duties for which the military commander is responsible within this framework is the duty to ensure that law is upheld in the territories."). See also Yesh Din v. Commander of IDF Forces in Judaea and Samaria, et. al, HCJ 2164/09, (26 Dec. 2011)("As is well known, Article 43 has been recognized in our jurisprudence as a quasi-constitutional framework provision that sets out the general framework for the way the duties and powers of the military commander must be exercised in occupied territory.").

[90] U.N. Human Rights Committee, *General Comment No. 34*, U.N. Doc. CCPR/C/GC/34, para. 35 (Sept. 12, 2011), *available at* http://www2.ohchr.org/english/bodies/hrc/docs/GC34.pdf

[91] SARAH JOSEPH, JENNY SCHULTZ, AND MELISSA CASTAN, THE INTERNATIONAL COVENANT ON CIVIL AND POLITICAL RIGHTS: CASES, MATERIALS, AND COMMENTARY, 825, para. 25.54 (2d ed. 2005).

[92] *See generally* Bankovic and Others v. Belgium, 2001-XII Eur. Ct. H.R. 333, *reprinted in* 123 I.L.R. 94 (2001); Francoise J. Hampson, Is *Human Rights Law of Any Relevance to the War in Afghanistan?*, THE WAR IN AFGHANISTAN: A LEGAL ANALYSIS, 85 NAVAL WAR COL. INT'L. L. STUD. 485 (Michael Schmitt, ed., 2009); Michael J. Dennis, *Application of Human Rights Treaties Extraterritorially in Times of Armed Conflict and Military Occupation*, 99 AM. J. INT'L L. 119 (2005); Michael J. Dennis & Andre M. Surena, *Application of the International Covenant on Civil and Political Rights in Times of Armed Conflict and Military Occupation: The Gap between Legal Theory and State Practice*, 13 EUROPEAN HUMAN RIGHTS L. REV. 714 (2008); Nigel Rodley, *The Extraterritorial Reach and Applicability in Armed Conflict of the International Covenant on Civil and Political Rights: A Rejoinder to Dennis and Surena*, 14 EUROPEAN HUMAN RIGHTS L. REV 628 (2009).

emergency. Respect for the right to life is not, however, such a provision. In principle, the right not arbitrarily to be deprived of [one's] life also applies in hostilities. The test of what is an arbitrary deprivation of life, however, then falls to be determined by the applicable *lex specialis*, namely, the law applicable in armed conflict which is designed to regulate the conduct of hostilities. Thus whether a particular loss of life, through the use of a certain weapon in warfare, is to be considered an arbitrary deprivation of life contrary to Article 6 of the Covenant can only be decided by reference to the law applicable in armed conflict and not deduced from the terms of the Covenant itself.[93]

Similarly, in the *Wall* opinion, the ICJ indicated in paragraph 106 that

the protection offered by human rights conventions does not cease in case of armed conflict, save through the effect of provisions for derogation of the kind to be found in Article 4 of the International Covenant on Civil and Political Rights. As regards the relationship between international humanitarian law and human rights law, there are thus three possible situations: some rights may be exclusively matters of international humanitarian law; others may be exclusively matters of human rights law; yet others may be matters of both these branches of international law. In order to answer the question put to it, the Court will have to take into consideration both these branches of international law, namely human rights law and, as *lex specialis*, international humanitarian law.[94]

We will say much more about the *lex specialis* test in Chapter 5.

The overriding purpose of the human rights mechanism is to ensure that States cannot impose restrictions that are applied or invoked in a manner that would impair the essence of a covenant right. From a human rights perspective, sovereign States that seek to curtail the rights of their citizens "must demonstrate their necessity and only take such measures as are proportionate to the pursuance of legitimate aims in order to ensure continuous and effective protection of Covenant rights."[95] When it comes to considering the inherent right to life, the lex lata law of armed

---

93 International Court of Justice, *Legality of the Threat or Use of Nuclear Weapons*, Advisory Opinion of July 8, 1996, ICJ Reports (1996) 226, para 25.

94 Legal Consequences of the Construction of a Wall in the Occupied Palestinian Territory, Advisory Opinion, 2004 I.C.J. 136, 177–81 (July 9), *reprinted in* 43 I.L.M. 1009, 1038–1039 (2004), *available at* http://www.icj-cij.org/docket/index.php?p1=3&

95 General Comment No. 31 [80] Nature of the General Legal Obligation Imposed on States Parties to the Covenant CCPR/C/21/Rev.1/Add.13, May 26, 2004, *available at* http://daccess-dds-ny.un.org/doc/UNDOC/GEN/G04/419/56/PDF/G0441956.pdf?OpenElement

conflict operates as the exact antithesis of this premise. Proportionality as a general premise of international law is not susceptible to one comprehensive definition, and that perhaps provides sufficient reason for scholars and practitioners to abandon efforts to achieve the elusive overarching definition in favor of deep immersion into its interdisciplinary uses.

4

PROPORTIONALITY IN THE JUST WAR TRADITION

IN THIS CHAPTER, we will critically discuss the way proportionality has traditionally been understood in the Just War tradition, a tradition that was primarily grounded in certain moral philosophies, such as the natural law approach, which itself was at best only quasi-legal. Nonetheless, the Just War tradition has had a very strong influence on international law. In that tradition, there are three branches, the *jus ad bellum* concerning justice of initiating war; *jus in bello* concerning justice of conducting war; and *jus post bellum* concerning justice at the end of war. In the first two cases, proportionality has played a major role; in the third case, there is an emerging literature concerning proportionality assessments at the end of war.

The Just War tradition is really several overlapping traditions that have their roots in Roman and early Medieval Christian thinking about the justifiability of killing. In this chapter, we will draw on significant contributions to the discussion of all three forms of proportionality contributed by the leading historical figures in the Just War tradition. In discussing the three branches of the proportionality principle, we are especially interested in how the principle's branches complement each other and also sometimes conflict. And we discuss how these largely moral and historical debates map onto the legal debates about proportionality today.

The Just War tradition involves proposed theoretical justifications for war often drawn in terms of sets of conditions that must be satisfied. The overriding object of a just war is the vindication of justice and the restoration of an enduring peace.[1] In a sense, this goal remained the underlying raison d'être for the centuries of

---

[1] *See* Roland H. Bainton, CHRISTIAN ATTITUDES TOWARDS WAR AND PEACE: A HISTORICAL SURVEY AND CRITICAL REEXAMINATION 33(1960).

moral and legal thought that followed. We will briefly examine the criteria for the non-proportionality conditions for each of the three branches of the Just War tradition, but will mainly focus on proportionality conditions. It is our contention that significant insights for international law can be gleaned from the debates about proportionality in earlier centuries. But we are also critical of some of the Just War ideas, especially war seen justified as punishment for offenses against natural law.

Proportionality has been understood in the Just War tradition, at least as far back as the very early sixteenth century, as involving three separate sets of conditions. The sixteenth century philosopher Francisco Vitoria said:

> When war for a just cause has broken out, it must not be waged so as to ruin people against whom it is directed, but only so as to obtain one's rights... When victory has been won and the war is over, the victory should be utilized with moderation and Christian humility.[2]

In this vein, for Vitoria, the dominant goal was to avoid war altogether. Even as the lust for gold drove Spanish soldiers to ravage the New World in a horrific pattern of brutality and betrayal, the king issued the so-called Requirement in 1513 proscribing that natives should not be converted by force nor killed for rejecting the gospel. Peace would be restored when the native inhabitants acknowledged the Roman Catholic Church as the ruler of the world, and the king of Spain as its authentic representative for the preaching of the faith. The underlying premise was that force ought to be focused on the achievement of the specified goals, and minimized to the degree necessary to vindicate those rights.

By the early seventeenth century, Francisco Suarez stated the core concept more concisely: "due proportion must be observed in its beginning, during its prosecution, and after victory." Suarez says he is following in the footsteps of Vitoria. Here is the division of Just War into *jus ad bellum, jus in bello,* and *jus post bellum,* which will form the organization of the first three sections of this chapter. In Section IV, we examine how these three branches of the Just War tradition intersect with each other. In Section V, we look at some specific applications of the Just War thinking for international law today.

---

[2] Francisco Vitoria, De Indus et de Ivre Belli Reflectiones, section 60, p. 187. (Reflections on Indians and on the Laws of War)(John Pawley Bate trans., Washington DC: The Carnegie Institution, 1917) (1557).

[3] Francisco Suarez, *On War* (Disputation XIII, De Triplici Virtue Theologica: Charitate), *in* Selections from Three Works Disputation XIII, Section I.7, 805 (Gladys L. Williams, Ammi Brown, and John Waldron, trans., Oxford: Clarendon Press, 1944)(1610).

I. *JUS AD BELLUM* PROPORTIONALITY

Those who work in the Just War tradition recognize five conditions that need to be satisfied for a war or armed conflict to be justly initiated: just cause, right intention, legitimate authority, last resort, and proportionality.[4] The debate about how a war might be justifiably initiated is conducted within the framework of how best to understand these conditions, and whether or not these are the right conditions. But the basic contours of the framework have been relatively stable for well over a thousand years. Their application in practice nevertheless remains debatable in the modern era.

First, the most significant of these *jus ad bellum* conditions is often said to be just cause. Augustine is thought to be the founder of the Just War tradition, although Cicero also has a claim on this title as well. According to Augustine, there were primarily two causes to go to war, self-defense and the defense of others. But he clearly favored the latter, since it was "a dutiful concern for the interests of others."[5] Augustine also spoke of "a war…either to correct or to punish their sins."[6] Today, both of these just causes, punishment and the defense of others, are controversial. The idea that punishment can be a just cause of war is now completely rejected. And the idea that defending others is a just cause, what is often called a humanitarian intervention, remains controversial if increasingly less so. But self-defense remains the paramount, if not the only just cause to initiate war.

Articulating the implications of such a just cause, Vitoria hinted at the difficulties that would later be caused by conflation of the *jus ad bellum* with the *jus in bello.* Vitoria extended the mandate of Exodus 23:7 which specified "the innocent and righteous slay thou not" to reason that the "basis of a war is a wrong done. But a wrong is not done by an innocent person. Therefore war may not be employed against him… [Moreover] it is not lawful in a state to punish the innocent for the wrongdoing of the guilty. Therefore, this is not lawful among enemies."[7]

Second, at the height of the middle ages, Thomas Aquinas championed the idea that in addition to a just cause to go to war, there must also be "legitimate authority" for instance "the authority of the sovereign." But even Aquinas recognized that legitimate authority could be satisfied by a "judge, or (as a public person) through zeal for

---

[4] Sometimes the condition of "reasonable likelihood of success" is also included.

[5] AUGUSTINE, THE CITY OF GOD (c. 420)(Henry Bettenson trans., Book XIX, Chapter 14, p. 874).

[6] *Id.*, section 15, p. 875.

[7] FRANCISCO VITORIA, DE INDIS ET DE IVRE BELLI REFLECTIONES (Reflections on Indians and on the Laws of War) (1557)(John Pawley Bate trans., Washington DC: The Carnegie Institution, 1917, section 3, para. 35, p. 178).

justice."[8] Today, there is considerable controversy about who is entitled to declare war and be considered a legitimate authority. This controversy arises at least in part because wars and armed conflicts are often civil wars or have at least one party that is not a recognized State, and hence lacks a sovereign leader. Many contemporary theorists do not list legitimate authority as a condition of the *jus ad bellum*, but there remains a recognition that armed conflict and terrorism are different and something like the old legitimate authority condition could be used to aid in distinguishing these cases.

Indeed, one might plausibly trace the thread of the legitimate authority requirement directly to Article 51 of the Charter of the United Nations (UN Charter or Charter). Though nothing in the UN Charter or international custom "shall impair the inherent right of individual or collective self-defence," the plain text of Article 51 imposes a temporal limitation "until the Security Council has taken measures necessary to maintain international peace and security." Furthermore, the UN Charter expressly states that "[m]easures taken by Members in the exercise of this right of self–defence shall be immediately reported to the Security Council" nor shall they "in any way affect the authority and responsibility of the Security Council under the present Charter to take at any time such action as it deems necessary to maintain or restore international peace and security." Though these principles are often acknowledged only in the breach, they represent the vestigial remains of the Just War legitimate authority condition.

Third, Aquinas also held that it was a condition of a just war that there is "a rightful intention so that they intend the advancement of good, or the avoidance of evil."[9] Aquinas especially wanted to rule out wars being waged for "wicked intentions," such as "the passion for inflicting harm, the cruel thirst for vengeance."[10] One could have the aim of helping others and yet act in behalf of these others for the wrong intentions or motives, Aquinas believed. Today, few theorists separate just cause and rightful intention in the way that Aquinas did, and many have dropped the rightful intention condition altogether. It is often thought to be sufficient that the war aims at helping innocent others or at self-defense since motives are often mixed even in the best of cases, and it would be too much to restrict just war to those fought for wholly pure motives.[11]

---

[8] AQUINAS, SUMMA THEOLOGICA (1265-1273), Pt. II-II, Qu. 49, Art. 1 (Fathers of the English Dominican Province, London: Burns, Oates, and Washburn, trans. 1936, p. 1354).

[9] *Id.*

[10] *Id.*

[11] Although states have intervened in the name of humanitarian motives for centuries, the historical practice is littered with the use of the humanitarian motive as pretext to advance geopolitical interests or to subjugate foreign peoples in the name of "civilizing" them. Hans Köchler, *Humanitarian Intervention in the Context of Modern Power Politics* 4 (Int'l Progress Org., Studies in Int'l Relations XXVI) (2001), *available at* http://i-p-o.org/koechler-humanitarian-intervention.pdf. Following the end of the Cold War, the UN authorized many

Fourth, there has been near universal agreement that wars must only be fought as a last resort. Aquinas talks of it being unlawful if a man, even in self-defense, "uses more than necessary violence."[12] Here necessity and last resort are linked conceptually. But even if *jus ad bellum* necessity, or last resort, can be satisfied, Aquinas tells us, it is not justified to kill an innocent person. As early as the seventeenth century, theorists like Alberico Gentili challenged this idea, by saying that "a legitimate cause of fear" even without any real danger, is sufficient to justify the use of lethal force.[13] And today, there is considerable interest in this topic, especially as it relates to the killing of "human shields" as we will see in Chapter 9.

Diplomatic and other uses of non-lethal force that are short of war must either be tried and shown to have failed, or be deemed useless on very good grounds. One need only recall the bitter political discord that surfaces in the run-up to almost every war to appreciate the lasting power of this precept. From the calls to give the UN weapons inspectors more time prior to the 2002 War in Iraq to the now discredited efforts of the British Prime Minister Neville Chamberlin to preserve peace within Europe before the Second World War, there has seldom been unequivocal agreement about how best to avoid the competing extremes of appeasement in the face of aggression and undue abandonment of reasoned restraint in the rush towards war.

So, we now get to the fifth condition of the *jus ad bellum*, proportionality. For our purposes, this is the most salient condition even as it is inevitably commingled with other considerations. The goal is balanced harmony among objectives or, as the Oxford English Dictionary posits, "symmetry." Aquinas discusses this condition when he says, "And yet, though proceeding from a good intention, an act may be rendered unlawful, if it be out of proportion to the end."[14] According to Aquinas, "if he repel force with moderation his defense will be lawful."[15] In *jus ad bellum* discussions since Aquinas's time, more than mere moderation has been required to satisfy the proportionality condition.

Hugo Grotius, writing in 1625, gives us a good place to start in understanding proportionality as a modern *jus ad bellum* precept. At one point, Grotius quotes

Chapter VII actions. Based on the "grave concern" expressed over the repression of the Kurdish population in Iraq in 1991, the United States, the United Kingdom, and France intervened, establishing safe havens and imposing no-fly zones. The resolution did not expressly authorize the intervention. S.C. Res. 688, U.N. Doc. S/RES/688 (Apr. 5, 1991). The no-fly zones designed to protect the Kurds represented at the time "a single partial exception in a half-century of non-intervention on humanitarian grounds." Michael Byers & Simon Chesterman, *Changing the Rules About Rules? Unilateral Humanitarian Intervention and the Future of International Law, in* HUMANITARIAN INTERVENTION 184 (J.L. Holzgrefe & Robert Keohane eds., 2003).

[12] *Id.* Pt. II-II, Qu. LXIV, Art. 6, p. 1464.
[13] ALBERICO GENTILI, DE JURE BELLI (On the Law of War) (1598), translated by John C. Rolfe, Oxford: Clarendon Press, 1933, Bk. I, Ch. 14, pp. 62–63.
[14] AQUINAS, SUMMA THEOLOGICA, Pt. II-II, Qu. 49, Art. 1.
[15] *Id.*

Seneca: "it is not for a man to put his fellow man to a wasteful use."[16] Since wars involve massive destruction of life, they should only be initiated if what the wars aim to accomplish outweighs all of this expected killing, so that lives are not merely wasted. For example, on September 11, 1864, the citizens of Atlanta pleaded with Union General William Tecumseh Sherman to cancel the pending attack because the "inconveniences, loss, and suffering attending it…will involve in the aggregate consequences appalling and heart-rending."[17] Sherman famously reinforced the cautionary function of *jus ad bellum* proportionality in his reply, which read in part:

> You cannot qualify war in harsher terms than I will. War is cruelty, and you cannot refine it; and those who brought war into our country deserve all the curses and maledictions a people can pour out. I know I had no hand in making this war and I know I will make more sacrifices today than any of you to secure peace…. You might as well appeal against the thunderstorm as against these terrible hardships of war. They are inevitable and the only way the people of Atlanta can hope to live in peace and quiet at home is to stop the war…you deprecate its horrors, but did not feel them when you sent car-loads of soldiers and ammunition, and moulded shells and shot, to carry war into Kentucky and Tennessee, to desolate the homes of hundreds and thousands of good people who asked only to live in peace at their old homes and under the Government of their inheritance. I want peace, and believe it can only be reached through union and war, and I will ever conduct war with a view to perfect and early success.[18]

The traditional understanding of *jus ad bellum* proportionality calls for a weighing of what the entire war is expected to achieve against the losses that are also expected if the war is initiated. General Sherman understood this implicitly, though it is worth noting that these common sense precepts formed part of the mandatory part of his curriculum while he studied at West Point.[19] The aims of the war have to first pass the just cause test. The *jus ad bellum* framing of proportionality requires that

---

[16] Hugo Grotius, The Law of War and Peace, at ch. 2, 577 (Francis W. Kelsey trans., Oxford Clarendon Press 1925) (1625).

[17] William Tecumseh Sherman, Memoirs of General W.T. Sherman 598 (The Library of America 1990) (1875).

[18] *Id.*, pp. 601–602.

[19] Patrick Finnegan, *The Study of Law as a Foundation of Leadership and Command: The History of Law Instruction at the United States Military Academy at West Point*, 181 Mil. L. Rev. 112 (2004)(noting that the West Point curriculum required four hours of discussion per week on legal, ethical, and philosophical topics that included both Vattel and Kent's *Commentaries on American Law*).

a lawful resort to force be proportional to the asserted *casus belli*.[20] A provocation sufficient to trigger a right to use military force in self-defense[21] must be designed to eliminate the threat presented and carefully calibrated to achieve that objective. In this context, for example, it is notable that no nation on earth criticized the war in Afghanistan on proportionality grounds during the debates in the UN Security Council following the 9/11 attacks or in the decade of UN General Assembly meetings after the attacks on the New York World Trade Center towers.[22]

But there is a further sense that the proportionality condition influences what counts as just cause, or how just cause is limited, in that if the cause is just but results in only a trivial good, the just cause will result in a disproportionate war, on the assumption that human life and societal peace are always at grave risk in time of war. Hence, the foreseeable losses of inherently valuable human lives need to be outweighed by something more than a trivial aim of war. It is surely a good thing that trivial just causes are not grounds for war, given war's devastation.

One of the most difficult questions raised in more recent Just War literature is whether the traditional *jus ad bellum* proportionality condition is too strong in that most wars would be ruled out. This theme resurfaces in the debate over the human rights implications of its application to *jus in bello* that will be discussed in Chapter 6. Some, like legal scholar Yoram Dinstein, have suggested that the *jus ad bellum* proportionality principle should be understood merely to call for "reasonableness in the response to force by counter-force."[23] Others, such as the moral philosopher Douglas Lackey, have suggested that we liberalize *jus ad bellum* proportionality because it is so hard to calculate in a manner likely to gain universal accolade. The liberalized standard of proportionality will be met "unless it produces a *great deal* more harm than good."[24] Yet, as Lackey and others recognize, proportionality will nonetheless rule out many wars that have just cause to be initiated. If *jus ad bellum* proportionality is taken seriously, even on the liberalized view of it, there will have to be adjustments in how we view just wars today.

In a later section of the current chapter, we will say more about how the three proportionality conditions relate to each other. Suffice it here to say that just as *jus ad bellum* proportionality considerations can rule out wars with just causes, so too can *jus in bello* and *jus post bellum* proportionality. Just cause may be the most important

[20] Oscar Schachter, *In Defense of International Rules on the Use of Force* (1986) 53 Univ. Chi. L.Rev.113, 132 (1986)("[A]cts done in self-defense must not exceed in manner or aim the necessity provoking them.")

[21] Michael N. Schmitt, *Asymmetrical Warfare and International Humanitarian Law*, 62 Air Force L. Rev. 1, 297 (2008).

[22] Tarcisio Gazzini, The changing rules on the use of force in international law 198–199 (2005).

[23] Yoram Dinstein, War, Aggression, and Self-Defense 184 (3rd ed. 2001).

[24] Douglas P. Lackey, The Ethics of War and Peace, 40–41 (1989)(emphasis in original).

consideration of all the conditions of just war, but proportionality is nearly as significant especially since it can greatly restrict what counts as a just cause, or how just
cause is limited. Indeed, *jus ad bellum* proportionality, when applied strictly, would
be tantamount to pacifism, or at least contingent pacifism. And when we consider
the uses of lethal force during war, the strict application of the classic just war criteria
means that very few wars would be justifiable in contemporary times, particularly
in light of the modern prohibitions on inter-State aggression embedded in the UN
Charter. This problem is exacerbated by the enormous technological leaps that seek
to make killing in war more efficient and often more impersonal.[25]

II. *JUS IN BELLO* PROPORTIONALITY

Today, it is recognized that there are three *jus in bello* conditions one needs to satisfy in order to conduct war justly: discrimination (or distinction), necessity, and
proportionality. Each of these principles is well established in international law, as
we will see in later chapters. It is often said that the principle of discrimination that
guarantees civilian immunity is the key *jus in bello* condition because, in requiring
that civilians not be directly targeted, war can be conducted humanely. Yet, as we
will see in this section and in other chapters, *jus in bello* proportionality has lately
been viewed as at least as important if not more important than the discrimination
principle, also called the distinction principle in legal writings.

   Theorists in the Just War tradition strongly condemned the killing of the innocent
during war. Francisco Suarez states the general view that "no one may be deprived
of his life save for reason of his own guilt."[26] Suarez extended this category of people who are innocent to include those who carry weapons as long as "they have not
shared in the crime nor in the unjust war."[27] Grotius also articulated a very strong
and encompassing principle: "No action should be attempted whereby innocent
persons may be threatened with destruction."[28]

   The key discrimination consideration, then as well as now, concerns who should
count as innocent. Often, this group is considered civilian, but there is a long history of worrying about whether all civilians during war are indeed innocent and

---

[25] *See* Larry May, "Contingent Pacifism: Human Rights, Conscience, and International Law," book manuscript
   in draft, 338 MS pages.
[26] Francisco Suarez, *On War* (DISPUTATION XIII, DE TRIPLICI VIRTUE THEOLOGICA: CHARITATE), *in*
   SELECTIONS FROM THREE WORKS Disputation VII.14, 845 (Gladys L. Williams, Ammi Brown, and John
   Waldron, trans., Oxford: Clarendon Press, 1944)(1610).
[27] *Id.,* p. 846.
[28] HUGO GROTIUS, THE LAW OF WAR AND PEACE, Bk. III, Ch. 11, Sec. VIII, p.734 (Francis W. Kelsey trans.,
   Oxford Clarendon Press 1925) (1625).

therefore entitled to protection from the effects of conflict insofar as possible. In the parlance of the Geneva Convention for the Protection of the Civilian Population in Times of War, this class of civilians is termed "protected persons" whose status conveys a defined set of rights as well as duties. In other words, the definition of the class of persons to whom states owe specific legal duties is not universal based on their humanity, but is narrowed by the treaty texts that define those duties and obligations. And there has also been considerable debate about whether the targeting only includes intentional acts and whether collateral damage to civilians counts as violating the principle of discrimination. If collateral damage cannot be justified under any moral or legal analysis, then most wars, and indeed almost all uses of military power, are unjust. We shall have much more to say on this theme in Chapter 9.

The second *jus in bello* condition, necessity, also has a long and distinguished pedigree in the Just War tradition. Aquinas held that "if a man in self-defense uses more than necessary violence, it will be unlawful."[29] This echoes some of the very recent attempts to introduce human rights constraints on *jus in bello* conditions, as we will see in Chapter 6. And Grotius tries to specify what a necessity principle requires when he says: "The danger again must be immediate and imminent in point of time."[30] He follows this up by saying: "I maintain that he cannot lawfully be killed, either if the danger can in any other way be avoided, or if it is not altogether certain that the danger cannot be otherwise avoided."[31]

The kind of necessity, sometimes lumped into the overarching concept of military necessity, involves a double necessity: The objective must be necessary for winning a just war, and the tactic must be necessary for achieving that objective. In Chapter 5, we will spend considerable time discussing how *jus in bello* necessity relates to proportionality in contemporary international law. Suffice it to summarize here that necessity precedes *jus in bello* proportionality in that the tactic or weaponry has to be necessary, in both senses, before it even makes sense to ask about whether the tactic or weapon is disproportionate. At the same time, it cannot be forgotten that the concept of necessity in *jus in bello* is one that accords the war-fighter with a broad range of discretion based upon what is reasonable under the circumstances in light of the available information. It is not intended to function as a tactical straightjacket as we shall see in Chapters 5 and 7.

This brings us to *jus in bello* proportionality about which most of the rest of our book is concerned. In the Just War tradition, *jus in bello* proportionality was

---

[29] THOMAS AQUINAS, *SUMMA THEOLOGICA*, II-II, Qu. LXIV, Art. 7, p. 1465.
[30] HUGO GROTIUS, THE LAW OF WAR AND PEACE Bk. II, Ch. 1, Sec. V., p. 173 (Francis W. Kelsey trans., Oxford Clarendon Press 1925) (1625).
[31] *Id.*, p. 175.

increasingly seen as very important and also it has come to be regarded as highly contentious. Grotius stated one version of the concern with *jus in bello* proportionality when he talked of "reasons that are weighty and will affect the safety of many."[32] This reference to the weightiness of considerations is one of the core ideas in proportionality assessments. Yet, weighing alone is not the only consideration in how proportionality was understood in the Just War tradition as well as for many contemporary moral and legal theorists.

In addition to weighing the likely consequences of a strategy or tactic, there are the deontic considerations identified by contemporary philosophers. Simply put, the value of the consequences matters, especially in terms of the special duties that may be owed to one class of person but not another. A soldier who is a co-national may have special deontic weight. More controversially differential weight might attach to the fact that the soldier is on the morally wrong side of a war and is hence a kind of "unjust combatant." Such soldiers may be treated differently in the proportionality assessment than someone who is a "just combatant," as is also true if a person guilty of a crime is treated differently, and even has different rights than one not guilty of a crime.

Historically, the Just War tradition has not generally embraced the view, sometimes taken today, that enemy soldiers are "free targets" who can be killed regardless of whether the loss of their lives is offset by the greater gains of the military objective. For the moral philosophers writing about war over the centuries, only the lives of the "guilty" could be taken with impunity, and enemy soldiers were not guilty merely because they were on the side of a war that a "just" State opposed. Indeed, in general, it was not accepted that the unjustness of the war tainted the soldiers who served, reducing their lives to mere cannon fodder.

Jus in bello proportionality in the Just War tradition was what was thought to render war humane, not merely in the way civilians were treated as was true for the principle of discrimination, but in the way that soldiers were treated as well. Grotius is well known for having started the tradition that stresses that soldiers should not be subjected to cruel or useless suffering, a tradition that is now embodied in humanitarian law and became one of the cornerstones of the Geneva Conventions.

The savagery of the Thirty Years' War provided the moral impetus for Grotius as he made plain in the "Prologema" to his most famous work, *De Jure Belli ac Pacis*:

I have had many and weighty reasons for undertaking to write upon this subject. Throughout the Christian world I observed a lack of restraint in relation

---

[32] Hugo Grotius, The Law of War and Peace Bk. III, Ch. 11, Sec. 8, p. 733–734 (Francis W. Kelsey trans., Oxford Clarendon Press 1925) (1625).

to war, such as even barbarous races should be ashamed of; I observed that men rush to arms for slight causes, or no cause at all, and that when arms have been taken up there is no longer any respect for law, divine or human; it is as if, in accordance with a general decree, frenzy had openly let loose for the committing of all crimes.

Grotius linked honor with the kind of humaneness that is the cornerstone of proportionality assessment today.[33] In other words, the intrinsic value of human life cannot be completely discounted on the basis of mere usefulness or military convenience. Thomas Hobbes, often associated with an amoral view of war, also called for a prohibition on cruelty. In *De Cive*, Hobbes says: "But there are certain natural laws, whose exercise ceaseth not even in the time of war. For we cannot understand what drunkenness or cruelty, that is, revenge that respects not the future good, can advance toward peace, or the preservation of any man."[34] And Hobbes also says: "But to hurt another without reason... is contrary to the fundamental law of nature.... Now the breach of this law is commonly called cruelty."[35] Here, the assertion is that one's life has special weight by virtue of being a fellow human being who has a certain dignity. Historically, Immanuel Kant was the most important philosopher to make a case for this position.

The moral tension between evolving technology and the precise application of the moral and legal imperatives to minimize cruelty and inhumanity during conflict represents one of the enduring threads within the field going back to the efforts of the Second Lateran Council to ban the crossbow from medieval battlefields as anathema and "hateful to God" because "men of non-knightly order could fell a knight."[36] The concrete formulations of Articles 22 and 23 of the 1907 Hague Regulations provided a fitting positive end to this very long developmental arc in specifying that:

Article 22
The right of belligerents to adopt means of injuring the enemy is not unlimited.

---

[33] For discussion of Grotius's impact on Just War thinking, see LARRY MAY, WAR CRIMES AND JUST WAR, (2007).
[34] Thomas Hobbes, *De Cive* EW II Ch. 3, para 26, note. *See also* Larry May, *A Hobbesian Account of Cruelty and the Rules of War*, 26 LEIDEN J. INT'L L.1 (2013); LARRY MAY, LIMITING LEVIATHAN: HOBBES ON LAW AND INTERNATIONAL AFFAIRS (2013).
[35] EW II Ch. 3, para. 11.
[36] G.I.A.D. Draper, *The Interaction of Christianity and Chivalry in the Historical Development of the Law of War* X INT. REV. OF THE RED CROSS 3, 19 (1956).

Article 23

In addition to the prohibitions provided by special Conventions, it is especially forbidden

(a) To employ poison or poisoned weapons;

(b) To kill or wound treacherously individuals belonging to the hostile nation or army;

(c) To kill or wound an enemy who, having laid down his arms, or having no longer means of defence, has surrendered at discretion;

(d) To declare that no quarter will be given;

(e) To employ arms, projectiles, or material calculated to cause unnecessary suffering;

(f) To make improper use of a flag of truce, of the national flag or of the military insignia and uniform of the enemy, as well as the distinctive badges of the Geneva Convention;

(g) To destroy or seize the enemy's property, unless such destruction or seizure be imperatively demanded by the necessities of war;

(h) To declare abolished, suspended, or inadmissible in a court of law the rights and actions of the nationals of the hostile party. A belligerent is likewise forbidden to compel the nationals of the hostile party to take part in the operations of war directed against their own country, even if they were in the belligerent's service before the commencement of the war.

Similarly, there are myriad specific treaty-based condemnations that derive from this tradition such as the prohibitions on the use of "any weapon the primary effect of which is to injure by fragments which in the human body escape detection by X-rays."[37]

But we should not be led to think that humaneness and avoiding cruelty is all that is involved with *jus in bello* proportionality. We shall have more to say about this in Chapter 5. Indeed, the idea that superfluous and unnecessary suffering are to be prohibited constitutes only the most minimal part of what *jus in bello* proportionality has meant. For not only must the useless killing of soldiers be stopped, so must any killing that is not proportionate to the good that is to be achieved by a particular military strategy. And as we will see in subsequent chapters, the killing of civilians as well as soldiers is ruled out by *jus in bello* proportionality in many situations that are not cruel but merely insufficiently outweighed by what is the expected gain from the military strategy or tactic in question.

---

[37] United Nations Convention on Prohibitions or Restrictions on the Use of Certain Conventional Weapons Which May Be Deemed to Be Excessively Injurious or to have Indiscriminate Effects, Protocol I, 19 I.L.M. 1523 (1980)(U.N. Doc. A/Conf.95/15 of October 27, 1980).

Think of soldiers who are retreating. It is sometimes said that if they are soldiers they are *free targets*. In a strictly technical sense of the law (*lex lata*), the armed forces of the enemy remain lawful combatants that may be targeted based only on that status for so long as they choose to retain that status. Enemy combatants in the context of international armed conflicts may gain affirmative protections from targeting either through capture or surrender or by falling into the hands of the adversary when medically incapacitated (termed *hors de combat*). But what is to be gained by killing them, rather ✻ than taking them captive? Extending the Just War tradition's *jus in bello* proportionality principle to include combatants not participating in conflict might mean that the killing of these soldiers would need to be outweighed by a military objective of greater value. Given that these soldiers are already retreating, it may well be unclear how the calculation can be successfully made in a way that does not make their killing disproportionate. The key to thinking in this *lex ferenda* vein is that the burden of proof would shift towards the commander seeking to target such retreating combatants.

Recall our earlier discussion of context. In the face of persistent enemy efforts to take advantage of the good faith compliance by one side with the laws and customs of warfare in order to gain military advantage, it is wholly warranted to require a definitive intent to abandon the fight before the use of lethal tactics are suspended. The experiences peculiar to each conflict and specific identity of those waging war may well be the determinative factor. It is accordingly difficult to declare an unequivocal rule; but all acts of war must be undertaken in light of the enormously important need to minimize wanton cruelty and indiscipline.

It is against this backdrop that some observers criticized US actions during the Gulf War as Iraqi forces began to withdraw from Kuwait as required by UN Security Council Resolution 660. Iraqi soldiers mingled with a column of panicked civilians who had commandeered any form of transportation to leave Mutlai, Kuwait, and escape to Basra, Iraq. Responding to Iraqi small arms fire, a 5-mile long column of retreating Hammurabi Division forces was attacked. As the coalition land assault began to the west, US airpower disabled vehicles at the front and rear of the convoy thereby creating a 7-mile long traffic jam. Unknown numbers of Iraqi soldiers and civilians died in the seven hours of subsequent strafing along what became known as the Highway of Death.[38] General McCaffrey's official report concluded that 34

---

[38] For discussion of the estimated casualties caused to Iraqi military on the Highway of Death, see Carl Connetta, The Wages of War: Iraqi Combatant and Noncombatant Fatalities in the 2003 Conflict, Project on Defense Alternatives Research Monograph # 8, Appendix 2, Iraqi Combatant and Noncombatant Fatalities in the 2003 Conflict (October 20, 2003), *available at* http://www.comw.org/pda/0310rm8ap2.html#5. The Highway(s) were estimated to have caused the Iraqi military casualties in the range of 6 to 10 percent, and eyewitness descriptions recounted that "T-55 tanks lay blown apart like Chinese firecrackers, their turrets and main gun barrels blown 50 feet away and their hulking steel bodies disintegrated into pieces of shrapnel small enough to pick up with one hand."

tanks, 224 trucks, 41 armored personnel carriers, 43 artillery pieces, 319 anti-tank guns were destroyed, and an estimated 400 Iraqi soldiers were killed, with no loss of American life.

Though one American general later wrote that the attacks were controversial and disproportionate,[39] the *lex lata* legal rule remains that "fleeing soldiers of today are likely to regroup tomorrow as viable military units" and thus remain appropriate military targets so long as the commander's estimate of the military advantage gained is in good faith.[40] In Chapter 10, we address this issue in considerably more detail as part of a discussion that contrasts the alternatives of capturing soldiers with killing them, the latter euphemistically termed *targeted killings*.

Jus in bello proportionality is much more significant than is normally thought. Indeed, even if we just think of it as a minimal restraint, as apparently Grotius did,[41] many military strategies will be ruled out by the humane considerations of not allowing lives to be wasted. In that vein, consider the decision made by President George H.W. Bush to announce the ceasefire to end the 1991 Gulf War. Central Command informed the White House that a mishmash of Iraqi equipment was trapped waiting to cross the pontoon bridges near Basra and escape the oncoming coalition forces. American commanders were loath to spare the equipment on the grounds that "sooner or later those tanks would be put to malicious use." However, General Schwartzkopf later wrote that there was "no doubt in anybody's mind that we'd won decisively, and we'd done it with very few casualties. Why not end it? Why get somebody else killed tomorrow? That made up my mind."[42] The Iraqi units were spared with the assent of the White House and thus ended the combat phase of the 100-hour war. When we add a more robust notion of *jus in bello* proportionality, as was true of some Just War theorists, commanders would have to be more careful in calculating what would outweigh the loss of lives of enemy soldiers, to say nothing of their own soldiers, than they are now.

III. *JUS POST BELLUM* PROPORTIONALITY

In recent times, the *jus post bellum* has begun to get attention; yet this branch of the Just War tradition was certainly countenanced and discussed in earlier times as well. Today, there is the beginning to be recognition that there are at least six *jus post*

---

[39] LTG Ricardo Sanchez, Wiser in Battle 80 (2008).

[40] Yoram Dinstein, *Legitimate Military Objectives Under the Current Jus in Bello in* Legal and Ethical Lessons of NATO's Kosovo Campaign, 78 Naval War Col. Int'l. L. Stud. 153 (Andru Wall ed., 2002).

[41] Although see Larry May, *Grotius and Contingent Pacifism*, Journal of the History of Ethics, on-line journal.

[42] General H. Norman Schwartzkopf with Peter Petre, It Doesn't Take a Hero 469–470 (1992).

bellum principles: retribution, reconciliation, rebuilding, restitution, reparations, and proportionality.[43] This part of the Just War tradition is not nearly as well settled as the other two parts. Indeed, there is not even consensus on what the conditions are, or even whether they are conditions of the same sort as those of the *jus ad bellum* and *jus in bello*. As in previous sections of this chapter, we will first discuss the non-proportionality conditions before turning to *jus post bellum* proportionality.

After war is over, one of the most important and most difficult conditions to satisfy is that of retribution—the bringing to account those who committed wrongs either by initiating an unjust war or by waging war unjustly. This is especially problematic because holding criminal trials, for instance, often makes the second condition of the *jus post bellum*, reconciliation, very difficult also to satisfy.[44] But it is hard to comprehend what *post bellum* justice would involve if it did not have some accounting of the wrongs done during the war or armed conflict that has now ended. Vitoria argues that wrongs committed during war should be punished "proportionate to fault,"[45] thereby linking retribution with *jus post bellum* proportionality. And he argued that a guide to whether to seek retribution is whether it "be for the public good."[46]

Closure is hard to achieve if there is not a public reckoning for those who used the war as an occasion to commit wrong, or who chose to conduct war in a wrongful way, for there needs to be a just peace. The major theorists of the Just War tradition rarely talked about criminal trials, but certainly were focused on punishment of some kind for the wrongdoers after war ends. Grotius talks about some kind of tribunal in this respect, but there would be another three hundred years before the International Military Tribunal sat at Nuremberg.

The second condition of the *jus post bellum* is reconciliation. After war or armed conflict is over, another key consideration of the *jus post bellum* is that the parties come to a peace marked by mutual respect for rights. Vitoria is concerned with the effects of punishing those who have done wrong during war, and argues that punishment must be mitigated by "moderation and Christian humility" so as best to achieve a secure and just peace.[47] Reconciliation was also recognized by Grotius, as when he discusses the conditions for which clemency rather than punishment should be meted out.[48] Today, reconciliation is again taking center stage in the *jus*

---

[43] *See* LARRY MAY, AFTER WAR ENDS: A PHILOSOPHICAL PERSPECTIVE (2012).

[44] *See* Michael A. Newton, *A Synthesis of Community Based Justice and Complementarity, in* INTERNATIONAL CRIMINAL JUSTICE AND LOCAL OWNERSHIP: ASSESSING THE IMPACT OF THE JUSTICE INTERVENTION (Carsten Stahn, ed., 2013).

[45] Vitoria, section 56, p. 185.

[46] Vitoria, section 47, p. 182.

[47] Vitoria, section 60, p. 187.

[48] HUGO GROTIUS, THE LAW OF WAR AND PEACE Bk. III, Ch. 11, Sec. III., p. 725 (Francis W. Kelsey trans., Oxford Clarendon Press 1925) (1625).

post bellum Just War debates, as well as in the related debates about transitional justice, with the idea of a return to the rule of law as a major subcategory.[49]

The third condition of the *jus post bellum* is rebuilding. Rebuilding is the condition that calls upon all those who participated in devastation during war to rebuild as a means to achieve a just peace. Grotius says that "all the soldiers that have participated in some common act, as the burning of a city, are responsible for the total damage."[50] One of the most difficult issues in the *jus post bellum* debates over the centuries is whether both the just and unjust sides of a war have obligations to rebuild. Vitoria addressed this issue straightforwardly when he said that "injured states can obtain satisfaction" even if they are those who have done wrong because "fault is to be laid at the door of their princes" not among those who acted in good faith in following the dictates of these princes.[51] Although some in the Just War tradition called for the wrongful vanquished State to be severely treated, Vitoria and others were concerned that rebuilding was necessary for a just and lasting peace. This was also true of how the Allies responded to winning World War II, namely by funding the rebuilding of cities in defeated Axis Powers of Germany and Japan.

The fourth condition of the *jus post bellum* is restitution. Vitoria addresses this condition when he urged that we distinguish between those goods that can be carried away and "immovables" in determining what the victor can legitimately demand.[52] Vitoria believed that restitution was due only in certain situations because he generally thought that the victors get to keep "movables" insofar as they are necessary for paying compensation for what the war has cost. In this regard, Vitoria says that "he who fights a just cause is not bound to give back his booty."[53] When it comes to land that has been seized, though, most theorists believed that this should be returned as a matter of restitution after war ends, as long as it is not necessary "as a deterrent."[54]

This position on restitution is sometimes also held today, although it is becoming more common to think that the restitution of land is normally owed at wars' end. There are exceptions, such as Israel's refusal to give back the West Bank and Golan Heights after the 1967 Six Day War. After launching its preemptive attack and decisively defeating numerically superior enemies, Israel claimed that these lands provided a necessary buffer to deter future aggression. Once again, the context matters because the Six Day War was the third of Israel's defensive wars and was initiated

---

[49] *See* COLLEEN MURPHY, A MORAL THEORY OF POLITICAL RECONCILIATION (2010); Elizabeth Edenberg and Larry May, *Introduction*, JUS POST BELLUM AND TRANSITIONAL JUSTICE (Larry May and Elizabeth Edenberg, eds. 2013).

[50] Grotius, Bk. III, Ch. 10, Sec. IV, p. 719.

[51] Vitoria, section 60, p. 187.

[52] Vitoria, section 50, p. 184.

[53] Vitoria, section 51, p. 184.

[54] Vitoria, section 52, p. 184.

against Egyptian, Syrian, and Jordanian forces massed along the border. Given the surprise attacks that followed from Arab armies in the 1973 Yom Kippur War, successive Israeli leaders have vowed that "Israel will not return to the indefensible lines of 1967."[55] Israel, in essence, has followed Vitoria's understanding of restitution.

The fifth condition of the *jus post bellum* is reparations. Suarez says that "in order that reparation of the losses suffered should be made to the injured party" war may be declared.[56] But reparations are more typically discussed as due after a war is over. Indeed, Grotius says that "there are certain duties which must be performed toward those from whom you have received an injury."[57] This remark is mainly addressed at prohibiting cruelty but it can easily also be seen as a way to view reparations, such that even the just victor may have duties of reparation to the unjust vanquished.[58] Grotius proposes the principle of *meionexia*, not to demand all that is one's due, as a way to understand how to see reparations from the standpoint of the just victors. Reparations are crucial for reestablishing trust among the parties after wars' end.

And now we turn to the sixth *jus post bellum* condition, proportionality. One way to understand *jus post bellum* proportionality is as applying to each of the other five conditions. Whatever is required by the application of other normative principles of *jus post bellum* must not impose more harm on the population of a party to a war than the harm that is alleviated by the application of the other postwar principles. In this sense then the *jus post bellum* principles are not necessary conditions so much as they are desiderata, to use the favored term of Lon Fuller in describing the components of the rule of law.[59] Desiderata differ from necessary or sufficient conditions in that they need not be satisfied, at least not to their fullest extent, for a war to be justly ended. But each of the desiderata must at least be partially satisfied nonetheless. So, the proportionality principle calls for a determination of how much each of the other *jus post bellum* principles should be applied in light of the overall consequences.

Jus post bellum proportionality is perhaps closer to a meta-principle than the other two Just War proportionality principles. But this proportionality principle still is

[55] Abba Eban famously termed the 1967 boundaries "Auschwitz borders." Prime Minister Netanyahu's May 2011 speech to the Joint Session of the US Congress can be read in full at http://www.mfa.gov.il/MFA/Government/Speeches+by+Israeli+leaders/2011/Speech_PM_Netanyahu_US_Congress_24-May-2011.htm

[56] Francisco Suarez, *On War* (Disputation XIII, De Triplici Virtue Theologica: Charitate), *in* Selections from Three Works Disputation XIII, Section IV.4, 817 (Gladys L. Williams, Ammi Brown, and John Waldron, trans., Oxford: Clarendon Press, 1944)(1610).

[57] Hugo Grotius, The Law of War and Peace Bk. III, Ch. 11, Sec. I., p. 722 (Francis W. Kelsey trans., Oxford Clarendon Press 1925) (1625).

[58] Brianne McGonigle Leyh, Procedural Justice?: Victim Participation in International Criminal Proceedings (2011).

[59] *See* Lon Fuller, The Morality of Law (1964).

about weighing and context as was true for the other proportionality principles. Yet, *jus post bellum* proportionality focuses on the other *jus post bellum* conditions, unlike the other proportionality conditions. One of the reasons for this is that military operations have ceased, and so the actions that proportionality will concern are some of the very components of the larger *jus post bellum*, such as reparations and retribution. We are asked to consider whether the operation of these other *jus post bellum* principles might not do more harm than good. A just and lasting peace is one in which demands are not disproportionate.

Think again about restitution and reparations. This is often seen as a key to post-war justice and an important dimension of achieving reconciliation. But if the losing side of a war is already devastated and cannot easily repay the winning side what it would normally be thought to be owed, then there is reason to think that demanding that full reparations be made is in some sense disproportionate. One classic example would be Articles 231 to 247 of the Treaty of Versailles by which a defeated Germany was required to "make compensation for all damage done to the civilian population of the Allied and Associated Powers and to their property during the period of the belligerency [referring to the First World War]" that was "imposed upon them by the aggression of Germany and her allies."

The question is, in what sense is it disproportionate to demand reparations payments from those who are already devastated by the effects of a long war? And one answer is that demanding full reparations will pose a greater burden on the losing side than it will benefit the winning side. Indeed, for this and related reasons, Grotius proposed that *meionexia* described above could be seen as a principle of postwar justice. For demanding less than what is one's due can be crucial for avoiding disproportionate settlements at the end of a war or armed conflict. *Jus post bellum* proportionality is the condition, or desiderata, which is aimed at aiding in the avoidance of overly severe peace settlements in order to attain a just and lasting peace.

IV. THE THREE JUST WAR PROPORTIONALITY PRINCIPLES

What could be at the base of all three of these proportionality principles that would make us think that they are about the same thing or of the same sort despite their evident differences? As we have already seen, each proportionality principle is about weighing the consequences of an action or series of actions against what is hoped would be accomplished. This seems unexceptional; but there is more here as well. For one of the interesting connections among these principles is that they force us to think about how the three branches of the Just War tradition relate to each other. Given the assumption that war must end justly to be proportionate, those contemplating the initiation of a war should consider the conditions and results at the end of that war in weighing what will be lost or risked.

The proportionality of initiating war must then at least, in some sense, take into account the proportionality of ending the war. Considering the three proportionality principles together means that more consequences must need to be considered and more wars are less likely to be just than would normally be thought to be true. Considering the three Just War proportionality principles together would counsel that those initiating or conducting a war think very seriously about how their choices will affect the possibility of ending the war justly. This might mean, for instance, that the use of certain tactics or weaponry that unnecessarily antagonizes the enemy should not be employed because of the likely adverse effects of achieving reconciliation at the end of war. And this is especially relevant to questions of how the use of various tactics, which risked civilian casualties that are normally allowed given the immediate military objective, might make the ultimate ending of an insurgency more difficult to achieve. The justice of war's end thus becomes relevant for the justice of war's initiation, as well as the conduct of war.

The shifting role of airpower over Afghanistan represents precisely this kind of values driven adjustment. In the first week of the war to drive the Taliban from power, US Navy Commander Layne McDowell dropped some 6,000 pounds of ordnance from his carrier-based plane. Reflecting on his previous experiences in the First Gulf War and in Kosovo, he says, "Our culture is a fangs-out, kill-kill-kill culture." "That's how we train. And back then, the mind-set was: maximum number of enemy killed, maximum number of bombs on deck, to achieve a maximum psychological effect."[60] In his perspective, considerations of how the use of various tactics will be perceived, after a war is over, are now in the forefront of military strategizing.

After a decade of coalition warfare in Afghanistan, Cdr. McDowell's usual mission is now simply to "overwatch," which consists of scanning the ground via infrared sensors and radioing what he sees to troops below. Indeed, according to press reports, in 953 close-air support sorties by the 44 F/A-18 Super Hornets aboard the aircraft carrier John C. Stennis, aircraft attacked only 17 times, and flew low- or mid-elevation passes only 115 times. The shifts in missions and tactics partly reflect adaptations by the Taliban, but also the evolving Rules of Engagement (ROE) that emphasize proportionality and restraint. Commenting on the need to be precise in target selection and minimize civilian casualties, Cdr. McDowell admits that, "So much has changed from when I was here the first time. Now I prefer not dropping— if I can accomplish the mission in other ways." He might well have never heard the

---

[60] International Herald Tribune, Jan 17, 2012, p. 1.

term *jus post bellum*, but the changing mission profiles and professional perspectives derive in part from its normative power.

Considering the three Just War proportionality conditions together is a way to think about how the Just War can be thought of as a coherent theory of the justice of war, and not merely a separate set of constraints on various aspects of war or armed conflict. It remains true that war can be initiated justly but conducted unjustly, or conducted unjustly but ended justly. Yet, bringing the three branches together as seems inevitable when one realizes the effect of applying *just post bellum* proportionality in particular means that, in most cases, there should not be isolated discussions of what is occurring at each stage of a war or armed conflict. The beginning, middle, and end of war will each have effects on the other, leading to a unified theory of the overall justice of war. One need only think of the continuing gestalt surrounding the Vietnam War or the repercussions of the Second Gulf War to grasp this point.

One might ask why it is important to have a unified theory of the Just War. We will attempt to address this issue in the remainder of this short section. In the history of the Just War tradition, the various branches that we recognize today were not well distinguished from each other. To take the most prominent example, Suarez set out the conditions of initiating a just war to include conducting the war justly. In his treatise on war, that interestingly was part of a much larger volume on charity, Suarez provides the basis for a unified theory of the Just War.

Here is the longer quotation from Suarez that contains a passage we began this chapter with:

in order that a war may be justly waged, a number of conditions must be observed, which may be grouped under three heads. First the war must be waged by a legitimate power; secondly, the cause itself and the reason must be just; thirdly, the method of its conduct must be proper, and due proportion must be observed at its beginning, during its prosecution and after victory. The underlying principle of this general conclusion, indeed, is that, while war is not in itself evil, nevertheless, on account of the many misfortunes which it brings in its train, it is one of those undertakings that are often carried on in an evil fashion; and that therefore it requires many [justifying] circumstances to make it righteous.[61]

---

[61] Francisco Suarez, *On War* (Disputation XIII, De Triplici Virtue Theologica: Charitate), *in* Selections from Three Works Disputation XIII, Section I.1, 805 (Gladys L. Williams, Ammi Brown, and John Waldron, trans., Oxford: Clarendon Press, 1944)(1610).

Notice that Suarez mixes together considerations from all three branches of the Just War into what seems to be a single set of conditions. The first and second of his conditions are normally seen as *jus ad bellum* conditions; the third is a *jus in bello* condition; and the fourth is a mixture of *jus ad bellum, jus in bello*, and *jus post bellum* proportionality conditions.

So, despite the fact that many theorists today working in the Just War tradition separate the various branches, some of the most respected theorists in the historical Just War tradition did not clearly separate the branches and their various conditions. Indeed, for Suarez, proportionality, the central focus of our study, was seen as spanning the three branches of the Just War. And Grotius speaks of good faith as spanning all three branches of the Just War as well, saying that peace should always be at the forefront of all considerations having to do with war.[62] In a similar vein, the Judgment of the International Military Tribunal at Nuremberg said that, "To initiate a war of aggression is not only an international crime, it is the supreme international crime, differing only from other war crimes in that it contains within itself the accumulated evil of the whole."

If Grotius and Suarez are representative of the historical Just War tradition, these various branches of the Just War are not kept separate. They are linked together under the considerable requirement that war must in all of its aspects be directed at peace. This is the essence of the sentiment expressed by General Sherman on the outskirts of Atlanta some century and a half ago. It is our view that theorists today need to heed this advice and think about proportionality especially as a Just War condition, or perhaps desiderata, which spans the three branches or phases of war. Throughout what follows in subsequent chapters we will strive to provide a unified account of proportionality in armed conflict situations.

V. SIGNIFICANCE FOR INTERNATIONAL LAW

The debates in the Just War tradition have had a profound impact on the development of international law over the centuries. Grotius was a central figure in the Just War debates in the seventeenth century, and is recognized as the founder of international law today which is why practitioners commonly refer to momentous changes in the legal order as Grotian Moments.[63] The nineteenth century debates about the

---

[62] Grotius, DE JURE BELLI AC PACIS, Bk. III, Ch. XX, sec. 1, p. 804, and Bk. III, Ch. XXV, Sec.2, p. 861.

[63] MICHAEL P. SCHARF, CUSTOMARY INTERNATIONAL LAW IN TIMES OF FUNDAMENTAL CHANGE: RECOGNIZING GROTIAN MOMENTS 13 (2013)(tracing the development of the concept of the Grotian moment in customary international law and observing that Grotius wrote his book as a response to "those who regard international law with contempt, as having no reality except an empty name.")

principles of international law and morality governing the way wars were waged mirrors rather well the similar debates about the *jus in bello* branch of the Just War in the seventeenth century, so it is no wonder that Grotius is the common touchstone. Indeed, the Lieber Code and the first Geneva conventions originated from the development of a unified Just War theory that we have been describing. Article 16 of the 1863 Lieber Code exemplifies this commingling by stating that "[m]ilitary necessity does not admit of cruelty, that is, the infliction of suffering for the sake of suffering or for revenge, nor of maiming and wounding except in fight, nor of torture to extort confessions. It does not admit of the use of poison in any way, nor of the wanton destruction of a district. It admits of deception, but disclaims acts of perfidy; and, in general, military necessity does not include any act of hostility which makes the return to peace unnecessarily difficult."[64] Here, we have an account of *jus in bello* necessity that is interdependent with intentional *jus post bellum* considerations.

The way the proportionality conditions fit with each other is one of the more intriguing developments of Suarez and some of the other Just War theorists. These developments might have significance for a host of issues similar to the way the Lieber Code extends the reach of the *jus post bellum* back into *jus in bello* necessity considerations. In Chapter 6, we will explore how proportionality and necessity should be thought to work together. Suffice it here to say that *jus in bello* proportionality considerations should take into account factors such as whether the use of certain tactics or weapons will so antagonize the enemy population as to make peace much more difficult to attain and sustain. The point is not that such *jus post bellum* issues trump other important *jus in bello* proportionality and necessity concerns, but that such *jus post bellum* considerations as how choices of tactics or weapons will affect reconciliation should at least be part of the thinking of commanders in deciding what weapons or strategies to use.

More directly relevant to *jus in bello* deliberations is that proportionality should be seen to sweep more widely than is often thought. The Just War tradition has set the stage for the *lex ferenda* debate in international law today about the extent to which the lives of enemy soldiers should be seen as integral to proportionality calculations. In the Just War tradition, many soldiers are seen as innocent and hence cannot be killed except in cases in which it is necessary for a significant military objective. The major figures in the Just War tradition were opposed to merely seeing all soldiers as free targets because of the strong concern for the protection of innocent lives even of soldiers during war or armed conflict.

And the emerging international law concerning aggression as a crime could also benefit from some of the considerations we have rehearsed earlier. Self-defense

---

[64] John Fabian Witt, Lincoln's Code: The Laws of War in American History 377 (2012).

considerations are often thought today to be paramount in *jus ad bellum* deliberations. But the Just War tradition looks to proportionality as at least as important as
just causes like self-defense. What is important at the moment is to see that all three
proportionality conditions are relevant to deciding whether a war is initiated justly
or is a war of aggression.

In addition, there are important lessons to be learned for current debates about
transitional justice from the Just War tradition. The field of international law closest
to the *jus post bellum* today is transitional justice, and especially the law that is emerging known as the Responsibility to Protect. In this area, rebuilding and reconciliation, as well as new modes of accountability and retribution, are discussed in ways
that would benefit from the parallel discussions in *jus post bellum*.[65] The debates about
proportionality in the Just War tradition are especially important since transitional
justice often involves the kind of amelioration and compromise that has also been the
hallmark of Just War proportionality at least as far back as Grotius. Indeed, Grotius
wrote of the justifiability of a people rebelling against a sovereign leader if their own
preservation and livelihoods were being undermined.[66] And he cautioned a sovereign
ruler from "openly show[ing] himself [as] the enemy of the whole people."[67]

In this vein, Grotius would certainly have opposed the assaults on a population
by the leaders of a State, a premise that has recently become the incentive to discuss
transitional justice in terms of a recovery after mass atrocity. Grotius wrote passion-
ately at times, for instance saying that "in a lawful war certain acts are devoid of
moral justice," speaking of justice in this sense in terms of limits on what can be done
even to one's enemies.[68] And at the end of his *De Jure Belli ac Pacis*, Grotius defended
the principle of humanity as the main guidance for sovereigns as well as soldiers.[69]
The branch of international law that is often called international humanitarian law
is also indebted to Grotius and others in the Just War tradition.

---

[65] LARRY MAY, AFTER WAR ENDS: A PHILOSOPHICAL PERSPECTIVE, Cambridge University Press, 2012.
Brian Orend, *Jus Post Bellum: A Just War Theory Perspective* in JUS POST BELLUM: TOWARDS A LAW
OF TRANSITION FROM CONFLICT TO PEACE 31(Carsten Stahn & Jan K. Kleffner eds., T.M.C. Asser
Press 2008).

[66] *See* Grotius, DE JURE BELLI AC PACIS, Bk. I, Ch. 4.

[67] *Id.*, Bk. I, Ch. 4, Sec. XI, p. 157.

[68] *Id.*, Bk. III, Ch. 11, Sec. 1, p. 722.

[69] *Id.*, B. III, Ch. 11, Sec. VII, p. 733. In the context of modern debates over humanitarian intervention he also
famously noted that

Though it is a rule established by the laws of nature and of social order, and a rule confirmed by all the records
of history, that every sovereign is supreme judge in his own kingdom and over his own subjects, in whose
disputes no foreign power can justly interfere. Yet where a Busiris, a Phalaris or a Thracian Diomede provoke
their people to despair and resistance by unheard of cruelties, having themselves abandoned all the laws of
nature, they lose the rights of independent sovereigns, and can no longer claim the privilege of the law of
nations. Ibid., p. 288.

Throughout this chapter, the Just War tradition, which spans two thousand years, has been described as a source of inspiration for contemporary legal debates about proportionality. Proportionality was seen as a limit, indeed a humanitarian limit, on the initiation, conduct, and ending of war. In subsequent chapters, we will build on some of the insights from the Just War tradition, as we aim to emulate Grotius in describing a humanitarian doctrine that takes account of humaneness as well as human rights.

5

PROPORTIONALITY IN INTERNATIONAL HUMANITARIAN LAW

AS WE OBSERVED at the outset of our book, proportionality admits of more meanings than nearly any concept in the lexicon of international law and morality. The term recurs as one of the most basic and accepted terms of art in a number of legal and moral frameworks. It is important initially to explore the scope of current *jus in bello* understandings of the principle in international law, since this will give us the clearest baseline of proportionality in international law today. In fact, a proclamation by a layperson, a newscaster, or editorial that this strike or that attack is disproportionate, may well be the point of departure for thinking about these issues, though seldom explained as a reference to *jus in bello* standards. In modern State practice, proportionality debates during the conduct of armed hostilities have presented policymakers and commanders with visceral and enduring controversies.

This is especially true in the context of asymmetric attacks by determined enemies that deliberately exploit the protections derived from the laws and customs of warfare by commingling their hostile activities among otherwise protected civilians in order to facilitate attacks. During fighting in 2004, for example, insurgents inside Fallujah used 60 percent of the mosques in the city as fighting positions and weapons caches. There is now overwhelming evidence that Hamas has used civilian houses, schools, and other protected places in the Gaza Strip to launch indiscriminate rocket attacks into Israel.[1]

---

[1] Here is what Italian reporter Lorenzo Cremonesi reported that citizens of the Gaza Strip reported about Hamas statements to them about the situation during Operation Cast Lead:

"Get away! Get away from here! Do you want the Israelis to kill everyone? Do you want our children to die under the bombs? Take your missiles and weapons away," the inhabitants of the Gaza Strip yelled at the Hamas militants and their allies in Islamic Jihad. The more courageous were organized and blocked the entrances to their courtyards and locked the doors to their buildings, barricading quickly and furiously the

Recent international criticisms over the legality of extraterritorial drone strikes conducted by US forces, with their quite significant operational ramifications, further illustrate this tension.[2] At the time of this writing, there have been 307 acknowledged US drone strikes in Pakistan since 2004, of which 44 occurred during the George W. Bush presidency. In all these cases, *jus in bello* proportionality was at the forefront of public debate. We discuss the use of human shields in Chapter 9 and the use of drones in Chapter 10. The current chapter sets the stage for an understanding of these especially difficult cases.

In this chapter, we will first frame the debates about *jus in bello* proportionality by discussing the relation between *jus in bello* and *jus ad bellum* proportionality. Section II discusses the historical origins of the contemporary doctrine of *jus in bello* proportionality. In Section III, we discuss the important relation between professionalization and proportionality. In Section IV, we discuss major sources of *jus in bello* proportionality in treaty law. In Section V, we discuss the famous Lieber Code, the touchstone for contemporary *jus in bello* proportionality discussions. And we end with an account of the most recent sources of *jus in bello* proportionality, including the Rome Statue of the International Criminal Court (ICC). We aim to provide clarity to the most contentious area of proportionality, its application in armed conflict.

I. FRAMING THE *JUS IN BELLO* AND *JUS AD BELLUM* LEGAL DEBATES

Jus in bello proportionality must be understood at the outset in contrast to its older and more esoteric cousin, *jus ad bellum* proportionality. Chapter 4 explored the evolution of *jus ad bellum* proportionality in the roots of philosophical discourse. *Jus ad bellum* debates originated in the philosophical deliberations over the medieval perspective on the contours and causes of human war making. Over time, considerations of Just War and the lawful threshold for conducting warfare became important components of secular moral and political decision-making and dialogue in the modern era.

---

stairs to the highest rooftops. But for all of that the guerrillas didn't listen to anyone. "Traitors, collaborators with Israel, spies of Fatah, cowards! The soldiers of the holy war will punish you. And in any case you will all die, like us. Fighting the Zionist Jews we are all destined for paradise. Do you not wish to die with us?" This is what they yelled furiously as they broke down doors and windows, hiding themselves on high floors, gardens, using ambulances and barricading themselves near the hospitals, schools and buildings of the UN. In extreme cases Hamas militants shot those who sought to block them from their streets and houses to save their own families, or they beat them savagely.

[2] Justin Elliott, ProPublica, *Washington's Silence Creates doubts on deaths*, SYDNEY MORNING HERALD, June 23, 2012, pg. 11.

Embodying the classical conception of hostilities, Hugo Grotius quoted Cicero for the proposition that *Inter bellum ac pacis nihil est medium* s (e.g., "there is no medium between war and peace").[3] This classical conception of conflict in turn led to the sharp cleavages drawn between the Law of War and the Law of Peace.[4] The traditional demarcation between peace and warfare was marked by objectively clear manifestations such as a declaration of war, followed by a breach of diplomatic relations and onset of active hostilities. But this view is unsustainable in the modern era, in which declarations of war rarely occur, just as we saw the same to be true of the Just War *jus ad bellum* principle of legitimate authority.

Modern armed conflicts can be characterized as often involving non-State actors that share common ideological and religious motivations yet transcend regional or territorial delineations. In addition, transnational economic and ethnic integration, the decline of colonialism, and the rise of social networking and embedded communication across continents show why the old model of conflicts needed to change. This has given rise to shifting perceptions of the rights and obligations incumbent on sovereign States as a result of the ongoing human rights revolution, which we will discuss in the next chapter.

Today, many legal and moral theorists have argued that *jus ad bellum* proportionality should take account of the war's overall goals in human rights terms. When we come to consider *jus in bello* proportionality, as we argued earlier, there is a connection with *jus ad bellum* in that the larger goals of the war are infused into the deliberation of the intermediate goals on the battlefield. Winning a particular battle is the measure against which civilian or combatant casualties has to be weighed in *jus in bello* proportionality, but the value of winning that battle is in part determined by the value of winning the overall war, which was the main basis of *jus ad bellum* justifications.

Jus ad bellum sets limits on when war may be initiated, whereas *jus in bello* sets limits on how war can be waged. There are quite significant differences conceptually as well as legally with these two domains. Conceptually, once war has been justly initiated, there is a prima facie justifiability to tactics undertaken in prosecution of that war. There is no similar prima facie justification at the initiation of war. In this way of thinking, it matters quite a bit whether war has indeed been initiated and whether this was a justified initiation. Yet, the main marker of whether war has been initiated, the formal declaration of war, is increasingly obsolete.

---

[3] HUGO GROTIUS, THE LAW OF WAR AND PEACE Bk. III, Ch. XX, p. 832 (Francis W. Kelsey trans., Oxford Clarendon Press 1925) (1625).

[4] Notice that the very title of Hugo Grotius' classic work framed the issue in precisely this manner because that was the intellectual and philosophical fissure that he sought to explicate.

There has been no formal declaration of war for two generations at the time of this writing, yet armed hostilities remain an omnipresent facet of international relations and human existence. Some commentators have accordingly argued there is no need to draw a distinction between proportionality as a determinative principle in *both* *jus ad bellum* and *jus in bello* in modern warfare. As Oliver O'Donovan has stated, "[t]his...is a secondary casuistic distinction, not a load-bearing one."[5] From this perspective, the central principle of proportionality is the same regardless of when it arises in the course of conflict and preserving arbitrary prescriptive categories with different criteria causes undue confusion. We respectfully disagree.

We recognize that the *jus ad bellum* and *jus in bello* frameworks have heretofore "continued along parallel tracks without converging toward a unified and theoretically satisfying standard."[6] These two frameworks have been reinforced in a number of notable cases to the point that it constitutes "absolute dogma" in the words of Louise Doswald Beck.[7] There is, however, an inescapable logic to this historic trend. Two differing standards of proportionality apply to different actors, at varying decision points on the spectrum of conflict; and (as we will discuss later) employ very different valuations and assumptions.[8] *Jus ad bellum* proportionality decisions are made by sovereign rulers, or at least by political leaders of some weightiness, whereas *jus in bello* proportionality decisions are made by commanders and even by soldiers.

As a noted US federal judge observed in a recent decision related to the application of *jus in bello* principles, "Clarity in law is a virtue. In the context of war, that virtue becomes a life-and-death necessity."[9] Phrased another way, we see affirmative dangers in the conflation of concepts. Specifically, commanders should not have to be responsible for the decision to enter into war but only for the calculations concerning the intermediate goals of battle. It is unfair to hold commanders so responsible, even as we recognize that their *jus in bello* proportionality calculations must in part be based on the larger goals of the war. Similarly, commanders cannot be held responsible for perceived violations of *jus ad bellum* proportionality ordered by the appropriate (generally civilian authorities). Military practitioners are responsible for

---

[5] OLIVER O'DONOVAN, THE JUST WAR REVISITED 15 (2003). For a nice critique of this position, particularly as it collides with Waltzer's views see Jeremy Waldron, *Post Bellum Aspects of the Laws of Armed Conflict*, 31 LOY. L.A. INT'L & COMP. L. REV. 31 (Winter 2009).

[6] Evan J. Criddle, *Proportionality in Counterinsurgency: A Relational Theory*, 87 NOTRE DAME L. REV. 1073, 1076 (2012).

[7] L. Doswald Beck, *International Humanitarian Law and the Advisory Opinion of the International Court of Justice on the Legality of the Threat or Use of Nuclear Weapons*, INT'L REV. OF THE RED CROSS, No. 316, Feb 28, 1997.

[8] But remember our discussion in Chapter 4 about how these proportionality principles connect to each other.

[9] *Al-Bihani v. Obama* (Al-Bihani III), 619 F.3d 1, 4 (D.C. Cir. 2010)(Judge Brown explaining the denial of en banc review for the underlying decision reported at Al-Bihani v. Obama (Al-Bihani II), 590 F.3d 866 (D.C. Cir. 2010)).

creating a culture of compliance with the laws and customs of war, which necessarily include the good-faith application of the *jus in bello* proportionality standards we will explain more fully below.

Courts and commentators have increasingly begun to squeeze the margins of *jus in bello* proportionality using the model provided by the *jus ad bellum* and human rights formulations, which impose very high standards of specific justification. Nonetheless, there has been a notable, and what some might regard as a counterintuitive, *increase* in the miscommunications, misperceptions, and misapplications of the standards, if any, for restraining combatants. We conclude that the corrosion of *jus in bello* proportionality as a distinct concept of war fighting, as long as wars will still be waged, endangers the lives of both innocent civilians and the war fighters responsible for properly applying the legal construct, even in the midst of horrific conflict.

II. THE ORIGINS OF *JUS IN BELLO* PROPORTIONALITY

The 1868 Declaration of St. Petersburg outlawed the use of exploding bullets based on the premise that

> The only legitimate object which states should endeavor to accomplish during war is to weaken the military force of the enemy; for this purpose, it is sufficient to disable the greatest number of men; this object would be exceeded by the employment of arms which uselessly aggravate the suffering of disabled men, or render their death inevitable; the employment of such arms would, therefore, be contrary to the laws of humanity.[10]

This tenet echoed a strand of Just War thinking about how to define the proper bounds for waging war that can be traced at least to the time of Augustine, who wrote that peace "is not sought in order to provoke war, but war is waged in order to attain peace. Be a peacemaker, then, even by fighting, so that through your victory you might bring those whom you defeated to the advantages of peace."[11] The Brussels Declaration of 1874 extended this notion with the formal recognition of the customary principle that "the laws of war do not recognize in belligerents an unlimited power in the adoption of means of injuring the enemy."[12]

---

[10] Declaration of St. Petersburg, Documents on the Laws of War (Adam Roberts and Richard Guelff, eds. Oxford University Press Third Edition 2001) 53.

[11] St. Augustine, Letter 189, to Boniface, *in* AUGUSTINE: POLITICAL WRITINGS (Indianapolis: Hackett, E.L. Fortin and D. Kries, eds., trans. M.W. Tkacz and D. Kries, 1994), 220.

[12] The Brussels Project of an International Declaration Concerning the Laws and Customs of War art. 12, *reprinted in* DIETRICH SCHINDLER & JIRÍ TOMAN, THE LAWS OF ARMED CONFLICTS 21–28 (2d ed. 1981).

Notice that the restriction on the *jus in bello* historically begins with the idea that disabling the enemy, not killing the enemy, is the right way to understand just conduct during battle. We will comment more on this idea in the next chapter on human rights. In a sense, there is a common beginning for both international humanitarian law and human rights law: that only those actions are justified that are necessary for achieving a given military objective. As we will document, the human rights and humanitarian law models diverged quite a bit, just as some are now urging they converge again as we will see in the next chapter.

The well-known Martens Clause appeared in the Preamble to the 1899 Hague Regulations and was substantially replicated in many other treaties:[13]

> Until a more complete code of the laws of war is issued, the High Contracting Parties think it right to declare that in cases not included in the Regulations adopted by them, populations and belligerents remain under the protection and empire of the principles of international law, as they result from the usages established between civilized nations, from the laws of humanity, and the requirements of public conscience.

The Russian publicist, jurist, and diplomat Fyodor Fyodorovich Martens proposed the compromise language as something of a diplomatic pressure-relief valve to alleviate the sharp disputes between nations during negotiations, especially those concerning the relationship between civilians and combatants.

Perhaps because of its evasive yet enduring phraseology, the Martens Clause has been widely cited by courts, international organizations, human rights advocates, tribunals, and individuals. Its contortions in both domestic and international jurisprudence led the late jurist Antonio Cassese to say that the Martens Clause has become one of the "legal myths of the international community."[14] The clause nevertheless reflected an underlying and notably enduring consensus that the humanitarian aspiration, even in the midst of conflict cannot be completely discounted on the basis of expediency or artful treaty drafting.

By 1907, this terminology was changed into the terms of Article 22 of the Hague Regulations that "the right of belligerents to adopt means of injuring the enemy is not unlimited."[15] The modern formulation of this foundational principle is captured in Article 35 of Additional Protocol I of the Geneva Conventions, as follows: "In any

---

13 See the Preamble to the 1907 Hague Regulations, all four Geneva conventions of 1949, the Preamble of the 1977 Additional Protocol II, Article 1, para. 2 of the 1977 Additional Protocol I, and the Preamble of the 1980 Conventional Weapons Convention.

14 Antonio Cassese, *The Martens Clauses: Half a Loaf or Pie in the Sky*, 11 EUR. J. INT'L L. 187, 188 (2000).

15 1907 Hague Regulations, art. 22.

armed conflict, the right of the Parties to the conflict to choose methods or means of warfare is not unlimited."[16] Military codes and manuals of many States communicate the gravity and importance of such behavioral norms.[17]

In contrast, the modern articulations of proportionality as a discrete legal test with a widespread formulation accepted by consensus did not emerge until the negotiations that led to the 1977 Additional Protocols to the Geneva Conventions. However, and this is a vital insight, the *idea* of *jus in bello* proportionality is as old as professionalized military practice. Though the treaty texts did not contain formulations of the word *proportionality* that could be dissected with precision until the conclusion of Additional Protocols in 1977, the practice of proportionality was entangled in the very notion of restraints applicable to hostilities.

The concept that hostilities should be constrained on the basis of an irrepressible humanitarian imperative has seemed naïve to many. Two thousand years ago, the Roman orator and philosopher Cicero said that antagonists will simply discount all notion of legal or moral constraints when facing *in extremis* situations; "*salus populwe supremus est lex*[18]. .. *silent enim leges inter armes*."[19] Restraint in warfare is also inescapably in tension with Carl von Clausewitz's modern view that

> war is an act of force, there is no logical limit in the application of force… Attached to force are certain self-imposed imperceptible limitations hardly worth mentioning, known as international law and custom, but they scarcely weaken it.… [In fact] kind-hearted people might… think that there was some ingenious way to disarm or defeat an enemy without bloodshed, and might imagine that this is the true goal of the art of war. Pleasant as it sounds, it is a fallacy that must be exposed; war is such a dangerous business that the mistakes which come from kindness are the very worst…[20]

von Clausewitz correctly anticipated that the fundamental nature of warfare would remain constant.

In the nineteenth century, Union General William Tecumseh Sherman said, "It is those who have neither fired a shot nor heard the shrieks and groans of the wounded who cry aloud for blood, more vengeance, more desolation. War is hell." He could

---

[16] Protocol I, art. 3.

[17] W. Michael Reisman & William K. Leitzau, *Moving International Law from Theory to Practice: The Role of Military Manuals in Effectuating the Laws of Armed Conflict*, THE LAW OF NAVAL OPERATIONS, 64 NAVAL WAR COL. INT'L. L. STUD. 1, 5–6 (Horace B. Robertson, Jr. ed., 1991).

[18] *De Legibus*, III, iii, 8.

[19] *Pro Milone*, IV, xi.

[20] CARL VON CLAUSEWITZ, ON WAR, Bk. I, ch.1, ¶ 2, 3, & 75,(1833)(Michael Howard and Peter Paret, trans., Princeton: Princeton University Press, 1976).

not foresee that the accepted practices of States and the expectations of professionalized militaries would form the fabric of the binding treaties into which the humanitarian precepts would become melded. Even as restraining factors, the laws of war explicitly incorporate a built in dimension of deference to the commanders and to the lawful pursuit of victory.

To return to one of our examples from Chapter 1, US Marines killed 24 unarmed Iraqi civilians in the village of Haditha by entering their homes following the death of one Marine from an improvised explosive device. The official investigation documented a command culture that devalued the lives of Iraqi civilians, which both contributed to the incident and made the follow-up a low priority. What should have been a swift arc of investigative efficiency became bogged down with rationalizations that only shifted after the shock of public revelation and recrimination.

In the official terminology of General Eldon Bargewell: "All levels of command tended to view civilian casualties, even in significant numbers, as routine and as a natural and intended result of insurgent tactics."[21] The pervasive attitude that all Iraqis were either the enemy or supporters of the enemy, removed the incentive for individual Marines to follow ROE that mandate ceaseless efforts to distinguish between combatants and noncombatants. One Marine, SSgt Frank Wuterich (who entered a plea of guilty at his court martial but was sentenced to only 90 days' confinement, which was not served pursuant to a pretrial agreement, reduction to the lowest enlisted rank, and forfeiture of $984.06 per month for three months) remarked that "As for the PID (Positive Identification of civilians versus combatants), we didn't want my Marines to check if they had weapons first. We told them to shoot first and deal with it later."[22] His court-martial conviction was based on issuing the unlawful order, which violated the ROE and in legal terms violated the principle of distinction.

---

[21] *US Dep't of the Army, Major General Eldon A. Bargewell, Investigation*, "Simple Failures" and "Disastrous Results" p. 18 (June 15, 2006), 25. The first investigation under US Army Major General Eldon Bargewell was notable simply because a well- regarded army general was charged with investigating allegations of US Marine misconduct. The official investigation resulted in the removal of Lieutenant Colonel Jeffrey Chessani, the commanding officer, and the company commander, Captain Luke McConnell along with another commander, Captain James Kimber, from their duties, along with subsequent courts martial for key Marines. General Bargewell concluded that: "Statements made by the chain of command during interviews for this investigation, taken as a whole, suggest that Iraqi civilian lives are not as important as U.S. lives, their deaths are just the cost of doing business, and that the Marines need to get 'the job done' no matter what it takes. These comments had the potential to desensitize the Marines to concern for the Iraqi populace and portray them all as the enemy even if they are noncombatants." This excerpt is from Army Major General Eldon A. Bargewell's report, *Washington Post*, April 21, 2007, http://www.washingtonpost.com/wp-dyn/content/article/2007/04/20/AR2007042002309.html linked from http://en.wikipedia.org/wiki/Haditha_killings#cite_note-32 (accessed June 21, 2011).

[22] Sworn Statement of SSgt Frank D. Wuterich (taken Feb. 21, 2001).

In the context of the Haditha massacres, the Marine commander aided in creating a culture that led to criminality by largely ignoring the potential negative ramifications of indiscriminate killing based on his stated view that the Iraqis and insurgents "respect strength and power over righteousness."[23] These attitudes not only led to a culture that socialized soldiers not to stop and think prior to indiscriminately killing civilians, but a culture that also saw limited value in retrospectively punishing Marines for acting in such a way. In the face of an entrenched command climate that discounted the lives of enemy civilians, one must question whether more formalized classroom discussions of morality or law would be a sufficient antidote.[24] One might also wonder whether the oft-stated discretion given to commanders also contributed to the problem. There was certainly an utter failure to investigate promptly and properly report the facts as they developed to superior command channels. The commanders at both battalion and company level, as well as the battalion legal advisor, were charged with dereliction of duty in relation to the reporting failures.

In this context, one must note that Additional Protocol I expanded on earlier provisions of the law with regard to concrete obligations for its training and dissemination.[25] Article 83 included more sweeping provisions focused on closing the gap between the textual provisions of law and their realization in practice:

1. The High Contracting Parties undertake, in time of peace as in time of armed conflict, to disseminate the Conventions and this Protocol as widely as possible in their respective countries and, in particular, to include the study thereof in their programmes of military instruction and to encourage the study thereof by the civilian population, so that those instruments may become known to the armed forces and to the civilian population.

---

[23] Bargewell Report, at 19. An initial Marine Corps communique reported that 15 civilians were killed by the bomb's blast and eight insurgents were subsequently killed when the Marines returned fire against those attacking the convoy. However, other evidence uncovered by the media contradicted the Marines' account. http://www.time.com/time/world/article/0,8599,1174649,00.html

[24] Alex Vernon, Editorial, *The Road From My Lai*, N.Y. Times, June 23, 2006, at A7 ("With all due respect to the general, does he really think that such training will appease those who believe the Americans at Haditha and Hamdaniyah, and our soldiers and agents elsewhere, are guilty of atrocities?").

[25] *See*, e.g., Geneva Convention for the Amelioration of the Condition of the Wounded and Sick in Armed Forces in the Field, *opened for signature* Aug. 12, 1949, 75 U.N.T.S. 31, 6 U.S.T. 3114, art. 47 (replacing previous Geneva Wounded and Sick Conventions of 22 August 1864, 6 July 1906, and 27 July 1929 by virtue of Article 59); Geneva Convention for the Amelioration of the Condition of Wounded, Sick, and Shipwrecked Members of Armed Forces at Sea, *opened for signature* Aug. 12, 1949, 75 U.N.T.S. 85, 6 U.S.T. 3217, art. 48 (replacing Hague Convention No. X of 18 October 1907, 36 Stat. 2371); Geneva Convention Relative to the Treatment of Prisoners of War, *opened for signature* Aug. 12, 1949, 75 U.N.T.S. 287, 6 U.S.T. 3316, art. 127 (replacing the Geneva Convention Relative to the Protection of Prisoners of War of 27 July 1929, 47 Stat. 2021); Geneva Convention Relative to the Protection of Civilians in Time of War, *opened for signature* Aug. 12, 1949, 75 U.N.T.S. 287, 6 U.S.T. 3516, art. 144.

2. Any military or civilian authorities who, in time of armed conflict, assume responsibilities in respect of the application of the Conventions and this Protocol shall be fully acquainted with the text thereof.

Taken together, these provisions are intended to effect a comprehensive mechanism for training military professionals in the obligations inherent in the law of armed conflict as well as a systematic and authoritative implementation of those principles even during the heat of battle and the flow of rapidly evolving operations. In the next section, we explore more fully the connection between the principle of *jus in bello* proportionality and the professionalization of soldiers in modern international law.

III. PROPORTIONALITY AND PROFESSIONALIZATION

Commanders throughout history recognized that the humanizing influence of the norms for conducting conflict is a vital dimension of a healthy and combat effective unit that should not be ignored or devalued. In other words, Cicero was simply incorrect when he said that the law was silent during war; or in the best possible light, his opinion betrayed an inaccurate appreciation for the dynamics of waging war. In contrast, Seneca, also writing in the Roman period, called for significant restraint especially during times of armed conflict in his essays, "On Anger" and "On Mercy."[26]

Even in the face of the powerful psychological tendencies that are the *sine qua non* of combat, the principles of the law of armed conflict became an embedded aspect of military professionalism. The *jus in bello* obligates an individualized consideration of the propriety of each and every military action against the backdrop of an established normative framework. Thus, we wholeheartedly concur with the admonition in the training materials for the US Army Officer Candidate School that leaders must focus "on the impropriety of the motives of vengeance, cruelty, and hatred. A generalized hatred toward the enemy leads too quickly to events like those at Beirut or My Lai. Once the enemy is viewed as something less than human, atrocities are more likely to occur."

There are two important pragmatic reasons for this linkage between proportionality and professionalization, which over time led to the development of the

---

[26] Seneca, *On Anger*, in SENECA: MORAL AND POLITICAL ESSAYS 97–98 (John M. Cooper and J.F. Procope, eds., 1995); and *On Mercy*, pp. 132–134. Also see NANCY SHERMAN, STOIC WARRIORS (2005); Jefferson D. Reynolds, *Collateral Damage on the 21st Century Battlefield: Enemy Exploitation of the Law of Armed Conflict, and the Struggle for a Moral High Ground*, 56 A.F. L. REV. 1, 8 (2005).

concretized obligations inherent in the modern proportionality formulation. In the first place, the modern conception of proportionality originated from the quest for commanders to inculcate a disciplined professionalism that facilitated the accomplishment of a military mission. As early as 500 B.C., Sun Tzu wrote that commanders have a duty to ensure that their subordinates conduct themselves in a civilized manner during armed conflict.[27]

Writing in 1625, Hugo Grotius documented the Roman practice that "it is not right for one who is not a soldier to fight with an enemy" because "one who had fought an enemy outside the ranks and without the command of the general was understood to have disobeyed orders," which offense "should be punished with death."[28] Grotius explained the necessity for such rigid discipline as follows: "The reason is that, if such disobedience were rashly permitted, either the outposts might be abandoned, or, with the increase of lawlessness, the army or a part of it might even become involved in ill-considered battles, a condition which ought absolutely to be avoided." These precepts echoed the State action component of the prevalent Just War thinking of his era, though he explicitly made the leap from *jus ad bellum* into *jus in bello* usages. Grotius later in the same text, *De Jure Belli ac Pacis*, also offered a critique of this position, becoming one of the first to call for humane conduct during the course of battle.[29]

Historically, the idea of the professionalization of soldiers that included the restraining effects of proportionality is well documented. During the Thirty Years' War, Gustavus Adolphus, the Swedish king, mandated that, "no Colonel or Captain shall command his soldiers to do any unlawful thing; which who so does, shall be punished according to the discretion of the Judge."[30] Military success can never be guaranteed by a sense of professionalized discipline, but wars are won by disciplined and determined forces that are shaped by the will of the commander.

Writing some two decades after the American Civil War, General Sherman sought to capture the key military lessons of that conflict for posterity. As the

---

[27] Brandy Womack, *The Development and Recent Application of the Doctrine of Command Responsibility: With Particular Reference to the Mens Rea Requirement, in* INTERNATIONAL CRIME AND PUNISHMENT: SELECTED ISSUES (vol. 1) 101, 113 (Sienho Yee ed., 2003).

[28] HUGO GROTIUS, THE LAW OF WAR AND PEACE Bk. III, Ch. XVIII, p. 788–789 (Francis W. Kelsey trans., Oxford Clarendon Press 1925) (1625). In this respect, Grotius is consistent with Cicero who conditioned his Just War rationale in part on the identity of the participants by declaring that only the state could properly conduct warfare and that a "soldier not inducted by oath could not legally serve." Roland H. Bainton, CHRISTIAN ATTITUDES TOWARDS WAR AND PEACE: A HISTORICAL SURVEY AND CRITICAL REEXAMINATION 41(Abingdon Press, Nashville 1960).

[29] See the discussion of Grotius's complex position concerning the law of war in LARRY MAY, WAR CRIMES AND JUST WAR (2007).

[30] M. CHERIF BASSIOUNI, CRIMES AGAINST HUMANITY IN INTERNATIONAL CRIMINAL LAW 59 (2d. ed. 1999) (quoting Gustavus Adolphus, Articles of War to be Observed in the Wars (1621)).

commander of a disciplined fighting force, General Sherman's observation that excessive "courts-martial in any command are evidence of poor discipline and inefficient officers" rings as true today as it did in 1885.[31] Lack of discipline breeds military and strategic disaster, as the United States has learned in the aftermath of the Haditha massacres, and other crimes committed at Abu Ghraib, Hamdiniyah, and in Afghanistan.

The law of armed conflict developed as a restraining and humanizing necessity to facilitate commanders' ability to accomplish the military mission even in the midst of fear, fatigue, factual uncertainty, moral ambiguity, and horrific violence conducted under the dual impulses of surging adrenaline and inculcated training.[32] The historical grounding of the laws and customs of war as deriving from the unyielding demands of military discipline under the authority of the commander or king explains why the legal status of lawful combatant was reserved for the armed forces fighting for a State or to paramilitary forces incorporated into those armed forces.[33]

The responsibility of commanders is a clear implication of the command relationship, independent of the geographical context or the intersovereign nature of the hostilities. Hence, it was no accident that the legal right to conduct hostilities was premised on the command of a person responsible for the conduct of subordinates, i.e., the commander, the orchestrator of lawful violence. As a corollary, the US Supreme Court found in 1946 that "the law of war presupposes that its violation is

---

[31] WILLIAM TECUMSEH SHERMAN, MEMOIRS OF GENERAL W.T. SHERMAN 888 (The Library of America 1990) (1875).

[32] See THE LAWS OF ARMED CONFLICTS: A COLLECTION OF CONVENTIONS, RESOLUTIONS, AND OTHER DOCUMENTS vii (Dietrich Schindler & Jiri Toman eds., 1988).

[33] This statement is true subject to the linguistic oddity introduced by Article 3 of the 1907 Hague Regulations, which makes clear that the armed forces of a State can include both combatants and non-combatants (meaning chaplains and medical personnel), and that both classes of military personnel are entitled to prisoner of war status if captured ("[t]he armed forces of the belligerent parties may consist of combatants and non-combatants. In the case of capture by the enemy, both have a right to be treated as prisoners of war"). The Hague Regulations embodied this legal regime as follows:

Article 1. The laws, rights, and duties of war apply not only to armies, but also to militia and volunteer corps fulfilling the following conditions:

1. To be commanded by a person responsible for his subordinates;
2. To have a fixed distinctive emblem recognizable at a distance;
3. To carry arms openly; and
4. To conduct their operations in accordance with the laws and customs of war.

In countries where militia or volunteer corps constitute the army, or form part of it, they are included under the denomination "army."

For a side by side comparison of the evolution from the 1899 language to the 1907 multilateral text, see J.B. SCOTT (ED.), THE HAGUE CONVENTIONS AND DECLARATIONS OF 1899 AND 1907, 100–127 (1918). It should be noted, though, that there is a difference between the way the term "combatant" was used in the law of the Hague Convention and the way it is used today in the law of Additional Protocol I.

to be avoided through the control of the operations of war by commanders who are to some extent responsible for their subordinates."[34]

The current context of armed conflict presents commanders with the challenge of implementing humanitarian restraints in an environment marked by an adversary's utter disregard for those bounds. In our view, the complexity of modern asymmetric conflicts makes the normative power of restraint during conflict more rather than less relevant. General David Petraeus, in essence, corrected von Clausewitz by clarifying that restraint during violent combat operations is an integral *aspect* of the mission rather than an inconvenient hindrance.

Addressing a letter to all coalition forces serving in Iraq,[35] General Petraeus wrote to "Soldiers, Sailors, Airmen, Marines, and Coast Guardsmen serving in Multi-National Force-Iraq":

> Our values and the laws governing warfare teach us to respect human dignity, maintain our integrity, and do what is right. Adherence to our values distinguishes us from our enemy. This fight depends on securing the population, which must understand that we—not our enemies—occupy the moral high ground. This strategy has shown results in recent months. Al Qa'ida's indiscriminate attacks, for example, have finally started to turn a substantial proportion of the Iraqi population against it.

We would once again note the implicit reference to *jus post bellum* considerations in determining *jus in bello* restraints.

From the modern perspective, the overall mission will often be intertwined with political, legal, and strategic imperatives that cannot be accomplished in a legal vacuum or by undermining the threads of legality that bind together diverse aspects of a complex operation. The crimes committed at Abu Ghraib emphatically demonstrate the strategic costs of such war crimes, and provide an enduring example of what General Petraeus has described as "non-biodegradable events."[36]

---

[34] *In re Yamashita*, 327 U.S. 1, 15 (1946).

[35] *See*, e.g., Letter from Gen. David H. Petraeus, Commanding Officer of Multi-National Force-Iraq, to Multi-National Force-Iraq (May 10, 2007), *available at* http://www.humanrightsfirst.org/2009/0 2/05general-petraeus-what-sets-us-apart-is-how-we-behave/

[36] *One-on-One with General David Petraeus: One of Our Most Powerful Military Leaders Talks About Iraq and Afghanistan*, VU Cast Vanderbilt University's News Network (Mar. 5, 2010), *available at* http://news.vanderbilt.edu/2010/03/watch-vucast-extra-one-on-one-with-general-david-petraeus-108942/; *see also* Uthman al-Mukhtar, *Local Sunnis Haunted by the Ghosts of Abu Ghraib*, Sunday Herald, Dec. 26, 2010, http://highbeam.com/doc/1P2-28566487.html; Joseph Berger, *U.S. Commander Describes Marja Battle as First Salvo in Campaign*, N.Y. Times, Feb. 21, 2010, http://www.nytimes.com/2010/02/22/world/asia/22petraeus.html.

The US doctrine for counterinsurgency operations,[37] perhaps reflecting the ghost of von Clausewitz, makes this clear in its opening section:

> Globalization, technological advancement, urbanization, and extremists who conduct suicide attacks for their cause have certainly influenced contemporary conflict; however, warfare in the 21st century retains many of the characteristics it has exhibited since ancient times. Warfare remains a violent clash of interests between organized groups characterized by the use of force. Achieving victory still depends on a group's ability to mobilize support for its political interests (often religiously or ethnically based) and to generate enough violence to achieve political consequences. Means to achieve these goals are not limited to conventional forces employed by nation-states.

The very essence of the commander's relationship with subordinates reflects the second, and much more subtle, reason that restraints during warfare become so embedded in professional practice. The bond between commander and commanded embodies an underappreciated and often unrecognized (at least in the academy) symbiosis.

Proportionality emerged as a tenet of military pragmatism because the authentic military leader has a paramount obligation to do all that is possible to "take care of subordinates." This is, in essence, a solemn bilateral recognition that the leaders will issue orders based on the best assessment of the pathway to victory, and subordinates will obey such orders to the best of their ability. An effective commander issues plans and guidance prior to the onset of operations, and sets a command climate of professionalism in which he or she empowers subordinates as the conflict unfolds.[38] The universal feeling among military men and women of all ranks and regions when deployed is that "when this is over we want to go home"[39] and they must trust in a leadership that seeks the same goal.

Commanders have the most at stake in the success of the mission both personally and professionally. *To command* is an active verb. The independent emergence of

---

[37] Dep't of the Army, Field Manual No. 3-24, Marine Corps Warfighting Publication No. 3-33.5, Counterinsurgency 1 (2007).

[38] Commentary to Protocol I, Art 87, ¶ 3550, available at http://www.icrc.org/ihl.nsf/COM/470-750001?OpenDocument ("Undoubtedly the development of a battle may not permit a commander to exercise control over his troops all the time; but in this case he must impose discipline to a sufficient degree, to enforce compliance with the rules of the Conventions and the Protocol, even when he may momentarily lose sight of his troops.")

[39] For a trenchant and piercingly honest exploration of the psyche of the infantryman in battle see Karl Marlantes What It Is Like To Go To War (2011). His work builds on the masterpieces of an earlier era such as, *inter alia*, Dave Grossman, On Killing: The Psychological Cost of Learning to Kill in War and Society (1995) and John Keegan, The Face of Battle (1983).

the principle that the commander's orders operate with the force of law to limit the application of violence in widely disparate cultures and historical periods suggests that it is more than just a legal technicality, but instead is fundamental to the nature of warfare itself. Of course, the commander does not always speak with the authority of law behind him or her. But the best commanders are those that convey the proper sense of the restraints of proportionality for all of those who serve under them.

The commander is responsible both for decision-making needed to employ a disciplined force and for the sustained combat readiness and training of those whom he or she is privileged to lead. As famed historian S.L.A. Marshall noted, "when an officer winks at any depredation by his men, it is no different than if he had committed the act."[40] The implicit permission given by a present authority figure by acquiescence and silent approbation has been labeled "atrocity by connivance."[41] This principle extends to command at all levels, and in all contexts and applies without limitation to commanders who assume control of organizations by conventional means or after the death or incapacitation of a previous leader. Despite von Clausewitz's demeaning of values in war, each individual military actor remains an autonomous moral figure with personal responsibility. This explains the bright line principle that there is no defense of superior orders in response to allegations of war crimes.[42]

Restraint during the conduct of hostilities helps to preserve the humanity of the war fighter even as it helps to minimize unavoidable civilian suffering and damage. Conversely, compliance with the legal and moral imperatives for waging war determines the dividing line between pride in one's service and shame that cannot be discarded like a dirty uniform. This subtle need to protect the humanity of the war fighter was epitomized by a photograph that appeared during the early phases of the coalition drive to Baghdad in early 2003 of an American Marine, in the middle of the combat zone, holding up a notarized letter directing him to report at a specific date and time for jury duty. The young Marine is grinning at the stark reality that the grinding normality of life in a combat zone might as well be occurring in a parallel universe from the normality of life at home.

An inculcated climate of discipline helps hone a combat effective unit with the result that the force has confidence in the command. The goal is to win the war as quickly as possible with the fewest casualties as possible and the most favorable peace terms that lead to a sustainable peace. This tenet of military practice helps explain why the law of occupation has never conveyed a carte blanche authority to

---

[40] GEN. S.L.A. MARSHALL, THE OFFICER AS LEADER 274 (1966).

[41] MARK OSIEL OBEYING ORDERS 189 (1999).

[42] Report of the International Law Commission Covering its Second Session, June 5–July 29, 1950, U.N. GAOR, 5th Sess., Supp. No. 12, U.N. Doc. A/1316, *reprinted in* The Laws of Armed Conflicts: A Collection of Conventions, Resolutions, and Other Documents, at 1265–66 (Dietrich Schindler & Jiri Toman eds., 1988).

an occupying power to exercise unlimited discretion over the civilians within the previously hostile territory.[43]

As a corollary to this duty to take care of subordinates, modern research indicates that a command climate that tolerates war crimes and the abuse of civilians violates the "psychological contract within the military unit." Many soldiers that serve in units in which cruelty and lack of discipline are the norm may feel disenfranchised from the mission and the military institution, and also betrayed, causing them to question their role in the organization. How many grandfathers or grandmothers will recount stories of having served at Abu Ghraib to their families? By extension, some military researchers attribute the rising rates of suicides to the failure to inculcate a climate of professionalism and restraint with some units.[44] Commanders that truly care about their subordinates will do all they can within their power to inculcate and sustain a climate in which proportionality is a central tenet of operational planning and sustained combat effectiveness.

IV. THE EMERGENCE OF PROPORTIONALITY IN TREATY LAW

Proportionality, like many other norms found in modern international humanitarian law, represents the divide between the unyielding aspiration to protect civilians during conflicts and the stark realization that legal tenets never provide an impenetrable guarantee of protections. Bombs and bullets will strike innocent people, even if only by mistake. Combat readiness can be achieved only by melding individuals from disparate backgrounds into a disciplined unit with a fine-edged warrior ethos focused on overcoming any obstacle in order to accomplish the mission.

The formal articulation of proportionality as a term of treaty law is the pinnacle of the legal imperatives that developed over time as nations sought to negotiate legal documents to address the moral complexities of combat. The textual requirements of proportionality crystallized from different sources in a piecemeal fashion over more than 150 years, culminating in the text of the 1977 Additional Protocols. The principle of proportionality developed as one of the primary mechanisms to protect noncombatants in conflict. Though the term proportionality does not appear as such in the treaty, the concept is clearly present in a number of key provisions.

---

[43] In 2012, the ICRC completed an extensive set of discussions among experts regarding the proper latitude enjoyed by an occupying power during its temporary authority, see Experts Report, Occupation and Other Forms of Administration of Foreign Territory (2012), available at http://lgdata.s3-website-us-east-1.amazonaws.com/docs/905/474159/ICRC_expert_meeting_-_occupation.pdf

[44] George R. Mastroianni and Wilbur J. Scott, *Reframing Suicide in the Military*, PARAMETERS 6 (Summer 2011).

The idea of proportionality is enshrined in Article 51 of Protocol I, which in its initial clause implements the categorical admonition that

> the civilian population and individual civilians shall enjoy general protection against dangers arising from military operations. To give effect to this protection, the following rules, which are additional to other applicable rules of international law, shall be observed in all circumstances.

The negotiating text that became Article 51 in the final text of Protocol I was adopted by a vote of 77 votes in favor, one against (France) and 16 abstentions.

French opposition was premised on the position that the very complexity of the proportionality test would seriously hamper military operations against an invader and prejudice the exercise of the sovereign and inherent right of defense as recognized by Article 51 of the United Nations Charter. In particular, the French delegation pointed out that it would be difficult to define the dispositive limits of a "specific military objective."[45] Even the phrasing of Article 51 indicates that proportionality is to be considered as only one piece, albeit perhaps the most prominent and controversial piece, of an interconnected mosaic of protections for the civilian population. The overarching prohibition is followed by the more specific and pointed application in Article 51(4) that "indiscriminate attacks are prohibited."

Article 51(5) of Protocol I, then defines indiscriminate attacks, using the non-exhaustive caveat that "among others the following types of attacks are to be considered as indiscriminate":

(a) an attack by bombardment by any methods or means which treats as a single military objective a number of clearly separated and distinct military objectives located in a city, town, village or other area containing a similar concentration of civilians or civilian objects; and

(b) an attack which may be expected to cause incidental loss of civilian life, injury to civilians, damage to civilian objects, or a combination thereof, which would be excessive in relation to the concrete and direct military advantage anticipated.

This language of "incidental loss of civilian life ... excessive in relation to ... the military advantage anticipated," is the core of the modern doctrine of what counts as disproportionate response.

---

[45] Official Records of the Diplomatic Conference on the Reaffirmation and Development of International Humanitarian Law Applicable in Armed Conflicts, Geneva (1974–1977), vol. 3, 161–162, paras. 110-116 (ICRC Bern 1978)(referencing concerns raised by the Polish delegation among others)

The balancing test of Article 51(5)(b) represents the modern basis for assessing a proportionate, hence permissible attack. Article 51(5)(b) must be understood and implemented as only one piece of the modern mosaic of protections that coexist alongside the permissive bounds of the law of warfare. When the composite snippets of Protocol I are consolidated and considered as a whole, the tenets of proportionality change from discordant pieces into a clear road map that can help military decision-makers accurately judge the lawfulness of their conduct and effectively protect civilians.

As only one other illustration of this interconnected set of legal imperatives, consider the duty imposed upon an attacking force by Article 57(2)(c) to provide "effective advance warning" of any attacks "which may affect the civilian population, unless circumstances do not permit." The scope of this duty to warn civilians and the obligations incumbent on an attacker are most controversial in light of the Israeli efforts in the Gaza Strip and the findings of the Goldstone Report but, for our purposes, the key factor to understand is that the duty to warn civilians operates alongside and often juxtaposed to the proportionality principle found in other aspects of the law.

Proportionality therefore represents the product of two historical developments. In the first place, the baseline principle of distinction protects civilians from the intentional infliction of harm. Article 51(2) specifies that

> [t]he civilian population as such, as well as individual civilians, shall not be the object of attack. Acts or threats of violence the primary purpose of which is to spread terror among the civilian population are prohibited.

This entitlement functions properly only against the backdrop of the modern principle of distinction, or discrimination as the philosophers call it, captured in the ringing imperative of Article 48:

> In order to ensure respect for and protection of the civilian population and civilian objects, the Parties to the conflict shall at all times distinguish between the civilian population and combatants and between civilian objects and military objectives and accordingly shall direct their operations only against military objectives.

Any modern force that intentionally directs attacks against civilians or civilian objects, irrespective of the pretext of military necessity, commits a war crime. No responsible commander ever intentionally directs attacks against protected persons or objects. This is one reason why the claims that such and such drone strike intentionally killed X number of civilians is so damaging; the perception remains that North Atlantic Treaty Organization (NATO) forces in Afghanistan for example simply murder civilians when it suits them. This narrative in turn, feeds the Al Qa'ida and Taliban accounts that the West is waging war upon Muslims in general. This generalized narrative is false, and would be grossly criminal and thoroughly prosecuted if it were true.

It must be recalled that these specific prohibitions operate in conjunction with the other dominant historical trend, which of course is implicit in the principle of distinction. International law restricts the class of persons against whom violence may be applied during armed conflicts, even as it bestows affirmative rights to wage war in accordance with accepted legal restraints. Because of the central importance of these categorizations, the standards for ascertaining the legal line between lawful and unlawful participants in conflict provided the intellectual impetus for the evolution of the entire field of law relevant to the conduct of hostilities.[46]

From the outset, States sought to prescribe the conditions under which they owed particular persons affirmative legal protections derived from the laws and customs of war.[47] The recurring refrain in negotiations can be described as "To whom do we owe such protections?" The constant effort to be as precise as possible in describing the classes of persons entitled to those protections was essential because the same criteria prescribe the select class who may lawfully conduct hostilities with an expectation of immunity. As noted above, the declarative humanitarian limitation that the "right of belligerents to adopt means of injuring the enemy is not unlimited"[48] is one of the organizing principles that unifies the framework of the law of armed conflict.

Persons outside the framework of international humanitarian law who commit warlike acts do not enjoy combatant immunity from prosecution and are therefore common criminals subject to prosecution for their actions.[49] The imperative that

---

[46] The field is frequently described as international humanitarian law. This vague rubric is increasingly used as shorthand to refer to the body of treaty norms that apply in the context of armed conflict as well as the less distinct internationally accepted customs related to the treatment of persons.

[47] GEOFFREY BEST, WAR AND LAW SINCE 1945 128–133 (1994).

[48] Hague Convention IV Respecting the Laws and Customs of War on Land, 1907, Annex art. 22, Jan. 26, 1910, *reprinted in* ADAM ROBERTS & RICHARD GUELFF, DOCUMENTS ON THE LAWS OF WAR 73, 77 (3d ed. 2000).

[49] In a classic treatise, Julius Stone described the line between lawful participants in conflict and unprivileged or "unprotected" combatants as follows:

> The…distinction draws the line between those personnel who, on capture, are entitled under international law to certain minimal treatment as prisoners of war, and those not entitled to such protection. "Non-combatants" who engage in hostilities are one of the classes deprived of such protection…Such unprivileged belligerents, though not *condemned* by international law, are not protected by it, but are left to the discretion of the belligerent threatened by their activities.

JULIUS STONE, LEGAL CONTROLS ON INTERNATIONAL CONFLICT 549 (1954).

logically follows is that the right of *non-belligerents* to adopt means of injuring the enemy is *nonexistent*. Those persons governed by the law of armed conflict derive rights and benefits but are also subject to bright line obligations. Prisoners of war, for example, enjoy legal protection *vis à vis* their captors; because they are legally protected, they have no right to commit "violence against life and limb."[50] Yet, lawful combatants become "war criminals" only when their actions transgress the established boundaries of the laws and customs of war.[51] Taken together, these principles form the backbone of the law of armed conflict (*lex lata*), and the foundational principle of military necessity defines the necessary predicate for the lawful application of force in pursuit of the military mission.

In sum, the detailed provisions of the modern laws of warfare relate back to the basic distinction between persons who can legally participate in conflict and the corresponding rights and obligations they assume. Hence, the law of war is integral to the very notion of professionalism because it defines the class of persons against whom professional military forces can lawfully apply violence based on principles of military necessity and reciprocity.[52]

Even against a lawless enemy, there are two essential questions professional military forces must ask in this new style of conflict:

(1) How may we properly apply military force?

(2) If lawful means of conducting conflict are available,[53] against whom may we properly apply military force?

---

[50] *See* Geneva Convention Relative to the Treatment of Prisoners of War, art. 93.

[51] *International Law Reports* 481 (E. Lauterpacht ed., 1971) ("Similarly, combatants who are members of the armed forces, but do not comply with the minimum qualifications of belligerents or are proved to have broken other rules of warfare, are war criminals as such ...."); Protocol I, art. 85 ("Without prejudice to the application of the Conventions and of this Protocol, grave breaches of these instruments shall be regarded as war crimes.").

[52] *See generally* Leslie C. Green, *What is—Why is There—The Law of War?, in* ESSAYS ON THE MODERN LAW OF WAR (2d. ed. 1999).

[53] Apart from other limitations found in applicable treaty regimes such as the Ottawa Landmines Convention, the Chemical Weapons Convention, and the 1980 Conventional Weapons Convention, the baseline of Article 35, Protocol I specifies that:

Art 35. Basic rules

1. In any armed conflict, the right of the Parties to the conflict to choose methods or means of warfare is not unlimited.

2. It is prohibited to employ weapons, projectiles and material and methods of warfare of a nature to cause superfluous injury or unnecessary suffering.

3. It is prohibited to employ methods or means of warfare which are intended, or may be expected, to cause widespread, long-term and severe damage to the natural environment.

Because only States enjoyed the historical prerogative of conducting warfare, the principles of lawful combat developed from the premise that only States had the authority to sanction the lawful conduct of hostilities.[54]

The intellectual roots of combatant immunity nevertheless remain grounded in the soil of State sovereignty. In laymen's terms, historically, one is either a civilian or a combatant. Propelled by the classic view that "the contention must be between States" to give rise to the right to use military force, the concept of combatant status developed to describe the class of persons operating under the authority of a sovereign State to wage war.[55] Then, as now, there was a stigma attached to being an unlawful combatant because the term carried implicit recognition that the sovereign power of the state was being thwarted without legal cause. For example, from 1777 to 1782, the British Parliament passed an annual act declaring that privateers operating under the license of the Continental Congress were pirates, *hosti humanis generis* (enemies of humanity), and as such could be prosecuted for their acts against the British Crown.[56]

Combatant status conveys the implication that lawful combatants enjoy protection under the laws of war to commit acts that otherwise would be unlawful, such as killing persons and destroying property. Two implications follow from the conceptual foundation of combatant immunity as an offshoot of State sovereignty. First, although the application of international humanitarian law has expanded from international to non-international armed conflicts,[57] the concept of *combat* (and its associated benefit: combatant immunity for acts conducted in compliance with legal norms) has been strictly confined to international armed conflicts.

Second, even as there have been efforts to extend legal protections (and combatant immunity) for irregular forces that do not line up in military uniforms on a parade field, participants in non-international armed conflicts, as a matter of *lex lata,* remain completely subject to domestic criminal prosecution for their warlike acts. Protections found in domestic law are grounded not on the status of a person, but on the basis of actual activities, because no one in international law has a "right to participate in hostilities" in a non-international armed conflict.[58] Again, this position is something that is being challenged from a human rights perspective, as we will see in the next chapter.

---

[54] L. Oppenheim, *International Law: A Treatise* 203 (H. Lauterpacht ed., 7th ed. 1952).

[55] *See* Geneva Convention Relative to the Treatment of Prisoners of War, Article 4. It should be noted, though, that not all of the persons that benefit from the protections of this Geneva Convention are properly termed *combatants.*

[56] Alfred P. Rubin, The Law of Piracy 154 (1988).

[57] *See,* e.g., Rome Statute of the International Criminal Court art. 8(2)(e), July 1, 2002, 2187 U.N.T.S. 90, 139.

[58] Marco Sassòli & Antoine Bouvier, How Does Law Protect in War? 208 (Int'l Comm. of the Red Cross 1999).

V. THE LIEBER CODE AND ADDITIONAL PROTOCOL I

The historical effort to define the scope of lawful participation in war and armed conflict resulted in the first concrete steps to create legal forms that communicated the normative duties of forces in the field. The tactical uncertainty faced by Union forces waging a campaign against rebel forces during the American Civil War thrust lawyers, and sound legal analysis, into the spotlight. The first comprehensive effort to describe the law of war in a written code, the Lieber Code, began as a request from the General-in-Chief of the Union Armies, based on his confusion over the distinction between lawful and unlawful combatants.[59]

General Henry Wager Halleck recognized that the law of armed conflict never accorded combatant immunity to every person who conducted hostilities, yet could provide little guidance to those under his command over whom they should target much less protect as civilians in the face of the changing tactics of war in what was a civil war not an international war. He knew, however, that the war could not be won without clear delineation to the forces in the field regarding the proper targeting of combatants and a correlative standard for the treatment of persons captured on the battlefield based on the legal characterization of their status.

On August 6, 1862, General Halleck wrote to Dr. Francis Lieber, a highly regarded law professor at the Columbia College in New York, to request his assistance in defining guerrilla warfare. This request, which can be described as the catalyst that precipitated more than one hundred years of legal effort resulting in the modern web of international agreements regulating the conduct of hostilities, read as follows:

> My Dear Doctor: Having heard that you have given much attention to the usages and customs of war as practiced in the present age, and especially to the matter of guerrilla war, we hope you may find it convenient to give to the public your views on that subject. The rebel authorities claim the right to send men, in the garb of peaceful citizens, to waylay and attack our troops, to burn bridges and houses and to destroy property and persons within our lines. They demand that such persons be treated as ordinary belligerents, and that when captured they have extended to them the same rights as other prisoners of war; they also threaten that if such persons be punished as marauders and spies they will retaliate by executing our prisoners of war in their possession. We particularly request your views on these questions.

---

[59] Letter from General Halleck to Dr. Francis Lieber, Aug. 6. 1862, *reprinted in* RICHARD SHELLY HARTIGAN, FRANCIS LIEBER, LIEBER'S CODE AND THE LAW OF WAR 2 (1983).

The Union Army issued a disciplinary code governing the conduct of hostilities, known worldwide as the Lieber Code, as General Orders 100 Instructions for the Government of the Armies of the United States in the Field (General Orders 100), in April 1863.[60] General Orders 100 was the first comprehensive military code of discipline that sought to define the precise parameters of permissible conduct during conflict. From this baseline and to this day, the principle endures in the law that persons who do not enjoy lawful combatant status are not entitled to the benefits of legal protections derived from the laws of war, including prisoner of war status, and are subject to punishment for their warlike acts.

Lieber embedded the protections that later became known as the principles of military necessity, distinction, and proportionality into the code in several, occasionally overlapping provisions (emphasis added):

Art. 14. Military necessity, as understood by modern civilized nations, consists in *the necessity of those measures which are indispensable for securing the ends of the war*, and *which are lawful according to the modern law and usages of war.*

Art. 15. *Military necessity admits of all direct destruction of life or limb of "armed" enemies, and of other persons whose destruction is incidentally "unavoidable" in the armed contests of the war*; it allows of the capturing of every armed enemy, and every enemy of importance to the hostile government, or of peculiar danger to the captor; it allows of all destruction of property, and obstruction of the ways and channels of traffic, travel, or communication, and of all withholding of sustenance or means of life from the enemy; of the appropriation of whatever an enemy's country affords necessary for the subsistence and safety of the army, and of such deception as does not involve the breaking of good faith either positively pledged, regarding agreements entered into during the war, or supposed by the modern law of war to exist. *Men who take up arms against one another in public war do not cease on this account to be moral beings, responsible to one another and to God.*

Art. 16. *Military necessity does not admit of cruelty*—that is, the infliction of suffering for the sake of suffering or for revenge, nor of maiming or wounding except in fight, nor of torture to extort confessions. It does not admit of the use of poison in any way, nor of the wanton devastation of a district. It admits of

---

[60] For descriptions of the process leading to General Orders 100 and the legal effect it had on subsequent efforts, *see generally* Grant R. Doty, *The United States and the Development of the Laws of Land Warfare*, 156 MIL. L. REV. 224 (1998); George B. Davis, *Doctor Francis Lieber's Instructions for the Government of Armies in the Field*, 1 AM. J. INT'L L. 13 (1907).

deception, but disclaims acts of perfidy; and, *in general, military necessity does not include any act of hostility which makes the return to peace unnecessarily difficult.*

Art. 18. When a commander of a besieged place expels the noncombatants, in order to lessen the number of those who consume his stock of provisions, it is lawful, though an extreme measure, to drive them back, so as to hasten on the surrender.

Art. 19. *Commanders, whenever admissible, inform the enemy of their intention to bombard a place, so that the noncombatants, and especially the women and children, may be removed before the bombardment commences.* But it is no infraction of the common law of war to omit thus to inform the enemy. Surprise may be a necessity.

Art. 20. Public war is a state of armed hostility between sovereign nations or governments. It is a law and requisite of civilized existence that men live in political, continuous societies, forming organized units, called states or nations, whose constituents bear, enjoy, suffer, advance and retrograde together, in peace and in war.

Art. 21. The citizen or native of a hostile country is thus an enemy, as one of the constituents of the hostile state or nation, and as such is subjected to the hardships of the war.

Art. 22. Nevertheless, as civilization has advanced during the last centuries, so has likewise steadily advanced, especially in war on land, the distinction between the private individual belonging to a hostile country and the hostile country itself, with its men in arms. *The principle has been more and more acknowledged that the unarmed citizen is to be spared in person, property, and honor as much as the exigencies of war will admit.*

Art. 23. *Private citizens are no longer murdered, enslaved, or carried off to distant parts*, and the *inoffensive individual is as little disturbed in his private relations as the commander of the hostile troops can afford to grant in the over-ruling demands of a vigorous war.*

Art. 24. The almost universal rule in remote times was, and continues to be with barbarous armies, that the private individual of the hostile country is destined to suffer every privation of liberty and protection, and every disruption of family ties. *Protection was, and still is with uncivilized people, the exception.*

Art. 25. In modern regular wars of the Europeans, and their descendants in other portions of the globe, protection of the inoffensive citizen of the hostile country is the rule; privation and disturbance of private relations are the exceptions.

In passing, it should be noted that Lieber's description of unlawful combatant status is notable in light of operational uncertainties that have been prominent in current antiterrorist operations. Though this language is dated, it suggests the al-Qa'ida tactics in evocative terms:

> Men, or squads of men, who commit hostilities, whether by fighting, or inroads for destruction or plunder, or by raids of any kind, without commission, without being part and portion of the organized hostile army, and without sharing continuously in the war, but who do so with intermitting returns to their homes and avocations, or with the occasional assumption of the semblance of peaceful pursuits, divesting themselves of the character or appearance of soldiers—such men, or squads of men, are public enemies, and therefore, if captured, are not entitled to the privileges of prisoners of war, but shall be treated summarily as highway robbers or pirates.[61]

This position runs contrary to the modern International Committee of the Red Cross (ICRC) and International Court of Justice (ICJ) view of the matter and of course conflicts with the subsequent development of human rights law. With respect to the lawful right to conduct hostilities and enjoy combatant status, Lieber's formula is probably still the dominant view of lex lata law of armed conflict, though of course detaining states have no right summarily to execute such persons based on an abundance of modern international law prohibitions.

There is a direct line between the Lieber Code and Additional Protocol I of the Geneva Conventions. In addition to the precepts embedded in Articles 51 and 48 of Protocol I of 1977, described above, Articles 57 and 58 crystallized the concept of proportionality for the first time in any treaty text in relation to the duties incumbent on the commander:

Art 57. Precautions in attack

1. In the conduct of military operations, constant care shall be taken to spare the civilian population, civilians and civilian objects.
2. With respect to attacks, the following precautions shall be taken:
   (a) those who plan or decide upon an attack shall:
      (i) do everything feasible to verify that the objectives to be attacked are neither civilians nor civilian objects and are not subject to special protection but are military objectives within the meaning of

---

[61] Lieber Code, art. 82.

paragraph 2 of Article 52 and that it is not prohibited by the provisions of this Protocol to attack them;

    (ii) take all feasible precautions in the choice of means and methods of attack with a view to avoiding, and in any event to minimizing, incidental loss or civilian life, injury to civilians and damage to civilian objects;

    (iii) refrain from deciding to launch any attack which may be expected to cause incidental loss of civilian life, injury to civilians, damage to civilian objects, or a combination thereof, which would be excessive in relation to the concrete and direct military advantage anticipated;

(b) an attack shall be cancelled or suspended if it becomes apparent that the objective is not a military one or is subject to special protection or that the attack may be expected to cause incidental loss of civilian life, injury to civilians, damage to civilian objects, or a combination thereof, which would be excessive in relation to the concrete and direct military advantage anticipated;

(c) effective advance warning shall be given of attacks which may affect the civilian population, unless circumstances do not permit.

3. When a choice is possible between several military objectives for obtaining a similar military advantage, the objective to be selected shall be that the attack on which may be expected to cause the least danger to civilian lives and to civilian objects.

4. In the conduct of military operations at sea or in the air, each Party to the conflict shall, in conformity with its rights and duties under the rules of international law applicable in armed conflict, take all reasonable precautions to avoid losses of civilian lives and damage to civilian objects.

5. No provision of this article may be construed as authorizing any attacks against the civilian population, civilians or civilian objects.

Art 58. contains precautions against the effects of attacks:
The Parties to the conflict shall, to the maximum extent feasible:

(a) without prejudice to Article 49 of the Fourth Convention, endeavor to remove the civilian population, individual civilians and civilian objects under their control from the vicinity of military objectives;

(b) avoid locating military objectives within or near densely populated areas;

(c) take the other necessary precautions to protect the civilian population, individual civilians and civilian objects under their control against the dangers resulting from military operations.

Against the backdrop of treaty development and customary practice, the reader should be little surprised to learn that the judges of Allied war crimes trials in the post–World War II era grappled with the complexities of assessing the appropriate balance between military imperatives and the bounds of humanity. There are a number of notable criminal precedents that shaped the emerging perceptions of what the good-faith war fighter can reasonably accomplish in the balancing of often competing priorities.

A great many controversies remain: What is feasible? Is incidental damage a different category than the common media term "collateral"? Whose perspective is determinative when assessing the military advantage to be gained? How does one determine the difference between a calculated campaign of cruelty to civilians, and the unfortunate necessities of urgent combat? Who bears the burden of proof? What should nations and the media do with respect to the public disclosure of information related to the planning and conduct of questionable attacks? Does an asymmetric conflict in which the defender intentionally commingles combatant-like activities with the civilian population affect the legal duties? When does a moral or tactical perspective counterbalance the strict application of the legal tests? Does the introduction of human shields affect the analysis? We shall address some of these questions in later chapters, but want to focus the reader on what is perhaps the most enduring question in modern practice.

Protocol I created the first specific text that set out the tenets of proportionality as noted above. It also extended criminal liability for disproportionate attacks as a "grave breach" of its provisions. Article 85(3) of the Protocol makes a willfully conducted attack a crime if it results in "death or serious injury to body or health." The grave breach is defined as either:

(a) making the civilian population or individual civilians the object of attack;
(b) launching an indiscriminate attack affecting the civilian population or civilian objects in the knowledge that such attack will cause excessive loss of life, injury to civilians or damage to civilian objects, as defined in Article 57, paragraph 2 (a)(iii);
(c) launching an attack against works or installations containing dangerous forces in the knowledge that such attack will cause excessive loss of life, injury to civilians or damage to civilian objects, as defined in Article 57, paragraph 2 (a)(iii);

The scope of Article 85 exemplifies the intimate relationship between the principles of distinction and proportionality that this chapter has sought to explain.

Setting aside the obvious circularity of the text, given that Article 57(2)(a)(iii) merely describes a prohibited disproportionate attack rather than defining such an attack with precision, the importation of a consequence element introduces a troubling degree of imprecision. Do States truly accept that there is such a sharp distinction between prohibited disproportionate attacks and the commission of the crime of launching a disproportionate attack? Would the public agree with such a formalistic distinction? Do the lives of terrorists or unlawful participants in conflict count? What about human shields? We take up the first issue in the next section and the issue of human shields in Chapter 9.

Conclusion

VI. THE INTERNATIONAL CRIMINAL COURT FRAMING OF THE CRIME OF DISPROPORTIONATE ATTACKS

Finally, it should be noted that the formulation in Protocol I has been superseded in practice by the adoption of the 1998 Rome Statute of the International Criminal Court (ICC). At the time of this writing, there are 122 States Party[62] that have adopted the statute, and the Elements of Crimes required by the treaty were adopted by the consensus of all states, including the United States, China, and other major non-States Party. Article 8(2)(b)(iv) describes proportionality in a manner consistent with modern State practice following the adoption of Protocol I as:

> Intentionally launching an attack in the knowledge that such attack will cause incidental loss of life or injury to civilians or damage to civilian objects or widespread, long-term severe damage to the natural environment which would be *clearly* excessive in relation to the concrete and direct *overall* military advantage anticipated." (emphasis added)

In addition, the Elements of Crimes (adopted by consensus as mentioned above) included a key footnote that reads as follows:

> The expression "concrete and direct overall military advantage" refers to a military advantage that is foreseeable by the perpetrator at the relevant time. Such advantage may or may not be temporally or geographically related to the object of the attack. The fact that this crime admits the possibility of lawful incidental

---

62 As of this writing, ICC States Party include 34 African nations, 18 from the Asia-Pacific realm, 18 from Eastern Europe, 27 from Latin American and the Caribbean, and 25 from Western Europe.

injury and collateral damage does not in any way justify any violation of the law applicable in armed conflict. It does not address justifications for war or other rules related to *jus ad bellum*. It reflects the proportionality requirement inherent in determining the legality of any military activity undertaken in the context of an armed conflict.

The inclusion of a proportionality requirement to mark off a specific war crime under the Rome Statute is significant for two reasons. In the first place, the consequence required for conviction of a grave breach under Protocol I is omitted. The crime is committed simply by the deliberate initiation of an attack, provided that the prosecutor can produce evidence sufficient for the finder of fact to infer that the perpetrator believed that the attack would cause an anticipated disproportionate result. The *actual* result is not necessarily relevant.

Unlike the grave breach formulation found in Protocol I, the criminal offense in the Rome Statute is completed based on the intentional initiation of a disproportionate attack. The highest possible *mens rea* standard implicitly concedes that some foreseeable civilian casualties are lawful. Thus, the Rome Statute standard strongly mitigates against the inference of a criminal intent just based on evidence sufficient to show that the commander might have had knowledge that a particular attack might cause some level of damage to civilians or their property.

In addition, the Elements of Crimes include an explicit footnote to stipulate that the perpetrator must intentionally launch the attack, i.e., as a volitional choice, and do so in the knowledge that the attack would be expected to cause disproportionate damage. Footnote 37 of the ICC Elements of Crimes makes plain that the perpetrator's knowledge of the foreseeably disproportionate effects of an attack requires an explicit value judgment. Nevertheless, the standard for any post hoc assessment of the action taken by an alleged perpetrator is clear: "An evaluation of that value judgment must be based on the requisite information available to the perpetrator at the time." This distinction within the *jus in bello* makes proportionality analysis during wartime a distinctively different exercise than in other contexts, as we will explore more fully in Chapter 7.

Second, the Rome Statute crime of disproportionate attack widens the scope of the military advantage that can be considered in the proportionality analysis (through inclusion of the word overall) and narrows what level of collateral damage is considered excessive (by specifying that the damage needs to be *clearly* excessive to generate criminal liability). These revisions to the treaty terminology employed by the drafters of Protocol I could be discounted as an ICC specific clause of convenience. In other words, similar to the heated debates that led to the compromise language related to proportionality in Protocol I, one might well discount the caveats introduced into the Rome Statute as a *sui generis* necessity based on diplomatic convenience. But this assumption would be inaccurate.

In fact, the text of the Rome Statute reflects the broadly accepted view of State practice. To be more precise, the text of the Rome Statute, as understood in light of the Elements footnote adopted by consensus, accurately embodies preexisting customary international law. This is true in two equally important dimensions. In the first place, the governments of the United Kingdom, the Netherlands, Spain, Italy, Australia, Belgium, New Zealand, Germany, and Canada each published a virtually identical reservation with respect to Articles 51 and 57 as they acceded to Protocol I.[63] The overwhelming weight of the reservations made clear that State practice did not intend to put the war fighter into a straightjacket of rigid orthodoxy. The New Zealand reservation for example (virtually identical to those of other States listed above) reads as follows:

> In relation to paragraph 5 (b) of Article 51 and to paragraph 2 (a) (iii) of Article 57, the Government of New Zealand understands that the military advantage anticipated from an attack is intended to refer to the advantage anticipated from the attack considered as a whole and not only from isolated or particular parts of that attack and that the term "military advantage" involves a variety of considerations, including the security of attacking forces. It is further the understanding of the Government of New Zealand that the term "concrete and direct military advantage anticipated," used in Articles 51 and 57, means a bona fide expectation that the attack will make a relevant and proportional contribution to the objective of the military attack involved.

Second, in reaching the legally defensible assessment of proportionality, the perspective of the commander (or war fighting decision maker) is entitled to deference based on the subjective perspective reservation prevailing at the time. The Italian declaration with respect to Protocol I states that in "relation to Articles 51 to 58 inclusive, the Italian Government understands that military commanders and others responsible for planning, deciding upon or executing attacks necessarily have to reach decisions on the basis of their assessment of the information from all sources which is available to them at the relevant time." This understanding is replicated in a number of other State pronouncements. Another reservation from the government of Austria declares that "Article 57, paragraph 2, of Protocol I will be applied on the

---

[63] The numerous texts of state declarations expressing similar views using almost identical language is at <http://www.icrc.org/ihl.nsf/WebSign?ReadForm&id=470&ps=P>

understanding that, with respect to any decision taken by a military commander, the information actually available at the time of the decision is determinative."

The language of the United Kingdom Law of War Manual summarizes the state of the law that was captured in the prohibition of Article 8(2)(b)(iv) as it should be understood in light of the Elements of Crimes,[64]

> The military advantage anticipated from the attack refers to the advantage anticipated from the attack considered as a whole and not only from isolated or particular parts of the attack. The point of this is that an attack may involve a number of co-ordinated actions, some of which might cause more incidental damage than others. In assessing whether the proportionality rule has been violated, the effect of the whole attack must be considered. That does not, however, mean that an entirely gratuitous and unnecessary action within the attack as a whole would be condoned. Generally speaking, when considering the responsibility of a commander at any level, it is necessary to look at the part of the attack for which he was responsible in the context of the attack as a whole and in the light of the circumstances prevailing at the time the decision to attack was made.

Military advantage is described as an objective component of proportionality but it is shifting due to the relative comparisons of relevant information available to individual commanders. The International Security Assistance Force (ISAF) policy on air strikes in Afghanistan nicely illustrates the deference accorded to the commander's assessment of the mission within the discretionary bounds of *jus in bello* proportionality. General Stanley McChrystal issued his 2009 Tactical Directive in his capacity as the ISAF Commander (overall commander of all NATO forces in Afghanistan). In it, he implemented restrictions on the use of artillery, helicopter gunships, and close air support. "I recognize that the carefully controlled and disciplined employment of force entails risk to our troops—and we must work to mitigate that risk wherever possible. But excessive use of force resulting in an alienated population will produce far greater risks."[65] McChrystal's order continued: "I expect leaders at all levels to scrutinize and limit the use of force like close air support (CAS) against residential compounds and other locations likely to produce civilian casualties in accordance with this guidance."[66]

---

[64] The Joint Service Manual of the Law of Armed Conflict, ¶ 5.33.5 (2004).
[65] Stanley McChrystal, COMISAF Tactical Directive, July 6th, 2009.
[66] Stanley McChrystal, COMISAF Tactical Directive, July 6th, 2009.

One way to defend McChrystal against his critics is to point out that he was simply doing what any commander is permitted to do: Employ a higher standard than what is required by law. And the rationale for such a higher standard for operations in Afghanistan, which were increasingly counterinsurgency operations, could be defended on straightforward *jus post bellum* grounds, as we discussed earlier. As one American officer reportedly said in 2011, if the goal is stabilizing the nation "it's pretty hard to do that when you're dropping bombs on innocent people."[67] Counterinsurgency operations succeed if the people in the region of the armed conflict accept the actions of the foreign military operatives working there.

From a different perspective, it might also have been well within General McChrystal's prerogatives to frame an aggressive alternate policy based on a different articulation of the overall military advantage anticipated based upon the information reasonably available to him. For instance, when apologizing to Afghan officials for the September 2009 bombing that killed seventy-two civilians, General McChrystal's explanation was interrupted by a council chairman named Ahmadullah Wardak. According to the *Washington Post* account, General McChrystal was "caught off guard" as Wardak asserted that the allies had been "too nice to the thugs" and demanded a more aggressive policy to protect the Afghan people.[68]

Anecdotal evidence suggests that this is not an isolated sentiment either. An anonymous Pakistani sounded a similar theme to the Wall Street Journal some years later, "I am a government official so I can't say it publicly, but I really want the drones to increase because they have eliminated all of the bad people."[69] Another American commander told us that the Afghans in his area of operations "only respect strength. The people expected us to swing a large baseball bat and make the insurgents go away. They praised us every time we and the Afghan National Army did just that. They chided us each and every time about the overall lack of security in all the areas" we patrolled. General McChrystal might well have focused on the willingness of local leaders to work with the coalition and the Afghan government as the operational center of gravity. If the military objective was reframed to be providing tangible encouragement to the law-abiding Afghans that seek to ally with the government against the depredations and human rights violations of the Taliban, one might well imagine a radically different ISAF Tactical Directive.

---

[67] Anne Mulrine, *How Afghanistan Civilian Deaths have Changed the Way the US Military Fights*, THE CHRISTIAN SCIENCE MONITOR, June 27, 2011, *available at* http://www.csmonitor.com/USA/Military/2011/0727/How-Afghanistan-civilian-deaths-have-changed-the-way-the-US-military-fights

[68] Rajiv Chandrasekaran, Sole Informant Guided Decision on Afghan Strike, WASH. POST, Sept. 6, 2009, at A1.

[69] Dion Nissenbaum, *In Former Taliban Sanctuary, An Eerie Silence Takes Over*, WALL STREET JOURNAL, Jan. 26-27, 2013, at A1.

Jus in bello proportionality is best preserved when it is understood to be an integral dimension of the mission. Accomplishing the mission is a nonnegotiable necessity which in turn breeds a military culture that prizes the selfless pursuit of duty. Correctly applying the precepts of proportionality should seldom if ever force good-faith war fighters into an absolute choice. The Israeli Supreme Court summarized this notion by noting that the authority of military commanders "must be properly balanced against the rights, needs, and interests of the local population: the law of war usually creates a delicate balance between two poles: military necessity on one hand, and humanitarian considerations on the other."[70]

Proportionality becomes an embedded aspect of war fighting on both the horizontal level (by linking disparate units and national contingents) and on the vertical (by binding the strategic, operational, and tactical goals of a military operation). The ICRC categorically maintains that State practice has proven the principle of proportionality to be a norm of customary law applicable in both international and non-international armed conflicts.[71] Furthermore, the preamble of Additional Protocol II "recalls the humanitarian principles" enshrined in Common Article 3, and it therefore has been argued that the principle of proportionality has to be taken into account when applying Additional Protocol II.

The ICTY noted in its *Galić* Trial Judgment "an attack on civilians can be brought under Article 3 by virtue of customary international law."[72] The broad application of proportionality is further warranted by the fact that Article 3(8)(c) of Amended Protocol II to the Convention on Certain Conventional Weapons also contains the principle. The ICTY Trial Chamber in the *Kupreškić* Case (though only in dicta) further underlined the principle of proportionality as a transcendent norm in noting that "certain fundamental norms still serve unambiguously to outlaw (widespread and indiscriminate attacks against civilians), such as rules pertaining to proportionality."[73]

In modern international law, it is inarguable that the principle of proportionality applies to all conflicts, whether international or non-international. The war fighter's

---

[70] Beit Sourak Village Council v. the Government of Israel, [2004] HCJ 2056/04, ¶34 <http:elyon1.court.gov.il/files_eng/04/560/020/A28/04020560.a28.htm>(*quoting* Yoram Dinstein Legislative Authority in the Administered Territories, 2 lyunei Mishpat (1973) 505, 509).

[71] JEAN-MARIE HENCKAERTS, LOUISE DOSWALD-BECK, CUSTOMARY INTERNATIONAL HUMANITARIAN LAW VOL 1: RULES, Rule 14, 46ff (2005)("Launching an attack which may be expected to cause incidental loss of civilian life, injury to civilians, damage to civilian objects, or a combination thereof, which would be excessive in relation to the concrete and direct military advantage anticipated, is prohibited.").

[72] Prosecutor v Stanislav Galić, Case No. IT-98-29, Judgment, ¶ 63(Int'l Crim. Trib. For the Former Yugoslavia Dec. 5, 2003).

[73] Prosecutor v. Kupreškić, Case No. IT-95-16, Judgment, ¶ 513 (Int'l Crim. Trib. For the Former Yugoslavia Jan. 14, 2000).

role is demanding, but the standard remains that only clearly excessive strikes are prohibited per se. The discretion remains vested in reasonable persons who share a professional ethos that obligates them to balance competing goals in complex circumstances with incomplete or inaccurate information. It is clear that *jus in bello* proportionality cannot be isolated to a particular narrow tactical context, nor can it automatically be assumed to be identical to other disciplines. Any responsible military commander must attempt to orchestrate hostilities in just such an integrated manner.

To summarize—Proportionality provides no license to recklessly destroy civilian lives and property; neither should it serve as an impenetrable cipher designed to ensnare soldiers attempting to perform their mission with endless allegations of criminality and interminable investigations. The non-derogable right to life of innocent civilians is balanced against the mandate to accomplish the mission, for which one must be prepared to sacrifice selflessly. Theorists have long noted that insurgent propagandists make the most of government excesses, "so that the burning of a few shops and homes [becomes] magnified into the rape of entire villages."[74]

In one of his most poignant observations from the context of the Algerian insurgency, David Galula noted that the "asymmetrical situation has important effects on propaganda. The insurgent, having no responsibility, is free to use every trick; if necessary, he can lie, cheat, exaggerate. He is not obliged to prove, he is judged by what he promises, not by what he does."[75] This fact has been reiterated with often tragic results around the world; from the streets of Fallujah to the outskirts of Kandahar the insurgent "casts himself in the role of David, and makes it his business to force the enemy into the role of Goliath in the public mind."[76] Not so for the lumbering forces of the government. "Counterinsurgents seeking to preserve legitimacy must stick to the truth and make sure that words are backed up by deeds; insurgents, on the other hand, can make exorbitant promises and point out government shortcomings, many caused or aggravated by the insurgency."[77] United States doctrine is stunningly concise and correct in the conclusion that the "contest of internal war is not *fair*; many of the *rules* favor insurgents."[78]

The problem is that as the legal regime applicable to the conduct of hostilities has matured over the last century, the legal dimension of conflict has at times overshadowed the armed struggle between adversaries. US Secretary of Defense Robert

---

[74] Robert Taber, War of the Flea: The Classic Study of Guerilla Warfare 104 (2002).

[75] David Galula, Pacification in Algeria 1956–1958 9 (RAND Corporation 2006) (1963).

[76] Robert Taber, War of the Flea: The Classic Study of Guerilla Warfare 99 (2002).

[77] Dep't of Army, Field Manuel 3-24, Counterinsurgency Para. 1–1 (MCWP 3-33.5) (Dec. 2006) [hereinafter FM 3-24]. FM 3-24, Counterinsurgency, ¶ 1-13.

[78] FM 3-24, Counterinsurgency, ¶ 1-9 (emphasis added).

Gates noted that the "principal strategic tactic of the Taliban...is either provoking or exploiting civilian casualties."[79] In this manner, the globalized media can be misused to mask genuine violations of the law with spurious allegations and misrepresentations of the actual state of the law.

Proportionality is a complex construct designed to be employed in the midst of stress, inadequate information, and surging adrenaline. Terminological imprecision, taken to its logical end, marginalizes the precepts of international humanitarian law and therefore creates strong disincentives to its application and enforcement. We end with this intriguing insight of the modern difficulty of correctly understanding and implementing *jus in bello* proportionality and next take up the challenge to this model from human rights law and morality in Chapter 6. We then move, in Chapter 7, to explaining what is common to most interdisciplinary understandings of proportionality and then proceed to explain what is unique about *jus in bello* proportionality compared to the myriad other uses of proportionality in modern law.

---

[79] Secretary of Defense Robert Gates—Press Conference, Secretary of Defense Robert Gates & Chairman, Joint Chiefs of Staff Michael Mullen, Leadership Changes in Afghanistan (transcript), DEFENSELINK (May 11, 2009), http://www.defenselink.mil/transcripts/transcript.aspx?transcriptid=4424

6

PROPORTIONALITY IN HUMAN RIGHTS LAW AND MORALITY

IN CHAPTER 4, we set out the standard account of proportionality within the Just War tradition, especially in the *jus ad bellum*. In Chapter 5, we set out the standard account of *jus in bello* proportionality within the international humanitarian law tradition. In this chapter, we will explore the recent legal and moral controversy about a new paradigm in both *jus in bello* and *jus ad bellum* that argues that the laws and rules of war should become more homogenous and aligned with the human rights perspective. The human rights revolution is one of the most significant legal developments of the post-World War II era. In many ways, the entire field of legal development now termed *human rights* hearkens back to the threads of natural law argumentation that motivated Thomas Aquinas, Hugo Grotius, Immanuel Kant, and other philosophers.

At the moment, there are several major sources of international law that support the human rights turn in the law of armed conflict; but those sources mainly speak to what international law should become (*lex ferenda*) and do not yet constitute a new regime of international law (*lex lata*). According to the human rights model and contrary to the long history of thinking about war and armed conflict, necessity and proportionality considerations dictate that soldiers cannot merely be treated as cannon fodder according to some theorists and courts. In the domain of human rights, those initiating war, and those prosecuting a war, must take account of combatant as well as civilian casualties, because all people have rights. Furthermore, using that logic, soldiers as well as civilians enjoy precisely the same range of human rights.

From the human rights perspective, the traditional allocation of rights and privileges under the laws and customs of war that correlate to persons based on their status or their affiliation is thought to be unwarranted. Hence, proportionality should reflect this fact. In particular, the right to life is nonderogable and the pinnacle of the human rights domain. There is an abundance of human rights jurisprudence that supports this finding, but nowhere is there a comprehensive treatment of its implications for the proportionality principle. We will attempt to provide such a view here since we find many of these ideas intriguing, but will offer some cautions as well.

In this chapter, we will explain what proportionality and necessity assessments in war or armed conflict would look like if the human rights perspective were taken more seriously. In Section I of this chapter, we explain how the models of humanitarian law and human rights law differ. In Section II, we discuss why the human rights approach to armed conflict is so controversial today. In Section III, we discuss how taking human rights more seriously would affect current debates in Just War theory. In Section IV, we discuss two of the most prominent ways that theorists are pushing back against the human rights approach, the idea that soldiers forfeit their human rights and the idea that humanitarian law should override human rights law, but only in special circumstances (*lex specialis*). In Section V, we discuss the relationship between necessity and proportionality from the human rights perspective. And we end with a section on how even the crime of disproportionate assault could be changing due to the influence of human rights concerns. Throughout, we approach this highly controversial subject with caution and hope.

I. HUMANITARIAN LAW AND HUMAN RIGHTS LAW

In international humanitarian law, soldiers can be killed and hence do not retain the same rights they had when they were noncombatants, but there are many rights that soldiers retain even on the battlefield. Or to be more precise, the right to life of soldiers is protected using the rubric of the laws and customs of warfare. Thus, their right to be free from attempts to kill them is the exceptional circumstance grounded in the express authorities of the Geneva Conventions and customary practice. Soldiers retain the right not to be subjected to excessive or superfluous suffering in all circumstances. Soldiers retain the right not to be killed treacherously or perfidiously. If captured, soldiers have many rights as *prisoners of war*. Similarly, if they are wounded or otherwise disabled and in the custody of the enemy, soldiers also have many rights insofar as they are *hors de combat*. The principle that soldiers cannot be treated inhumanely is a cross-cutting norm that applies in all types of conflicts to all participants in armed conflicts. One might well ask, then, "Why have soldiers forfeited their rights to life, but retained their rights not to suffer?" This is one of several puzzles that motivates this chapter.

Additionally in international humanitarian law, soldiers whose activities have not crossed the armed conflict threshold, retain even the full protection of their right to life. Imagine a group of soldiers who engage in sporadic violence aimed at pressuring their government to give them higher wages and greater health benefits, or even aimed at toppling the government. The government does not have the right to kill these soldiers, except perhaps in an emergency, during which the self-defense of the State is jeopardized. Yet, once the soldiers constitute an insurgency that crosses the armed conflict threshold they can be legitimately killed by the security forces of the State, at least as a matter of *lex lata* international humanitarian law. One might here ask how it is that being a soldier, and yet still a human being, has changed because armed conflict is afoot—and the supposedly nonderogable right to life is no longer the preeminent norm that one enjoyed just a short while earlier? This is another piece of the landscape of interconnected law and morality we will try to portray and comment upon in this chapter.

In international human rights law, in contrast to international humanitarian law, people generally do not forfeit essential rights such as the right to life. Indeed, human rights law stands as a fairly strong contrast to humanitarian law in this respect. The Universal Declaration of Human Rights (UDHR), in Article 2, says that "Everyone has the right to life, liberty and security of person." The International Covenant on Civil and Political Rights (ICCPR) seeking to enforce the UDHR's rights, in Article 6.1 said "Every human being has the inherent right to life. This right shall be protected by law. No one shall be arbitrarily deprived of his life." From the human rights perspective, war is not generally regarded as a situation in which non-arbitrary deprivations of the right to life occur. In times of emergency that "threaten the life of the nation," during which the very essence of the State is jeopardized, there can be derogation of some of the rights guaranteed by the ICCPR. This is in contrast to the express reminder found in Article 15 of the European Convention on Human Rights and Fundamental Freedoms that the laws and customs of warfare lawfully permit killing in war. The derogation provisions of the ICCPR nevertheless do not provide for an unrestricted deprivation of the right to life as seems to occur in most wartime contexts.[1]

Any derogation from the normally dominant right to life under the human rights regime must be limited "to the extent strictly required by the exigencies of the situation." This provision implies strict temporal limits and mandates close scrutiny of the substantive scope of permissible action. The United Nations (UN) Human

---

[1] *See* EMILY CRAWFORD, THE TREATMENT OF COMBATANTS AND INSURGENTS UNDER THE LAW OF ARMED CONFLICT 132–133 (2010).

Rights Council made this explicit in paragraph 6 of its General Comment 31[2] issued in 2004:

> The legal obligation under article 2, paragraph 1, is both negative and positive in nature. States Parties must refrain from violation of the rights recognized by the Covenant, and any restrictions on any of those rights must be permissible under the relevant provisions of the Covenant. Where such restrictions are made, States must demonstrate their necessity and only take such measures as are proportionate to the pursuance of legitimate aims in order to ensure continuous and effective protection of Covenant rights. In no case may the restrictions be applied or invoked in a manner that would impair the essence of a Covenant right.

From the human rights perspective, proportionality provides the basis for determining the validity of a measure taken by a State to derogate from the human rights of those humans within the State's scope of authority.

The key is to delimit the domain of what counts as arbitrary deprivation of the right to life, or rather to understand what counts as the non-arbitrary deprivation of the right to life. This is especially important in determining how international criminal law will treat the killing of soldiers in various situations that are likely to arise increasingly in the new forms of asymmetric warfare that are emerging in the world today. In what follows in this section, we will discuss the recent trend to incorporate human rights considerations more and more into areas, such as armed conflict, that used to be the exclusive purview of international humanitarian law.

Since the end of World War II, international human rights law has developed to become the default norms defining the relationship between a State and its people, at least as a matter of international obligations and the expectations of other States.[3] This parallel body of legal and moral restraint has sometimes been seen as

---

[2] Human Rights Committee, *General Comment No. 31 [80], The Nature of the General Legal Obligation Imposed on States Parties to the Covenant*, Adopted on March 29, 2004 (2187th meeting), U.N. Doc. CCPR/C/21/Rev.1/Add. 13, available at http://daccess-dds-ny.un.org/doc/UNDOC/GEN/G04/419/56/PDF/G0441956.pdf?OpenElement

[3] Justice Scalia's concurrence in Sosa v. Alvarez-Machain correctly observed that the maturation of international human rights norms does not completely displace the normal democratic channels of constitutional governance:

> The notion that a law of nations, redefined to mean the consensus of states on *any* subject, can be used by a private citizen to control a sovereign's treatment of its own citizens within its own territory is a 20th-century invention of internationalist law professors and human rights advocates.... American law—the law made by the people's democratically elected representatives—does not recognize a category of activity that is so universally disapproved by other nations that it is automatically unlawful here, and automatically gives rise to a private action for money damages in federal court. That simple principle is

providing a challenge to international humanitarian law, particularly in the context of non-international armed conflicts in which each body of law may well be concurrently applicable. In this chapter, we will be especially concerned with the way that the lives of soldiers, and the rights of soldiers, are being treated and should be treated in international law. We shall return to place a particular emphasis at the end of the chapter on the treatment of the killing of soldiers in international criminal law because that topic remains a source of continuing controversy.

Let us start by considering a recent case from the Grand Chamber of the European Court of Human Rights (ECHR). In the *Case of Al-Skeini and Others v. The United Kingdom*,[4] decided on July 7 of 2011, the ECHR held that Article 2 of the Human Rights Act applied to States whose agents were acting outside the territorial boundaries of that State. In particular, the court held that the United Kingdom (UK) could be held liable for the arbitrary killing by its soldiers of civilians in Iraq. Armed conflict has historically been governed by humanitarian law, which also recognizes prohibitions on the arbitrary killing of civilians. What is noteworthy is that in *Al-Skeini*, the application was made in terms of violations of human rights law applicable during the period of occupation following the Iraq war, and the court allowed such an application, ultimately deciding in favor of the victims' families.

In *Al-Skeini*, the conventional provisions of the European Convention of Human Rights were extrapolated directly into the context of conflict waged in Iraq that have traditionally been governed by the occupation law provisions of the Fourth Geneva Convention. This extension was based on the jurisdictional ground that UK forces exercised effective control over that portion of Iraq under the laws of occupation. In effect, human rights principles displaced the default obligations of the occupying power. Unlike the civil liability at issue in *Al-Skeini*, violations of the international humanitarian law, i.e., war crimes, also carry personal criminal liability.

In *Al-Skeini*, the ECHR relied in substantial part on the International Court of Justice (ICJ) Advisory Opinion, *Legal Consequences of the Construction of a Wall in the Occupied Palestinian Territory* (July 9, 2004), which held that both international humanitarian law and human rights law applied in cases of armed conflict. In that case, the ICJ rejected Israel's claim that "humanitarian law is the protection granted to conflict situations such as the one in the West Bank and Gaza Strip, whereas human rights treaties were intended for the protection of citizens from their own government in times of peace." (para. 90). Human rights treaties do allow for derogation "in times of public emergency which threaten the life of the nation and the

---

what today's decision should have announced. Sosa v. Alvarez-Machain, 542 U.S. 692, 750 (2004)(Justices Scalia, Rehnquist, and Thomas concurring in judgment and filing separate opinion).

[4] Case of Al-Skeini and Others v United Kingdom, ECtHR (Grand Chamber), Application no. 55721/07, July 7, 2011, *available at* http://hudoc.echr.coe.int/sites/eng/pages/search.aspx?i=001-105606

existence of which is officially proclaimed." But, as noted above, such derogation is only allowed "to the extent strictly required by the exigencies of the situation." (para. 90).[5]

International humanitarian law, in contrast to human rights law, has largely followed the Just War tradition in regarding some wars as just even though war involves the intentional killing of humans. As long as the cause is just (normally, these days, understood to mean self-defense and, controversially, some cases of defense of innocent others) and the war is a last resort as well as proportional, then war is recognized as a legally just war. So, even though war often involves a massive killing of combatants and arguably the violation of their rights to life, according to international humanitarian law, some wars are seen as justifiable today. And *jus in bello* proportionality is not seen as concerned with the lives of enemy soldiers in armed conflict, but only with the incidental killing of civilians, along with damage to civilian property, or unwarranted long-term damage to the natural environment.

Judith Gardam captures the current state of international humanitarian law on combatants when she says:

Combatants are legitimate targets in armed conflict, whereas civilians are not. For this reason, the level of combatant casualties never became an issue in IHL [International Humanitarian Law] and remains a matter for the probability equation in the *jus ad bellum*. In IHL, it is the prohibition of means and methods of warfare that are of a nature to cause superfluous injury or unnecessary suffering that today purports to limit the impact of armed conflict on combatants.[6]

To put the point somewhat differently, proportionality in international humanitarian law today does not count the loss of lives of soldiers in *jus in bello* proportionality calculations. Instead, *jus in bello* proportionality only concerns whether the soldiers are treated cruelly in the sense that they experience unnecessary or superfluous suffering. International humanitarian law generally starts from the position that some wars can be justified even though there is lots of killing of combatants, but that it is important to diminish the level of suffering of soldiers and to curtail attacks on civilians. International human rights law starts from a very different assumption, namely, that all people have the right to life.

In an important book, *The Humanization of International Law*, Theodor Meron summarized and defended the myriad ways that human rights law has intruded into

---

5 We will return to a consideration of the ICJ's Wall case in the final section of this chapter.
6 Judith Gardam, Necessity, Proportionality and the Use of Force by States 14 (2004).

international law generally. Meron recognizes the primary problem we want to highlight in this chapter when he notes:

> To speak of the humanization of humanitarian law or the law of war is thus in many ways a contradiction in terms. Consider, for example, the law of war term "unnecessary suffering." To genuinely humanize humanitarian law, it would be necessary to put an end to all kinds of armed conflict. But wars have been part of the human condition since the struggle between Cain and Abel, and regrettably they are likely to remain so.[7]

Notice here that Meron forthrightly recognizes the radical potential of human rights law to change the very nature of the laws of war. Concerning proportionality, Meron sees the need for radical change if human rights are taken seriously, since "Classical international law allowed a State which had a just cause for war to apply the maximum degree of force and destruction to bring about a speedy victory."[8] This understanding comports with the deepest desires of the men and women who must carry on the conflict because it is they who bear its costs most directly and they who most earnestly desire a return to a sustainable peace.

Meron nonetheless states that "human rights norms have infiltrated the law of war to a considerable extent."[9] He traces this influence back into the natural law tradition, but its clearest modern influence is in the Martens Clause of the Hague Conventions. Meron says that the Martens Clause epitomizes the humanizing aspect of the law of war.[10] The Martens Clause appeared in the Preamble to the 1899 Hague Regulations and would be substantially replicated in the Preamble to the 1907 Hague Regulations, all four Geneva conventions of 1949[11], the Preamble of the 1977 Additional Protocol II, Article 1, paragraph 2[12] of the 1977 Additional Protocol I, and even the Preamble of the 1980 Conventional Weapons Convention. The Martens Clause states:

> Until a more complete code of the laws of war is issued, the High Contracting Parties think it right to declare that in cases not included in the Regulations

---

[7] Theodor Meron, The Humanization of International Law 9 (2006).

[8] *Id.*, p. 61.

[9] *Id.*, p. 6.

[10] *Id.*, p. 5.

[11] GC I: Art. 63; GC II: Art. 62; GC III: Art. 142; GC IV: Art. 158.

[12] "In cases not covered by this Protocol or by other international agreements, civilians and combatants remain under the protection and authority of the principles of international law derived from established custom, from the principles of humanity and from the dictates of public conscience."

adopted by them, populations and belligerents remain under the protection and empire of the principles of international law, as they result from the usages established between civilized nations, from the laws of humanity and the requirements of the public conscience.

The Martens Clause is often cited today by legal theorists who support the intrusion of human rights norms into international humanitarian law.

In particular, the reference to "the laws of humanity and the requirements of public conscience" are seen as principles of general international law that, in the words of a member of the ICJ, may change as "the outlook and tolerance level of the international community" changes.[13] Needless to say, this sliding scale of subjectivity gives no small degree of pause to the warfighter that faces personal criminal liability for violations of the laws and customs of warfare.

It does seem today that the tolerance for war is changing in international legal discussions, such that the ascendency of human rights will mean that fewer and fewer wars are considered to be legally justified. That is quite a different issue, however, than the application of established *jus in bello criteria* to the conduct of warfare by the individuals charged with enforcing international humanitarian law. Indeed, Meron ends this discussion by saying that, although the Martens Clause has had far-reaching effect, he is "far less confident, however, that the Martens Clause has had any influence on the battlefield."[14] We have already examined the Martens Clause in Part II of Chapter 5, as we considered its implications for the further development of *jus in bello*. For the moment, we remain focused on its relevance for the development of the human rights domain.

In the 1970 Report of the Secretary-General on Respect for Human Rights in Armed Conflict, there was a very strong statement about the intended effect of having the UN General Assembly examine armed conflicts in human rights terms. "It is an endeavor to provide a greater degree of protection for the integrity, welfare and dignity of those who are directly affected by military operations pending the earliest possible resolution of such conflicts."[15] Yet the examination on the effects of human rights in battlefield situations by the Secretary-General of the United Nations (Secretary-General) was mainly restricted to the protection of civilian lives, even though the lives of soldiers are certainly those that are most directly affected by military operations. Forty years after the Secretary-General's report, things seem to be changing.

---

[13] *Id.*, p. 20, quoting the ICJ's Advisory Opinion on Nuclear Weapons, dissenting opinion of Shahabuddeen.
[14] *Id.*, p. 28.
[15] Respect for Human Rights in Armed Conflict. Report of the Secretary-General, A/8052, para 13 (1970).

II. WORRIES ABOUT APPLYING HUMAN RIGHTS LAW TO
ARMED CONFLICT

Superimposing the human rights principles that the application of lethal violence is to be limited only to the narrowest possible extent onto the domain of active hostilities creates a great deal of uncertainty on the part of those who risk their own lives daily and are charged with winning the war while simultaneously respecting applicable legal and moral restraints. Proportionality is not merely a cost-benefit calculation in many cases. The upper limit of the cost-benefit calculus is determined by deontological factors such as the rights of the parties involved. We will say much more about this point as this chapter develops.

The formulation of the ECHR in *Khatsiyeva and others v. Russia*[16] captured the human rights standard nicely by holding that "[t]he use of force which may result in the deprivation of life must be no more than "absolutely necessary"... [which] indicates that a stricter and more compelling test of necessity must be employed than that normally applicable when determining whether State action is "necessary in a democratic society".... Consequently, *the force used must be strictly proportionate to the achievement of the permitted aims*."[17] (emphasis added) These criteria modify traditional *jus in bello* proportionality by limiting considerations of military advantage to the immediate confrontation with the enemy. Practitioners argue that the human rights model imposes a subjective straitjacket on persons during combat if applied stringently, and it is worth remembering that they are liable to be branded as war criminals for even inadvertent uses of force later determined to be excessive.

Furthermore, in the words of one experienced military practitioner, the related issue about whether there are rules derived from human rights principles that require capturing instead of killing unlawful combatants "is a highly relevant—and contentious—question for today's military commanders and lawyers" with the potential to undermine effective cooperation within western-led military coalitions.[18]

One way to make the human rights doctrine more palatable to soldiers is to note the difference between international and non-international armed conflict. Though the 1949 Conventions regulate armed conflicts conducted between "two or more of the High Contracting Parties," the treaty law applicable to non-international armed conflicts does not provide for combatant status, nor does it define combatants or

---

[16] App. No. 5108/02, 17 Jan. 2008 <http://cmiskp.echr.coe.int/tkp197/view.asp?item=1&portal=hbkm&action =html&highlight=Khatsiyeva&sessionid=91907041&skin=hudoc-en>

[17] *Id.* at ¶ 129 (emphasis added).

[18] Richard S. Taylor, *The Capture Versus Kill Debate: Is the Principle of Humanity Now Part of the Targeting Analysis When Attacking Civilians Who Are Directly Participating in Hostilities?*, THE ARMY LAWYER 103, 104 (June 2011).

specify a series of obligations inherent in combatant status.[19] Under the Geneva principles, anyone operating outside the authority of a State who participates in hostile activities can expect no form of automatic legal license or protection from prosecution.[20] Introducing the concept of "combatant immunity" in the context of non-international armed conflicts would grant immunity for acts which would be perfectly permissible when conducted by combatants in an international armed conflict, such as attacks directed at military personnel or property.[21] The concept of combatancy in an armed conflict not of an international character is a legal nullity.

The striking silence in the law applicable to non-international armed conflicts means that any effort to describe a "combatant engaged in a non-international armed conflict" is an oxymoron. There simply is no legal category of *combatant* in a non-international armed conflict, irrespective of the moral imperatives claimed by one party or the other to warrant hostile activities. In fact, a wide range of States coalesced around the effort to defeat the diplomatic draft applicable to non-international armed conflicts that was tabled in 1975 by the ICRC and supported by the United States and other Western European nations.

The group of States, which included Argentina, Honduras, Brazil, Mexico, Nigeria, Pakistan, Indonesia, India, Romania, and the then Union of Soviet Socialist Republics (USSR), succeeded in raising the threshold for the application of Protocol II (designed to regulate non-international armed conflicts) precisely because of fears that extending humanitarian protections to guerillas and irregular forces might elevate the status of rebel groups during such conflicts, thereby giving rise to the perception that they

---

[19] Geneva Convention Relative to the Treatment of Prisoners of War, art. 2.

[20] *Id.*

[21] Professor Bassiouni posits that

It is almost always the case that an attack by Israeli armed forces against Palestinian targets is presented in the public discourse as being legitimate both in purpose and in means, while a Palestinian attack upon on [*sic*] Israeli targets is almost invariably described in opposite terms. An attack upon military targets is permissible under IHL. Thus, if the Palestinians attack Israeli armed forces, they are legitimate targets. However, Israel always describes such attacks as terrorist attacks. For Israel to recognize the legitimacy of such attacks upon its armed forces would be a major political concession to Palestinian nationalistic claims and would add significantly to the legitimacy of their conflict against Israel as being a war of national liberation. Geneva Convention Protocol I would apply to such a conflict, thus giving the Palestinian combatants the status of POWs, which Israel has denied to date. The analogy in this case extends only with respect to Israeli armed forces. With respect to Israeli attacks on Palestinian targets, the target may be a civilian one, which is not authorized under IHL, or a legitimate military target, but attacked with disproportionate use of force that causes civilian casualties and destruction of private property, which would be prohibited by IHL. In both of these cases, the attack would be a violation of IHL, but is almost always presented as justified. Conversely, when the Palestinians attack a legitimate military target, it is almost always labeled an act of terrorism. Without question, if Palestinians attack a civilian target, that violates IHL.

M. Cherif Bassiouni, *The New Wars and the Crisis of Compliance with the Law of Armed Conflict by Non-State Actors*, 98 J. Crim. L. & Criminology 711, 786 n. 307 (2008).

enjoy combatant immunity (hence the right to kill lawfully).[22] Insurgents and other non-State actors do not benefit from combatant immunity even when they perpetrate violence seeking to accomplish goals similar to those of the sovereign State.[23] Thus, the normal range of domestic criminal law and human rights legislation remain in effect as a matter of law. *Jus in bello* provides an additional layer of rights and duties, but does not completely substitute for the underlying strata of human rights norms.

The field of human rights law puts great weight on the prohibition on violating the rights of individual persons, especially violations of the right to life. In this respect, if not in others as well, human rights law starts from a different position than does humanitarian law. From a human rights perspective, war is inherently difficult to justify given that war involves the intentional taking of innocent civilian life, even if it is often a matter of collateral damage rather than an intentional object of warfare. In addition, the killing of soldiers can be seen as initially problematic from a human rights perspective, since there is a presumption that all humans have rights that should be respected, arguably including soldiers.[24] Human rights are not absolute, but in human rights law the exceptions are few and largely restricted to cases of emergency.

The standard for permissible derogations from the established machinery of human rights protections is set intentionally high as being "public emergency that threatens the life of the nation." Even in that context, there are two key constraints

---

[22] David P. Forsythe, *Legal Management of Internal War: The 1977 Protocol on Non-International Armed Conflicts*, 72 Am. J. Int'l L. 272, 284 (1978). *See also* Eleanor C. McDowell, 1976 Digest of United States Practice in International Law 697 (1976) (documenting the US success in eliminating subjective qualifiers such as "significant" or "important" that might have permitted some States to selectively apply the provisions of Protocol II).

[23] We accept the widely recognized concept that terrorism is "the use or threat of use of anxiety inducing extra-normal violence for political purposes by any individual or group, whether acting for or in opposition to established governmental authority, where such action is intended to influence the attitudes and behavior of a target group wider than victims." Edward F. Mickolus et al., International Terrorism in the 1980s: Volume II 1984–1987 xiii (1989). For the purposes of this work:

> terrorist incidents are restricted to actions that purposely seek to spread terror in the population either by directly targeting noncombatants or by destroying infrastructures that may affect the life and well-being of the civilian population at large… Insurgent, revolutionary, and right-wing terrorism are generally included under the terrorism rubric. Insurgent terrorism refers to violent acts perpetrated by identifiable groups that attack governmental or other targets for short-term goals aimed at sparking widespread discontent toward the existing government. This kind of terrorism is often grounded on a defined ideology, and it seeks to unleash a process of revolution. Revolutionary terrorism defines terrorist actions that take place during existing struggles against a determined regime and develop as a guerrilla tactic. Right-wing terrorism refers to acts perpetrated by outlawed groups that do not seek a social revolution but resort to violence as a way to express and advance their political goals, such as ultranationalism and anticommunism.

Andreas E. Feldmann and Maiju Perala, *Reassessing the Causes of Nongovernmental Terrorism in Latin America*, 46 Latin Am. Pol. And Soc'y 101, 104 (2004).

[24] *See* Reuven Ziegler and Shai Otzari, Do Soldiers' Lives Matter? 45 Israel L. Rev. 53 (No. 1, 2012).

on the power of States to derogate, quite apart from the proportionality requirement mentioned above. Derogations are textually permitted only to the extent that they are "officially proclaimed" (which hearkens back to the legitimate authority prong of Just War theory). In addition, proportionate derogations are permitted "provided that such measures are not inconsistent" with other obligations under international law (of course obliquely referring the reader back to the laws and customs of war in particular).

Human rights law seemingly does not recognize the category of a just war, at least not given the way that wars are fought today. Indeed, William Schabas has argued that there is a "pacifist strain within human rights law" such that carried to its logical endpoint, human rights principles would prevent conflict altogether.[25] From the perspective of the war fighter, a US Army non-commissioned officer told George Will, in June 2010, that the Rules of Engagement (ROE) promulgated by the command structure were "too prohibitive for coalition forces to achieve sustained tactical success."[26] As only one of many examples, current ROE in Afghanistan require a positive identification of an enemy in the act of conducting hostilities. Taliban have learned to fire weapons at coalition forces and become safe from counterfire simply by throwing their weapons down or hiding them.

Based on the realities on the ground in Afghanistan, some have noted that a human-rights-centric approach seemingly overvalues the lives and property of enemy combatants and civilians and can thus create the conditions for military stalemate. This is particularly poignant if the enemy forces have no intention of complying with human rights norms or the precepts of the laws and customs of war. At a minimum, such restrictive ROE signal the increased willingness of commanders to sacrifice some degree of military efficiency and accept increased risk to the lives of friendly forces. There has been little recognition of the larger reality that prolonging conflict through restrictive ROE may in fact lead to much more suffering and human rights abuses over the longer term due to the inability to institute a sound basis for lasting peace.

And some other theorists have linked this human rights approach to the UN Charter, according to which war is virtually outlawed, except in those cases that are authorized by the UN itself. There remains one category of war that is supported by the Charter, namely, self-defensive war—the main case of emergency. But if the UN Charter is to embody a consistent human rights doctrine, even this exception would

---

[25] William Schabas, *Lex Specialis? Belt and Suspenders? The Parallel Operation of Human Rights Law and the Law of Armed Conflict, and the Conundrum of Jus ad Bellum*, 40 ISRAEL L. REV. 592(No. 2 2007).

[26] George Will, *Futility in Afghanistan: An NCO Fires off a Round of Illumination*, WASHINGTON POST, June 20, 2010, at A19.

be difficult to justify in many cases, at least if self-defensive war is understood as war fought for the self-defense of a State without the authorization of the UN. We shall have more to say on these matters in Chapter 11.[27]

From a human rights perspective, grounded in the rights of individual human persons, it does not appear that there should be a straightforward right to self-defense of States, despite the way international law is today often characterized. Of course, if the rights of States are merely shorthand for the rights of individuals that reside in States, or who are citizens thereof, there can be self-defense rights of the States in human rights terms. But the rights of States will be derivative rights. Yet, then this will mean that war will be hard to justify as a matter of the rights of self-defense of individuals, since war is primarily a collective enterprise, and seemingly must be justified as such. There are clear ways to respond to the challenges mentioned in this section. Before addressing these developments in international law further, let us next look at parallel developments in contemporary Just War theory.

III. JUST WAR THEORY AND HUMAN RIGHTS

The premise of the contemporary Just War theory that Michael Walzer has elaborated is supposedly a deep concern for human rights. Walzer begins his book, *Just and Unjust Wars*, by proclaiming that "the morality we shall expound is in its philosophical form a doctrine of human rights."[28] Walzer maintains this view contrary to what he regards as the dominant strain of realism in international relations theory. In this sense, Walzer seeks to humanize the discussion of war in a way similar that of scholars such as Theodor Meron, who have recently tried to humanize the discussion of war in international law, as we saw in the Section I of this chapter. Yet, when he comes to discussions of the lives of soldiers, Walzer defends the "central principle that soldiers have an equal right to kill."[29]

Walzer defends what he calls the moral equality of soldiers: Combatants have an equal right to kill and are themselves subject to be rightfully killed as well. The rationale offered by Walzer seems to be mainly a prudential one, although he calls it moral, namely, that without the recognition of such an equality of soldiers "war as a rule-governed activity would disappear."[30] For suffering to be minimized during war, we must recognize the legitimacy of war itself, most especially the killing of one

---

[27] *See also* Larry May, *The UN Charter, Human Rights Law, and Contingent Pacifism, in* 23 FLORIDA STATE UNIVERSITY J. INT'L L. (2014).

[28] MICHAEL WALZER, JUST AND UNJUST WARS xxii (1977).

[29] *Id.*, p. 41.

[30] *Id.*

soldier by another. Walzer's argument explicitly parallels the argument concerning traditional *jus in bello* legal reasoning in international humanitarian law, not what one might have expected, namely, the analysis provided in International Human Rights Law.

In Walzer's view, war can be defended in terms of the collective rights of people not to be forcibly subjugated. States have a right to go to war in order to defend sovereignty, just as individual people have an inherent right to engage in self-defensive killing. What Walzer calls the analogical argument explains why States have a right to engage in war. Such a right is significant for believing that soldiers can be killed in wars. And the main reason why soldiers can be legitimately killed is that they have forfeited their rights:

> the theoretical problem is not to describe how immunity is gained but how it is lost. We are all immune to start with, our right not to be attacked is a feature of normal human relationships. This right is lost by those who bear arms "effectively" because they pose a danger to other people. It is retained by those who do not bear arms at all.[31]

All people start with the human right not to be attacked or killed, but then what they choose to do can restrict or forfeit those rights in this view.

Walzer's view is premised in the idea that all soldiers have made themselves into the kind of dangerous men that can be killed without major worry about proportionality.

> He can be personally attacked only because he is already a fighter. He has been made into a dangerous man, and though his options may have been few, it is nevertheless accurate to say that he has allowed himself to be made into a dangerous man. For that reason he finds himself endangered…the risks can be raised to their highest pitch without violating his rights.[32]

In Walzer's view, soldiers forfeit their rights because of their "warlike activities."[33]

The parallel in international humanitarian law is that those persons governed by the law of armed conflict derive rights and benefits but are also subject to bright line obligations. Prisoners of war, for example, enjoy legal protection *vis-à-vis* their captors; because they are legally protected, they have no right to commit "violence

---

[31] *Id.*, p. 145, note.
[32] *Id.*, p. 145.
[33] *Id.*

against life and limb."[34] Conversely, lawful combatants become "war criminals" only if their actions transgress the established boundaries of the laws and customs of war.[35] International criminal law intervenes into battlefield killing not when one soldier kills another, but only when one soldier causes unnecessary suffering by killing, or when civilians are directly targeted and killed.

Walzer has said that proportionality will hardly ever come into effect because of the problem of incommensurability and because the threshold is so high that most military acts would satisfy it in any event.[36] Proportionality considerations are so hard to figure out that they come into play only in the most extreme and most clear-cut cases. Such considerations do not ever concern the calculation of the lives or rights of soldiers because those soldiers, in Walzer's view, have forfeited their human rights.

Another, more recent version of Just War theory, supported by Jeff McMahan and his followers, criticizes Walzer for failing to recognize that only those who fight in an unjust war have forfeited their rights and are hence liable to be attacked and killed. Those who fight in a just war retain their rights and cannot be killed except in extreme circumstances. In this respect, as we will see, this contemporary school of Just War theorists makes a radical departure from Walzer in that some soldiers retain the full range of their human rights, but only those who fight on one side, the just side, of a war.

McMahan claims to be driven by a concern for human rights even though he has also argued that so-called aggressive, or unjust, soldiers are liable to be killed in large numbers. Here is how McMahan characterizes his view:

> For a person to cease to be innocent in war, all that is necessary is the forfeiture of the right not to be attacked *for certain reasons*, by certain persons, in certain conditions. There is no loss of rights in general, nor even any loss of the right against attack, understood as the right that holds against all agents at all times. The right against attack is instead forfeited only in relation to certain persons acting for certain reasons in a particular context.[37]

---

[34] *See* Geneva Convention Relative to the Treatment of Prisoners of War, art. 93.

[35] 42 INTERNATIONAL LAW REPORTS 481 (E. Lauterpacht ed., 1971) ("Similarly, combatants who are members of the armed forces, but do not comply with the minimum qualifications of belligerents or are proved to have broken other rules of warfare, are war criminals as such...."); Protocol Additional to the Geneva Conventions of 12 Aug. 1949, and relating to the Protection of Victims of International Armed Conflicts (Protocol I), U.N. Doc. A/32/144, art. 85 (Dec. 7, 1979), *reprinted in* 16 I.L.M. 1391 (1977) [hereinafter Protocol I] ("Without prejudice to the application of the Conventions and of this Protocol, grave breaches of these instruments shall be regarded as war crimes.")

[36] *Id.*, p. 129.

[37] JEFF MCMAHAN, KILLING IN WAR 10 (2009).

This restricted view of rights forfeiture is meant to apply to those who fight in an unjust war, and is an objective determination—either it is true that one has forfeited one's rights by fighting in a war that is objectively unjust, or not. Since human rights are also supposed to be matters of objective morality, those who fight in an unjust war have objectively forfeited their rights whether they realize, or even could reasonably realize it, or not. Human rights obtain objectively, and, in McMahan's view, they can be objectively forfeited, although in a restrictive way, as well.

Concerning proportionality, McMahan has argued that there are two types, narrow and wide, but that neither places a serious limitation on what just combatants are entitled to do to unjust combatants during war. For McMahan, "Proportionality is a constraint on action that causes harm. In most cases, if an act that causes harm is to be justified, it must be instrumental to the achievement of some valuable goal against which the harm can be weighed and assessed."[38]

Narrow proportionality involves harms inflicted "on those who were potentially liable to lesser harms." Wide proportionality involves harms inflicted "on those who were not liable to any harm at all."[39] Harms inflicted in the narrow sense are normally intentional, whereas harms inflicted in the wide sense are normally unintentional. McMahan claims that only wide proportionality is relevant to wartime situations. In this, McMahan follows the traditional international humanitarian law model of focusing proportionality only on the collateral killings of civilians, not on the loss of lives of soldiers, at least if we are thinking of the lives of those who fight on the unjust side of a war. In international humanitarian law, any deliberate targeting and killing of civilians, or *protected persons,* (the term of the law of armed conflict), represents a separate war crime in itself. The war crime of targeting those who are legally protected is a completed offense at the moment the attack is intentionally undertaken, irrespective of its effects.

McMahan puts his finger on one of the main reasons for the traditional restriction of *jus in bello* proportionality to wide, that is, unintentional harm to those who are not at all liable to be harmed, namely, innocent civilians.

Harms inflicted on those who are liable to suffer them have traditionally been assumed to have no role in determining proportionality. Otherwise the resort to war might be ruled out if, for example, the number of expected killings of enemy combatants would exceed the number of people on one's own

---

[38] *Id.,* p. 19.
[39] *Id.,* p. 21.

side whose lives the war could be expected to save—an implication that to my knowledge no just war theorist has been willing to embrace.[40]

In what follows, we will indeed seriously consider such a position, even if we do not fully embrace it in the end. Only harms inflicted "on the innocent as unintended side effects—that is with collateral damage" is in practice part of the *jus in bello* proportionality assessment, in McMahan's view.[41]

But McMahan argues, contrary to the traditional view, that the killing of combatants is often part of *jus in bello* proportionality. He puts the point simply and clearly when he says: "acts of war by unjust combatants are in practice very unlikely ever to be proportionate in the wide sense."[42] So, at least in this sense, McMahan seems to go a long way toward taking the human rights of soldiers seriously. But again, notice that this is only true of the human rights of what he calls "just combatants," not of "unjust combatants." Unjust combatants have forfeited their rights, even if on his view this is not a general but a highly contextualized and conditional forfeiture.

In our view, Just War theory today does not take the individual rights of all soldiers seriously, at least in part because these views continue to think of soldiers as a class rather than as individuals. Walzer is quite explicit about this when he says that war is an enterprise of a "class" not of an individual.[43] McMahan, as in all such things, is much more subtle. McMahan has rather harsh things to say about collectivist approaches to the morality of war.[44] Yet, his view seems to treat soldiers in terms of whether they are just or unjust combatants, thereby treating them primarily based on what their States have done. Seemingly in a similar vein, Brian Orend has said that if the enemy State lacks just cause, then everything the enemy soldier does is tainted and seemingly disproportionate.[45] Let us now examine how legal and moral theorists have sought to limit the reach of human rights norms in wartime situations.

IV. *LEX SPECIALIS* AND FORFEITURES

Various responses have been given by theorists who want to keep human rights law and morality from encroaching too far into traditional humanitarian law and Just War domains. Legal theorists argue that the domain of humanitarian law is

---

[40] *Id.*, p. 19.

[41] *Id.*, p. 22.

[42] *Id.*, p. 27.

[43] MICHAEL WALZER, JUST AND UNJUST WARS 144 (1977).

[44] JEFF MCMAHAN, KILLING IN WAR 209 (2009).

[45] Brian Orend, *Jus Post Bellum: A Just War Theory Perspective, in* JUS POST BELLUM: TOWARDS A LAW OF TRANSITION FROM CONFLICT TO PEACE 38 (Carsten Stahn and Jenn Kleffner, eds., 2008).

lex specialis. Moral and political theorists argue that if one person unjustly threatens the life of another person, the first person has forfeited his or her rights and can be attacked or killed without violating human rights. We will take up these arguments in more detail now.

The *lex specialis* argument has been restated in several recent decisions of the ICJ. In the *Nuclear Weapons* Advisory Opinion, the ICJ said:

> In principle, the right not arbitrarily to be deprived of one's life applies also in hostilities. The test of what is an arbitrary deprivation of life, however, then falls to be determined by the applicable *lex specialis*, namely the law applicable in armed conflict which is designed to regulate the conduct of hostilities. Thus whether a particular loss of life, through the use of a certain weapon in warfare, is to be considered an arbitrary deprivation of life contrary to Article 6 of the Covenant [International Covenant on Civil and Political Rights], can only be decided by reference to the law applicable in armed conflict and not deduced from the terms of the Covenant itself.[46]

Here, then, is the expression of the *lex specialis* doctrine thought to save humanitarian law from being completely swamped by human rights law.

This principle is implicitly affirmed in the European Convention on Human Rights and Fundamental Freedoms. Article 2 makes clear that "Everyone's right to life shall be protected by law. No one shall be deprived of his life intentionally save in the execution of a sentence of a court following his conviction of a crime for which this penalty is provided by law." This seemingly categorical imperative is qualified by the caveat in Article 15, paragraph 2, that the right to life is paramount "except in result of deaths resulting from lawful acts of war." The term *lawful* refers to both the textual application of treaties dealing with the conduct of hostilities and the permissible choice of weapons. The term also includes broader resort to the established body of international customary law related to warfare.

The idea is that human rights law creates a kind of prima facie case for thinking that certain behavior, especially deprivation of the right to life, is to be proscribed. But the all things considered case is determined only after looking at the legal requirements that may be applicable to the specific kind of case in question. A case

---

[46] International Court of Justice, *Legality of the Threat or Use of Nuclear Weapons*, Advisory Opinion of July 8, 1996, ICJ Reports (1996) 226, para 25. Also see *Legal Consequences of the Construction of a Wall in the Occupied Palestinian Territory*, Advisory Opinion of July 92004, ICJ Reports (2004) 136, para 106; and *Case Concerning Armed Activities in the Territory of the Congo (DRC v. Uganda)*, Judgment of December 19 2005, para 216.

that falls directly under a specific provision of humanitarian law, can be justified by the laws of war, even though human rights may be abridged.

One recent commentator on this decision and the general doctrine of *lex specialis*, Marko Milanovic, has raised a skeptical question that we at least partially endorse:

> If human rights accrue to human beings solely by virtue of their humanity, why should these rights evaporate merely because two states, or a state and a non-state actor, have engaged in armed conflict? More limited these rights may be, but they cannot be completely extinguished or displaced if their basic universality premise, that they are immanent in the human dignity of every individual, is accepted.[47]

Notice, though, that Milanovic allows that human rights can be limited or restricted during war, but not that they can be extinguished, which is the position we support as well.

The *lex specialis* doctrine cannot carve out an area of human rights law such that these rights are never applicable to armed conflict and still allow human rights to have universal scope. So, the main question becomes, "How can human rights legitimately be restricted in certain situations in war or emergencies?" If the entirety of human rights law is suspendable on *lex specialis* grounds, there is a danger of undermining all human rights.

A restriction on humanitarian law considerations needs to be drawn so that the entire doctrine of human rights, or what is centrally important to it, is still operable for some wartime situations and other emergencies in which, clearly, the individuals who are involved still are recognized as human. In this vein, we note that there are indeed instances in which the affirmation of human rights is a central dimension of the military mission. In his Tactical Directive[48] of November 30, 2011, the International Security Assistance Force (ISAF) Commander, US Marine General John R. Allen, makes this explicit linkage:

> **Respect for Human Rights.** A significant component of our campaign is championing the respect for human rights and supporting GIRoA's development of institutional protections of every citizen's human rights in accordance with LOAC, international law, and the laws of Afghanistan. ISAF will

---

[47] Marko Milanovic, Norm Conflicts, International Humanitarian Law, and Human Rights, *in* International Humanitarian Law and International Human Rights Law 95, 101 (Oma Ban-Naftali, ed. 2011).

[48] COMISAF'S TACTICAL DIRECTIVE, 30 November 2011, http://lgdata.s3-website-us-east-1.amazonaws.com/docs/905/474743/ISAF__General_Allen__Tactical_Directive_of_Nov_2011.pdf

support and encourage GIRoA to hold those responsible accountable for their actions. These actions are vital in building the Afghan population's confidence and trust.

At the moment, international law is definitely unsettled about how precisely the doctrine of *lex specialis* is to limit human rights law in armed conflict situations. On most views, human rights remain fully in force during armed conflict, but the source of protections is seen as being embedded in the prevailing *jus in bello* framework. This view is largely satisfactory, but cannot account for the recurring collision between the core rights to life and liberty.

The conservative view is that human rights law only comes into effect if there are no rules of humanitarian law that could be applicable to a given situation. The emerging, more liberal view is that a rule of humanitarian law is clearly and unequivocally applicable only if human rights considerations are completely inapplicable in battlefield situations. The newer, more liberal view seems to us to be gaining ground and it is to this view that we will refer for guidance in how we should view human rights in the moral and legal debate about the applicability of human rights to armed conflict situations.

We now turn to the forfeiture argument advanced by most Just War theorists to try to blunt the effects of human rights on *jus in bello* considerations. The revisionist Just War theorists maintain that if a State is an aggressor, its soldiers have forfeited their right not to be killed. It is also often said that if a State or a soldier is acting in self-defense, many more action options are justifiable than otherwise. And such a position on self-defense calls into question the concern for the lives of enemy soldiers that we argue needs to be the human rights part of the proportionality assessment. In the remainder of this section, we will address the way self-defense is often understood in philosophical debates about killing in war.

Let us start by making an assumption drawn from criminal law and human rights law, namely, that if a person is attacked, that person is not justified in using whatever force he or she chooses. Self-defense does not automatically grant the one attacked the right to kill. Instead, the one attacked has the right to do what is necessary to stop the attack. Rather than discussing self-defense in terms of the right to kill, human rights law seems to call for a change that would instead posit the right to disable the attacker, rather than the right to kill the attacker. Thus, the attacker has made himself or herself liable to be disabled, not to be killed. It may turn out that the only way to disable the attacker before the attacker kills is to kill the attacker. But it is misleading to discuss this case by saying that the attacker has made himself or herself liable to be killed since this is only one of several ways that the attacker can be disabled.

The one who is the attacker should be granted fewer options than the one attacked, and in this sense there is a prima facie preference for the one attacked vis-à-vis the one doing the attacking. But, from a human rights approach, it is a mistake to think that the attacker has forfeited his or her right to life, or right not to be killed, even temporarily. It would be unnecessary and disproportionate for the one attacked to use lethal force when non-lethal force will fend off the attack. But beyond this clear line other choices are often not clear-cut.

Joel Feinberg was right to argue that certain basic rights are mandatory in the sense that they cannot be alienated by waiver. And his position on forfeiture of rights also seems to have at least initial appeal, namely, that even the most basic rights can be forfeited at least temporarily due to one's wrongful or negligent behavior. Rejecting the idea that one cannot waive the right not to be killed does not mean that one must also reject the idea that one cannot forfeit this right.[49] What is most important is over what period of time one forfeits one's right to life. If it is forfeited henceforth, then it is hard not to infer that it is also true that henceforth the person who has forfeited the right to life is also not truly a human any more.

The most defensible version of the rights-forfeiture view in Just War theory is that basic rights, such as the right not to be killed, can be forfeited only for a certain period of time, not permanently, as McMahan has contended. In McMahan's view the unjust combatant forfeits his or her right not to be killed for as long as he or she participates in an unjust war. And the forfeiture is only to those who fight in the just war. But why is the forfeiture to everyone else on the other side of the war? It seems that forfeiture should only occur to those who one is wronging at the moment. The salient question is to whom does each combatant forfeit the right to life for as long as that combatant participates in an unjust war?[50] Surely the forfeiture is not to everyone in the world, or even to everyone who is on the just side of the war. The wrong of participating in an unjust war is not exactly parallel to participating in an attack on another person. Not everyone on the other side has their lives threatened in the same way as in the two-person case of someone who must defend herself in a dark alley against an unknown assailant.

In the two-person case, the one who attacks with lethal force forfeits certain rights by one's wrongdoing. But from a restrained view encompassing human rights considerations, even in this case there is no automatic forfeiture of the right to life of the attacker. *Vis-à-vis* the one who is attacked, the attacker loses whatever rights would

[49] See Joel Feinberg, "Voluntary Euthanasia and the Inalienable Right to Life," The Tanner Lectures on Human Values, 1977, pp. 223–256.

[50] We here follow Cheyney Ryan's important insights about to whom one has forfeited rights in self-defense and extend some of his insights to situations of war. *See* Cheyney C. Ryan, *Self-Defense, Pacifism, and the Possibility of Killing*, 93 Ethics 508–524 (April 1983).

have otherwise prevented the one attacked from successfully and rightfully thwarting the attack. Things get even more difficult in the case of a soldier who participates in an unjust war. Here that soldier forfeits, if he or she forfeits at all, whatever rights would normally stand in the way of the soldiers on the just side of the war from preserving their lives and protecting their fellow citizens.

Soldiers fighting in an unjust war are jeopardizing the self-defense of enemy soldiers in quite variable ways over the course of participating in war. They are creating risks for their enemies, but like the two-person case, in many situations, what is needed to nullify the risk does not necessarily involve lethal action. Yet if soldiers can only be killed if they are highly dangerous or killing them is necessary for self-defense of others, those who attack them take a risk in that the soldiers attacked may not, at any given moment, have forfeited their rights not to be killed. To be clear, such an understanding would radically restructure the entire regime of humanitarian law to the extent that targeting during an international armed conflict may properly be made on the basis of affiliation with an entire group—termed combatants in the *jus in bello*. In any event, the key is the principle of necessity, along with related issues concerning the principle of proportionality, a topic to which we turn in detail in the next section.

In general, the terminology of forfeiture of rights seems inapt. There is a great risk that such talk will make us think that the so-called unjust combatant is deprived of his or her most basic rights. Yet, this is not true since the loss of rights only in certain limited contexts and only to a very restricted set of people is not a deprivation of rights that opens up a class of people to any general liability to be killed or harmed. From a human rights perspective, we should start from the position that all lives are to be treated the same. And we definitely do not think that the very limited forfeiture of rights means that the human rights of enemy soldiers can be dismissed or severely devalued in proportionality assessments. We next look at the relation between proportionality and necessity against this human rights background.

V. NECESSITY'S RELATION TO PROPORTIONALITY

Necessity seen through the prism of human rights sets a limit for all proportionality assessments. Lethal force can only be justified to begin with if it is the required strategy (and in this sense necessary) that can achieve a goal that is a significant one. Within the human rights domain, necessity carries with it the most literal interpretation in the narrow context of action. If this necessity threshold is not crossed, then it makes no sense to discuss whether the response is proportionate or not. *Necessity* has a double meaning: First, the strategy must be needed to accomplish a specific military objective, and second, this objective must itself be needed for some larger goal, normally winning the war. If human rights law is applicable, that larger goal will presumably be drawn in terms of the preservation of human rights. It might be thought that lethal force can be used if it is the least costly way to achieve a militarily necessary goal. But from a human rights perspective, lethal force is unjustifiable merely showing that it is least costly compared to all alternatives.

It is sometimes thought that as long as killing soldiers is militarily necessary then it can be justified—after all that is what war involves. But, again from a human rights perspective, war is not about killing soldiers; rather war is about achieving reasonable objectives through the least objectionable (again, in terms of human rights) use of force. Wars should be aimed at incapacitating enemy soldiers, but there is a range of tactics that can incapacitate, including the capture of enemy soldiers. If the incapacitation of the enemy is seen as the key to legitimate military objectives, the use of lethal force, even against other enemy soldiers, must itself be justified as necessary.[51] Full implementation of a human-rights-based model during armed conflict would necessitate shifting burdens onto the war fighter beyond those already found in the laws and customs of war. And proportionality assessments would therefore also be drawn in terms that take account of possible loss of soldiers' lives, even if those soldiers are enemies who are on the unjust side of a war.

In Part IX of its Interpretive Guidance on the Notion of Direct Participation in Hostilities under International Humanitarian Law (Interpretive Guidance), the International Committee of the Red Cross (ICRC) inserted an entire section addressing restraints on the lawful use of lethal force during armed conflicts. This section postulated that the "kind and degree of force which is permissible against persons not entitled to protection against direct attack must not exceed what is actually necessary to accomplish a legitimate military purpose in the prevailing circumstances."[52] This is the narrowest reading of necessity that we discussed above, i.e., necessity is a literal term drawn in the narrowest tactical terms.

Given the fact that there is no black letter law (*lex lata*) to support that assertion, the ICRC Interpretive Guidance relied on its assertion of moral authority (*lex ferenda*) and indirect application of the protections that are universally accepted as applying to persons who are not clearly combatants, in particular

---

[51] Taken literally, this principle could be extended to prevent destruction of enemy property when some other form of achieving the concrete and direct military advantage is warranted and reasonably available.

[52] ICRC, *Interpretive Guidance on the Notion of Direct Participation in Hostilities under International Humanitarian Law*, 77.

employing an expansive notion of the principle of necessity in the way we have just indicated.

> It would defy basic notions of humanity to kill an adversary or to refrain from giving him or her an opportunity to surrender where there manifestly is no necessity for the use of lethal force. In such situation, the principles of military necessity and of humanity play an important role in determining the kind and degree of permissible force against legitimate military targets.[53]

The ICRC also cited Jean Pictet for the idea that "'if we can put a soldier out of action by capturing him we should not wound him, if we can obtain the same result by wounding him, we must not kill him, if there are two means to achieve the same military advantage we must choose the one which causes the lesser evil.'" To be clear, prior to Part IX, there was no affirmative statement of this principle in any authoritative text, and the ICRC Interpretive Guidance did not carry with it the force of State consensus at the time of its promulgation, so it is *lex ferenda*, not *lex lata*.

Part IX is highly controversial, particularly insofar as the ICRC sought to cast its position in terms of preexisting customary international norms.[54] Military practitioners have sharply objected to this commingling of the nonderogable right to life derived from human rights norms with the notion of military necessity and lawful targeting inherent in the *jus in bello*. Experienced military practitioners argue that the ICRC created a precept that embeds the right to capture in *jus in bello*, thereby concluding that "the ICRC has lost sight of its role as trusted advisor and has assumed the position of international legislator."[55] In the words of one expert who participated in several years of meetings that preceded the issuance of the Interpretive Guidance, "Recommendation IX deals with a matter that the experts were not asked to decide, it was raised late in the expert process, was

---

[53] ICRC, *Interpretive Guidance on the Notion of Direct Participation in Hostilities under International Humanitarian Law*, 82.

[54] John B. Bellinger, III and William J. Haynes II, A US government response to the International Committee of the Red Cross study Customary International Humanitarian Law, 89 Int. Rev. Red Cross No. 866, June 2007, p. 443. Jann K. Kleffner, *Section IX of the ICRC Interpretive Guidance on Direct Participation in Hostilities: The End of Jus in Bello Proportionality as We Know It?*, 45 ISRAEL L. REV. 35 (2012); W. Hays Parks, *Part IX of the ICRC "Direct Participation in Hostilities" Study: No Mandate, No Expertise, and Legally Incorrect*, 42 N.Y.U. J. INT'L L. & POL'Y 769, 828 (2010); Dapo Akande, *Clearing the Fog of War? The ICRC's Interpretive Guidance on Direct Participation in Hostilities*, 59 INT'L & COMP. L. Q. 180, 192 (2010).

[55] Richard S. Taylor, *The Capture Versus Kill Debate: Is the Principle of Humanity Now Part of the Targeting Analysis When Attacking Civilians Who Are Directly Participating in Hostilities?*, THE ARMY LAWYER 103, 104 (June 2011).

strongly objected to by a substantial number of the experts present, was not fully discussed and so should not, in my opinion, have been included in the document."[56]

From the perspective of the ICRC and its defenders, this issue highlights one important litmus test for the application of human rights norms to battlefield situations. To see why proponents would maintain that even so-called unjust combatants cannot be killed if it is possible to capture them instead with little cost, consider the example of so-called "Stand your ground" laws that are currently the focus of intense public debate in the US. Even if an aggressor is wrongful, considering the aggressor as a person with rights rather than as someone primarily defined by his or her status (as an aggressor) makes a huge difference. That one does not want to retreat, and that one has in some sense the right not to retreat, is not dispositive. One does not respect the person who is the aggressor as a bearer of rights by allowing such considerations to trump the rights of even a person who is an aggressor. And when we move to considerations of war, there seems to be even less reason to say that anything other than necessity can override the rights of enemy soldiers, even those on the unjust side of a war.

War or armed conflict cannot be initiated or conducted unless it satisfies the necessity condition. It is relatively uncontroversial that the initiation of war (*jus ad bellum*) can only be justified if it is a last resort, that is, if all other strategies have been attempted or are patently unlikely to succeed in accomplishing a justified aim. According to many theorists, self-defense is the only aim that justifies war or armed conflict. Today, as well as historically, some have argued that defense of innocent others is also a "just cause" to initiate war.[57] Suffice it here to say that even in cases of self-defense, the strategy of using lethal force can only be justified if it is the last resort when the human rights domain is dominant.

The *jus in bello* condition of necessity has a strong affinity with this last resort principle in *jus ad bellum* considerations. Necessity establishes a threshold that must be crossed first in order for the use of lethal force to be justified. Only then does proportionality enter the picture. In the language of the Italian Criminal Code, no punishment may be imposed upon "persons who commit an offense when forced to do so by the need to defend their rights or the rights of others against a real danger of unjust attack, provided that the defensive response is proportionate to the attack."[58]

---

[56] A.P.V. Rogers, *Direct Participation in Hostilities: Some Personal Reflections*, 48 MIL. L. & L. OF WAR REV. 143, 158 (2009).

[57] *See* AUGUSTINE, THE CITY OF GOD, Book XIX, Chapter 14, 874 (translated by Henry Bettenson, trans., New York: Penguin Books, (c. 420); LARRY MAY, AGGRESSION AND CRIMES AGAINST PEACE (2008).

[58] *See* Case of Giuliani and Gaggio v Italy, (Application no. 23458/02), European Court of Human Rights (Grand Chamber): ECtHR (Strasbourg), para. 144, Decided March 24, 2011 (holding that the death of demonstrators at the hands of Italian carabinieri during protests surrounding the 2001 G8 Summit in Genoa did not violate the Convention).

Last resort and self-defense play important roles in how to understand necessity in a *jus in bello* context, just as is true in *jus ad bellum*. We can think of military necessity at both the initiation of a war, and also while war is conducted and intermediate military goals are being set. For these intermediate goals, such as clearing an area of enemy soldiers, necessity in its strictest sense requires that all other non-lethal avenues be exhausted, or shown to be clearly ineffective. From a human rights perspective, it is not sufficient that the soldiers to be attacked are enemies, or even unjust combatants. To be justified in attacking these soldiers with lethal force requires that the necessity threshold be crossed, i.e., the action is *forced* upon the participant to echo the verb used in Italian domestic law. This means that the dual aspects of necessity must be met: The goal cannot be achieved by any other means, and the goal itself is necessary for achieving the wider goal of winning the war. As we saw in Chapter 5, these human-rights-derived precepts do not accurately reflect the current *lex lata* of *jus in bello* because military necessity has a broader functional meaning based on pragmatic goals rather than a literal necessity limited to a particular context.

However, if we think of these goals in human rights terms, it becomes easier to determine whether proportionality is met. In the *jus ad bellum* context, the self-defense of a population against an aggressor can be understood rather straightforwardly. But what of the *jus in bello*? Here the military goals all have something to do with facilitating the larger goals of the war. Some of these goals are intermediate in that they are stages in the overall *jus ad bellum* plan, i.e., necessary to eliminate the ongoing threat posed by the enemy. And some of the military goals are merely necessary for achieving the *jus ad bellum* plan, such as not losing too many soldiers so that there are still enough troops to launch a successful offensive, for instance. Here the lives of one's own soldiers are weighed against the lives of enemy soldiers, but part of the value of the larger war's goal, seen in human rights terms, is also put into the balance.

Winning a war, as well as achieving an intermediate military objective, can often be accomplished by taking enemy soldiers as prisoners rather than killing them during battle. This is the heart of the debate because it touches on the areas of autonomy, presumption, and burden of proof that we discussed in Chapter 5. In the constitutional debates over the Obama administration policy of targeting American citizens overseas, the Department of Justice (DOJ) White Paper went so far as to argue that lethal force is lawful only when capture is "infeasible."[59] The White Paper defined the term "infeasible" loosely as follows: [C]apture would not be feasible if it could not be physically effectuated during the relevant window of opportunity.... Other

---

[59] US Department of Justice, White Paper: Lawfulness of a Lethal Operation Directed Against a U.S. Citizen Who Is a Senior Operational Leader of Al-Qa'ida or An Associated Force. Michael Isikoff, Justice Department Memo Reveals Legal Case for Drone strikes on Americans, Jan. 4, 2013, *available at* http://msnbcmedia.msn.com/i/msnbc/sections/news/020413_DOJ_White_Paper.pdf.

factors such as undue risk to US personnel conducting a potential capture operation also could be relevant."[60] This language does little to clarify whether the administration premises targeting primarily on the human rights model (as implied by the very notion of a duty to capture) or on the *jus in bello* regime (which can be inferred from the broad construction of military necessity).

It may also be completely correct to surmise that the administration policy is based on the human rights model insofar as it applies to American citizens while drawing its functional strength from *jus in bello*. In the sense that the policy even authorizes the intentional killing of American citizens, but does so without giving carte blanche authority to those ordering or planning the strikes, the Obama policy represents a sophisticated synthesis of the two approaches, albeit without clearly specifying the basis of legal authority. In that respect, it is troubling because it obscures precise application of proportionality, which is intellectually defensible and contextually appropriate.

It is often difficult to show that the necessity condition has been met for *jus in bello* killing in a narrow tactical sense based on the ICRC approach. And if we add considerations of proportionality, it is not clear that the use of lethal force to accomplish an intermediate military objective can easily be justified. The force must not only be a last resort but must also be such that, among other things, the loss of life of soldiers that is risked is less than the value of the goal to be accomplished. In human rights terms, then, it may be that what is necessary is still not justified because of it is disproportionate. Achieving a military objective, even one that is necessary for winning a war, may not be proportionate because accomplishment of the overall goal of the war may not be significant enough to justify the killing entailed. So, just because achieving a military objective requires lethal use of force, such use of force may still be disproportionate and hence unjustified.

Satisfying a threshold consideration is not sufficient for all justifications, only for *prima facie* justification. Proportionality is an independent concept from necessity; each is a condition in its own right, and each has a different threshold level. But these concepts are linked in the sense that although proportionality is not exhausted by necessity considerations, proportionality does not even apply to a given situation until the necessity condition has been satisfied. Similarly, once proportionality's threshold is crossed, other conditions may come into play before all justifications can be achieved. In human rights terms, this means that the lives of everyone affected are assessed at two distinct levels: whether the lives lost were necessary for a given objective, and whether the lives lost were proportionate, in the sense of having less value than the value of achieving the military objective.

---

[60] *Id.* at 8.

Lastly, consider *jus ad bellum* justification. Assume for a moment that a just cause to go to war has been established by a showing that the war will be one of self-defense. As indicated above, one must then show that the necessity condition has been satisfied, namely, that the war (which can involve lethal or non-lethal tactics) is the only way the State can indeed prevent itself from being conquered or destroyed. Many people would think that the justification is now firmly established. But there are proportionality considerations here as well even in cases of self-defense. Only proportionate strategies can be used to defend sovereign interests. Just as in the two-person case, where in the ICRC's view one is not permitted to kill an opponent if merely wounding him stops his attack, so in war or armed conflict, one cannot obliterate one's enemy if merely capturing some of its troops will accomplish the military mission. Indeed, this is the conceptual basis for the historically inarguable war crime of "declaring that no quarter will be given" (i.e., no prisoners taken alive).[61] At a minimum, one cannot simply discount the value of human lives irrespective of their role in the conflict. This, in our view, is how human rights concerns should affect both *jus ad bellum* and *jus in bello* considerations.

VI. THE CRIME OF DISPROPORTIONATE ATTACK

In this final section, we will discuss what recent international legal theorizing concerning international criminal law might also tell us about how human rights law could affect combat. The two main international courts have held somewhat different views of how to make proportionality assessments. In most cases, proportionality is limited to a consideration of the collateral damage to noncombatants. We will examine the proportionality criteria used by international courts to consider how a human rights approach could change international criminal law.

In the International Court of Justice advisory opinion on the Legal Consequences of Construction of a Wall in the Occupied Palestinian Territory,[62] the standard of proportionality adopted was very similar to the international humanitarian law as restricted by the human rights approach discussed in the Israeli High Court judgment. In that case the Israeli High court said:

> if a terrorist taking a direct part in hostilities can be arrested, interrogated or tried, those are the means that should be employed.[63]

---

[61] Rome Statute Article 8(2)(b)(xii).
[62] Case Concerning the Legal Consequences of a Wall in the Occupied Palestinian Territory, International Court of Justice, 9 July 2004.
[63] Targeted Killings Decision, ILDC 597 (IL 2006), para 40.

Concerning the necessity principle the ICJ quoted from its earlier *Gabcikovo-Nagymaros Project* case, which requires that the act being challenged be "the only way for the State to safeguard an essential interest against a grave and imminent peril."[64] In one sense, this is merely a logical extrapolation of the human rights precept that rights may be constrained only "to the extent strictly required by the exigencies of the situation."

The ICJ then said this about proportionality, quoting the Human Rights Committee of the United Nations: The restrictions "must conform to the principle of proportionality" and must be the least intrusive instrument amongst those which might achieve the desired result.[65] The ICJ concluded the opinion by finding that Israel's construction of the wall had not met either the necessity or proportionality principles so understood.

Notice that the ICJ construal of proportionality is stricter than most—namely, that the strategy or tactic is "the least intrusive." In earlier understandings of proportionality, the strategy or tactic merely had to cause less damage than would occur if the military objective were not accomplished by the strategy or tactic. In most cases, meeting the proportionality requirement would not have necessarily meant using the least intrusive strategy or tactic. The ICJ *Wall* case thus raises the bar considerably in terms of what is required for an action not to be disproportionate, at least from a human rights perspective.

The international criminal tribunals have partially followed the ICJ in how they have understood proportionality and necessity. The Rome Statute allows for criminal punishment for disproportionate attacks during armed conflict in the International Criminal Court (ICC). One of the most prominent violations of the laws of war—disproportionate attack—is defined as,

> Intentionally launching an attack in the knowledge that such attack will cause incidental loss of life or injury to civilians or damage to civilian objects or widespread, long-term and severe damage to the natural environment which would be *clearly* excessive in relation to the concrete and direct *overall* military advantage anticipated.[66]

---

[64] Case Concerning the Gabcikov-Najymaros Project (Hungary/Slovenia), International Court of Justice, 25 Sept. 1997, § 140.

[65] *Id*, § 136.

[66] Art. 8(2) ICCSt.

Proportionality here ranges over damages to civilian lives, to civilian objects, and even over the natural environment, but not over the lives of combatants.[67] By contrast, the ECHR is on record that lethal force is warranted in law enforcement operations only when it is "strictly proportional" and only in the absence of suitable alternatives.[68] As we previously noted, the ICRC is at the forefront of challenging the notion that combatant lives are completely disconnected from proportionality analysis by calling for a human rights approach to proportionality in armed conflict.

In addition, the ICC Elements of Crimes document contains a key footnote that reads as follows:

> The expression "concrete and direct overall military advantage" refers to a military advantage that is foreseeable by the perpetrator at the relevant time. Such advantage may or may not be temporally or geographically related to the object of the attack. The fact that this crime admits the possibility of lawful incidental injury and collateral damage does not in any way justify any violation of the law applicable in armed conflict. It does not address justifications for war or other rules related to *jus ad bellum*. It reflects the proportionality requirement inherent in determining the legality of any military activity undertaken in the context of an armed conflict.

Here, we see a reflection of what has traditionally been thought to be the domain of *jus in bello* proportionality assessments, at least as measured by state practice. However, the footnote itself, when given interpretive force as permitted under Article 21 of the Rome Statute could provide the basis for judges to impose the narrowest human rights understanding of proportionality based on the assumption of a *pactum tacitum* among the delegations.

The circularity of the last sentence of this extensively negotiated footnote could well be interpreted by future Trial Chambers to accord with a more human-rights-based orientation we have seen expressed in the ICJ opinions and the ICRC Direct Participation Guidelines. The ICC judges are vested with the normative uncertainty of determining what "the proportionality requirement in determining the legality of any military activity" actually means. In any event, it is clear to us that those provisions of the Rome Statute, if modified by the constituent elements of the actual crimes, support the conclusion that the modern understanding of *jus*

---

[67] The ICTY has reaffirmed the idea that proportionality must be observed in considering strategies in armed attack. See Review of the Indictment Pursuant to Rule 61, *Prosecutor v. Milan Martic*, ICTY Case No. IT-95-11-R61, 13 March 1996, § 18.

[68] *McCann v. United Kingdom*, App. No. 18984/91, 21 Eur. H.R. Rep. 97 (1995).

in bello proportionality must be made independently of the larger *jus ad bellum* circumstances.

In this light, Judith Gardham has made an important observation in commenting on how the ICC has come to understand proportionality:

> The Statute definition of the offense of launching a disproportionate attack adds the word "clearly" to the text of the provision as it appears in Additional Protocol I. This addition is intended to indicate to the Court that only obvious cases of disproportionate attacks should be punished.[69]

When we are in the realm of international criminal punishment, only *clearly* disproportionate attacks are prosecutable. For some commentators, that means that proportionality shrinks to include only obvious cases of collateral civilian deaths that are not outweighed by gains in military advantage.

But, we believe, it is important that the ICC has extended the domain of proportionality assessments from what had previously been understood. The term "overall" military advantage calls for an assessment that, as the note cited above indicates, takes in greater geographical and temporal dimensions than the immediate target of a particular attack. Such a broadening of the scope might well reach to include the idea that some lives of soldiers need to be taken into account in the proportionality assessment. Killing soldiers, who are in the geographical area but not necessary for accomplishing a mission, is the kind of disproportionate attack that might in the future trigger a criminal prosecution at the ICC if the judges interpose a human-rights-based concern for human life that includes the protection of combatants from the effects of combat operations. This arguably echoes the strands of Geneva Conventions law and military professionalism that abhor wanton cruelty that is either divorced from a focused pursuit of tactical or strategic advantage, or reflects indiscipline and inefficiency within a military command. This is also an important result for international criminal law of taking human rights seriously.

A more radical reading of the change is wrought by incorporating human rights considerations into international law. The Israel High Court decision in the *Targeted Killings* case, that seemed to follow the lead of the ICJ, said that the lives of terrorists needed to be considered in proportionality assessments. If the standard employed in the *Wall* case were to be applied to a broader range of cases than just those concerning terrorism, but to other combatants as well, it seems that not many killings could be justified since they would become per se disproportionate. In most cases, there are other strategies that can be adopted that would have the same military advantage,

---

[69] J. Gardham, Necessity, Proportionality, and the Use of Force by States 134 (2004).

such as capturing the targeted person. In any event, there would always have to be a showing that capture was not possible, or was overly risky, if killing is to meet the ICJ standard. This would shift the burden of proof onto the war fighter to affirmatively justify each tactical decision.

The upshot seems to be that it might some day be considered a disproportionate attack that would warrant international criminal prosecution if soldiers were killed who could be disabled for the same military effect. After all, if terrorists should be treated this way, then surely regular soldiers who happen to be on the unjust side of a war should not be treated any worse. In any event, this concludes our exploration of how to think about what changes should be made (*lex ferenda*) to the international law of *jus in bello* proportionality concerning human rights applied during armed conflict.

We will close with two caveats. First, the effort to interject human rights into the context of conflict is not artificial or imagined. These are very real trends that increase the uncertainty among international lawyers and academics over the precise bounds of what is required during conflict and indeed what is desirable. There are very few bright line boundaries, particularly in the domain of non-international armed conflicts, or in dealing with sustained insurgencies that wage war in an asymmetric manner by ignoring legal and moral constraints. This tension is particularly notable in the context of efforts by States to cooperate in preventing or responding to terrorist acts. The balance between the loss of innocent life necessitated by striking terrorist actors and the prevention of terrorist crimes that seek to destroy innocent lives is indeed irreducible to a formula or a neat decision matrix. In the memorable summation by Gary Solis, "such calculations are one of the burdens of high military command."[70]

Second, we cannot become so wedded to the aspirational goals of human rights law so as to ignore the reality faced by the soldier on the ground. For example, the US Army Counterinsurgency (COIN) Manual posits a context specific definition of proportionality that appears to be based on the human rights model,[71] but imposes what is in actuality nearly an impossible decision-making criterion onto the war fighter:

> In conventional operations, proportionality is usually calculated in simple utilitarian terms: civilian lives and property lost versus enemy destroyed and military advantage gained. But in COIN operations, advantage is best calculated not in terms of how many insurgents are killed or detained, but rather which enemies are killed or detained. If certain key insurgent leaders are essential

---

[70] GARY D. SOLIS, THE LAW OF ARMED CONFLICT: INTERNATIONAL HUMANITARIAN LAW IN WAR 280 (2010).

[71] Field Manual 3-24, para. 7-32.

to the insurgents' ability to conduct operations, then military leaders need to consider their relative importance when determining how best to pursue them. In COIN environments, the number of civilian lives lost and property destroyed needs to be measured against how much harm the targeted insurgent could do if allowed to escape. If the target in question is relatively inconsequential, then proportionality requires combatants to forego severe action, or seek non-combative means of engagement.

Requiring the decision-maker to make a precise assessment of "how much harm the targeted insurgent could do if allowed to escape" seems to put a tactical straightjacket on the average soldier in the field who operates with imperfect information and often in the midst of grave personal dangers. The law of proportionality cannot properly mean that soldiers are frozen in indecision as insurgents target them or deprive other innocent persons of *their* fundamental human rights. Similarly, requiring an absolute exhaustion of conceivable courses of action as necessary for any use of lethal force would constrict conflict to the point of extinction. Such a shifting would grant an unwarranted military advantage to the aggressor in a particular situation, especially an aggressor that sought to achieve an advantage by disregarding the laws and customs of warfare altogether. This does not seem to be a desirable objective, either from the human rights perspective or from goals of the *jus in bello*. Yet this seems to be the direction that human rights theorists are pushing international humanitarian law.

In this chapter, we have been exploring how considerations of human rights could affect proportionality assessments in times of war or armed conflict. To be sure, these are difficult conceptual and operational issues. When considering effects of battle, the lives of soldiers should not be ignored or severely discounted. There may well be circumstances in which enemy combatants are killed in large numbers pursuant to a just war and the military mission that flows from that cause. Nevertheless, if the lives of soldiers are being compared and weighed against military objectives, those lives should not be counted in a way that falls below what will still show respect for them as bearers of human rights. This seems commonsensical to us as one way of winning a war both in the near and long term, especially also from the perspective of *jus post bellum* considerations of reconciliation. And we should not shy away from admitting that such a view moves us close, perhaps dangerously close, to what some of us have recently called contingent pacifism.[72]

---

[72] *See* Larry May, *Contingent Pacifism and the Moral Risks of Participating in War*, 25 PUBLIC AFFAIRS QUARTERLY 95 (No. 2, 2011); Larry May, *Contingent Pacifism and Selective Refusal*, 43 JOURNAL OF SOCIAL PHILOSOPHY 1 (No. 3 Spring 2012); Larry May, CONTINGENT PACIFISM: HUMAN RIGHTS, CONSCIENCE, AND INTERNATIONAL LAW, book manuscript in draft.

7

THE UNIQUENESS OF *JUS IN BELLO* PROPORTIONALITY

THE GOAL OF this chapter is to consolidate the theoretical implications of the proportionality principle as it is applied. We will first set out the points of commonality that have become embedded in the term *proportionality* with a view to providing a common baseline of understanding of its accepted interdisciplinary attributes. We will then discuss the range of theoretical purposes served by the concept of proportionality with a view to explaining why it has become such a pervasive notion despite its generality. Then we will summarize the reasons why the *jus in bello* articulation of proportionality remains distinct from all other usages of the concept.

Previous chapters have described the baseline of the proportionality principle in its most common usages. Despite its linguistic consistency, the principle of proportionality does not provide a homogenous terminological template. Though the same term spans different disciplines, the one striking conclusion is that each unique usage of the concept is similar but simultaneously contrasting depending on the rights at stake, who is interfering with rights, and who is reviewing the action.

In this chapter, we will first briefly explain one attempt to provide a common understanding of proportionality across legal disciplines. In Section II, we will identify three common components of proportionality: (1) the use of negative rather than positive terminology, (2) the similarities of permissible discretion; and (3) the things that are typically left out in proportionality assessments. These attributes might well be thought of as the "common core" of proportionality. In Section III, we will identify three affirmative values that clearly expressed proportionality determinations advance: (1) the articulation of positive values; (2) the preservation of room for evaluating discretionary acts; and, (3) the establishment of a framework for interrelation.

And then in Section IV, we provide three reasons for seeing *jus in bello* proportionality as unique: (1) the contextual application of the principle, (2) the attribution of errors, and (3) the permissive nature of the entire body of law concerning *jus in bello* proportionality. The array of contextual applications of the same term could generate a seemingly natural drift towards commonality. We conclude that morphing *jus in bello* proportionality into an interdisciplinary straitjacket based on a desire for homogeneity of application would be undesirable and is actually unnecessary. *Jus in bello* proportionality is unique in its context, and a simplistic shift to make it operate precisely parallel to other usages would largely destroy its utility in the context of armed conflicts.

I. SUITABILITY, NECESSITY, AND PROPORTIONALITY

As we have seen, usages in several different legal disciplines apply variations of a three-prong test: suitability, necessity, and proportionality *stricto sensu*. To review this three-part test frequently used by many courts and commentators, proportionality is evaluated in a cumulative manner by considering (1) suitability (sometimes termed adequacy) for what it seeks to determine, i.e., whether the rule or action in question is practicable to achieving the desired end state; (2) whether it is the least restrictive, or least intrusive available means to achieve the end (at least as measured against those of similar efficiency); and (3) whether the balance is reasonable in light of its overall advantages and disadvantages.

Proportionality is reflected in French law as requiring "a balance between costs and benefits," in the adjudication of constitutional rights.[1] And Article 10 of the Spanish Constitution mandates that

> The principles relating to fundamental rights and liberties recognized by the Constitution shall be interpreted in conformity with the Universal Declaration of Human Rights and the international treaties and agreements thereon ratified by Spain

The Spanish Constitutional Court has accordingly noted that a state restriction on the right of the people is proportional *stricto sensu* if it is "pondered or balanced because more benefits or advantages for the general interest are derived from it than damages against other goods or values in conflict."[2] One Spanish scholar insists

---

[1] Juan Cianciardo, *The Principle of Proportionality: The Challenges of Human Rights*, 3 J. OF CIVIL STUDIES 177,

[2] S.T.C., May 8, 1995 (S.T.C., No. 66/1995) (Spain). In Spanish: "Ponderada o equilibrada por derivarse de ella más beneficios o ventajas para el interés general que perjuicios sobre otros bienes o valores en conflicto."

that this test of constitutionality requires a "well-adjusted relationship between the means and the ends in terms of costs and benefits."[3] There is a tendency to seek intellectual homogeneity based on the assumption that dissidence in law and morality is undesirable. However, the principle of proportionality is a far more nuanced and context-specific principle and efforts to reduce it to a formulaic trope are misplaced.

The careful reader of the previous six chapters will recognize the wisdom of Yoram Dinstein's admonition that we must focus our gaze on the power of proportionality as law not liturgy. The principle of proportionality has an array of applications with wholly specific variations depending on the actors and interests such as, *inter alia*, human rights, federalism, institutional competencies, and the appropriateness of judicial deference to other institutions."[4] In fact, as we have seen in the caselaw and in the operational examples from Afghanistan and Iraq, there are affirmative dangers in uncritically summoning forth the proportionality principle as a self-reinforcing and result-oriented mantra.

Before delving into the particularities of *jus in bello*, we want to highlight the common themes that emerge from an interdisciplinary assessment of proportionality. In other words, some aspects of proportionality are consistently replicated despite its different uses and considerations across contexts. Proportionality purports to provide a standard of non-arbitrariness by which to assess compelling operational, legal, or moral imperatives, as long as it is properly understood and implemented. At the same time, proportionality operates in close conjunction with other principles. For example, damage to civilians during military operations that is not grounded firmly in accompanying military necessity by definition cannot be proportionate. Because they are intended to be highly enforceable, the laws and customs of war are designed from the ground up to provide appropriate boundaries while embedding norms into military practice that can and will be followed. The laws and customs of warfare reflect the highest professional norms designed to hinder an endless cycle of violence and lawlessness that would lead to unending warfare.

At the same time, proportionality in conjunction with the concepts of distinction, military necessity, and the law of targeting must remain practicable because "rules that are incompatible with all effective military action risk being ignored and, thereby, not preventing any harm from occurring."[5] Thus, the starting point for an affirmative vision for preserving proportionality as a viable concept in practice is to

---

[3] Manuel Medina Guerrero, La Cinvulación Negativa del Lesislador a Los Derechos Fundamentales 132, 134 (1996).

[4] Jeremy Gunn, *Deconstructing Proportionality in Limitations Analysis*, 19 Emory Int'l L. Rev. 465, 467 (2005).

[5] On the need to construct enforceable rules of international humanitarian law, see Janina Dill & Henry Shue, *Limiting the Killing in War: Military Necessity and the St. Petersburg Assumption*, 26 Ethics & Int'l Aff. 311, 324 (2012).

identify its points of commonality across disciplines. This is rather like the process of identifying specific comparators when doing fingerprint analysis. After discussing commonalities among most types of proportionality in law, we will discuss the uniqueness of *jus in bello* proportionality

II. COMMONALITIES AMONG DIFFERENT USES OF PROPORTIONALITY

A. *The Pervasive Use of Negative Phraseology*

In the first place, it is notable that there is no area in which the law of proportionality is defined with clarity on an abstract basis—in large part because of a failure to capture the changing circumstances. This is integral to its very nature because proportionality always involves competing factors and shifting relationships between the values sought. There is accordingly no area in which a strict and unyielding assessment of proportionality is articulated in a positive and encompassing manner. By this, we do not mean to infer that there is no form or content to the principle, but that the actual content of proportionality in any given context is not subject to being reduced to a soundbite or easily extrapolated judicial test. This is precisely why the term retains such generality in definition even as it is so widespread in judicial and moral literature. Proportionality is an imperfect tool, but it is nonetheless essential in a wide variety of disciplines.

Because proportionality provides an indispensable balancing function, yet defies precise, overarching, and comprehensive description, it is most frequently expressed in the negative rather than the positive form as a rule of decision. This creates uncertainty over which of the objective formulations is appropriate in a given context. In Chapter 12, we will develop a theory of thresholds as a way of clarifying the rule of first resort for the various formulations of proportionality

In human rights parlance, governments may invoke inherent restrictions on the rights conveyed by the European Convention on Human Rights and Fundamental Freedoms only if "the means employed are not disproportionate."[6] To cite another example, in an International Centre for Settlement of Investment Disputes (ICSID)_ decision rendered on December 7, 2011, the tribunal compared the relative value of the costs incurred by the defendant against the damage caused to the Russian budget with the conclusion that "[t]he sequestration orders were legitimate and *not disproportionate.* [emphasis added] The tribunal finds no breach of the fair and equitable treatment requirement in respondent's treatment of the investment in this regard."[7]

---

[6] Mathieu-Mohin and Clerfayt v. Belgium, App. No. 9267, 10 Eur. H.R. Rep. 20, 23, P 52 (1987).

[7] Spyridon Roussalis (Claimant) v Romania (Respondent), ICSID Case No. ARB/06/1 (Award), ¶ 520 (Dec. 7, 2011), *available at* https://icsid.worldbank.org/ICSID/FrontServlet?requestType=CasesRH&actionVal=showDoc&docId=DC2431_En&caseId=C70

Similarly, the International Court of Justice (ICJ) relied upon the proportionality principle as the rule of decision in its first environmental law ruling in the *Case Concerning Gabcikovo-Nagymaros Project (Hungary/Slovakia)*[8] over the construction and operation of dams on the river Danube. In finding in Hungary's favor on the Slovak dam project, the court held that Slovakia's countermeasure to Hungary's breach of a prior treaty "failed to respect the proportionality which is required by international law" and was consequently unlawful.[9] In other words, Slovakia's countermeasure to Hungary's breach of the 1977 treaty was "not proportionate."[10] The majority opinion omitted discussion of the precise judicial methodology employed to reach this finding apart from merely comparing the economic damages foreseeably attributed to each side of the dispute.

In his dissent, Judge Vereschetin more clearly described proportionality as a "basic requirement for the lawfulness of a countermeasure," which is to be determined "in the circumstances of the case."[11] Quoting the International Law Commission, he conceded that "there is no uniformity...in the practice or the doctrine [in international law] as to the formulation of the principle, the strictness or flexibility of the principle and the criteria on the basis of which proportionality should be assessed." As a result, "reference to equivalence or proportionality in the narrow sense...is unusual in State practice...[which] is why in the literature and arbitral awards it is suggested that the lawfulness of countermeasures must be assessed by the application of such *negative criteria* as 'not [being] manifestly disproportionate,' or 'clearly disproportionate,' '*pas hors de toute proportion*' [quoting the original French text],'not out of proportion,' etc."[20]

The widespread practice in other arenas mirrors the intentional design of the *jus in bello* framework. The International Committee of the Red Cross (ICRC) Commentary on Protocol I notes with some understatement that the language applicable to precautions in the attack "gave rise to lengthy discussions and negotiations among delegations."[12] The 1973 ICRC working draft of what became the proportionality provisions in the 1977 Protocol, i.e., Articles 57(2) and 85(3) of Protocol

---

[8] ICJ Press Office, "Case concerning Gabcikovo-Nagymaros Project (Hungary/Slovakia)," Press Release No. 1997/10, (September 25, 1997) *available at* http://www.icj-cij.org/docket/index.php?pr=267&p1=3&p2=1&case=92&p3=6

[9] Case Concerning the Gabcikovo-Nagymaros Project (Hungary v. Slovakia), 1997 I.C.J. 7, 12 (September 25, 1997).

[10] *Id.* ¶¶ 85, 87.

[11] *Id.* at 223 (Vereschetin, J., dissenting).

[12] COMMENTARY ON THE ADDITIONAL PROTOCOLS OF JUNE 8, 1977 TO THE GENEVA CONVENTIONS OF AUGUST 12, 1949, Art. 57, at 683, ¶ 2204 (Sandoz et al, eds 1987), *available at* http://www.icrc.org/ihl.nsf/COM/470-750001?OpenDocument.

I, cautioned that lawful attacks were those deemed "not disproportionate to the direct and substantial military advantage anticipated."[13]

Geoffrey Best notes that although the textual incarnations of proportionality came after more than a century of development within the field, that gap should not be attributed to unfamiliarity with the basic precepts of the precautions expected to be taken by attackers and defenders alike. In his words, the treaty language was a developmentally delayed formulation "because it was thought to be too slippery and in its potential implications embarrassing to commit to a set form of words."[14] Thus, the rather wide range of discretion given to decision makers by the widespread use of the negative form "not disproportionate" reflects the sheer inability of drafters to define the term *proportionate* as a rigid concept. In that sense, the indeterminacy of its application is baked into the very design of the proportionality principle.

B. Breadth of Permissible Discretion

By extension, every field we have surveyed embeds a notably high threshold for a finding of disproportionality. Proportionality is, by its very nature, a comparative exercise as we have noted. Comparison is made more complex in a number of areas given the inherent difficulty of valuation that we described in Chapter 3. As Michael Schmitt points out "[h]ow does one, for instance, compare tanks destroyed to the number of serious civilian injuries or deaths caused by attacks upon them?"[15] The use of markedly strong modifiers is a core truism that recurs in our examination of the term. As the snapshot of examples we have considered already illustrates, decisions invalidate previous actions only upon the showing that they "grossly"[16] or "markedly" or "strikingly" or "plainly" lacked proportionality. The elevated threshold simultaneously empowers actors by recognizing the rightful boundaries of their discretion even as it places the burden of proof onto the plaintiff attempting to overturn or discredit the decision.

Judge Vereschetin's observation, quoted above, that international practice requires a finding that a particular countermeasure is "manifestly" or "clearly" out of balance is completely accurate. Perhaps more notable for our purposes, the qualifiers span courts and contexts. The European Court of Justice (ECJ) upheld a series of European Union (EU) agricultural directives in July 2012 reasoning that "notwithstanding the fact that they may involve adverse economic consequences for some

---

[13] *Id.*

[14] GEOFFREY BEST, WAR AND LAW SINCE 1945 323 (1994).

[15] Michael N. Schmitt, *Fault Lines in the Law of Attack, in* TESTING THE BOUNDARIES OF INTERNATIONAL HUMANITARIAN LAW 277, 293 (Susan C. Breau & Agnieszka Jachec-Neale, eds. 2006).

[16] R. *v.* Khawaja, 2012 S.C.C. 69, para.63 (2012).

traders, [the Directives] do not appear, in the light of the economic interests of those traders, to be *manifestly disproportionate* in relation to the aim pursued." [emphasis added][17] Similarly, in *Afton Chemical Limited v Secretary of State for Transport*, the disputed EU action was upheld because a "measure adopted in the exercise of that discretion, breaches the principle of proportionality only if it is manifestly unsuitable for achieving the objective pursued by the competent body, if there are clearly less onerous measures which are equally effective or if the measures taken are *clearly out of proportion* to the objectives pursued." [emphasis added][18]

Within the *jus in bello* realm, the United Kingdom (UK) included an express reservation to the grave breaches provisions of Protocol I, Articles 85(3)(c), and 56. The reservation rejected an absolute standard of protection for "works or installations containing dangerous forces" because States merely must "avoid severe collateral losses among the civilian population." In other words, rather than an absolute bar, a substantial degree of property damage or loss of life might well be permissible. The International Criminal Tribunal for the former Yugoslavia (ICTY) has indirectly reinforced this higher threshold by repeatedly declining to convict perpetrators on the basis of *post hoc* evaluations of their proportionality analysis. Of particular note, the ICTY Appeals Chamber overturned the conviction of Croatian Generals Ante Gotovina and Mladen Markač by holding that the Trial Chamber improperly created an evidentiary standard that then became the basis for inferring disproportionate and indiscriminate artillery attacks using its own judicial construction as the dispositive principle.[19] Though the majority decision generated vigorous dissents that are "perhaps unprecedented in international tribunal history decision" the Appeals Chamber was unanimous in finding that the judicially fabricated standard was inappropriate.[20]

Previous, ICTY opinions have based liability on an inference of direct intention to conduct prohibited attacks on civilians rather than second guessing a commander's proportionality assessments. For example, avoiding what would be a sticky proportionality analysis, the Blaškić Trial Chamber used the principle of distinction to conclude that an attack against civilians was criminal only if it was "conducted intentionally in the knowledge, or when it was impossible not to know that civilians or civilian property were being targeted not through military necessity."[21]

---

[17] Association Kokopelli v Graines Baumaux SAS, Case C-59/11, E.C.R., para. 68-69 [2012].

[18] Afton Chemical Limited v Secretary of State for Transport, Case C-343/09, E.C.R. I-07027, para. 57 [2010].

[19] Prosecutor v. Gotovina et al., Case No. IT-06-90-A, Appeal Judgment, ¶ 49-67 (Int'l Crim. Trib. for the Former Yugoslavia Nov. 16, 2012).

[20] Julian Elderfield, *Introductory Note to the International Criminal Tribunal for the Former Yugoslavia: The Prosecutor v. Gotovina et. al.* 52 I.L.M. 72 (2013).

[21] Prosecutor v. Blaškić, Case No. IT-95-14-T, Appeal Judgment, ¶ 180 (Int'l Crim. Trib. for the Former Yugoslavia March 3, 2000); *See also* Judgment, Prosecutor v. Galić, Case No. IT-98-29-A, ¶ 140 (Int'l Crim. Trib. for the Former Yugoslavia Nov. 30, 2006).

Based on this and other examples of state practice, the reader will recall that the drafters of the Rome Statute added the qualifier to the proportionality language in Article 8(2)(b)(iv) that the crime is committed only when the attack is intentionally launched in the knowledge that the foreseeable loss of civilian life or damage to civilian property will be "clearly excessive" in relation to the anticipated military advantage. Though they "leave a wide margin of discretion to belligerents" the proportionality provisions, to include the elevated comparative threshold, "do not appear to be contested by any State, including those which have not ratified" Protocol I.[22]

To further complicate the uncertainty of comparing what we term these "dissimilar dimensions," there is no strict sequence for the procedural steps that the decision-maker must make in assessing proportionality. The ICTY Final Report to the Prosecutor by the Committee Established to Review the NATO Bombing Campaign in Kosovo simply noted that

> It is unlikely that a human rights lawyer and an experienced combat commander would assign the same relative values to military advantage and to injury to noncombatants. Further, it is unlikely that military commanders with different doctrinal backgrounds and differing degrees of combat experience or national military histories would always agree in close cases. It is suggested that the determination of relative values must be that of the "reasonable military commander"[23]

As we have already indicated, this subjectivity is at least quasi-objective, though since it is presumed that not just any subjective judgment will do, but only those that are "reasonable" in the circumstances. If this were not presumed, then proportionality assessments would collapse into what a given decision-maker thought at the time, regardless of what the decision maker thought. And this kind of discretion would make proportionality useless as any kind of restraining influence.

On this score, the authoritative ICRC Commentary recognizes that in these subjective evaluations "the interpretation must above all be a question of common sense and good faith for military commanders. In every attack, they must carefully weigh

---

[22] KNUT DÖRMANN, ELEMENTS OF WAR CRIMES UNDER THE ROME STATUTE OF THE INTERNATIONAL CRIMINAL COURT 168 (2002).

[23] See FINAL REPORT TO THE PROSECUTOR BY THE COMMITTEE ESTABLISHED TO REVIEW THE NATO BOMBING CAMPAIGN AGAINST THE FEDERAL REPUBLIC OF YUGOSLAVIA (June 13 2000), reprinted in 39 I.L.M. 1258 (2000), at para. 50. For analysis, see Michael N. Schmitt, Precision Attack and International Humanitarian Law, 87 INT'L REV. RED CROSS 445 (2005).

up the humanitarian and military interests at stake."[24] As a result, in the Kosovo context, the North Atlantice Treaty Organization (NATO) launched more than 38,000 air sorties, of which some 10,484 were strike missions that dropped a total of 6,303 tons of ordinance and caused some 500 civilian casualties apart from destroying an array of military objectives.[25] The ICTY Expert Review of these incidents nevertheless reinforced the elevated threshold by concluding that "[a]lthough there will be room for argument in close cases, there will be many cases where reasonable military commanders will agree that the injury to noncombatants or the damage to civilian objects was clearly disproportionate to the military advantage gained." Of course, as we will indicate in our final chapter, the *jus in bello* self-defense threshold is especially high, and much higher than any other of the proportionality thresholds.

C. What Proportionality is Not[26]

The modern understandings of proportionality are seldom subject to being framed on the basis of dollar-for-dollar equality in any of the contexts we identified. This is why courts routinely consider a wide range of possible factors and the other potential options for countermeasures in assessing proportionality. In the media and popular perception, there is often a direct implication that civilian casualties represent the benchmark for inferring disproportionality during wartime. For example, *The Economist* published a direct comparison of Israelis killed as a result of rocket fire from Hamas in the Gaza strip and the number of Palestinians killed: From January 1, 2012 to November 11, 2012, the ratio was 1/78 and the ratio spiked to 3/95 during the period November 13-19, 2012, as hostilities flared and the Palestinians field tested a new rocket system capable of reaching Jerusalem.[27] Without knowing anything else about what feasible measures Israel took to avoid killing innocents, or how many of the weapons targeted were deliberately housed by Hamas in the midst of urban areas and basements, or the planning undertaken to minimize or eliminate civilian casualties, or the nature of the weapons employed, or the effects based targeting decisions

---

[24] COMMENTARY ON THE ADDITIONAL PROTOCOLS OF 8 JUNE 1977 TO THE GENEVA CONVENTIONS OF 12 AUGUST 1949, Art. 57, at 683–684, ¶ 2208 (Sandoz et al, eds 1987), *available at* http://www.icrc.org/ihl. nsf/COM/470-750001?OpenDocument.

[25] William J. Fenrick, *Targeting and Proportionality During the NATO Bombing Campaign Against Yugoslavia*, 12 EUR. J. INT'L L. 489 (No. 3 2001).

[26] We thank Gary Solis for this trenchant turn of phrase, GARY D. SOLIS, THE LAW OF ARMED CONFLICT: INTERNATIONAL HUMANITARIAN LAW IN WAR 280 (2010).

[27] http://www.economist.com/blogs/pomegranate/2012/11/israel-and-palestinians?fb_action_ids=10151332071194603&fb_action_types=og.likes&fb_ref=scn%2Ffb_ec%2Fgaza_abacus&fb_source=other_multiline&action_object_map={%2210151332071194603%22%3A168039173342619}&action_type_map={%2210151332071194603%22%3A%22og.likes%22}&action_ref_map={%2210151332071194603%22%3A%22scn\%2Ffb_ec\%2Fgaza_abacus%22}

or the communications between the parties during the conflict, often one cannot assess proportionality properly.

Just as there is no strict mathematical comparison possible in the contexts we examined in Chapter 2, media accounts that reduce military operations to a simple numerical comparison of casualty figures create misimpression over the nature of proportionality. For example, one account of the sinking of the Argentine cruiser *General Belgrano* during the Falklands War commented that the deaths of 368 seamen "seems all out of proportion to the threat posed by the ship at the time of the attack…Was this an instance of an excessive or disproportionate use of force?"[28] Though this simple numerical comparison is qualified as only presenting the appearance of disproportionality, it reinforces the erroneous impression that *jus in bello* proportionality is properly grounded in the immediate tactical threat posed by a particular military target. In any event, Yoram Dinstein is surely correct in his assertion that "[m]any people confuse excessive with extensive."[29]

In fact, with the exception of some instances of proportionality assessment in the human rights domain we have discussed, there is no usage of proportionality in the field whereby the larger context is irrelevant. The standard for *lex lata jus in bello* proportionality is "clearly excessive" and that measure is assessed against the broader "concrete and direct overall military advantage anticipated." (to recall the Rome Statute standard we discussed in Chapter 6). Thus, damage to civilians or their property can "be exceedingly extensive without being excessive, simply because the military advantage anticipated is of paramount importance."[30] Proportionality is not a prohibition on *extensive* damage or loss of civilian life if they are not clearly *excessive* in relation to the concrete and direct military advantage anticipated, assuming that the value of the military advantage is itself very high.

Last, proportionality is seldom if ever completely encapsulated without reference to a larger totality of the circumstances examined. There is a recurring issue with respect to the lawful resort to force by a state to thwart an imminent attack. There is of course, a duty on the part of a state to consider non-forcible measures before resorting to

---

[28] A.J. COATES, THE ETHICS OF WAR 209-10 (1997).

[29] LEGAL AND ETHICAL LESSONS OF NATO'S KOSOVO CAMPAIGN, 78 NAVAL WAR COL. INT'L. L. STUD. 215 (Andru Wall ed., 2002).

[30] *Id.* Gary Solis describes the instance where "bombing of an important army or naval installation (like a naval shipyard) where there are hundreds or even thousands of civilian employees need not be abandoned merely because of the risk to these civilians." GARY D. SOLIS, THE LAW OF ARMED CONFLICT: INTERNATIONAL HUMANITARIAN LAW IN WAR 280 (2010). *See also* Military and Paramilitary Activities in and against Nicaragua, Nic. v. U.S., Judgment, Dissenting Opinion of Judge Schwebel, 1986 I.C.J. 14 (Jun. 27), para. 9 ("To the extent that proportionality of defensive measures is required—a question examined below—in their nature, far from being disproportionate to the acts against which they are a defence, the actions of the United States are *strikingly proportionate*.") (emphasis added)

force. This obligation simultaneously implicates both the requirements of necessity and proportionality. Assessing proportionality between the force used and an attack that might (or might not) have taken place if the force had not been used poses tricky questions. However, proportionality in neither the *jus ad bellum* nor *jus in bello* usages operates as a categorical barrier to extensive damage or destruction. Robert Ago is correct in concluding that if a State is victimized by "successive and different acts of armed attack from another State, the requirement of proportionality will certainly not mean that the victim State is not free to undertake a single armed attack on a much larger scale in order to put an end to this escalating succession of attacks."[31]

The key, of course, is that proportionality always involves a comparative assessment. As the importance of the military objective is elevated, the right of people to enjoy complete freedom from the effects of hostilities diminishes; the peace and order of civilian life is inversely related to the "concrete and direct overall military advantage anticipated" by a particular strike or operation. Conversely, a minimal advantage may not lawfully be achieved with disproportionate force, thus these related considerations relate to each other rather like a seesaw. As one goes up, so the other declines. But there is no point on this spectrum at which either important value is conceptually extinguished. This raises the question that we will consider in the next section—What is the overall positive purpose of proportionality?

III. WHAT IS THE POSITIVE ROLE OF PROPORTIONALITY?

A. The Articulation of Cardinal Values

The proportionality principle provides affirmative authority for state action even as it defines its appropriate boundaries. In effect, proportionality functions as a rule of containment because its effects-based analysis requires consideration of the individual rights of those affected by State action while validating the deference normally accorded to the reasonable and good-faith actions of the State. Proportionality serves as an important basis by which to mitigate the otherwise unconstrained coercive power of States. By extension, it binds those that act in accordance with State mandates and those under the effective control of State authorities. The constraining effects of proportionality are only accomplished because its various formulations require clear articulation of the underlying values that are implicated in a particular context. This clarifying and defining function is crucial to the implementation of modern proportionality even as it is often subtle. The necessity for sharply identifying

---

[31] Addendum—Eighth Report on State Responsibility, para. 121, U.N. Doc. A/CN.4/318/Adds.5-7 (1980), *available at* http://legal.un.org/ilc/documentation/english/a_cn4_318_add5-7.pdf

and analyzing the fundamental values that are implicated by State action operates at a secondary level as a sort of filter that serves to create a climate of self-regulation.

There are many examples in which we see proportionality operating to require clear dissection of the goals and values underlying any State action. In the *DRC v. Uganda Case* we mentioned in Chapter 2, the ICJ confronted the relationship between what it termed "Uganda's legitimate security interests" and the operational objectives of Operation Safe Haven, during which Ugandan forces entered the Democratic Republic of the Congo (DRC) in response to the cross-border operations of insurgents.[32] The majority relied on an assessment of the limitations of a legitimate self-defense rationale in the absence of DRC's consent to the cross-border operations but did so by cataloging other relevant values. The ICJ recognized the indispensable role of the United Nations (UN) Security Council as the body charged with responding to international aggression. The ICJ then observed that "in August and early September 1998 Uganda did not report to the Security Council events that it had regarded as requiring it to act in self-defense" nor did it allege that the armed attacks were linked to the armed forces of the DRC.

This is important because of the core precept that the established law of sovereign self-defense must operate in consonance with the non-intervention principles of Article 2(4) of the UN Charter (Charter) that do "not allow the use of force by a State to protect perceived security interests beyond these parameters."[33] In other words, a purported, and in this instance wholly warranted, claim of self-defense does not provide a ready rationale for any action deemed to be expedient by the concerned State. The proportionality analysis required the linkage between the goals sought by the State and the actual measures taken to achieve those objectives. State self-defense ends at the point the threat is eliminated or ameliorated; unlawful aggression begins at that precise juncture. Thus, the analysis focused on the locations and presumed purposes of the military activities by Ugandan forces. This analysis was conducted in light of the larger effects of that intervention on other countervailing values such as the sanctity of sovereign borders and the importance of Security Council oversight as the vestigial remains of the just cause principle of *jus ad bellum* Just War thinking.

This decision has been controversial in its finding that, despite suffering what it termed "deplorable attacks," the "legal and factual circumstances for the exercise of a right of self-defense by Uganda against the DRC were not present." For our purposes, the key point is that the evaluation of proportionality prompted clarification of the values at stake in a given context. The importance of this recurring role

---

[32] Case Concerning Armed Activities in the Territory of the Congo (DRC v. Uganda), Judgment of December 19, 2005, para 113.

[33] *Id.*, at para. 145–146.

cannot be overlooked, especially insofar as states are not free simply to disregard the operation of proportionality as the backdrop of decision-making. In this manner, proportionality provides the basis for evaluating the moral and legal rightness of a particular choice. Thus, it is crucial in gaining and preserving a harmony, or symmetry, between equally important objectives. Neither is eliminated at the expense of the other.

B. *The Preservation of Space for Second Opinions Reevaluating Discretionary Acts*

As an important corollary to the values identification role, proportionality preserves jurisprudential space for the subsequent evaluation of discretionary actions. By prompting a clear delineation of the affected interests, proportionality validates the sequencing of those interests. For better or worse, the proportionality principle serves as the vehicle for subsequent ordering (or re-ordering) of those competing interests. Thus, commenting on the proportionality of punishments, "courts should not be quick to disturb the verdict of a jury where it is supported by substantial evidence, the weight and credibility of which is for the jury, unless the amount of the verdict is *manifestly out of proportion* to the injuries proven." [emphasis added][34] The relative hierarchy of values was preserved in this decision, and there are many occasions in which proportionality operates to restore the *status quo ante* to the greatest possible degree. This function in turn requires courts or commentators to reassess the relationship between affected interests in each particular context.

Even if the purpose of proportionality is to pursue overall equity in some contexts, it also serves as a limitation to the permissible subordination of values in other areas. This role is only possible because the proportionality principle obligates a clear-eyed assessment of the competing values in each context. There is, nevertheless, a danger that proportionality can serve as a useful substitute for what would otherwise be pejoratively labeled judicial activism. In other words, though a proportionality analysis serves as an appropriate placeholder for judicial oversight, it should not be permitted to become a tool for judicial law making.

Aharon Barak noted that what he called the "zone of proportionality" demarcates the proper lines "separating the legislator from the judge.[35] Proportionate conduct is wholly appropriate, and judges that intrude into that space display an aggressive activism that erodes judicial legitimacy. In this vein, Thomas Franck noted, in a

---

[34] Hoelzel v. Chicago, 85 S.W.2d 126, 133 (Mo. 1935).
[35] AHARON BARAK, PROPORTIONALITY: CONSTITUTIONAL RIGHTS AND THEIR LIMITATIONS 417 (2012), citing R. Farrakhan v. Secretary of State for the Home Department [2002] 3 WLR 481, 502.

seminal article in the *American Journal of International Law,* that although "tribunals and other commentators frequently endorse the principle of proportionality, they have been less than fastidious in explaining the exchange rate they have used to equate disparate integers."[36]

As one of the most famous early examples of this phenomenon, the judges of the Tokyo District Court rejected the arguments of the Japanese government. The Tokyo Court held that the atomic attacks on Hiroshima and Nagasaki were disproportionate in *Ruichi Shimoda* et. al. *v. The State.*[37] Some might argue that the court disregarded arguments that the bombings shortened the war, saved hundreds of thousands of lives (both military and civilian), and perhaps laid the foundation for a modern Japanese state able to enjoy a sustained peace by virtue of averting what would have been destruction on a vast scale as allied armies advanced across the Home Islands. Yet the court simply stated:

> It can be naturally assumed that the use of a new weapon is legal, as long as international law does not prohibit it. However, the prohibition in this context is to be understood to include not only the case where there is an express provision of direct prohibition, but also the case where the prohibition can be implied...from the interpretation and application by analogy of existing rules of international law (customary international laws and treaties). Further, the prohibition must be understood also to include the case where, in the light of principles of international law which are the basis of these positive rules of international law, the use of new weapons is admitted to be contrary to the principles...

Proportionality also provides an objectively described principle that permits arguably impartial judges properly to calibrate the optimal interaction between individuals and the state. However, as we have seen, the synthesis of competing interests as advocated by those parties most implicated by a given interaction is inherently incapable of reduction to a simple objective formula. Courts will always be caught in the difficulty of attempting to apply an objectively described test that depends upon at least partially subjective valuations and motivations for its intended operation. This provides ample opportunity for judicially imposed preferences. Indeed, one scholar lauded this reality by noting that "adjudication is one instance of government deployment of power that has the potential for genuine contextualism, for

---

[36] Thomas Franck, *On Proportionality of Countermeasures in International Law,* 102 AM. J. INT'L L. 715, 719 (2008).

[37] Ruichi Shimoda et. al. v. The State, *355* Hanrei Jiho 17 (1963), 32 I.L.R. 626, *translated in* 8 Jap. Ann. Int'l L. 231 (1964), *available at* http://www.icrc.org/ihl-nat.

December 28, 2008 alone; 2,500,000 leaflets overall, radio broadcasts, and another newly developed tactic involving non-explosive detonations known as "roofknocking."[46] Given a careful and good-faith articulation of these efforts in light of the effects of the Israeli attacks and the relevant context, neither side could argue that its interests were ignored or invalidated by a good-faith judicial application of the proportionality principle regardless of the ultimate decision.

IV. WHY *JUS IN BELLO* PROPORTIONALITY IS UNIQUE

We come now to one of the central questions of this work. Given the consistency with which the term proportionality recurs across disciplines, why should we not strive for a commonality of meaning across disciplines? Is there value in homogeneity of application across all of international law? To put the point more precisely, proportionality functions to examine the healthy tension between competing interests in a variety of applications, but does it follow that scholars and practitioners should strive to squeeze the margins of *jus in bello* proportionality into conformity with other accepted uses of proportionality in modern law? We are mindful of Shakespeare's admonition in King Lear: "Striving to better, oft we mar what's well."[47] To that end, the *jus in bello* usage should remain distinct from other applications, in our view. *Jus in bello* is the outlier if one maps out the various formulations as they relate to each other. The very nature of *jus in bello* proportionality is markedly different, notwithstanding the occasionally analogous approaches to other areas of international law.

The basis of the entire field of international humanitarian law is to build a careful balance between the ability of practitioners to lawfully accomplish the military mission in a manner that respects the enduring value of humanitarian considerations. There are three considerations that mandate the uniqueness of *jus in bello* proportionality, which we will respectively consider: (1) the contextual application of the principle, (2) the attribution of errors, and (3) the permissive nature of the entire body of law, which means that proportionality serves a different function within *jus in bello* than in other areas of law.

---

[46] Human Rights Council, Human Rights in Palestine and Other Occupied Arab Territories, Report of the United Nations Fact Finding Mission on the Gaza Conflict ¶ 498, U.N. Doc. A/HRC/12/48 (Sept. 15, 2009) [hereinafter Goldstone Report], *available at* http://www2.ohchr.org/english/bodies/hrcouncil/docs/12session/A-HRC-12-48.pdf. The number of fatal casualties as a result of Operation Cast Lead varies between nongovernmental organizations (NGOs), which report between 1,387 and 1,417 fatalities; Gaza authorities, which report 1,444; and the Government of Israel, which lists 1,166. *Id.*, ¶ 30.

[47] WILLIAM SHAKESPEARE, KING LEAR, act.i, sc. 4.

A. The Context of Armed Conflict

In every other discipline, the usage of proportionality depends upon the relationship between the relevant actors at the time of the action in question. In trade law, the governing treaty or agreement provides the grounds for decision because it defines the rights and relations between the parties. In the criminal arena, proportionality has variable meaning depending upon the crimes charged and the peculiar attributes of the victims and the perpetrators. Proportionality in the law of countermeasures is assessed in light of the aggregate circumstances of the particular harm inflicted on the victim and the range of feasible responses in light of their prior interactions.

Indeed, in one famous formulation related to the line between war and peace, necessity "is a defense when it is shown that the act charged was done to avoid an evil both serious and irreparable; that there was no other adequate means of escape; and that the remedy was *not disproportionate* to the evil."[48] In these and other areas, proportionality follows as a secondary consideration based on the relationship between the relevant actors. This should not be understood, of course, to imply that proportionality is not closely intertwined with the overall legality of the action.

In contrast, *jus in bello* proportionality depends on the larger context of armed conflict. This is at the heart of the ICJ characterization of the laws and customs of warfare as *lex specialis*. In other words, the precepts that flow from the laws and customs of warfare provide the evaluative basis for all actions undertaken when that body of law is applicable. The main question, then, does not deal with the particularities of the relationship between actors, but with the hierarchy of the choice of law rules. That is why it is intellectually at odds to limit the use of force in a particular combat engagement to the degree of force used by the enemy. Proportionality does not function as a rule of equity within armed conflict.

As we have seen, the relevant considerations are dissimilar: The concrete and direct military advantage sought as juxtaposed against the anticipated damage to civilian lives and property. This is the main reason why the asymmetric nature of modern conflicts does not require a wholly new *jus in bello* proportionality application. The established law contemplates a disparity of combat power and in no way mandates some form of equity as in other areas of international law.

The *lex lata* application of *jus in bello* norms is independent from the overarching *jus ad bellum* norms. In this way, even the most unlawful act of aggression that marks the onset of armed conflict operates to convey the entire range of rights, benefits, and obligations drawn from the laws and customs of warfare on every participant

---

[48] United States v. Krupp, 9 Trials of War Criminals Before the Nuremberg Military Tribunals Under Control Council Law No. 10, 1436 (1950).

in that conflict. This explains why each and every specific crime in Article 8 of the Rome Statute (which deals with the range of war crimes committed both in international and in non-international armed conflicts) requires the prosecutor to prove that the charged act was committed "in the context of and associated with" the armed conflict.   \ check (

The second circumstantial element that is embedded in every Rome Statute war crime logically follows; the prosecutor need not prove that the perpetrator made any specific legal conclusion about the nature of the conflict. Sufficient evidence of war crimes depends upon showing that "the perpetrator was aware of factual circumstances that established the existence of an armed conflict." In other words, there is a fundamental due process right that convictions may only be grounded in the perpetrator's knowledge that the *jus in bello* is applicable and should provide the signposts for acceptable conduct based on considerations of notice and fundamental fairness.

In summary, the actions of all participants in armed conflict are constrained by considerations of proportionality based on their relation to the conflict. There is no individualized assessment required because doing so might permit some degree of differentiation that would erode the humanitarian objectives of the law itself. There is no rationalization for failure to comply with the laws and customs of war, hence there is no recognized defense of military necessity unless the act comports with the actor's larger *jus in bello* obligations. Michael Waltzer is entirely correct in the conclusion that belligerent armies are "not entitled to do anything that is or seems to them necessary to win wars. They are subject to a set of restrictions that rest in part on the agreements of states but that also have an independent foundation in moral principle."[49]

In the context of armed conflicts proportionality operates as a single principle with little variation. Otherwise, proportionality and military necessity would become interlinked and unstoppable considerations that "would reduce the entire body of the laws of war to a code of military convenience."[50] Thus, there is no micro-analysis of the particularized circumstances related to the relationship of the relevant actors when applying the *jus in bello* either retrospectively in the course of criminal prosecution or disciplinary investigation or in the heat of battle. The contextual fact of an armed conflict is crucial and this distinguishes *jus in bello* proportionality from all other uses of proportionality in law.

---

[49] Michael Walzer, Just and Unjust Wars 131 (NY: Basic Books, 1977).
[50] Leslie C. Green, The Contemporary Law of Armed Conflict 353 (3d. ed. 2008).

B. *The Attribution of Acts*

The second unique feature of *jus in bello* proportionality is unavoidably linked to the principles we just explained. Regarding war crimes, there is an unbroken line of authority from the World War II era that supports the principle of individual responsibility. In other areas of international law, the ICJ has noted "the well-established rule, one of the cornerstones of the law of State responsibility, that the conduct of any State organ is to be considered an act of the State under international law, and therefore gives rise to the responsibility of the State if it constitutes a breach of an international obligation of the State."[51] It is of, course, true that States are responsible for the inculcation of the laws and customs of warfare within their armed forces. Neither can States escape their obligation to enforce the mandates of the law of war. However, just as participants in armed conflict bear the grievous personal costs associated with fighting, they also face individual punishment for any violation of the *jus in bello*.

Persons who commit war crimes cannot hide behind the shield of State sovereignty. In *Ilaşcu and others v Russia and Moldova*,[52] the European Court of Human Rights (ECHR) observed that in other contexts

> a series of wrongful acts or omissions attributable to a state under the international law of state responsibility constitutes an ongoing breach that "extends over the entire period starting with the first of the acts and continuing for as long as the acts or omissions are repeated and remain at variance with the international obligation concerned."[53]

Not so during armed conflict. If the *lex specialis* law of armed conflict is applicable, persons who violate its precepts are individually responsible for each and every violation and accordingly liable for punishment in the appropriate criminal forum.

This is important for our purposes because proportionality, during warfare, rests upon the individualized decisions and motivations of particular war fighters, but convictions cannot flow from fundamentally tainted proceedings no matter how horrible are the alleged facts. It follows that the right of every suspected war criminal to adequate time and facilities in the preparation of a vigorous defense represents

---

[51] Application of the Convention on the Prevention and Punishment of the Crime of Genocide (Bosnia and Herzegovina v Serbia and Montenegro), Judgment, para. 385 (Feb. 26, 2007).

[52] Ilaşcu and others v Russia and Moldova, Application No. 48787/99), Reports 2004–VII,

[53] *Id.* ¶ 320.

the quintessential expression of a systematic commitment to balance the ends of justice.[54]

In the Former Republic of Yugoslavia, for example, the Milosevic regime exercised power over the Yugoslav judicial system sufficient to prevent any potential accountability for the widespread violations of international law committed under its auspices. Thus, the UN Secretary-General concluded that the "particular circumstances" of impunity in the former Yugoslavia warranted the creation of the international tribunal[55] and the ICTY was born from this political mandate. The Secretary-General's report nevertheless made clear that it is "axiomatic that the International Tribunal must fully respect internationally recognized standards regarding the rights of the accused at all stages of the proceedings."[56] The essence of *jus in bello* proportionality ought to be viewed as the community property of all mankind. This requires a universalized commitment to its enforcement, but also motivates strongly towards an accepted due process framework for its application against individuals as a matter of punitive justice.

C. The Permissive Nature of the Jus in Bello Regime

Finally, and perhaps most importantly, *jus in bello* proportionality is properly understood as the quintessential expression of the laws and customs of warfare. Proportionality is permissive by its express terms insofar as it defines the limits of lawful authority rather than operating as an affirmative grant of authority. Unlike the varied applications of proportionality in other areas, the permissive nature of the legal regime applicable during armed conflicts is inextricably woven into the very fabric of such conflicts. This is not to say that the law is infinitely malleable based on the individualized will of combatants.

---

[54] Human Rights Comm., Zwaan-de Vries v. the Netherlands, Comm. No. 182/1984, U.N. Doc. CCPR/C/29/D/182/1984 (1987); Ofrer v. Austria, App. No. 524/59, 6 Y.B. Eur. Conv. on H.R. 680 (Eur. Ct. H.R.) ("equality of arms"). As U.S. Supreme Court Justice George Sutherland observed in *Powell v. Alabama*:
> The right to be heard would be, in many cases, of little avail if it did not comprehend the right to be heard by counsel. Even the intelligent and educated layman has small and sometimes no skill in the science of law. . . . He requires the guiding hand of counsel at every step in the proceedings against him. Without it, though he be not guilty, he faces the danger of conviction because he does not know how to establish his innocence. Powell v. Alabama, 287 U.S. 45, 68–69 (1932).

[55] UN Secretary-General, *Report of the Secretary General pursuant to paragraph 2 of Security Council Resolution 808*, ¶ 26, U.N. Doc. S/2-5704 (May 19, 1993). Similarly, Robert Jackson understood the iconic nature of the International Military Tribunal perhaps more clearly than any of his peers, but also believed that the prosecutions were a pragmatic necessity in defeating what he termed at the time "unregenerate and virulent" Nazism. ROBERT H. JACKSON, THAT MAN: AN INSIDER'S PORTRAIT OF FRANKLIN D. ROOSEVELT 170-71 (John Q. Barrett ed., 2003).

[56] *Id.* ¶ 106 (emphasis added).

The law of targeting does indeed evolve as the expectations of the international community change. Thus, following the World War II bombings of entire cities, modern law requires disaggregation of specific targets within a "city, town or village or other area containing a similar concentration of civilians or civilian objects" which in turn requires a series of discrete proportionality assessments for each target.[57] *Jus in bello* proportionality is a flexible standard but not nearly as flexible as is true of other uses of proportionality in modern law.

Even as there are abundant examples in *jus in bello* of express prohibitions subject to no caveats; combatants exercise what the ICRC has labeled a "fairly broad margin of judgment."[58] For example, medical care is due those in military custody only "to the fullest extent practicable and with the least possible delay."[59] Obligations are often couched in aspirational terms such as "whenever possible"[60] or "as widely as possible."[61] Other duties are couched in less than strident terms such as "shall endeavor"[62] or the duty to "take all practical precautions."[63] There are also express exceptions permitted for reasons of "imperative military necessity."[64]

For the purposes of proportionality, the most relevant permissive duties incumbent on those who order military strikes require them to "do everything feasible

---

[57] Protocol Additional to the Geneva Conventions of August 12, 1949, and relating to the Protection of Victims of International Armed Conflicts (Protocol I), June 8, 1977, Article 51(5)(a)(which classifies such intentional attacks as being per se indiscriminate and therefore prohibited). *See also* Volume II, ICRC Customary International Law Study: Practice <http://www.icrc.org/eng/assets/files/other/customary-international-humanitarian-law-ii-icrc-eng.pdf>. The Official ICRC Commentary to Additional Protocol I makes clear that the provisions of Article 51 flowed directly from the practices during World War II and the reactions thereto:

> The attacks which form the subject of this paragraph fall under the general prohibition of indiscriminate attacks laid down at the beginning of paragraph 4. Two types of attack in particular are envisaged here. The "first type" includes area bombardment, sometimes known as carpet bombing or saturation bombing. It is characteristic of such bombing that it destroys all life in a specific area and razes to the ground all buildings situated there. There were many examples of such bombing during the Second World War, and also during some more recent conflicts. Such types of attack have given rise to strong public criticism in many countries, and it is understandable that the drafters of the Protocol wished to mention it specifically, even though such attacks already fall under the general prohibition contained in paragraph 4. According to the report of Committee III, the expression "bombardment by any method or means" means all attacks by fire-arms or projectiles (except for direct fire by small arms) and the use of any type of projectile.

COMMENTARY ON THE ADDITIONAL PROTOCOLS OF 8 JUNE 1977 TO THE GENEVA CONVENTIONS OF 12 AUGUST 1949 Art. 51, ¶¶ 1967-68 (Sandoz et al, eds 1987).

[58] COMMENTARY ON THE ADDITIONAL PROTOCOLS OF 8 JUNE 1977 TO THE GENEVA CONVENTIONS OF 12 AUGUST 1949, Art. 57, ¶ 2187 (Sandoz et al, eds 1987).

[59] Protocol I, Article 10(2).

[60] Protocol I, Article 12(4).

[61] Protocol I, Article 83(1).

[62] Protocol I, Article 77(3).

[63] Protocol I, Article 56(3).

[64] Protocol I, Article 55(5).

to verify that the objectives to be attacked are neither civilians nor civilian objects"[65] and "take all feasible precautions in the choice of means and methods of attack with a view to avoiding, and in any event to minimizing, incidental loss of civilian life, injury to civilians and damage to civilian objects."[66] As a logical extension, "effective advance warning shall be given of attacks which may affect the civilian population, *unless circumstances do not permit.*" [emphasis added][67] The commander's actions "must be made in good faith and in view of all information that can be said to be reasonably available in the specific situation" according to the ICRC.[68]

This permissive *jus in bello* framing empowers those in the vortex of battle to balance the legitimate military needs against larger humanitarian imperatives. It is important to note that the benchmark for what is "feasible" is measured from the reasonable war fighter's point of view. In fact, modern international criminal law expressly preserves broad discretionary authority.

For example, Article 23 of the 1899 Hague II Convention stated that it was forbidden "[t]o destroy or seize the enemy's property, unless such destruction or seizure be imperatively demanded by the necessities of war."[69] The Rome Statute of the International Criminal Court repeated that same language in Articles 8(2)(b)(xiii) and 8(2)(e)(xii) (respectively applicable during international and non-international armed conflicts).[70] Based on their belief that the concept of military necessity ought to be an unacceptable component of military decision-making, some civilian delegates sought to introduce a higher subjective threshold by which to second-guess military operations.[71] They proposed a verbal formula for the Elements of Crimes that any seizure of civilian property would be valid only if based on "imperative military necessity."[72]

There is no evidence in the *traveaux* of the Rome Statute that its drafters intended to alter the preexisting fabric of the laws and customs of war.[73] Introducing a tiered

---

[65] Protocol I, Article 57(2)(a)(i).

[66] Protocol I, Article 57(2)(a)(ii).

[67] Protocol I, Article 57(2)(c).

[68] ICRC, *Interpretive Guidance on the Notion of Direct Participation in Hostilities under International Humanitarian Law*, at 75.

[69] Michael A. Newton, *Modern Military Necessity: The Role & Relevance of Military Lawyers*, 12 Roger Williams U. L. Rev. 877, 896 (2007).

[70] Rome Statute of the International Criminal Court, U.N. Doc. A/CONF.183/9 (July 17, 1998), 37 I.L.M. 999, *available at* http://un.org/law/icc/index.html [hereinafter Rome Statute].

[71] Mike Newton, *Humanitarian Protection in Future Wars, in* 8 International Peacekeeping: The Yearbook of International Peace Operations 349, 358 (Harvey Langholtz et al. eds., 2004).

[72] Knut Dörmann, Elements of War Crimes Under the Rome Statute of the International Criminal Court 249 (2003).

[73] William A. Schabas, The International Criminal Court: A Commentary on the Rome Statute 240–241 (2010)(noting that the provisions of the Rome Statute referencing military necessity were "quickly agreed to at the Rome Conference" and that the concept may be invoked only when the laws of armed conflict provide so and only to the extent provided by that body of law).

gradation of military necessity as proposed would have built a doubly high wall that would have had a paralyzing effect on military operations. A double threshold for the established concept of military necessity would have clouded the decision-making of commanders and soldiers who must balance the legitimate need to accomplish the mission against the mandates of the law.

From the practitioners' perspective,[74] requiring "imperative military necessity" as a necessary condition for otherwise permissible actions would have introduced a wholly subjective and unworkable formulation that would foreseeably have exposed military commanders to after the fact personal criminal liability for their good-faith judgments. The ultimate formulation in the Elements of Crimes translated the 1899 phrase into the simple modern formulation "military necessity" that every commander and military attorney understands. The important point for our purposes is that the twin concepts of military necessity and feasibility preserve *jus in bello* as a practicable body of law that balances humanitarian and military considerations, at least when applied by reasonable, well-intentioned, and well trained forces.[75]

By comparison, human rights law defines with particularity the comprehensive set of circumstances in which lethal force may be used. As we explained in Chapter 6, the human rights regime restricts lethal force to those circumstances in which such force is absolutely necessary as a last resort in order to protect life rather than merely reasonably related to an acceptable military purpose. By contrast, *lex lata* lethal force in armed conflict is presumed to be permissible whenever reasonably necessary to achieve a military objective absent evidence of some prohibited purpose or unlawful tactic.[76] The human rights regime requires a statement of affirmative authority, while *jus in bello* operates on a permissive basis subject to express limitations. As an additive requirement, lethal force under the human rights paradigm must be proportionate to the immediate context, meaning that the force used is directly proportionate to the risk posed by the individual at the moment force is employed. As we have seen, *jus in bello* proportionality by definition and accepted State practice will very likely depend upon the broader contextual set of aggregate circumstances, which in turn inform the commander's assessment of the "overall military advantage anticipated."

Violations of these standards subject the State to responsibility for any deaths resulting from unauthorized or inappropriate lethal force in the human rights domain.[77] Thus,

---

[74] The authors have somewhat different views of this issue.
[75] *See* Michael A. Newton, *The International Criminal Court Preparatory Commission: The Way It Is & The Way Ahead*, 41 VA. J. INT'L L. 204, 211–212 (2000).
[76] Nils Meltzer, *Targeted Killing or Less Harmful Means?—Israel's High Court Judgment on Targeted Killing and the Restrictive Function of Military Necessity*, 9 YEARBOOK OF INT' HUM. L. 109 (2006).
[77] *See Gulec v. Turkey*, Judgment, 28 Eur. H.R. Rep. 121, ¶71 (1998), *available at* http://www.unhcr.org/refworld/publisher,ECHR,,TUR,3ae6b6a918,0.html; *Ergi v. Turkey*, App. No. 2388/94, Judgment, 232 Eur.

we see that proportionality operates in a very different manner and for distinctive reasons within *jus in bello*. Unlike the relatively determinate measures that frame the comparisons needed to evaluate proportionality in every other context, *lex lata jus in bello* proportionality often shifts depending on the operational assessments made by differing commanders, based on newly received information or in response to the changing importance of a particular military objective. Any change in the rules of engagement cannot therefore be automatically interpreted as an admission of culpability by the relevant commander.

Rather than serving as a necessary basis for a positive articulation of lawful force as an exception to the norm, *jus in bello* proportionality delineates the outer boundaries of the commander's appropriate discretion. Aharon Barak, of the Israeli Supreme Court summarized this aspect of proportionality, and we leave you with his thoughts before we examine the applications of the proportionality principle over the next five chapters:

> The court will ask itself only if a reasonable military commander could have made the decision that was made. If the answer is yes, the court will not override the military commander's security discretion within the security discretion of the court. Judicial review regarding military measures to be taken is within the regular review of reasonableness. True, "military discretion" and "state security" are not magic words that dismiss judicial review. However, the question is not what I would decide under the given circumstances, but rather whether the decision that the military commander made is a decision that a reasonable military commander is permitted to make. In that realm, special weight is to be granted to the military opinion of the official who bear responsibility for security....Who decides on proportionality? Is it a military decision to be left to the reasonable application of the military, or a legal decision within the purview of the judiciary? Our answer is that the proportionality of military means used to fight terror is a legal question to be left to the judiciary... . Proportionality is not an exact science; at times there are a number of ways to fulfill its conditions so that a zone of proportionality is created; it is the boundaries of that zone that the court guards.[78]

H.R. Rep. 388 (1998), *available at* http://www.unhcr.org/refworld/topic,4565c225b,459e72b12,3ae6b6291c, 0,,,TUR.html 32 Eur. H.R.

[78] Aharon Barak, President (ret'd) Supreme Court of Israel, Address at the Jim Shasha Center of Strategic Studies of the Federmann School for Public Policy and Government of the Hebrew University of Jerusalem, (Dec. 18, 2007).

8

COUNTERMEASURES AND COUNTERINSURGENCY

THE TERM *PROPORTIONALITY* recurs across an array of disciplines and usages; each conveys legally distinct meanings and applications as a technical matter. Chapters 4 and 5 contrasted the applications of proportionality in both *jus ad bellum* (the law and morality of resort to force) and within *jus in bello* (the normative doctrines applicable for using force in the midst of conflicts). The same term has very different meanings with often profound and context specific implications. In Chapter 7, we discussed what proportionality assessments in law have in common and how *jus in bello* proportionality assessments are unique.

In this chapter, we discuss two cases that are especially problematic. The first concerns countermeasures that seem to be better handled according to *jus ad bellum* than *jus in bello* matters. The second is an area that is even more fraught with controversy, namely the *jus in bello* proportionality of counterinsurgency. We remind the reader that the *jus in bello* proportionality and the *jus ad bellum* proportionality need to be kept distinct, even as we embark on a discussion in which it is often difficult to maintain this distinction. In earlier chapters, we suggested that there was a common core of similarity in these two domains that now poses various conceptual puzzles.

In Section I of this chapter, we will begin by discussing controversial countermeasures that one State takes against another State. We will explain why the *jus in bello* model has not been deemed appropriate in this context. In Section II of the chapter, we provide three compelling examples of the implications for incomplete or inaccurate implementation of the *jus in bello* proportionality principle drawn from the decade of war in Afghanistan. The counterinsurgency examples provide a challenge to the way that *jus in bello* proportionality has been understood in international law.

In subsequent chapters, we will then discuss additional problematic areas of armed conflict that have raised *lex ferenda* challenges to the *lex lata* of *jus in bello* proportionality concerning human shields, targeted killing, and cyber attacks.

I. PROPORTIONATE COUNTERMEASURES

We begin by looking at one of the most significant and controversial applications in international law of *jus ad bellum* Just War thinking, countermeasures among States that have been wronged. Article 51 of the Draft Articles on the Responsibility of States for Internationally Wrongful Acts states the overarching proposition that countermeasures "must be commensurate with the injury suffered, taking into account the gravity of the internationally wrongful act and the rights in question."[1] The law of countermeasures focuses on the parameters for lawful State responses to previous illegal actions by other States or non-State actors. In this section, we consider the law of proportionality as it has been developed in State responses to threats of force or actual uses of force that warrant responses based on the inherent and sovereign right of self-defense. In a sense, this is a micro application of the macro issues we discussed in Chapter 4 concerning *jus ad bellum*.

There is some support in theory for the position that the law of countermeasures and the standard for proportionality are inextricably linked at the outset. The International Court of Justice (ICJ) in the *Nuclear Weapons* case put that connection front and center by stating in *dicta* that "a use of force that is proportionate under the law of self-defense, must, in order to be lawful also meet the requirements of the law applicable in armed conflict."[2] By definition, the larger "law applicable in armed conflict" necessarily includes proportionality.

James Crawford, later published the definitive commentary on the Draft Articles and noted what the default intent is.[3]

> Considering the need to ensure that the adoption of countermeasures does not lead to inequitable results, proportionality must be assessed taking into account not only the purely "quantitative" element of the injury suffered, but also "qualitative" factors such as the importance of the interest protected by

---

[1] General Assembly Resolution 56/83 of December 12, 2001, and corrected by document A/56/49(Vol. I)/Corr.4. International Law Commission, Draft Articles on Responsibility of States for Internationally Wrongful Acts, *available at* http://legal.un.org/ilc/texts/instruments/english/draft%20articles/9_6_2001.pdf.

[2] International Court of Justice, *Legality of the Threat or Use of Nuclear Weapons*, Advisory Opinion of July 8, 1996, ICJ Reports (1996) 226, 245 para 42.

[3] JAMES R. CRAWFORD, THE INTERNATIONAL LAW COMMISSION'S ARTICLES ON STATE RESPONSIBILITY, Article 51, para. 6 (2002).

the rule infringed and the seriousness of the breach. Article 51 relates proportionality primarily to the injury suffered but "taking into account" two further criteria: the gravity of the internationally wrongful act, and the rights in question. The reference to "the rights in question" has a broad meaning, and includes not only the effect of a wrongful act on the injured State but also on the rights of the responsible State. Furthermore, the position of other States which may be affected may also be taken into consideration."

Prior to delving into the important ways that proportionality has been developed in the law of countermeasures, there are two prefatory notes we believe will aid the reader. First, one gleans from Crawford's notes that consideration of the term *commensurate* is not subject to a precise mathematical comparison. In this sense, the means–ends analysis requires a rough contextual approximation rather than an objective evaluation. This is important, because the proportionality principle functions not only as an after-the-fact standard of review but as a basis for decision-making that can help guide a State as it evaluates its available options for responding to the actions of another State (or States). Hence, commensurate countermeasures are those that would in essence be deemed to be appropriate by the reasonable State policymakers acting in light of the information and assessments reasonably available to them to inform good-faith decision-making.

Second, the evaluative standard to be applied both in hindsight and to contemporaneous decision-making is that permissible countermeasures are those in which the likelihood of success is plausible. By that, we mean lawful countermeasures are those employed to achieve the wholly legitimate purpose of restoring the *status quo ante*. At a deep conceptual level, countermeasures derive from the Just War principles because the injured state is obliged to call upon the responsible wrongdoer to comply with its obligations, inform it of the pending countermeasures, and offer to negotiate in good faith.[4] This Just War linkage is particularly important if the contemplated countermeasures are designed to vindicate the self-defense rights of States or individuals.

Crawford notes that countermeasures are properly taken "as a form of inducement not punishment."[5] By extension, inappropriate countermeasures are, in our view, either (1) those that are either based on impermissible motivations such as revenge, territorial acquisition, or purely as a pretext to serve other political interests, or (2) countermeasures that impose wholly inappropriate sanctions if measured by their severity or scope and in light of their context. In this vein, the latitude

---

[4] Draft Articles on Responsibility of States for Internationally Wrongful Acts, *supra*, art. 52(1).

[5] Crawford, *supra* note, art. 49, para. 7.

accorded to permissible countermeasures under Article 51 of the United Nations (UN) Charter (Charter) has been recognized as binding customary international law based on state practice and the wide variety of its applications.[6]

The High Level Panel of Experts appointed to examine UN reform by UN Secretary-General Kofi Annan recognized that the "inherent" right of states to defend themselves and their interests buttressed the widely shared view on the issue of preemptive defense. The panel report noted that "a threatened State, according to long- established international law, can take military action as long as the threatened attack is imminent, no other means would deflect it, and the action is proportionate.[7] The High Level Panel did set an extremely high bar of necessity, which we believe was appropriate for countermeasures but as a matter of *lex lata* cannot be extrapolated into the *jus in bello* context for reasons we described in the previous chapter. The presumption that the tactical war fighter may not use deadly force unless previously establishing that there is "no other means" to achieve the immediate objective is nowhere found in the laws and customs of war. But that is a matter of *lex lata* and we will also say quite a bit about possible *lex ferenda* reasons to change this standard.

For the moment, it is sufficient to note that based on the background International Law Commission (ILC) Draft on the Law of State Responsibility, Robert Ago obliquely referenced the fissure between the proportionality of countermeasures (or preemptive action based on necessity) and deterrence of misconduct by commenting that if

> a State suffers a series of successive and different acts of armed attack from another State, the requirement of proportionality will certainly not mean that the victim State is not free to undertake a single armed attack on a much larger scale in order to put an end to this escalating succession of attacks[8]

---

6 *See* United States—Definitive Safeguard Measures on Imports of Circular Welded Carbon Quality Line Pipe from Korea, Report of the Appellate Body, WTO doc. WT/DS202/AB/R. para. 259 (WTO Appellate Body Feb 15, 2002). The Appellate Body also observed in passing that 'the United States has acknowledged this principle elsewhere. In its comments on the International Law Commission's draft articles, the United States stated that "under customary international law a rule of proportionality applies to the exercise of countermeasures" (id.)'.

7 *A more secure world: our shared responsibility*, Report of the High-level Panel on Threats, Challenges and Change, (2004) UN Doc A/59/565, para. 188, *available at:* http://www2.ohchr.org/English/bodies/hrcouncil/docs/gaA.59.565_En.pdf.

8 Addendum—Eighth Report on State Responsibility, para. 121, U.N. Doc. A/CN.4/318/Adds.5-7 (1980), *available at* http://legal.un.org/ilc/documentation/english/a_cn4_318_add5-7.pdf.

Thus, according to the Rapporteur of the ILC Draft articles, proportional uses of force may be tailored (the means) to achieve the goal of ending the ongoing pattern of attacks (the ends). For us, this does not completely address the moral and legal priority, which is to prevent violations in the first place.

Deterrence is an inevitable aspect of the proportionality decision. For the sake of clarity, it is clear that *jus ad bellum* proportionality as a limitation on a lawful countermeasure requires that actions undertaken in self-defense by the sovereign State do not exceed the scope or level needed to eliminate the imminent or ongoing threat. This roughly accords with the High Level Panel "no other means" formulation. Although seemingly uncontroversial, the larger question of the relationship between deterrence of future misconduct by the aggressor State and the accepted level of proportional acts by the victim State remains opaque.

The invocation of proportionality by the ICJ in the context of countermeasures has done little to clarify its precise boundaries. On the one hand, it is well established that the submission of the exercise of the right of self-defense to the conditions of necessity and proportionality is a rule of customary international law. As the ICJ stated in the case concerning *Military and Paramilitary Activities in and against Nicaragua (Nicaragua v. United States of America),* "there is a "specific rule whereby self-defense would warrant only measures which are proportional to the armed attack and necessary to respond to it, a rule well established in customary international law."[9] This dual condition applies equally to any use of force as a responsive right grounded in the *inherent* sovereign right of self-defense, to borrow the qualifier from Article 51 of the UN Charter.

In its seminal decision in the *Nuclear Weapons* case, the ICJ avoided clarifying this thorny issue. The ICJ stopped short of categorically proscribing the use of nuclear weapons because it could not judge "definitively whether the threat or use of nuclear weapons would be lawful or unlawful in an extreme circumstance of self-defense, in which the very survival of a State would be at stake."[10] The majority nevertheless had no hesitation (appropriately in our view) in accepting the *jus in bello* cardinal principle that "States must never make civilians the object of attack and must consequently never use weapons that are incapable of distinguishing between civilian and military targets."[11] The majority further declared that the fundamental rules related to targeting during armed conflicts "are to be observed by all States whether

---

[9] (I. C. J. *Reports 1986,* p. 94, para. 176)

[10] International Court of Justice, *Legality of the Threat or Use of Nuclear Weapons,* Advisory Opinion of July 8, 1996, para. 105(2)(E), ICJ Reports 226 (1996). For a sharp critique of the implications that this decision portends for the future of the laws and customs of warfare, see Michael Reisman, *Holding the Center of the Law of Armed Conflict,* 100 AM. J. INT'L L. 852 (2006).

[11] Legality of Nuclear Weapons, para. 78.

or not they have ratified the conventions that contain them, because they constitute intransgressible principles of international customary law."[12]

In her separate Dissenting Opinion, Judge Higgins expressly stated what the majority meant only by implication in her passing observation that proportionality "even if finding no specific mention, is reflected in many provisions of Additional Protocol I to the Geneva Conventions of 1949. Thus, even a legitimate target may not be attacked if the collateral civilian casualties would be disproportionate to the specific military gain from the attack."[13]

On the other hand, in considering issues of *jus ad bellum* proportionality, the ICJ has repeatedly demonstrated a tendency to conflate the necessity prong of sovereign self-defense with a quantitative view of proportionality. In finding that the attacks by insurgents across the border were not attributable to the Democratic Republic of the Congo (DRC) government, the ICJ concluded[14] that

> [f]or all these reasons, the Court finds that the legal and factual circumstances for the exercise of a right of self-defense by Uganda against the DRC were not present. Accordingly, the Court has no need to respond to the contentions of the Parties as to whether and under what conditions contemporary international law provides for a right of self-defense against large-scale attacks by irregular forces. Equally, since the preconditions for the exercise of self-defense do not exist in the circumstances of the present case, the Court has no need to enquire whether such an entitlement to self-defense was in fact exercised in circumstances of necessity and in a manner that was proportionate. *The Court cannot fail to observe, however, that the taking of airports and towns many hundreds of kilometres from Uganda's border would not seem proportionate to the series of transborder attacks it claimed had given rise to the right of self-defense, nor to be necessary to that end.* (emphasis added)

The highlighted ICJ language is dicta to be taken for what it is worth in the sense that it did not contribute to the legal resolution of the case. But it hints at a much deeper and more troubling erosion of the established law of countermeasures.

Proportionality in the law of countermeasures is best understood as a prohibition against excesses rather than a requirement for equivalence or mathematical equity.

---

[12] Legality of Nuclear Weapons, para. 79.
[13] Legality of Nuclear Weapons, para. 587.
[14] Case Concerning Armed Activities in the Territory of the Congo (DRC v. Uganda), Judgment of December 19 2005, para 147.

As only one of a number of recent examples, the UN Special Rapporteur conducted a simple numerical assessment to disregard the Israeli claim to self-defense during Operation Cast Lead in the Gaza strip conducted from December 27, 2008, to January 18, 2009, in response to indiscriminate rocket fire against Israeli villages launched by Hamas from the Gaza area. Without analysis of the circumstances, the conclusion that the attacks were disproportionate relies on the finding that a "total of 1,434 Palestinians were killed, of whom 235 were combatants. Some 960 civilians reportedly lost their lives, including 288 children and 121 women; 239 police officers were also killed, 235 in air strikes carried out on the first day. A total of 5,303 Palestinians were injured, including 1,606 children and 828 women (namely, one in every 225 Gazans was killed or injured, not counting mental injury, which must be assumed to be extensive)."[15] There is no analysis of the context or the lawful scope of military response by the Israelis.

We here cite again the words of Daniel Webster, that the act "justified by the necessity of self-defense, must be limited by that necessity, and kept clearly within it."[16] The *jus ad bellum* framing of proportionality *also* requires that a lawful resort to force be proportional to the asserted *casus belli*.[17] In speaking of proportionality between states in the realm of *jus ad bellum*, John Rawls noted that the "aim of war is a just peace, and therefore the means employed must not destroy the possibility of peace or encourage a contempt for human life that puts the safety of ourselves and of mankind in jeopardy."[18] As in the law of transnational trade, the proportionality of responses must be calibrated to eliminate the prior threat. If the purpose is to achieve broader diplomatic objectives or revert to the retributive model of punishment the countermeasure is unwarranted. By this standard, the fact that Ugandan forces attacked military objectives "hundreds of kilometers" from the border may or may not be legally relevant to an assessment of whether these attacks were directed towards the appropriate goal of ending rebel incursions from DRC territory. Again, we see the costs of imprecision in applying the proportionality principle.

By extension, this trend helps explain why there is a logical consistency to the efforts of some commentators to define *jus ad bellum* proportionality in a limited manner

---

[15] Human Rights Situation in Palestine and Other Occupied Arab Territories, Report of the Special Rapporteur on the situation of human rights in the Palestinian territories occupied since 1967, U.N. Doc. A/HRC/10/20 (Feb. 11, 2009).

[16] R.Y. Jennings, *The Caroline and McLeod Cases*, 32 AM. J. INT'L L (1938) 82, 89.

[17] Oscar Schachter, *In Defense of International Rules on the Use of Force*, 53 UNIVERSITY OF CHICAGO LAW REVIEW 113, 132 (1986)("[A]cts done in self-defense must not exceed in manner or aim the necessity provoking them.").

[18] RAWLS, A THEORY OF JUSTICE 379 (Cambridge, Massachusetts: The Belknap Press of Harvard University Press, 1971).

to mean that "the intensity of self-defense must be about the same as the intensity defended against."[19] During the Israeli incursion into Lebanon in 2006, for example, Kofi Annan condemned air strikes aimed at bridges as "a disproportionate act of force" despite Israeli explanations that the goal was to interdict the flow of ammunition and communications to the Hezbollah terrorists that rained down indiscriminate rocket fire onto Israeli cities. Whether the Israeli argument was factually merited is rather beside the point for our purpose. The UN and western media simply accepted the conclusion without discerning debate or consideration of the relevant factors.

Writing in the *Washington Post*, columnist Eugene Robinson cast the attacks as a form of collective punishment based on a presumed need for equitable equivalence of action saying "[o]f course Israel has the right to defend itself against Hezbollah's rocket attacks. But how can this utterly disproportionate, seemingly indiscriminate carnage be anything but counterproductive."[20] We maintain that a simple numerical or qualitative comparison fails to capture the essence of permissible proportionate responses. In practice, this "atomized" view, to borrow Robert Sloan's term,[21] is ill-conceived and thus unsustainable in practice. It has the fatal disadvantage of remaining divorced from the larger context by relying only on superficial comparators. The application of proportionality in the *jus ad bellum* context is far more nuanced than to rely on mere tactical comparisons.

We end this section by providing another example to show that although the law is clear in the abstract, and the general applicability of proportionality accepted, the residual ambiguities in the theory of proportionate countermeasures are similar to those we have seen in other disciplines. In the *Oil Platforms* case, the United States argued that a series of attacks against Iranian oil platforms were a lawful defensive effort taken in response to a series of attacks on US and neutral shipping which the US attributed to Iran.[22] In light of the Iranian argument that lawful self-defense is limited to the time the attack is in progress, the *US Memorial* argued that the Iranian attacks on the ships had lasted only a few seconds and that the "*status quo ante* could not be restored simply by driving an attacking force back across the border from whence they came."[23]

---

[19] Frederic L. Kirgis, *Some Proportionality Issues Raised by Israel's Use of Armed Force in Lebanon*, ASIL INSIGHTS, Aug. 17, 2006, http://www.asil.org/insights060817.cfm.

[20] William Safire, *On Language: Proportionality* N.Y. TIMES, Aug. 13, 2006.

[21] Robert Sloane, *The Cost of Conflation: Preserving the Dualism of Jus ad Bellum and Jus in Bello in the Contemporary Law of War*, 34 Yale J. Int'l L. 47, 109 (2009).

[22] *See* Natalia Ochoa-Ruiz and Esther Salamanca-Aguado, *Exploring the Limits of International Law relating to the Use of Force in Self-defence*, 16 EUROPEAN J. INT'L L. 499, 516 (2005)(describing US reliance on this theory in the *Oil Platforms* case), *available at* http://www.ejil.org/pdfs/16/3/306.pdf.

[23] *Oil Platforms case, Counter-memorial and counter-claim submitted by the United States of America,* 23 June 1997, at 140, *available at* www.icj-cij.org/docket/index.php?p1=3&p2=3&k=0a&case=90&code=op&p3=1.

Mindful of the perception that the resort to force could be a mere subterfuge for an otherwise unlawful punitive goal, the US argued that the oil platforms had been used for military purposes to identify and target vessels for attack. In reply, Iran contested the US claim that it had been subjected to an armed attack because there was insufficient evidence to establish state attribution and that only a specific armed attack rather than a series of smaller attacks generates a right of self-defense.

More important for our purposes, Iran argued that "self-defense is limited to that use of force which is necessary to repel an attack," and that "once an attack is over, as was the case here, there is no need to repel it, and any counter-force no longer constitutes self-defense. Instead it is an unlawful armed reprisal or a punitive action."[24]

We agree with Sloane in the conclusion that

> This parsimonious, almost *lex talionis*, position leads to absurd results and does not conform to state practice. In *Oil Platforms*, for example, it meant that once the attack on the *Sea Isle City* ended, so too did any necessity for self-defense. Any subsequent response would perforce be needless and disproportionate were it directed against an Iranian target other than the source of the Iranian missile. No state, in practice, would accept this conception of *ad bellum* proportionality if faced with repeated assaults from another state's territory, notwithstanding *Nicaragua* and its progeny.[25]

We will explore the implications of this sentiment in more detail in Chapter 12.

II. EXAMPLES OF DIFFICULT COUNTERINSURGENCY CASES

We next turn to very difficult and controversial cases of counterinsurgency, that is, where one State is fighting an armed conflict with a non-State actor that is trying to overthrow a legitimate State. We present three extended examples that are meant to show how factors such as *jus post bellum* as well as media perception turn out to make *jus in bello* proportionality assessments even harder than in the cases we have examined already.

---

[24] *Oil Platforms case, Reply and Defence to Counter-claim submitted by the Islamic Republic of Iran*, i, 10 Mar. 1999, at 136, available at: www.icj-cij.org/docket/index.php?p1=3&p2=3&k=0a&case=90&code=op&p3=1.

[25] Robert Sloane, *The Cost of Conflation: Preserving the Dualism of Jus ad Bellum and Jus in Bello in the Contemporary Law of War*, 34 YALE J. INT'L L. 47, 109 (2009).

First, during 2009, an American Armored Cavalry unit was stationed in a strategically important area of Afghanistan. The platoon established an observation post that overlooked a valley known for its enemy activity. The valley was particularly important because a major supply route cuts down its center and connects two provinces. The following sequence is not fictitious, though we have chosen to keep unit identities and the location anonymous to protect privacy. On an early April afternoon, one of the platoons encountered stiff and sustained enemy fire, and the firefight continued into the late evening. The American unit remained in close engagement with the enemy force and pursued it to a large qalat [Afghan home]. The platoon isolated the enemy combatants in the qalat and awaited further instructions.

The higher level headquarters ordered an attached special operations element to enter and clear the qalat. This American unit was augmented by a second special operations force from a key coalition ally. The team arrived on site around 3:00 A.M. and began to determine the appropriate course of action. The US Special Forces team was supported by two AH-64 attack helicopters that were able visually to confirm an enemy combatant with a RPK pointed directly at the front door from inside of the qalat. Insurgent forces in Afghanistan have commonly established hardened fighting positions just inside the entry points of domestic dwellings.[26] Based on the unbroken engagements throughout the afternoon and early evening, all levels of the command knew that the dwelling contained multiple armed enemies. The team of US Special Forces requested that the target be destroyed with a "gun run" by one of the attack helicopters flying overhead, but the request was denied by higher headquarters based on the worry that there could be civilians inside the qalat.

After a lengthy protest from the attached special operations element, the cavalry unit commander ordered dismounted entry into the structure. The commander had what military practitioners term operational control (OPCON)[27] of the attached special operations elements, which gave him authority to order them to assault the structure despite their tactical recommendations. The team decided to enter the

---

[26] Mark Owen and Kevin Maurer, No Easy Day: The Firsthand Account of the Mission That Killed Osama bin Laden 64 (2012).

[27] See Dep't of Defense, Dictionary of Military and Associated Terms, Joint Publication 1-02 (8 November 2010, as amended through 31 January 2011), *available at* http://ra.defense.gov/documents/rtm/jp1_02.pdf:

> Command authority that may be exercised by commanders at any echelon at or below the level of combatant command. Operational control is inherent in combatant command (command authority) and may be delegated within the command. Operational control is the authority to perform those functions of command over subordinate forces involving organizing and employing commands and forces, assigning tasks, designating objectives, and giving authoritative direction necessary to accomplish the mission.

qalat from the second-floor via a ladder. Immediately upon entering the home, the team received heavy fire which inflicted a severe chest wound on an allied officer and multiple gunshot wounds on an American noncommissioned officer. After suffering these casualties within steps of the point of entry, the coalition force evacuated its wounded and was driven back from the qalat.

Only after this predictable setback did the higher level commander authorize the attack helicopter to attack the qalat. The AH-64 destroyed the building rapidly using a Hellfire missile. The allied officer died as a result of his wounds while the American survived after surgery. The point is this: An allied officer died because of a speculative fear that some civilian might have been hurt by a strike from the air. During the battle damage assessment, a sister platoon discovered that at least one Afghan woman was killed during the engagement. An administrative investigation into the civilian fatality immediately followed, which is the standard operating procedure within International Security Assistance Force (ISAF).

In this instance, the lawfulness of the helicopter attack would have been unquestionable at the outset. The International Committee of the Red Cross (ICRC) Commentary to Protocol I of the Geneva Conventions notes that the application of proportionality during combat "is not always as clear as one might have wished" but clarifies that the law leaves "some margin of appreciation to those who have to apply the rule."[28] Though it is clear that the correct application of the proportionality principle in combat depends "to a large extent upon the good faith of the belligerents and on their wish to conform to the requirements of humanity,"[29] the circumstances of this incident were directed "against a military objective with means that are not disproportionate in relation to that objective."[30] The ICRC Commentary goes one step further by admitting that "putting these provisions into practice...will require complete good faith on the part of the belligerents, as well as the desire to conform with the general principle of respect for the civilian population."[31]

Operational control includes authoritative direction over all aspects of military operations and joint training necessary to accomplish missions assigned to the command. Operational control should be exercised through the commanders of subordinate organizations. Normally this authority is exercised through subordinate joint force commanders and Service and/or functional component commanders. Operational control normally provides full authority to organize commands and forces and to employ those forces as the commander in operational control considers necessary to accomplish assigned missions; it does not, in and of itself, include authoritative direction for logistics or matters of administration, discipline, internal organization, or unit training. Also called *OPCON*.

[28] Commentary to Protocol I, Art 87, ¶ 1835 available at http://www.icrc.org/ihl.nsf/COM/470-750001? OpenDocument.

[29] *Id.*

[30] Commentary to Protocol I, Art 51, ¶ 1979 available at http://www.icrc.org/ihl.nsf/COM/470-750001? OpenDocument

[31] *Id.* para. 1978.

From the perspective of the cavalry unit commander on the scene who had already suffered casualties, the elimination of the enemy fighters outweighed the possible loss to civilian lives or property. From the higher level perspective of the superior commanders (who certainly had larger missions and mandates), considerations of the overall welfare to civilians outweighed the near certainty of additional combatant casualties, at least at the outset. The two commanders gave differing values to the military advantage to be gained and weighed the hypothetical damage to civilian lives and property differently, which in turn affected their proportionality findings.

In our view, the law of armed conflict is not a suicide pact. Proportionality requires weighing loss of lives of civilians against the value of the military objective. In this case, it turned out that coalition combatant casualties could have been prevented by a recognition that the combatant casualties were nearly certain and the civilian casualties were not. The probability assessment must be part of a proper proportionality assessment. Indeed, proportionality could well be extended, as a matter of common sense, to include the foreseeable effects of military decisions on the innocent civilians the combatants' mission was trying to protect, or the families of the combatants as well as those caught in the vortex of battle.

We are unaware of any analysis of proportionality that seeks to extend proportionality as an umbrella concept to capture the foreseeable effects of conflict on the families of soldiers. But such an extension might well be appropriate if we begin to take seriously the human rights of those military personnel. This incident does reveal one striking truism. To the extent that the law of armed conflict grants a range of deference to the decision-maker in the heat of battle, the proportionality principle would ideally provide a common basis of analysis regardless of the level of command. If, indeed, the more senior commanders sincerely but incorrectly believed that proportionality requires deference to the mere possibility of civilian casualties, absent any indicators or intelligence that a particular attack would be expected to cause such damage, combatants were wounded and killed because of the disconnect between the principle of proportionality and its practice. This is why, in an earlier chapter, we spent so much time discussing the emerging *lex ferenda* that calls for all relevant lives, especially the lives of soldiers, to be part of the proportionality calculus.

Second, Australian forces attacked a Taliban enclave on February 12, 2009.[32] During the firefight with Taliban enemy forces, Australian SAS (special operations forces) threw a hand grenade at a group of Taliban that killed the enemy but also

---

[32] Gregory Rose, *Irregular warfare blows hole in Geneva rules*, THE AUSTRALIAN pp. 33–34 (Aug. 26, 2011).

caused the deaths of five children in the room from which the Taliban fighter was engaging the Australians. Three Australian Army 1st Commando Regiment troops were accused of murder by the members of the family and an Australian broadcast agency. Facing charges for manslaughter for negligently causing the civilian deaths, the Australian soldiers maintained that they had every lawful right to defend themselves and that, in the middle of a direct engagement with enemy forces, they were not culpable for the deaths of persons not known to have been present. On these facts, no credible prosecutor could have sustained charges based on the International Criminal Court (ICC) charge of "intentionally launching an attack… in the knowledge" that forcible engagement would foreseeably cause disproportionate damage or loss of life.

During the investigation of the incident, the Australian Army Judge Advocate determined that the soldiers did not owe an additional duty of care to the Afghan children beyond that mandated by the laws and customs of war. The laws and customs of war are designed to provide the basis for assessing military action that protects a range of rights during conflict even as it imposes correlative duties on a range of actors. This is the essence of the *lex specialis jus in bello* that serves to displace normal principles of tort law and to varying degrees the default obligations flowing from the human rights regime. Nevertheless, it took Australian authorities some 30 months (until May 2011) to clear the soldiers. The case reinforced the *lex specialis* principle that the laws and customs of war provide the primary source of humanitarian constraints during battle.

To speak of tortious conduct during war reflects the gravest possible commingling of legal and moral duties. Hence, accidental civilian deaths cannot be held to an additional civil duty of care subject to the assessments of *post hoc* political expediency or administrative recrimination. The incident nevertheless disrupted the combat effectiveness of the unit and the controversy damaged the professional reputations of those involved. Of perhaps more grave concern, it likely chilled the efforts of other forces engaging in lawful combat operations, which in turn could easily have increased casualties.

The paradox is that overweening fear of causing suffering to support ostensibly humanitarian purposes might well have resulted in more human rights abuses at the hands of Taliban who otherwise would have perished at the hands of coalition forces. But there is also a *jus post bellum* element here that needs to be addressed. The killing of children is an especially difficult problem for later reconciliation after the armed conflict has ended. We do not support the idea that, in the Australian case, overriding weight should have been attached to the lives of children. But giving great weight to those lives as a matter of *jus post bellum lex ferenda* is understandable even as it was also not required by *lex lata jus in bello* proportionality. Here is one of the most striking disconnects between *lex lata* and *lex ferenda* understood through the window of *jus post bellum*.[33]

Finally, a third example is that on August 16, 2007, Polish military vehicles came under fire near the village of Nangar Khel, located in the Paktika province of Afghanistan. Six Polish commandos serving in the 18th Stormtrooper Battalion from Biesko-Biala were charged with manslaughter; with a seventh accused of "opening fire at an undefended object" in what became Europe's first war crimes trial from Afghanistan. Though trial did not begin until February 2, 2009, the soldiers were widely excoriated in the media and political circles. What some termed the Nangar Khel Massacre caused something of a national reexamination as Poland's proud martial traditions and its post-Cold War emergence as a key North Atlantic Treaty Organization (NATO) ally became the focus of intense internal debate. In fact, the trial into the events at Nangar Khel was the first time in Polish history that soldiers were charged with war crimes for the deaths of civilians during battle. Those charged, as in other armies, faced the erosion of their careers as peers questioned their professionalism and integrity. They were ostracized and publicly castigated.

The soldiers were ultimately acquitted in the Military District Court in Warsaw on June 1, 2011, based on a finding that there was insufficient evidence to establish deliberate targeting of the civilians; the Polish Supreme Court subsequently reaffirmed the acquittals of three soldiers, believing that "they have committed no crime" but referred the cases of the others back to the lower court for further examination. During the case, Defense Minister Bogdan Klich stood by the accused soldiers, stating that they had merely performed a "fatal error" and as such should be judged as not guilty.

The commander of the Polish Land Forces, General Waldemar Skrzypczak, threatened to quit his post if the seven soldiers were convicted, and added further his own personal guarantee that the accused are innocent.[34] The general was promptly sacked as his remarks were understood as undue pressure on the military court's proceedings. The trial was a media spectacle that sent shockwaves across the international coalition of NATO forces in Afghanistan.

---

[33] *See* Larry May, After War Ends (2012)(especially Chapters 5 and 7). The authors of the current book on proportionality are somewhat at odds over the proper proportionality judgment of the Australian case just described, but the example is included to illustrate the importance of developing common understandings of the legal and moral principles involved to permit good faith debate over the relevant facts as they emerge).

[34] Miroslaw Czech, *Gentlemen, Do Not Play With the Army*, GAZETA WYBORCZA (May 6, 2008) (quoting General Waldemar Skrzypczak, "If those seven (soldiers accused of war crimes at Nangar Khel) are convicted, I do not see any place for myself in the army," and stating further that he personally vouched for their innocence).

Wikileaks released confidential documents on the incident declaring that, "[The Polish soldiers] fired a total of 26 rounds according to one report. They fired over and then short and then three rounds impacted within a compound." This reflected standard military practice around the world as they employed the technique known as *bracketing* to pinpoint fire on the desired objective. The terrorists that killed the American ambassador to Libya used the same technique in Benghazi in 2012. At Nangar Khel, one mortar round impacted on the roof of the house, one impacted in the court yard, and the last went through the roof and detonated within the house. There was a wedding celebration going on in the house, which explains the high number of casualties. Six Afghans died in the mortar attack, including a pregnant woman and three children, and seriously injured three other women.[35]

The residents of Nangar Khel were reportedly thought to be secretly harboring Taliban insurgents, casting the shadow of My Lai and Haditha over the media frenzy. Given that the attack took place only two days after a Polish soldier was killed in Afghanistan, there was also some speculation in the news media that the killings may have been an act of revenge.[36] In fact, Polish forces on a joint patrol with an American unit were attacked by improvised explosive devices (IEDs) earlier in the morning, and another group of Polish soldiers had been sent to reinforce the patrols that were waiting with their damaged vehicles. The reinforcements opened fire with their mortar, killing the civilians.

The incident became a national scandal fueled in part by the fact that the soldiers initially claimed to have been returning fire. Though there was testimony at trial that the patrol did come under fire from the village and that Polish forces returning fire stopped immediately upon realizing that civilians were hit, one member of the prosecution team, Lt. Col. Zbigniew Rzepa, said that the evidence showed that "We already know that this is not true."[37] The unit was under the OPCON of American commanders.[38] Though there was no serious suggestion of American involvement in the civilian deaths, Poles wondered about the uniformity within NATO of the commitment to the laws and customs of war.

The tragedy at Nangar Khel revealed deep disquiet over the Polish mission in Afghanistan, and the accompanying command lines needed to integrate smaller

---

[35] Mare Wasiński, *Odpowiedść Prawna Polki za incydent w Nangar Khel* a stwo i prawo miesie c ni organ r es enia prawni w pols ich 26 ńóś

[36] Nicholas Kulish, An Afghanistan War-Crimes Case Tests Poland's Commitment to Foreign Missions, N.Y. TIMES, Nov. 26, 2007, http://www.nytimes.com/2007/11/29/world/europe/29poland.html?_r=0

[37] Nicholas Kulish, *An Afghanistan War-Crimes Case Tests Poland's Commitment to Foreign Missions*, N.Y. Times, Nov. 29, 2007, at A 12.

[38] *Supra* note 27 (providing the doctrinal definition of OPCON).

coalition units into an ISAF lead by American forces. One Polish General, Jerzy Wójcik, described the effects of Nangar Khel syndrome:

> The men slated to travel out on successive missions are now wondering: what for? So that I will be afraid to draw my weapon and shoot? They are not saying this outright, but one can already sense it when talking to the soldiers. We are having trouble putting together full contingents for the successive rotations to Afghanistan. Instead of close-knit units, we will be sending out a hodgepodge of people from throughout Poland.[39]

Though the Polish commander's tone was heated, there can be no mistaking his perception that the application of proportionality has direct effects within and without a combat unit. Ordinary young men and women strive to perform to the highest standards of tactical and technical professionalism in moments of stress and given inadequate information and time. They struggle to balance the clear demands of the military mission and military necessity against the larger pallet of the laws and customs of war. At Nangar Khel, the loss of reputations and respect were not the most significant costs given the larger strategic uncertainties and the lasting erosion of Polish support for the NATO coalition.

The overarching lex lata *jus in bello* law applicable to Nangar Khel and other incidents in Afghanistan is indeed clear. The conjoined principles of proportionality and distinction are fundamental and inalterable. The *Galić* Trial Chamber in the International Criminal Tribunal of the former Yugoslavia (ICTY) hinted at what became the dispositive issue in Nangar Khel writing that "certain apparently disproportionate attacks may give rise to the inference that civilians were actually the object of attack,"[40] and that "in determining whether an attack was proportionate it is necessary to examine whether a reasonably well-informed person in the circumstances of the actual perpetrator, making reasonable use of the information available to him or her, could have expected excessive civilian casualties to result from the attack."[41] The judge in the Nangar Khel trial acquitted the soldiers in part because of a lack of evidence needed to establish precisely from where the shots had been fired, or the precise placement of witnesses. Proportionality provided the decisive test both for the contemporaneous response of the Polish unit and the judicial assessment of those decisions.

---

[39] Marcin Gorka and Adam Zadworny, *Afraid to Shoot*, GAZETA WYBORCZA (April 28, 2008).

[40] Prosecutor v Stanislav Galić (Judgment and Opinion) ICTY-98-29 (5 December 2003) 60.

[41] *Id.* para. 58.

The *Galić* Trial Chamber specifically recalled that "the rule of proportionality does not refer to the actual damage caused or to the military advantage achieved by an attack, but instead uses the words reasonably 'expected' and 'anticipated.'"[42] This entirely correct application of the proportionality principle was disputed by the Polish Prosecutor, Colonel Jakub Mytych, who argued that the defendants committed war crimes as well as violations of Polish law because "Stating that [the soldiers] were aiming at another target is merely a line of defense."[43] The prosecutor is entirely erroneous in his perception of *jus in bello* proportionality at least insofar as the relevant standard of the Rome Statute of the ICC, in Article 8(2)(b)(iv), provides the dispositive standard in Polish law.

The prosecutor's statement reveals an incorrect conflation between the principles of distinction and proportionality. For the prosecutor, and perhaps from the wider public perspective often informed by insurgent media narratives, any civilian deaths during combat are presumed to have been purposely caused and therefore criminal. In fact, delegates during the Protocol I negotiations made clear that the definitions of distinction and proportionality are separately delineated in the treaty because they are wholly distinct aspects of war fighting. For example, the Ukrainian delegation made clear that attacks against civilians were only impermissible as a violation of the principle of distinction if this was the primary reason for the attack, as opposed to a collateral consequence.[44]

Western delegations made it clear that there is a difference between intentionally engendering civilian lives and property and inadvertently doing so on the basis of military necessity. The United Kingdom delegation made a similar intervention on this vital point:

His delegation also welcomed the reaffirmation in paragraph 2, of the customary law rule that civilian objects must not be the direct object of attack. It did not, however, interpret the paragraph as dealing with the question of incidental damage caused by attacks directed against military objectives. In its view, the purpose

---

[42] *Id.* para. 109.

[43] http://www.thenews.pl/1/10/Artykul/25214,Seven-Polish-soldiers-acquitted-in-Nangar-Khel-trial-

[44] *See Ukrainian Soviet Socialist Republic Statement*, 6 OFFICIAL RECORDS OF THE DIPLOMATIC CONFERENCE ON THE REAFFIRMATION AND DEVELOPMENT OF INTERNATIONAL HUMANITARIAN LAW APPLICABLE IN ARMED CONFLICTS, GENEVA (1974-1977) 200–201 (1978) [hereinafter cited as OFFICIAL RECORDS OF THE DIPLOMATIC CONFERENCE] ("In common with the previous articles of this Section, Article 46 widens the scope of protection for the civilian population and individual civilians, who under no circumstances shall be the object of attack. In particular, paragraph 2 explicitly prohibits acts or threats of violence the *primary* purpose of which is to spread terror among the civilian population; this is in line with the generally recognized rules of international law, which lay down that Parties to the conflict shall not make the civilian population an object of attack") [emphasis added].

of the first sentence of the paragraph was to prohibit only such attacks as might be directed against non-military objectives.[45]

Delegations from the American,[46] German,[47] the Netherlands,[48] and Canada,[49] repeated this understanding using almost identical language.

The reader might well wonder why we include these extended *jus in bello* examples in this chapter. These three incidents each reveal the difficulties of properly applying the proportionality principle from a slightly different angle. In fact, there is little that is routine about applying the proportionality principle from the perspective of the authority figures charged with winning a conflict using all lawful means, those caught in the vortex of battle, or the broader public expectations. We include all three to illustrate the diversity of applications of the principle and the consequences of noncompliance in the midst of conflict. Whose assessment is dispositive? What information or assumptions warrant military action (or inaction)? What are the larger consequences for the practice of proportionality that ought to inform its use during warfare? These three instances demonstrate in the aggregate the inherent imprecision applying what is a conceptually simple principle.

In the wake of Nangar Khel, the commanding general of the Polish contingent in Afghanistan, Brig. Gen. Slawomir Wojchiechowski, observed that

we never knew if we were in the right or not, according to the law, in using force…In the past, soldiers sometimes decided it was easier to be hurt or dead than to act and be potentially jailed because you reacted to something. It wasn't fair to send people here without proper rules of engagement.

---

[45] *See United Kingdom Statement*, 6 OFFICIAL RECORDS OF THE DIPLOMATIC CONFERENCE, *supra* note 457, at 169.

[46] *See United States of America Statement*, 6 OFFICIAL RECORDS OF THE DIPLOMATIC CONFERENCE, *supra* note 457, at 204 ("The first sentence of Article 47 paragraph 2 prohibits only such attacks as may be directed against non-military objectives. It does not deal with the question of collateral damage caused by attacks directed against military objectives.")

[47] *See Federal Republic of Germany Statement*, 6 OFFICIAL RECORDS OF THE DIPLOMATIC CONFERENCE, *supra* note 457, at 188 ("Article 47…The first sentence of Article 47, paragraph 2 is a restatement of the basic rule contained in Article 43, namely that the Parties to a conflict shall direct their operations only against military objectives. It does not deal with the question of collateral damage caused by attacks directed against military objectives."

[48] *See Netherlands Statement*, 6 OFFICIAL RECORDS OF THE DIPLOMATIC CONFERENCE, *supra* note 457, at 195 ("Furthermore, it is the view of the Netherlands delegation that the first sentence of Article 47, paragraph 2, prohibits only such attacks as maybe directed against non-military objectives and consequently does not deal with the question of collateral damage caused by attacks directed against military objectives.").

[49] *See Canada Statement*, 6 OFFICIAL RECORDS OF THE DIPLOMATIC CONFERENCE, *supra* note 457, at 179 ("Article 47…In the view of the Canadian delegation, a specific area of land may also be a military objective if, because of its location or other reasons specified in Article 47, its total or partial destruction, capture

As we have noted, proportionality is a recurring analysis yet it carries grave and almost always uncertain implications.

The ICRC Commentary on Protocol I notes that although the targeting constraints embedded in the treaty were in some ways an imperfect product of difficult negotiations "[i]f it had not been possible to impose limitations on certain methods of combat, there would have been reason to fear that the credibility of humanitarian law would suffer seriously as a consequence."[50] The problem is that the very imprecision of the proportionality principle as it has been applied, and frequently misapplied, in modern conflicts leads directly to a loss of credibility for the normative power of humanitarian law. In other words, misinterpretation of the proportionality principle undermines the legitimacy of the larger body of law and undermines its laudable goals by undermining respect for its legal and moral imperatives.

Nevertheless, given the strong incentive of compliance in professional military organizations, the consequences for misunderstanding the proportionality principle and mistakenly applying its tenets can be severe. Humanitarian law is, after all, buttressed by the principle of individual criminal responsibility. Careers are ended by war crimes allegations, and convictions generally lead to personal punishments. By extension, actions that are perceived to be disproportionate can generate erosion of unit discipline and a honed fighting edge that in turn lead to strategic setbacks. On the other hand, lives are lost and international coalitions are strained by mistakes over the practice of proportionality. Our concern is for the human beings caught in this difficult situation. There are real people, both civilian and military, whose lives and property are endangered by misapprehension over the proper bounds of proportionality. We will devote the next three chapters to extended analysis of other highly visible and controversial applications of the proportionality principle.

---

or neutralization, in the circumstances ruling at the time, offers a definite military advantage. It is also our understanding that the first sentence of paragraph 2 prohibits only attacks that could be directed against non-military objectives. It does not deal with the result of a legitimate attack on military objectives and incidental damage that such attack may cause.").

[50] Commentary on the Additional Protocols of 8 June 1977 to the Geneva Conventions of 12 August 1949, Part IV, Sec. 1, ¶ 1835 (Sandoz et al, eds 1987), *available at* http://www.icrc.org/ihl.nsf/ COM/470-750001?OpenDocument.

9

HUMAN SHIELDS AND RISK

IN THIS CHAPTER and the two that follow, we take up more cases that are especially challenging on proportionality grounds. We begin with the problem of human shields. Proportionality assessments are often made under a certain kind of forced-choice situation insofar as the circumstances of war force many people to make decisions that they would normally not want to make. And there are certain circumstances of war that are especially difficult because of the contrived forced choices that occur. The problem of human shields is one of the most difficult of these situations. Indeed, from the narrow perspective of the required proportionality analysis, the problem of human shields seems almost insoluble due to the inevitable controversies surrounding injuries or deaths to civilians even if those persons have voluntarily placed themselves in close proximity to valid military objectives. War fighters seem to face these dilemmas more often, as we shall see. And, as a general observation, we note that the controversies are far from resolved, despite the time and expertise devoted to the debates.

In this chapter, we will try to explain why questions concerning human shields seem so intractable and then to offer some modest suggestions about how to address some of these cases. Throughout, we will be guided by the Vattelian principle that "the law of nature…does not favor oppressors."[1] On the basis of this principle, we will argue that if human shields are used to increase the likelihood of oppression, they should be severely sanctioned. In other words, the law of armed conflict

---

[1] EMER DE VATTEL, *LE DROIT DES GENS, OU PRINCIPES DE LA LOI NATURELLE*, APPLIQUÉ À LA CONDUITE ET AUX AFFAIRES DES NATIONS ET DES SOUVERAINS (THE LAW OF NATIONS, OR PRINCIPLES OF THE LAW OF NATURE, APPLIED TO THE CONDUCT AND AFFAIRS OF NATIONS AND SOVEREIGNS), Bk. IV, Ch. IV, §37, 357 (Charles G. Fenwick trans. 1916)(1758).

principles should not be distorted to incentivize choices that intentionally increase the human costs of conflicts.

Human shields involve, by definition, a forced choice. Here is one relatively uncontroversial definition of human shields:

> the intentional use of a party to a conflict of one or more human beings, usually civilians or captured members of the adversary's forces…placed between the adversary and themselves in a way meant to deter an attack against the forces using the human shields, for fear of killing or harming the unarmed shields. The shields are in effect hostages used for strategic purposes.[2]

Civilians or prisoners of war placed in front of a military target creates a forced choice for the party that has to decide whether to attack that target.

It is useful to distinguish involuntary from voluntary human shields. In the latter case, civilians have chosen to place themselves in front of the target, rather than being forced into this position. The classic example of this phenomenon was the hundreds of civilians that flocked onto the bridges in Belgrade during the 78-day North Atlantic Treaty Organization (NATO) air campaign against the Milosevic regime. In that context, the NATO commander was adamant that "no responsible commander wishes to kill civilians…Every day we did our very, very best to limit collateral damage and limit the loss of life on the adversary's side."[3]

Whereas human shields force a choice upon the party that needs to pursue the military target, now the civilians, rather than the other party to the war, have forced the choice. It is true that voluntary human shields seek to assist the military efforts of one of the belligerent states, but absent evidence of coercion or state coordination, it is difficult directly to attribute their actions to the responsibility of the belligerent state. All forms of human shields are artificial, contrived circumstances under which a party must decide between two unappealing prospects that would not be the only options but for the human shields. This artificiality in turn affects the hostilities in profound ways.

Human shields force a false choice upon the military force that wishes to apply the laws and customs of warfare in good faith. Much like the war crime of perfidy,[4] by

---

[2] H. Victor Conde, A Handbook of International Human Rights Terminology 114 (2nd ed. 2004), *quoted in* Ammon Rubinstein and Yaniv Roznai, Human Shields in Modern Armed Conflicts: the Need for Proportionate Proportionality, 93 Stanford L. & Pol'y Rev. 94 (2011)

[3] Lieutenant General Michael Short, *Operation Allied Force From the Perspective of the NATO Air Commander,* in Legal and Ethical Lessons of NATO's Kosovo Campaign, 78 Naval War Col. Int'l. L. Stud. 19, 23 (Andru Wall ed., 2002).

[4] Protocol I, Article 37; Jean-Marie Henckaerts, Louise Doswald-Beck, Customary International Humanitarian Law Vol I: Rules, Rule 65 (2005), *available at* http://www.icrc.org/customary-ihl/eng/docs/v1_rul_rule65.

which one side attempts to achieve a military advantage by exploiting the adversary's good-faith compliance with the laws of warfare, human shields create tension between the competing core assumptions of humanitarian law. On the one hand, the commanders have the lawful right to seek military advantage by attacking lawful military objectives using lawful weapons and techniques. On the other hand, the humanitarian imperatives require that civilians be shielded from the effects of hostilities to the greatest degree possible. Of course, it is never permissible intentionally to direct attacks against civilians. The question we will address is whether, and to what extent, the fact of a forced choice changes the proportionality assessment concerning this situation. And we will also be especially concerned about how the legal and moral landscape changes if serious risk of harm or loss of life is imposed on civilians by States or other political organizations.

In Section I, we describe the problem of forced choices and to what extent human shield cases are significantly different from other cases in wartime. In Section II, we discuss the somewhat unsettled position of international law concerning human shields. In Section III, we discuss the difficult case of voluntary human shields. In Section IV, we discuss the problem of involuntary human shields. In Section V we discuss a further complication that arises from the risks that must be undertaken on the part of civilian individuals and populations. In Section VI, we relate the various forms of human shields to the Vattelian principle. We will argue that human shields are not an intractable problem concerning proportionality but rather a problem that requires us to adjust how we understand civilian immunity and the principle of discrimination or distinction. We will conclude with a somewhat amended idea of how to conceive of proportionality in morality and international law. These clarifications with respect to the relevance of human shields as a factor in targeting decisions are increasingly important as asymmetric conflicts become more prevalent.

I. FORCED CHOICES

Let us begin by thinking about a very simple forced choice situation: A gunman approaches a woman and says, "Your money or your life." That a person feels compelled to give up her money does not establish anything about the moral status of the money now having been given to the gunman. As H.L.A. Hart has famously argued, this is a classic case of being *obliged* to do something even though we would never say that one was *obligated* to do so. Pragmatically, one feels compelled to accede to the gunman's demand, but we would not say that she had a moral duty to comply. And most important, those who perpetrate such forced choices are thought to act wrongly although the victim felt obliged to act as demanded and did so act.[5]

But what exactly is wrong with forced choices? In some respects, we act on the basis of forced choices all of the time. Most decisions are made with fewer options than a person would have otherwise preferred. Indeed, we make many choices on the basis of greatly restricted options, or at least without what could be understood as reasonable options. Yet, it is especially problematical if our options are restricted by the intentional actions of others, and the restrictions are such that there are no other reasonable options. We have then been forced into a situation in which all of our options are unreasonable. And, of course, our decisions in this situation are made all the more unpleasant by the realization that our actions did not contribute to the difficulty of the dilemmas we face. This is the kind of forced choice situation that human shields sometimes represent: there are no reasonable options, one feels one has to choose nonetheless, and the limiting of choices that created this situation was caused by the intentional and wrongful actions of other people. The liberty-limiting feature of forced choice situations is what makes them especially problematic in moral and legal theory.

Forced choices are wrong in the same way that coercion is wrong: One person's range of choices is adversely affected by a second person's intentional actions, eliminating all reasonable options, such that the first person is effectively forced to accept the wishes of the second person. The greatest wrong with forced choices is that a person's liberty is adversely restricted contrary to that person's desires. And the wrong-making characteristic that is crucial is the liberty-restricting aspect of the forced choice.[6] For our purposes, the wrong is compounded by the manipulation of the humanitarian norms, thereby discrediting their legal and moral force, or at least eroding the chances for overall compliance. Human life has been endangered needlessly by direct exposure to the reality of warfare.

If we move from the case of individuals influencing one another at the interpersonal level to States and other group-actors influencing other States or group actors, some differences arise, but these are not as significant as it often seems. States can manipulate the options of other States, just as is true of other groups and individuals. And to do so by leveraging legal and moral norms in a way that adversely affects another's interests is to act wrongfully. In part, such action is a violation of the right to self-determination of States, which is the group-based analogue of adversely influencing the right to be autonomous for individual persons. Self-determination of States is not as morally significant as the autonomy of individual persons, but is

---

[5] See H.L.A. HART, THE CONCEPT OF LAW (1960).
[6] See DAVID RODIN, WAR AND SELF-DEFENSE, ch 3 (2002).

still an important moral concept, since it often encompasses the aggregate rights of individuals to be autonomous. And harm occurs if self-determination or autonomy is infringed by the intentional actions of a person or group.

The various types of human shields all force a choice on the party that needs to attack the military target being shielded. The party that is contemplating attacking the military target would normally have to consider the value of the target compared to the likely collateral damages in terms of civilian lives lost as an indirect result of attacking the target. But with human shields in place, direct losses of civilian lives will result from the attack. So it appears that the attacking party would have to violate the philosophical principle of discrimination, or the legal concept of distinction, since one might well conclude that the attack was intentionally targeting civilian lives. Of course, it could also be said that the human shields are not being directly targeted if the direct target is a military target, such as an artillery unit, or the bridges in Belgrade. But it is hard to call civilian deaths merely collateral damage if it was known with certainty that an action would result in those deaths.

In cases of human shields, the proportionality assessment also looks more complicated and, it is fair to remember, controversial. If there are enough human shields surrounding a military target, it appears that the attack on the target would, in many cases, be deemed disproportionate. In any event, the value of destroying the military objective may well be undermined by the foreseeable negative consequences to the larger strategic or operational context from the deaths of the human shields. Yet, this result seems counterintuitive since the proportionality calculation is being manipulated by the party who has placed the human shields in harm's way. The fact that it is a forced choice seems to make it a different kind of case than it otherwise would be. But standard proportionality calculations would not allow for a variation based on such forced choice and manipulation conditions. In the standard proportionality calculations, all that matters is the assessment of the value of the military objective weighed, or perhaps also the likely costs in soldiers' lives if one remains aware of their human right to life, as assessed against the anticipated value of the likely collateral damages.

So, we could adjust the weights to reflect the fact that the human shields are a forced choice that renders the normal proportionality assessment artificial and subject to direct manipulation. But this would fail to respect the distinction between voluntary and involuntary human shields, if only the latter is a forced choice situation that is being manipulated by a State or political organization. It seems to matter, in terms of whether and how much to discount the lives of the civilians in the proportionality assessment, if the human shields are voluntary or involuntary. In part this is because proportionality, as we have understood it, involves not just a consequentialist tallying up but also a consideration of deontological factors, such as whether any of the parties were wrongdoers.

Proportionality, as we have seen, is intentionally designed to function properly if the participants in conflict make their decisions based on a good-faith implementation of their obligations under humanitarian law. From this perspective, it seems wholly unsatisfactory to reinforce a bright line rule by which sufficient numbers of human shields can seemingly immunize an otherwise valid military target. Civilians are entitled to protections from the effects of hostilities in general, and that humanitarian purpose is achieved through an interwoven network of carefully balanced obligations and norms. In psychological terms, one should avoid the positive reinforcement of otherwise disfavored activities. Human shields represent an important point of friction for the various protections of humanitarian law, and simplistic assessments risk undermining the careful compromises that keep the whole body of law alive and relevant. We turn next to a discussion of the legal status of human shields, before looking separately at each of these categories of human shields in terms of the possible wrongdoing of the human shields or those who place them. We will then tackle the way that the principles of proportionality and discrimination are impacted by human shields.

II. INTERNATIONAL LAW AND HUMAN SHIELDS

The International Committee of the Red Cross (ICRC) has issued a set of rules that describes its view of settled customary international law. Rule 97 is simply stated: "The use of human shields is prohibited." The definition given is also illustrative:

> [T]he use of human shields requires an intentional co-location of military objectives and civilians or persons *hors de combat* with specific intent of trying to prevent the targeting of those military objectives.[7]

The ICRC lists a large number of treaties and military manuals of States as supporting this rule, as well as the following summation: "No official contrary practice was found."[8] In other words, no nation on earth supports the assertion that civilians may lawfully be used to shelter military objectives.

---

[7] JEAN-MARIE HENCKAERTS, LOUISE DOSWALD-BECK, CUSTOMARY INTERNATIONAL HUMANITARIAN LAW VOL I: RULES, Rule 97 (2005), *available at* http://www.icrc.org/customary-ihl/eng/docs/v1_rul_rule97 http://www.icrc.org/customary-ihl/eng/docs/v1_rul_rule97.

[8] *Id.*

Notice that this ICRC definition of human shields confines the term to what are involuntary shields and excludes voluntary shields. It is fair to say that international law is well settled about the prohibition on involuntary human shields, but is in quite a bit of flux about the legal standards relevant to voluntary shields. In addition, and most importantly, the state of international law is also unsettled about what responsibilities attacking States have when confronted with human shields. The reason for this uncertainty is that the placement of a sufficient number of human shields in front of military targets seemingly makes any attempt to destroy those military targets disproportionate. Yet, this obvious result of the application of the proportionality principle is deeply counterintuitive for most commentators, particularly those with military experience or highly specialized knowledge of the *jus in bello*.

One might well imagine the emergence of an affirmative duty imposed upon state actors and agencies to prevent voluntary human shields from getting close to military objectives, based on the strength of the prohibitions on human shields in areas where they exercise effective control. To date, there is no such affirmative burden embedded in law or existing state practice. An emerging affirmative duty along these lines would, in our view, be wholly in keeping with human rights principles and the expanded conception of human rights we articulated earlier.

In discussing the legality of human shields we begin by looking to treaties, arguably the first source of international law. It is common to begin by citing to the Geneva Conventions of 1949 and Additional Protocol I of 1977. Article 19 of the Third Geneva Convention (on the Treatment of Prisoners of War) states:

> Prisoners of war shall be evacuated, as soon as possible after their capture, to camps situated in an area far enough from the combat zone for them to be out of danger. Only those prisoners of war who, owing to wounds or sickness, would run greater risks by being evacuated than by remaining where they are, may be temporarily kept back in a danger zone. Prisoners of war shall not be unnecessarily exposed to danger while awaiting evacuation from a fighting zone.

This provision of the Third Geneva Convention, which was ratified by nearly all States, clearly rules out the use of prisoners of war as human shields, since such prisoners are not to be moved into the combat zone or into danger and, if they are in a dangerous area, these prisoners of war are to be evacuated promptly.

Article 23 of the Third Geneva Convention makes direct reference to the exploitation of the protected status of prisoners of war in order to seek military advantage by specifying, "No prisoner of war may at any time be sent to, or detained in, areas where he may be exposed to the fire of the combat zone, nor may his presence be used to render certain points or areas immune from military operations." Similarly,

Article 28 of the Fourth Geneva Convention Relative to the Protection of Civilian Persons in Time of War mandates that the "presence of a protected person may not be used to render certain points or areas immune from military operations." This has been settled international law concerning prisoners of war and innocent civilians since at least World War II. Read as textual admonitions, these articles mean that even if a defender abuses the status of otherwise protected prisoners of war or civilians to leverage an undeserved military advantage the military objective is not thereby made "immune from military operations." Of course, this does not remotely settle the proportionality determinations.

Additional Protocol I to the Geneva Conventions of 1977 has not been ratified by nearly as many States as the Geneva Conventions themselves. But Protocol I is nonetheless also a source of customary international law and states the rule clearly for all civilians in Article 51 as we noted previously.

1. The civilian population and individual civilians shall enjoy general protection against dangers arising from military operations. To give effect to this protection, the following rules, which are additional to other applicable rules of international law, shall be observed in all circumstances....

3. Civilians shall enjoy the protection afforded by this Section, unless and for such time as they take a direct part in hostilities....

7. The presence or movements of the civilian population or individual civilians shall not be used to render certain points or areas immune from military operations, in particular in attempts to shield military objectives from attacks or to shield, favor or impede military operations. The Parties to the conflict shall not direct the movement of the civilian population or individual civilians in order to attempt to shield military objectives from attacks or to shield military operations.

Here, there is an explicit rule against the use of civilians as involuntary human shields. When Saddam Hussein abducted foreign nationals and placed them in the vicinity of military objectives during the First Gulf War in August 1990, the fact that he termed them "special guests" in no way changed the illegality of his actions, which the United Nations (UN) Security Council unanimously condemned.[9]

The literature on this prohibition interestingly asks whether mere co-location is sufficient to trigger the application of the prohibition, or whether specific intent is also required as the summary of customary international law by the ICRC indicates.[10]

[9] See UN. Sec. Council Resolution 664 (Aug 18, 1990). *Available at* http://www.un.org/ga/search/view_doc.asp?symbol=S/RES/664(1990)
[10] *See* Stephanie Bouchie de Belle, *Chained to Canons or Wearing Targets on their T-shirts: Human Shields in International Humanitarian Law*, 90 INT'L REV. RED CROSS, 883, 888 (no. 872, 2008).

The incidental movement of civilians into a war zone does not seem to trigger the prohibition. But the issue in cases of involuntary human shields is that a State or other party has intentionally placed civilians in harm's way to protect military objectives from attack. This is the reason that the ICRC definition in the Customary Law Study is actually better than the one with which we began.

Article 58 of Additional Protocol I also addresses human shields but in a somewhat different way from Article 51:

> The Parties to the conflict shall, to the maximum extent feasible:
>
> (a) without prejudice to Article 49 of the Fourth Convention, endeavor to remove the civilian population, individual civilians and civilian objects under their control from the vicinity of military objectives;
> (b) avoid locating military objectives within or near densely populated areas;
> (c) take the other necessary precautions to protect the civilian population, individual civilians and civilian objects under their control against the dangers resulting from military operations.

Michael Schmitt argues that Article 58 complements Article 51 in that an affirmative obligation is added to States to remove civilians from harm's way. But Schmitt also argues that Article 58 does not seem to require specific intent:

> Failure to either move civilians away from military objectives or refrain from emplacing them near civilians, when doing so is feasible in the attendant circumstances, breaches the norm. Furthermore, violation of the human shielding prohibition constitutes a war crime, whereas noncompliance with Article 58's requirements is not.[11]

This point is especially relevant to proportionality as we will see.

The status of human shields as war crimes is specifically addressed in the Rome Statute of the International Criminal Court (ICC) in Article 8(2)(b), in which war crimes during international armed conflicts include:

> (xxiii) Utilizing the presence of a civilian or other protected person to render certain points, areas or military forces immune from military operations;

---

[11] Michael N. Schmitt, Human Shields in International Humanitarian Law, Israel Y'book on Human Rights, pp. 17–59, especially pp. 28–29.

The analogous Rome Statute war crime applicable to the use of involuntary human shields during armed conflicts not of an international character is found in Article 8(2)(e)(viii), which prohibits

> Ordering the displacement of the civilian population for reasons related to the conflict, unless the security of the civilians involved or imperative military reasons so demand.

Of course, the taking of hostages remains unlawful in all conflicts, and as a result, the abduction of civilians for the purpose of using them as human shields is a separate war crime in all circumstances. As we have seen, it would be irrational for a state to argue that "imperative military reasons" included the authority to commit a known war crime through the use of human shields to protect otherwise lawful military objectives. As with all crimes under the jurisdiction of the ICC, there is an intent requirement here as we explained earlier.

The US Military Tribunal at Nuremberg reinforced the importance of these protections by prosecuting one defendant, in part, for what was alleged to be the intentional use of involuntary human shields. The *Von Leeb* Case (The High Command Trial) in 1948 prosecuted Hermann Hoth, *inter alia*, for the crime of ill treatment of prisoners of war. The following was reported:

> Under date of 29 October 1941, in the war diary of the Oberquartiermeister of Hoth's 17th Army, appears the following:
> *"The billeting of PW's captured in the city and some of the inhabitants of the country in the building used by our own troops has proved to be a useful countermeasure against the time bombs put there by the enemy. It has been our experience, that, as a result of this measure, the time bombs were found and rendered harmless in a very short time by the prisoners and/or the inhabitants of the country."*
> To use prisoners of war as a shield for the troops is contrary to international law.

Hoth said he gave no orders that this be done and he did not think it was done in his army. However, he admits knowing that prisoners of war were used as a shield for German troops in another army and states that he thought his Oberquartiermeister was reporting on that.

It will be recalled that Kurt Student was charged, *inter alia*, "with...the use...of British prisoners of war as a screen for the advance of German troops," when tried by a British Military Court at Luneberg. Although he was found not to have been responsible for such acts and although the charge also alleged that certain of the prisoners were killed while being used as a shield, there seems little doubt that, if proved, the mere act of forcing prisoners of war to go ahead of advancing enemy troops, thereby acting as a shield to the latter, would itself constitute another type of war crime.[12]

Here is one of the first courts to recognize the war crime of using involuntary human shields. This case, along with Article 23 of the Third Geneva Convention and Article 28 of the Fourth Geneva Convention, as distilled into the Protocol I provisions noted above, reinforce the essence of the debate. Humanitarian law clearly prohibits attempts to leverage its legal protections designed to benefit persons in enemy control into a tool for achieving military advantage during conflict. This nicely accords with Vattel's caution about not favoring oppressors, noted above.

Though international law recognizes that the use of involuntary human shields is prohibited, very few sources discuss voluntary human shields, as we next see. But there is a problem in even the nearly unanimous condemnation of the use of involuntary human shields, namely, how the prohibited use affects the responsibilities of the attacking party. As the British Manual of the Law of Armed Conflict makes clear:

> Even where human shields are being used, the proportionality rule must be considered. However, if the defenders put civilians or civilian objects at risk by placing military objectives in their midst or by placing civilians near the military objectives, this is a factor that must be taken into account in favor of the attackers in considering the legality of attacks on those objectives.

At the same time, as clarified later in this chapter, the problem is that there is also near unanimity that proportionality requires States not to attack military objectives if the likely loss of civilian life clearly outweighs the anticipated value of the military objective. The precise applications of proportionality if human shields are implicated remains highly uncertain, and this chapter seeks to add clarity on the appropriate moral and legal considerations.

III. VOLUNTARY HUMAN SHIELDS

The case of voluntary human shields raises several difficult conceptual questions, perhaps the most important of which concerns the difference between civilians and soldiers, or between combatants and noncombatants. If a person intentionally places himself or herself in front of a military target, such as an artillery unit, with

---

[12] US Military Tribunal Nuremberg, Judgment of October 27, 1948, *in* LAW REPORTS OF TRIALS OF WAR CRIMINALS, Selected and Prepared by the United Nations War Crimes Commission, Vol. XII The German High Command Trial, London: United Nations War Crimes Commission, 1949, pp. 104–105.

212 Proportionality in International Law

the purpose of preventing enemy forces from destroying that military target, it appears that the civilian is not, strictly speaking, a noncombatant. The actions of the voluntary human shield seem to be directed at achieving a military objective, namely, preventing the destruction of weaponry or of public works that serve a military purpose of the enemy. The act of using a protected status to seek protection for a lawful military objective is in itself a violation of the laws and customs of war as we have seen. This volitional action seems to make a difference in the status of the civilian, perhaps transforming the civilian into a combatant, or at least a vicarious participant in the conflict.

Yet, this civilian is not really a member of the military making decisions about military affairs. In fact, it might well be argued that the voluntary human shield is acting immorally by seeking to gain a military advantage at some point, and return to home and hearth at his/her convenience with a presumable expectation of protection from the effects of hostilities. And, of course, the civilian is not an *active* participant in the conflict. So, at most, the voluntary human shield is a mixed case, in which someone has partially changed his or her status by his or her actions and inactions but in which the transformation is not complete.

The standard definition of combatants used in international law and drawn from the Just War tradition is that they wear uniforms, carry weapons openly, and are subject to a chain of command. Of particular note for our purposes, what the ICRC describes as these "well known conditions"[13] added the requirement that combatant status is attained by the combination of these factors with the additional condition "of conducting their operations in accordance with the laws and customs of war." Voluntary human shields do not fit any of the conditions of being a soldier, hence it is difficult to argue that they have transformed their status to the degree that they may be intentionally targeted, based on that status alone. From a layperson's perspective, the category of combatant is not a precise term of legal significance, but a broader descriptor of anyone who participates in the war effort. There is a related group of civilians who may foreseeably become casualties due to their connection to the conflict, even though they do not fit any of the conditions of being a soldier, including those who work in munitions factories. Those who work in munitions factories or who design bombs are often integral to the war effort, and in a sense may be seen as taking a direct part in the hostilites, in that they make a difference in terms of whether their State or political organization will be able to achieve various military objectives.

---

[13] COMMENTARY ON THE ADDITIONAL PROTOCOLS OF JUNE 8, 1977 TO THE GENEVA CONVENTIONS OF AUGUST 12, 1949, Art. 44, at 541, ¶ 1722 (Sandoz et al, eds 1987).

The immunity from attack that civilians have been granted for many centuries is grounded in the idea that most civilians are innocent in that they do not substantially contribute to the war effort or take a direct part in hostilities. To adapt a phrase from Michael Walzer, they have not made themselves into dangerous men or women.[14] Insofar as a person does make a substantial contribution to the war effort, or take a direct part in hostilities, and thereby makes himself or herself dangerous to the enemy, that person is generally thought to lose that immunity. Indeed, the principle of discrimination or distinction is firmly enforced only for those civilians who are not able to defend themselves and who are innocent in either the sense of not participating in the war effort or not taking a direct part in the hostilities.

Voluntary human shields seem to have chosen to directly participate in the war effort, even though they do not wear uniforms, carry guns openly, or follow a chain of command. Indeed, by placing themselves in the line of fire, voluntary human shields move onto the battlefield and even directly to the precise point at which the effects of hostilities are anticipated. It is true that once they are on the battlefield, they are passive rather than active, but they intend to affect the war by their passivity, and passivity is often even more efficacious than those soldiers who are carrying weapons and are actively ready to fire them.

The NATO air commander during the Kosovo campaign noted that despite the best efforts of the coalition, every time civilians were killed in air strikes "the reaction by political leaders was hysterical."[15] Though they may look like civilians to the cameras of a curious media, voluntary human shields seem to come as close to being combatants as one can get, in terms of the effects of what they do, and still not wear uniforms or carry weapons openly. It would thus be inconsistent with the broader legal and moral principles to reward such intentional misconduct by requiring the attacker to ignore the changed role of the otherwise protected civilians.

Yet, it is worth at least raising the issue of whether voluntary human shields are truly acting in a voluntary manner. In recent cases, voluntary human shields seem to have been strongly influenced by the war propaganda of their States. It is, of course, still true that the overwhelming reality is that they are now dangerous—whether voluntarily or not is of secondary importance. But if the voluntary status of the act is supposed to justify disregarding their rights, then it may be worth inquiring further to see, in individual cases, to what extent a person has voluntarily chosen this role. It is theoretically possible for organized armed groups to be effectively incorporated

---

[14] MICHAEL WALZER, JUST AND UNJUST WARS 145 (1977).
[15] Lieutenant General Michael Short, *Operation Allied Force From the Perspective of the NATO Air Commander,* in LEGAL AND ETHICAL LESSONS OF NATO'S KOSOVO CAMPAIGN, 78 NAVAL WAR COL. INT'L. L. STUD. 19, 23 (Andru Wall ed., 2002).

into the organized structures of the State and operate under the effective control and authority of State agencies, but such groups would not constitute truly voluntary human shields in either the legal or moral sense.

To be a voluntary human shield, a person must intentionally seek to put herself or himself between a likely attack and a military target. This epitomizes the essence of the principle from Article 51(3) of Protocol I that civilians "shall enjoy the protection afforded" by the laws and customs of war "unless and for such time as they take a direct part in hostilities." Indeed, the temporal caveat in Protocol I that such civilians may be targeted "for such time as" they participate in hostilities seems particularly appropriate for the human shields that forsake the safety of their homes in order intentionally to endanger their safety in an effort to serve the military interests of a party to the conflict. Accordingly, in our view, those who merely happen to be present, or who choose not to leave a battle zone, are not properly thought of as voluntary human shields. Of course, refusing to leave the battle zone, intending thereby to remain in between a military target and the attacking forces, may be the equivalent of becoming a human shield. Normally, though, the voluntary human shield has done something active to become a shield, even though the very act of shielding a military target is defined by inactivity, i.e. simple presence suffices. There is a perception that people who are milling around a military target might be similar to involuntary human shields. Nevertheless, a truly valid example of involuntary human shielding must entail an intentional exploitation of these people by the State or political organization. More is discussed about this issue in the next section.

In order to see how the voluntary human shields matter significantly for traditional proportionality assessment, one must realize that as a matter of *lex lata jus in bello* proportionality, only civilian lives that are indirectly lost can be outweighed by more significant military objectives. Under the principle of distinction, the deliberate killing of civilians as a result of specific targeting cannot be justified by reference to the greater value of meeting certain military objectives of any sort. And it is at least questionable whether the deaths of voluntary human shields can be seen as collateral damage. Even though the voluntary human shields appear to place themselves in harm's way, it also appears that they are covered by traditional views about civilian immunity. Of course, the traditional legal regime was generally framed without considering the problem of voluntary human shields. In any event, the vast majority of civilians do not wish to put themselves into harm's way and thereby risk death or great harm.

So, how should proportionality assessments change if the civilian in harm's way is a voluntary human shield? One way is to think of them as people who risk their own lives for a particular military or political objective. In this sense they are not significantly different from freedom fighters or other insurgents, i.e., persons who participate in hostilities but do not enjoy combatant immunity or benefit from the full range of rights that accrue to lawful combatants. If we think of proportionality as only calculating likely casualties or harms to civilians, then the likely deaths to voluntary human shields would not be a factor. Neither the principle of discrimination nor the principle of proportionality would apply to these people if they were no longer classifiable as civilians. This part of the problem of human shields can be resolved in a relatively straightforward way, at least concerning traditional interpretations of the principles of discrimination or distinction and proportionality.

In Chapter 6, we explored a more expansive notion of proportionality that takes into account all of the human rights involved in a particular case. And we have argued that not all people in a battlefield situation forfeit their rights to life. So, in this nonstandard view of proportionality, it might seem that we must, even more so than in the traditional view of proportionality, take into account the lives of voluntary human shields. And that is indeed correct in the nontraditional view of proportionality.

Voluntary human shields should not be understood to have waived or forfeited their human right to life. Yet, we can still discount the human shields' lives because of the wrongful way, if it is demonstrably wrongful, that these individuals have acted, even as we keep the larger framework of humanitarian law intact. Hence, the attacking commander must do his best to avoid harming them, perhaps by changing the choice of weaponry or the time of attack, or by vigorous advance warning. But that does not mean that the rights of voluntary human shields trump every countervailing consideration. If the lives of combatants have inherent value, undue warnings could lead to suicide missions in which the presence of voluntary human shields enhances the enemy war effort even more. And we should take account of the wrongful way States or political organizations have potentially manipulated their civilian populations in cases of voluntary human shields. We discuss what difference the wrongful conduct makes in the Section VI of this chapter.

IV. INVOLUNTARY HUMAN SHIELDS

The case of involuntary human shields is much more difficult than the case of voluntary human shields at least in part because involuntary human shields clearly remain civilians and noncombatants. You do not lose your status as a civilian because of what someone else does to you. Involuntary human shields are civilians who have been victimized even more than civilians usually are during wartime, because they are endangered by the government that has the legal and moral duty to protect them from the effects of hostilities. Some involuntary human shields are endangered by an organization or political party within a state at war, but even in those circumstances, the government has an overarching obligation to protect civilians. Yet, though involuntary human shields may find themselves in harm's way contrary to their intentions, they are no less an impediment to the attacking forces who would never have asked for such a situation of forced choice. Indeed, the situation of involuntary human shields creates risks both for the civilians who are forced to be shields as well as for the political community that finds it necessary to attack a military target guarded by the shields and is more reluctant to do so than might be good for the community in question.

Why are these cases of involuntary human shields any different from normal collateral damage cases or cases if there are hostages that have been seized by one party in a war? We will first explain why involuntary human shields are different from but similar to these other cases before developing a response to the question of how they should be treated in terms of the principles of proportionality and distinction or discrimination. Hostage taking does not necessarily put the hostage-civilians' lives in jeopardy. In at least one common form of hostage taking, the strategy is merely to say that the civilians will not be returned until a particular demand is met. It is true that sometimes the threat is that the hostages will be killed unless the demand is met, and this brings these hostage cases closer to involuntary human shield cases. But this risk of death is not a necessary feature of hostage taking, whereas it is so in human shield cases.

Involuntary human shields who have been forced to guard military installations qualitatively shift normal collateral damage considerations by transforming an established likelihood that civilians will be killed or harmed into a near certainty. After all, the very goal of the defender is to place them in positions in which their lives would be forfeited in the midst of an otherwise appropriate use of enemy force against lawful military targets. Those who are involuntary human shields should still be afforded the status of having civilian immunity because they did not willfully forfeit that protected status. In this sense, though it may literally be true that they are "directly participating" in the conflict, their status cannot completely shift because of the implicit condition that they do what they are forced to do so. So, involuntary human shields can be analogized to conscripts with the important difference that conscripts who are forced into the armed forces of the enemy (and thus combatants) are always at liberty to regain their protected status by surrendering to the enemy, hence becoming protected persons under the Third Geneva Convention. And, in addition, conscripts are given weapons to protect themselves, unlike involuntary human shields

Even in the case of involuntary human shields, civilian immunity is never absolute during wartime. Remember that collateral damage can be justified if the anticipated military value is sufficiently significant. That is exactly what proportionality calculations have traditionally addressed. Like the collateral damage deaths of normal civilians caused by lawful attacks using lawful means of targeting, the deaths of involuntary human shields might be justifiable as well. Collateral damage seems to be different than direct targeting though. So, we need to explore what makes these cases distinguishable.

If deaths are the direct effect, and not merely the indirect effect of military action, the lives lost cannot be easily ignored as extraneous because the action was a direct targeting rather than a foreseen but unintentional consequence of the military action. And the direct targeting, as opposed to the collateral damage of civilians has been uniformly banned in international law and condemned in the Just War tradition as well. And here is the dilemma: It seems counterintuitive to allow one side to engage in wrongdoing, placing its citizens in harm's way, and yet give that party a kind of exemption from having its military targets attacked that it only receives because of its wrongdoing. The question is whether or not we can sustain the absolute ban on human shields in such cases as that of involuntary human shields, discussed in Section II, even as we preserve the unequivocal protections due to civilians caught in the midst of conflict. Before answering that question, let us look further at the often-used analogy to involuntary human shields, the case of hostage-taking.

Hostage-taking is like involuntary human shields in that people are coerced into positions in which it is clear that their lives will be jeopardized if a third-party engages in the legal activities that it contemplates pursuing. For thousands of years, there has been a prohibition on hostage taking in war or at least a strong condemnation of the abuse of hostages, for instance by putting them in harm's way. Hostages are to be treated as prisoners of war or as kidnapped members of one's own country. In both cases, there is no justification for placing them in harm's way. To place hostages in harm's way is a further harm to them compounding what was already the harm of kidnap or capture. One of the key moral considerations here is that a person has been forced to bear an unacceptable and unwanted risk. We will take up this issue of risk and related issues in the next section.

The absolute ban on the direct targeting of civilians needs to be conceptualized in combination with allowing the indirect targeting of civilians that often gets called collateral damage. This distinction assumes that there is a firm line between direct and indirect targeting. But in practice, the application of these clear concepts is murky in the context of human shields. If one knows that an action will almost certainly result in a certain consequence and one chooses to do that action, it is odd to say that one has only indirectly sought the nearly certain consequence. One cannot indirectly intend that which one knows to be nearly certain to occur as a result of taking a certain course of action. Collateral damage is about what *might* result from what we directly aim at and intentionally target. But if there is a consequence that is *almost certain* to result, that consequence is no longer merely something that might result as a side effect of our directly aim. The side effect that is nearly certain becomes part of what one's direct aim. In this sense, some of those who defend the doctrine of double effect have simply misidentified the relevant moral considerations.

The difference between direct and oblique intention was explored already by Jeremy Bentham at the end of the eighteenth century.[16] In his account, one can aim at one thing and nonetheless do another thing that one did not aim at. The aim, or the intention, is key to determining whether something is a direct or oblique intention. If it is merely a matter of intention, then to adapt an argument once used by Elizabeth Anscombe,[17] all you would need to do is to furrow your brow and clench your fists so as to indicate that you fervently do not intend to do something in order to make it only an indirect effect of your action. Though there may be a difference in meaning between direct and oblique intent, the difference is generally not as important as has sometimes been thought in the Just War tradition and international law. Obviously, more needs to be said to make this fully defensible, but this is beyond the scope of the current work.

The killing of involuntary human shields cannot be treated merely as acceptable collateral damage in all circumstances. The US Joint Targeting Manual adopts this approach by recognizing that while an enemy cannot lawfully

> use civilians as human shields in an attempt to protect, conceal, or render military objects immune from military operations or force them to leave their homes or shelters to disrupt the movement of an adversary.

The principle of proportionality nevertheless remains fully applicable in its conventional application (i.e., permitting attacks unless the collateral damage is clearly excessive in relation to the concrete and direct overall military advantage anticipated). There may be some sense in which it is indirect rather than direct targeting. But since the killing is an integral part of the destroying of the military target that is surrounded, it is too much a part of the direct intention for it to be seen as completely collateral to the destroying of the military target.

Hence, it may appear that in cases of involuntary human shields, the principle of discrimination or distinction is primarily implicated rather the principle of

---

[16] *See* JEREMY BENTHAM, INTRODUCTION TO THE PRINCIPLES OF LAW AND MORALS (J.H. Burns and H.L.A. Hart, eds. 1996).

[17] *See* Elizabeth Anscombe, *War and Murder, reprinted in* THE MORALITY OF WAR, (Larry May, Erik Rovie, and Steve Viner, eds. 2006).

proportionality. This is particularly true from the standpoint of public perceptions and political will. A number of adjustments must be made in applying the principles of discrimination or distinction if adhering to civilian immunity creates severe risks for loss of life or harm for other civilians. And one type of adjustment is to allow proportionality into the discussion of the application of the principle of discrimination or distinction. As we will next see, the key factor is the risks to civilians, both those targeted and those on the side of the attackers.

V. RISK AND CONCERN ABOUT CIVILIANS

There is a major type of risk that is relevant to human shield cases. The party who is planning the attack on a military target now faces the prospect of not being able to do so because of a concern for the human shields. In Afghanistan and Iraq, insurgents commonly seek to sway public opinion by forcing civilians to remain in danger so that the inevitable civilian casualties can, in effect, become another "weapon of war." Israel has repeatedly voiced this concern about the tactics of Hamas in Gaza, especially as they have increasingly set up military installations in the heart of very crowded cities. During Operation Cast Lead, there were accounts of children used as human shields by Hamas fighters,[18] weapons caches in mosques and houses, and improvised explosive devices used by Hamas in urban areas.[19]

Israel claims that it would not be able properly to defend its own civilians, who are subject to rocket attacks from Gaza, if it granted involuntary human shields and unknowing human shields the full civilian immunity normally required under international law and Just War theory.[20] The risk to its own civilians by not targeting artillery installations, even knowing that enemy civilians will surely be killed by such attacks, is said to be the key consideration that should allow for an adjustment in the way the principles of proportionality and discrimination or distinction are applied.

Hamas, which claims to be at war with Israel, has said that it was forced to launch rockets from populated areas because Israel has closed the borders of Gaza and yet the population continues to grow, and because Hamas lacks the resources to mount a more conventional attack on Israel. This is offered not so much as an excuse for launching rockets at Israeli civilians as a reason for some to believe that Hamas is not

---

[18] *See* Hamas Exploitation of Civilians as Human Shields, Israeli Ministry of Foreign Affairs, *available at* http://www.youtube.com/watch?v=70Oqo_wmuGo; Hamas Human Shields Confession, *available at* http://www.youtube.com/watch?v=gowJXf2nt4Y.

[19] Lawrence Wright, *Letter From Gaza: CAPTIVES—What really happened during the Israeli attacks*, THE NEW YORKER 47 (Nov. 9, 2009).

[20] For a defense of the Israeli position see Ammon Rubinstein and Yaniv Roznai, *Human Shields in Modern Armed Conflicts: the Need for Proportionate Proportionality*, 93 Stanford L. and Pol. Rev. 94 (2011).

engaging in wrongdoing by putting its citizens in harm's way. Hamas is in effect making the argument that the adjustment in how proportionality is calculated needs to be in its favor because of the nature of the conflict. The asymmetrical nature of the war is the key factor, according to that logic, rather than the protected nature of civilians and the duties thereby imposed on the combatants.[21]

Involuntary human shields and unknowing shields are especially likely to occur during asymmetrical war, as has seemingly been true of the use of poisons over the centuries, even though such weapons are banned. The weaker side of a war or armed conflict, especially an insurgency, will seek to blunt the stronger party's superiority in weaponry by inexpensive means. Poisons, as Grotius pointed out almost four hundred years ago,[22] are very inexpensive, and can be used by insurgent groups against much better armed defenders of the princes of the world. It may be that asymmetric warfare spawns arguments about the expediency of means that evade legal or moral barriers. Today, we see an increasing use of involuntary and unknowing human shields among insurgent groups that lack the sophisticated weapons of the defenders of the State's sovereign. In our view, we should be unsurprised by such strategies in light of the severe imbalances in resources between two sides to a war. But this is not the most important factor in many cases; instead, it is merely a factor that should not be overlooked.

The main problem, legally and morally, is that civilians are being used by States or political organizations in a way that greatly increases the risk of death and major harms for these civilians. And the rules of war, in both international law and Just War theory, are focused on the diminishment of suffering by civilians, and hence on the decrease in the risk of death or serious harm to civilians. The use of involuntary human shields of all kinds is a prima facie violation of civilian immunity that should cause us to reassess how proportionality is often grounded. But it should also make us wonder whether the traditional rules of war can be sustained in the face of asymmetric warfare. In our view, Hamas has a point in this respect, but so does Israel. Both sides involved in an asymmetric war face difficulties that strain the traditional rules of war. Yet, in the end, though some changes are needed, they are not as major as many have concluded.

Let us discuss whether there is a significant difference between involuntary human shield cases and what some have called "unknowing human shield cases" in which a civilian population has been put at risk but is unaware that the population is now in harm's way. In general, it is a mistake to think that there is no salient difference

---

[21] *See* Michael Gross, MORAL DILEMMAS OF MODERN WAR: TORTURE, ASSASSINATION, AND BLACKMAIL IN AN AGE OF ASYMMETRIC CONFLICT, ch. 7 (2010).

[22] Hugo Grotius, *De Jure Belli Ac Pacis* (On the Law of War and Peace) (1625), translated by Francis W. Kelsey, Oxford: Clarendon Press, 1925, p. 652.

between firing artillery from densely populated areas, where civilians are unknowingly put in harm's way, and involuntary human shield cases. These cases are somewhat similar in their effects on enemy military forces in that enemy military leaders become much more unwilling to launch the attacks they had planned out of concern for civilian casualties. But the case of unknowing risk to civilians is much more common and more difficult than one might first think.

It is not unknown for leaders to risk their own civilians' lives for securing a military advantage, even in cases that would not normally be seen as asymmetric wars. The principle of discrimination or distinction has rarely been invoked in such cases because the civilians put in harm's way were one's own, not those of the enemy. Consider two examples drawn from World War II: Churchill did not warn his citizens of Nazi planes approaching Coventry. Some conspiracy theorists postulate that Roosevelt failed to warn American civilian and military forces at Pearl Harbor of the impending Japanese attacks. These were not cases of unknowing human shields used to protect specific targets, but are better characterized as the sacrifice of civilian lives by their own rulers so as to seek military advantage.

In the case of the British, it is alleged that Winston Churchill did not warn the citizens of Coventry of an imminent Nazi attack because he wanted to provide evidence of Hitler's barbaric acts.[23] The purported military advantages might have been articulated as the need to preserve the secrecy of the Enigma program that permitted the Allies to decode German radio traffic. In the conspiratorial theory, Roosevelt's actions may have stemmed from a need to garner popular support for a foreseeably difficult war. The term *targeting*, normally at the center of these disputes, does not really apply. In any event, to be intellectually consistent, we might well apply the same proportionality formulation to the duty of the government toward its own citizens as to the duty to warn "when circumstances permit."

We need a different principle than the traditional principle of discrimination or distinction for situations in which a State or political organization puts its own civilians at risk. Indeed, the key consideration is that this is a case of assumed risk. In order to see what this category concerns and why it is important, we can turn back to the case of voluntary human shields. We have argued in an earlier chapter that we should not countenance the idea that people can generally forfeit their human rights. The possibility of abuse is too great to allow this theoretical framing of the issues. But the act of a person voluntarily placing his or her life at risk is most certainly relevant in how we assess things. The voluntary assumption of risk shifts the majority of the responsibility for the harm or death of the voluntary human shields to themselves.

---

[23] *See* Christopher Hutchens, *The Medals of his Defeats*, ATLANTIC MONTHLY, April 2002.

If we shift some of the responsibility onto the civilians if there is a voluntary assumption of risk in cases of voluntary human shields, we should similarly shift some of the responsibility onto the States or political organizations if they force their citizens to be involuntary human shields. Not only is the political organization forcing its citizens to be involuntary human shields, but its actions force unwanted choices upon their enemies as well. Such considerations should call for adjustments in the way these States or political organizations are regarded both legally and morally. In the next section, we provide more argumentation for the view that responsibility has shifted significantly in human shield cases, as well as indicate how the principles of proportionality and discrimination or distinction should be adjusted in cases of human shields.

VI. ADJUSTING THE RULES OF WAR SO AS NOT TO FAVOR OPPRESSORS

Vattel provides us with an important insight in trying to decide how to evaluate the use of human shields especially during asymmetric war. He contends that adjustments must be made so that we do not favor oppressors.[24] The reason is that if we have to disfavor someone, it should be those who have already done wrong. An extension of the Vattelian principle would say that adjustments need to be made in the application of the principles of proportionality and discrimination or distinction so that wrongdoers and those who assume risks for themselves are not unduly favored either. In psychological terms, if an enemy attacks a military target, even though human shields have been forced to remain in the face of warnings, an attack would be seen as a form of positive punishment designed to end the unwanted behavior. The humanitarian concerns of innocent civilians ought to be equally shared by all parties to the conflict at all times.

The Vattelian principle and its extension are supported by the general principle that has governed theorizing about law since at least the Ancient Greeks, namely that no one should be allowed to profit from his or her own wrongdoing.[25] In technical, but often overlooked terms, this principle is reflected in Article 49(1) of Protocol I, by which the term *attacks* is defined as "acts of violence against the adversary, whether in offence or in defense." The legal and moral duties are uniformly applicable, and thus should be respected equally by both parties to the conflict. Vattel's

---

[24] EMER DE VATTEL, *LE DROIT DES GENS, OU PRINCIPES DE LA LOI NATURELLE*, APPLIQUÉ À LA CONDUITE ET AUX AFFAIRES DES NATIONS ET DES SOUVERAINS (THE LAW OF NATIONS, OR PRINCIPLES OF THE LAW OF NATURE, APPLIED TO THE CONDUCT AND AFFAIRS OF NATIONS AND SOVEREIGNS), Bk. IV, Ch. IV, §37, 357 (1758) (translated by Charles G. Fenwick, trans. 1916).
[25] *See* LARRY MAY, AFTER WAR ENDS, ch. 3 (2012).

principle is strengthened if one adds that the person or organization is profiting because the wrongdoing in question involved coercion through forced choice. There is a double sense of wrongdoing that should not be countenanced by the laws and customs of war. In this final section, we set out more of the argument for this view and then indicate how those rules should be adjusted or refined.

As we indicated earlier, the laws and customs of war aim at diminishing the likelihood that civilians and soldiers will suffer during war or armed conflict. Hence if the application of these rules results in greater risk of suffering by civilians and soldiers, something has gone awry and the rules need to be adjusted. The principle of discrimination or distinction is supposed to reduce greatly the suffering of civilians by prohibiting that they be targeted during battle. The principle of proportionality is supposed to minimize the suffering of combatants by restricting the use of armed force to that which does not cause superfluous or unnecessary suffering.

For both civilians and soldiers, the application of these norms to the use of human shields undermines the aim of reducing suffering. The forced choice aspect of human shields means that there will be greater loss of life as a result of the planned military strike and the attendant harm to the human shields surrounding the military target. And if the attack does not take place then presumably the civilians where the attack was to be launched are made more insecure than if the attack had occurred as they continue to live in fear and unable resume normal civilian activities. And in the case of involuntary human shields, they remain essentially in captivity so long as the conflict continues or the military object to be protected remains sufficiently important to the defender.

In any case, we are assuming that the commander will abide by the obligation to take all feasible measures for avoiding civilian casualties and the duty to deliver an "effective advance warning…of attacks which may affect the civilian population, unless circumstances do not permit."[26] As far as soldiers go, there is the strong possibility that more suffering will occur there too because the forced choice occasioned by the use of human shields means that the normal calculations that put priority on civilians over soldiers will be skewed because of the increased likelihood of the two kinds of civilian casualties just mentioned.

One refinement or adjustment in the rules or laws of war that would seem to make sense, given the analysis provided so far, would be to lift the civilian immunity for any civilians who are in the act of serving as voluntary human shields. Just as they chose to participate directly in the hostilities by seeking a military advantage for the benefit of one party to the hostilities, they have perfect freedom to reclaim the protections that accrue to innocent civilians who remain neutral in the sense that they

---

[26] Protocol I, Art. 57(2)(c).

do not strive to directly gain military advantage for either party to the conflict. In that sense, civilians are innocent and fully protected from the deliberate conduct of *both* parties as we have observed. The main rationale is that voluntary human shields are now operating much more like combatants than standard innocent civilians. In addition, they have assumed the risk by their voluntary actions. Continuing to provide voluntary human shields with civilian immunity seems to be not in keeping with their own behavior, which has changed their status, at least in the eyes of these civilians themselves.

It seems appropriate to regulate human shields under the law in the manner they conceive of their own role in the hostilities. In fact, just as combatants can regain legal protections from being targeted by relinquishing their combatant status, so too voluntary human shields can regain their protected status by returning to their homes and avoiding known military objectives. Again, insofar as this behavior is itself wrongful, the laws and customs of war should not allow for these people to profit from their own wrongdoing.

We are aware that the ICRC definition and its subsequent Interpretive Guidance stopped short of declaring that voluntary human shields are actually functioning as direct participants in the hostilities and thus forfeit their wholly protected status. It is also true that some of the military experts who participated in the Interpretive Guidance, and others with operational experience, strongly disagreed with that conclusion and lengthy deliberations failed to achieve consensus on this point. Nevertheless, suspending the immunity of voluntary human shields "for such time" as they are protecting military objectives with their bodies would comport with Article 51(3) in our view. And this adjustment would hopefully deter such behavior in the future, thereby actually serving to preserve human rights and dignity in the long term. It would also have the virtue of providing clarity to all members of a multinational coalition when unanimity is required for specific targeting decisions, as it was during the Kosovo air campaign.

A second refinement or adjustment in the rules or laws of war is to allow calculations of proportionality in terms of collateral damage to be made even if the targeting of human shields might best be seen as direct targeting rather than indirect or oblique targeting. If the actions of the political organization or its citizens intentionally blur the border between direct and indirect effects sought by the adversary, then the laws and customs of war should be adjusted to reflect the imposition of the forced choice scenario on these adversaries. In other words, adversaries who are facing human shields should be permitted to respond in a measured and proportionate way, rather than feeling that they are prohibited from responding at all to the threat to their own population posed by the military target. After all, the point of humanitarian law is to immunize civilians from the effects of hostilities so far as possible, and an adversary should not benefit from deliberately distorting that goal through the use of human shields.

In any event, the foreseeability of civilian deaths if human shields are employed cannot be the only dispositive factor unless one is willing to rewrite the law of war by conflating the principles of distinction and proportionality. Discrimination or distinction is legally separate from proportionality, and neither subsumes the other. The grave breach provisions of Protocol I specifically preserve these dual lines of liability.[27] Article 85(3)(a) makes it a war crime to intentionally attack civilians. The leading commentary on the Additional Protocols concludes that the commander may be charged with a grave breach when the evidence indicates "directing an attack against the protected persons 'as such.'"[28] According to the Commentary on the Two 1977 Protocols Additional to the Geneva Conventions of 1949 (Commentary), attacks against lawful military targets with secondary effects on civilians are dealt with by subparagraphs (b) and (c) of Article 85, even if those secondary effects are foreseeable.[29] And as we noted earlier, it is significant that the criminal prohibition found in the grave breach provisions requires that the death or serious bodily injury to civilians "be committed willfully."

As the authoritative Commentary notes, "A high degree of precaution is required. A grave breach on the other hand presupposes more: the knowledge (not only the presumption) that such attack *will cause* excessive losses in kind."[30] This standard makes sense in light of all that we know of proportionality, which is crafted precisely to address attacks if there is "recognition that collateral civilian casualties or damage to civilian objects may be expected."[31] A disproportionate attack by definition involves collateral damage that is envisioned by the commander before the attack is launched. A lawful (i.e., proportionate) strike involves precisely the same *ex ante* decision with differing valuation of the military advantage anticipated.

The critical point with respect to human shields is that even if the killing of civilians is foreseeable, the very act of considering the number of deaths that will be proportionate or disproportionate does not necessarily violate the principle of distinction. Intentionally directing a prohibited attack against civilians means far more than being able to predict, even with some near certitude, the likely deaths of civilians. On the other hand, creating a new legal standard by which no military action

---

[27] *See* Michael Bothe, Karl Josef Partsch, & Waldemar A. Solf (eds), NEW RULES FOR VICTIMS OF ARMED CONFLICTS: COMMENTARY ON THE TWO 1977 PROTOCOLS ADDITIONAL TO THE GENEVA CONVENTIONS OF 1949 511–522 (1982).

[28] *Id., citing* Article 51(2).

[29] *Id.*

[30] *Id.*

[31] *Id.*, at 366.

may be undertaken unless there is a "near certainty that no civilians will be killed or injured" would corrode the very foundations of laws of war. Violating the principle of distinction requires the willful targeting of protected persons. The proportionality principle provides a different standard than one that focuses only on foreseeable civilian deaths. Conflating these principles by presuming criminality in every instance of foreseeable collateral damage (by virtue of anticipating some predictable degree of damage to civilian lives and/or property) would elevate the principle of distinction over the proper proportionality analysis. This would rewrite *jus in bello* and make proportionality into a rule of desuetude, or complete obsolescence.

A third refinement or adjustment in the rules or laws of war is to employ the rule of Article 8(2)(b)(xxiii) of the ICC Statute and begin holding State leaders criminally responsible for coercing their citizens into being involuntary human shields or offering undue influence to get their citizens to become voluntary human shields. In our view, one of the most useful innovations in this area would be a shared commitment to punishing leaders for the use of human shields in domestic forums along with firm commitments between States to assist such investigations and prosecutions. Such a change in practice, if not in law, would also hopefully act to deter States and other political organizations from coercing their own civilians into such risky and dangerous behavior as is manifest if these civilians become involuntary human shields.

A fourth adjustment or refinement in the rules or laws of war is to allow for the calculation of harm or death to one's own soldiers to count in proportionality assessments in human shield cases, shifting from the principle of discrimination or distinction in such cases to that of proportionality. This would effectively enhance the anticipated military advantage anticipated of a particular strike, and thereby countenance a higher number of permissible human shields to be killed or injured. Note that this is distinct from an automatic erosion of the human rights of involuntary human shields.

In Chapter 6, we discussed the limited application of a human rights based approach to the principle of proportionality that takes seriously the lives of soldiers as well as those of civilians. In the case of human shields that are intentional acts of either civilians or their political organizations, we should not allow for soldiers on the other side to be put at greater risk due to the forced choice foisted on the leaders of these soldiers. And this is especially true if the civilians treat themselves as voluntary participants in the conflict by serving as human shields. One side to a war should not be allowed to make war more risky for the soldiers on the other side by how they treat their own civilians as instruments of war. A limited human rights approach, developed earlier, will help to ground such a change.

Finally, we do not favor major adjustments in the rules or laws of war for so-called cases of "unknowing" human shields, who are not really human shields at all. It should, as it already can, be a war crime for political organizations to intentionally not warn their citizenry, thereby greatly increasing the likelihood of casualties that could be avoided. If not, then some adjustment should be made to clarify that this behavior is indeed a war crime that can be sanctioned in a variety of ways by the international community.

The use of human shields is routinely condemned in international law and the Just War tradition. We have given reasons to continue this way of responding, in most cases, to the use of human shields. But we wish to end by again highlighting the problem of asymmetry that is particularly relevant in the modern era. If one side of an asymmetric war lacks resources to match weaponry with its adversary, and that side also is hemmed in so that it cannot wage effective war without risking civilian casualties, determining what is disproportionate calls for a nuanced approach.

We do not mean to suggest that the requirement to warn these civilians is diminished; indeed, we think it is heightened. But if the already artificial conditions of war or armed conflict are exacerbated by the poverty of one side *vis-à-vis* the other, the impoverished and constrained party should not be penalized to the point that it is effectively rendered legally and morally powerless to defend itself by the rules or laws of war. These rules and laws should not take sides in this way. In this respect, we follow Vattel but also Grotius, surely the greatest thinker to have written on the dual aspects of these problems, both moral and legal, that we have addressed.

10

TARGETED KILLINGS AND PROPORTIONALITY IN

LAW: TWO MODELS

THE INCREASING USE of drones for targeted killing of high-profile leaders in the war on terrorism has highlighted several serious problems in international law and Just War theory concerning proportionality. Targeted killings seem to float between the two legal models for thinking of justified killing, a domestic law enforcement[1] model and an international humanitarian law (IHL) model. Targeted killings seem to follow the IHL model insofar as they are often perpetrated against the leaders of terrorist groups who are fighting against the State that targets them. But targeted killings also seem to follow the domestic law enforcement model insofar as they are perpetrated against individuals because of what they are alleged to have done rather than merely who they are. Since proportionality is understood differently in domestic law enforcement versus IHL models, it is not clear how to approach targeted killing. In this chapter, we explore various problems that arise because of the mixing of models that occurs in this domain and propose some tentative solutions to these problems.

At the outset of this chapter, we note that there is no prohibition in the laws and customs of warfare against the intentional targeting of individuals, provided that the means to conduct such lethal operations are lawful and the interconnected considerations of the legal and moral norms are met. Indeed, if one takes the human rights view with respect to the rights of combatants seriously, it might

---

[1] Throughout, we use the Anglo-American criminal justice system as our model of how to understand the domestic law enforcement framework, although much of what we say is found in other domestic criminal justice frameworks as well.

well be best to target individuals rather than massed units of the enemy. However, in the absence of declared warfare between States, drone strikes are the nexus for a complex interrelationship of law, morality, strategy, evolving technology, and international consensus.

We will explore three problems. First, how can targeted killings, understood on the law enforcement model, be conducted without violating due process concerns? If the targeting is based on the conduct or behavior of the person targeted, then it seems that a judicial determination of the facts is required. And in any event, the killing, rather than the arrest, of the person targeted would rarely be justified on a law enforcement model. Second, under the IHL model are targeted killings no different from other battlefield killings in war or armed conflict? Here, one of the salient issues is to satisfy proportionality that seems to require that the least lethal means be used consistent with military necessity. Third, under what conditions, if any, would targeted killings be subject to international criminal prosecution? If targeted killings fail to be proportionate, are those who carry out targeted killings liable to prosecution under the Rome Statute of the International Criminal Court (ICC) articulation of the war crime of disproportionate killing?

We will draw heavily on a distinction between status, on the one hand, and conduct or behavior, on the other hand, to help understand when the domestic law enforcement versus the IHL frameworks apply. Throughout, we argue that a nuanced approach is required if those who are targeted because of their status can be killed without major due process worries. But if the person targeted is picked out because of what he or she allegedly did, then due process concerns should be a dominant consideration. In addition, the possibility of criminal prosecution, either in the ICC or the courts of some other domestic State, under the rubric of the IHL, may raise especially difficult problems because a conviction requires a finding that the killing was clearly disproportionate. We make one important suggestion for addressing these tensions in the final section of this chapter.

In Section I of this chapter, we explain some of the reasons why targeted killing, especially by drones, is so controversial. In Section II, we highlight the debate about how combatant status is understood in IHL. In Section III, we explore the debate about the expanded Protocol I definition of who is a combatant in IHL. In Section IV, we explore the other dominant model, the law enforcement model that focuses on behavior or conduct. In Section V, we explain why the due process restraints of the law enforcement model are so important for proportionality assessments and not to be disregarded except in extreme cases. In Section VI, we discuss how self-defense figures in the debate about targeted killings. In Section VII, we discuss possible prosecutions for targeted killing in the ICC, before then drawing some general conclusions.

I. THE DRONE STRIKES CONTROVERSY

The United States takes the view that it is engaged in an armed conflict "not of an international character" with Al Qa'ida (to use the accepted phraseology of Common Article 3 of the Geneva Conventions). This threshold is legally signifi-cant insofar as it established the relevance of *jus in bello* as the applicable regime in certain limited circumstances. The International Criminal Tribunal for the former Yugoslavia (ICTY) described such an armed conflict as "protracted armed violence between government authorities and organized armed groups or between such groups within a State."[2] International law is absolutely clear that the default rules of law enforcement can be displaced under certain circumstances, as we shall see. But in our view, the *lex specialis* law of armed conflict means what its title says. *Lex specialis* is applicable only in the context of an armed conflict. Thus, the burden of proof for establishing the utility of *jus in bello* lies with the state advocating what is essentially the abnormal body of law rather than the default structures of human rights and its accompanying law enforcement domain.

Derived from the authority of the laws and customs of war, the use of drones dramatically escalated during the Obama presidency, beginning in 2009. The inter-active website, Out of Sight, Out of Mind, allows users to roll over graphics describ-ing every documented drone strike since July 17, 2004, along with data for the 3,207 alleged deaths, of which only an estimated 2 percent were high-value targets.[3] These percentages might well be much higher if the basis for categorizations were explained to the public. In any event, it is almost certainly the case that the category of *high-value target* is not coextensive with the much larger group of targets based either on their voluntary efforts to shield high-value targets or on some other uncon-troversial basis for the assertion that they were directly participating in hostilities. Despite the uncertainty over who is actually targeted under what precise circum-stances, a March 2013 Gallup poll revealed that some 65 percent of the American

---

[2] Prosecutor v. Tadic, Case No. IT-03-66-T, Decision on the Defense Motion for an Interlocutory Appeal on Jurisdiction, ¶ 70 (Int'l Trib. For the Former Yugoslavia Oct. 2, 1995). *See also* Hamdan v. Rumsfeld, 548 U.S. 557, 662–631 (2006).

[3] *See* http://drones.pitchinteractive.com/. At the time of this writing, apart from the 47 high-value fatalities (1.5 percent), the interactive website documents 2,348 unexplained casualties (75.6 percent of the total), 535 civilians (17.2 percent), and 175 children (5.6 percent). It is unclear how our analysis of the human shields problem we discussed in Chapter 9 might affect these totals. *See also* INTERNATIONAL HUMAN RIGHTS AND CONFLICT RESOLUTION CLINIC AT STANFORD LAW SCHOOL AND GLOBAL JUSTICE CLINIC AT NYU SCHOOL OF LAW, LIVING UNDER DRONES: DEATH, INJURY, AND TRAUMA TO CIVILIANS FROM US. DRONE PRACTICES IN PAKISTAN (September 2012), *available at* http://www.livingunderdrones.org.

people support the use of drones for targeted killings of suspected terrorists pro-vided that they are directed against suspects outside the United States.[4]

One thing is clear from the public record, and highly problematic in our view. Targeted killings seem to float between the two legal models for thinking of justified killing, a domestic law enforcement model and an IHL model. Recently, many peo-ple, including us, have been troubled by the accounts of the Obama Administration's efforts to repair the perception of American terrorism policy by shifting attention away from Guantanamo Bay and dramatically increasing drone strikes.[5] Drone strikes must be evaluated on the independent merits of each and every target when applying the best available information and stringent standards of proof.

The current rationale for the use of drones for targeted killing largely centers on self-defense against known threats framed in the context of a larger global struggle against organized non-State enemies. The Obama Administration white paper on drone policy adopts a hybrid approach by asserting that

> the President has authority to respond to the imminent threat posed by al-Qa'ida, and its associated forces, arising from his constitutional responsibil-ity to protect the country, the inherent right of the United States to national self-defense under international law, Congress' authorization of the use of all necessary and appropriate military force against this enemy, and the existence of an armed conflict with al-Qa'ida under international law.[6]

As we have noted, an armed conflict between the US and a non-State actor is at best an "armed conflict not of an international character." This leaves the adminis-tration in a somewhat uncomfortable position because there is scant support for a broad-based displacement of all human rights norms if there is a transnational war against a non-State organized terrorist group. The US administration is left to piece

---

[4] http://www.gallup.com/poll/161474/support-drone-attacks-terrorists-abroad.aspx/.

[5] Adam Entous, *Special Report: How the White House Learned to Love the Drone*, REUTERS, May 18, 2010 ("Besides putting an end to harsh interrogation methods, the president issued executive orders to ban secret Central Intelligence Agency (CIA) detention centers and close the Guantanamo Bay prison camp. Some cur-rent and former counterterrorism officials say an unintended consequence of these decisions may be that cap-turing wanted militants has become a less viable option. As one official said: 'There is nowhere to put them.' "); *See also* DANIEL KLAIDMAN, KILL OR CAPTURE: THE WAR ON TERROR AND THE SOUL OF THE OBAMA PRESIDENCY 126–127 (2012)("The inability to detain terror suspects was creating perverse incentives that favored killing or releasing suspected terrorists over capturing them. 'We never talked about this openly, but it was always a back-of-the-mind thing for us,' recalled one of Obama's top counterterrorism advisers. 'Anyone who says it wasn't is not being straight.' ").

[6] US Department of Justice, White Paper: Lawfulness of a Lethal Operation Directed Against a U.S. Citizen Who Is a Senior Operational Leader of Al-Qa'ida or An Associated Force, *available at* http://msnbcmedia. msn.com/i/msnbc/sections/news/020413_DOJ_White_Paper.pdf.

together a hodgepodge of legal rationales derived from established international law rationales but applied in a new, evolved post-9/11 environment. The Obama Administration white paper restates the widely accepted view, drawn from the law of countermeasures, that "targeting a member of an enemy force who poses an imminent threat of violent attack to the United States is not unlawful. It is a lawful act of self-defense."[7]

Nonetheless, the white paper seems to stretch the bounds of imminence into highly controversial imprecision by clarifying that

> [t]he condition that an operational leader presents an "imminent" threat of violent attack against the United States does not require the United States to have clear evidence that a specific attack on U.S. persons or interests will take place in the immediate future.[8]

For our purposes, the obvious challenge is that the proportionality analysis requires differing articulations with shifting substantive support as the overall rationale moves between the law of countermeasures, the ordinary *jus in bello* usage, or an extension of US constitutional prerogatives based on preemptive self-defense.

Seeking to justify the dramatic expansion of the concept of imminence, John Brennan defended the current approach on the grounds that:

> In practice, the U.S. approach to targeting in the conflict with al-Qa'ida is far more aligned with our allies' approach than many may assume. This Administration's counterterrorism efforts outside of Afghanistan and Iraq are focused on those individuals who are a threat to the United States, whose removal would cause a significant—even if only temporary—disruption of the plans and capabilities of al-Qa'ida and its associated forces. Practically speaking, then, the question turns principally on how you define "imminence."[9]

At its core, the targeted killings policy seems to vacillate between the IHL model discussed above and the domestic law enforcement law model, insofar as they are perpetrated against individuals because of what they are alleged to have done rather than merely who they are.

---

[7] *Id.*

[8] *Id.*, at 7.

[9] John O. Brennan, Ass't to the President for Homeland Security and Counterterrorism, Strengthening Our Security by Adhering to Our Values and Laws, Address at Harvard Law School (Sept. 16, 2011).

Since proportionality is understood differently in domestic law enforcement versus IHL models, the glibness with which the distinctions are glossed over makes it difficult precisely to evaluate the Obama Administration's approach to authorizing and conducting targeted killing. To be clear, the domestic law enforcement model of proportionality largely mirrors that drawn from the international law of self-defense against imminent threats. However, a blanket assertion of uncontested executive authority to direct lethal strikes against anyone in the world deemed to be hostile to the US, and who possesses some loose nexus to the armed conflict against al-Qa'ida, comes perilously close to an assertion that targeted killings are conducted at the convenience of the president in pursuit of undefined national interests and applying uncertain legal standards. In other words, self-defense is a sovereign right of the US and a solemn duty of the president, but it is not a black hole that swallows all intellectually consistent applications of existing international law and morality.

The Obama Administration white paper, on the grounds of pragmatism, muddles these considerations by finding that

> The United States would be able to use lethal force against a U.S. citizen, who it located outside the United States and is an operational leader continually planning attacks against U.S. persons and interests, in at least the following circumstances: (1) where an informed, high level official of the U.S. government has determined that the targeted individual poses an imminent threat of violent attack against the United States; (2) where a capture would be infeasible—and where those conducting the operation continue to monitor whether capture becomes feasible; and (3) where such an operation would be conducted consistent with applicable law of war principles. In these circumstances, the "realities" of the conflict and the weight of the government's interest in protecting its citizens from an imminent attack are such that the Constitution would not require the government to provide further process to such a U.S. citizen before using lethal force.

We accept that the last clause referring to "applicable law of war principles" is intended to incorporate the familiar principles of distinction, feasible precautions, the definitions of military objectives, and of course proportionality. The problem for us is that although each part of this policy statement might be sufficient to withstand critical analysis, it becomes a morass of muddled rationale. Is the correct test of proportionality to be drawn from the authority based on defensive countermeasures to prevent an imminent threat? In that event, do policymakers accept that the lawful scope of force would extend only to the immediate harm the drone strike aimed to ameliorate?

Is the proportionality principle to be extrapolated from the law enforcement context, which might be logical, given the reference to the duty to arrest such a terrorist if "feasible." In that event, the burden of proof would shift to the commander to demonstrate the absolute necessity of the strike and the use of the least possible measure of force. Or, is the law of proportionality to be drawn from the larger context of *jus in bello*, such that the lethal force need not be the very last resort, and need not be limited by the immediate threat posed by the particular terrorist. Under the *jus in bello*, the permissible proportionate damage would be based not on the nature of the imminent attack, but on the larger military advantage to be gained from the death of one who "is an operational leader continually planning attacks against U.S. persons and interests." This formula itself contains the seeds of controversy and confusion because the terrorist leader could be targeted both on the basis of status and conduct, thus obscuring the true test for proportionality. And to recall the articulation of proportionality in the Rome Statute, how much of the larger strategic context is relevant when evaluating the "overall" military advantage anticipated through the death of a particular member of a transnational terrorist organization?

What some have called the imperial presidency in the United States has exacerbated the problem of the use of drones. Presidents in the last 40 years have felt increasingly unrestrained by congressional or judicial oversight in matters of armed conflict. At a minimum, we ought to expect the executive branch to operate a process-based, information-driven interagency approach that produces a consensus justification for each and every strike.[10] Oversight by an impartial and independent judicial process might be the most desirable way to determine whether a particular strike actually was disproportionate under the relevant legal standard. However, the Article III courts have commonly avoided constitutional collision between the coequal branches of the federal power by invoking the political question doctrine in the context of drone strikes.

In one of the most pointed invocations of the power of the commander-in-chief, President Clinton authorized the bombing of targets in Sudan, Iraq, and Afghanistan in response to terrorist actions against US interests.[11] In reviewing Clinton's actions, the Court of Appeals in the DC Circuit reiterated in an *en banc* decision rendered in June 2010, that "[u]nder the political question doctrine, the foreign target of a military strike cannot challenge in court the wisdom of retaliatory military action taken by the United States."[12] Yet, this decision did not muffle

[10] Michael A. Newton, *Inadvertent Implications of the War Powers Resolution*, 45 CASE WES. RES. J. INT'L L. 173, 188–193 (2012).

[11] Michele L. Malvesti, *Bombing bin Laden: Assessing the Effectiveness of Air Strikes as a Counter-Terrorism Strategy*, FLETCHER F. WORLD AFF., Winter-Spring 2002, at 18–19.

[12] El-Shifa Pharm. Indus. Co. v. United States, 607 F.3d 836, 851 (D.C. Cir. 2010) (en banc).

the growing number of voices who object to the use of drones for targeted killing. Indeed, our chapter merely reflects a current, and growing, drumbeat of worry about the US use of drones.

II. STATUS AND CONDUCT: INTERNATIONAL HUMANITARIAN LAW AND DOMESTIC LAW ENFORCEMENT

A distinction has been drawn between " 'personality' strikes aimed at named, high value terrorists" and " 'signature" strikes that targeted training camps and suspicious compounds in areas controlled by militants."[13] When strikes are aimed at named individuals, we can also distinguish two variations. The named target may be identified on the basis of his or her role in a particular organization, such as Al Qa'ida, or on the basis of his or her alleged behavior, such as being responsible for setting off a bomb on the USS Cole or some other US warship. Some strikes might be justified as a hybrid model that identifies the target in terms of both behavior and status. In this section, we provide a normative argument for thinking that there is a significant difference between targeting based on status, such as group membership, rather than conduct or behavior, i.e., on what one allegedly has done.

One of the first questions that arises when thinking about warfare is why soldiers or combatants are treated differently than the ways we would treat persons in contexts other than war. One of the historical reasons is that the soldier was seen as merely an extension of the sovereign State, not as a person who acted on the basis of his or her personal decisions. As the old expression had it, soldiers were mere "cannon fodder," insofar as they were to be treated as people who would kill in order to protect their States, and they were people who could be killed or wounded by their State's enemies. Michael Walzer summarized the long tradition of thinking in the Just War tradition by saying that wars were not the responsibility of soldiers. Rather, States were responsible for war and soldiers were only responsible for obeying the orders of their states to fight in those wars.[14]

This is important because, in the traditional view, targeting large bodies of combatants with no possibility of civilian damage or death simply does not implicate *jus in bello* proportionality concerns. The accepted subordination of individual rights to those of the State reflects the entrenched dichotomy between the *jus ad bellum* and *jus in bello*, by which every actor in conflict remains a moral agent accountable to his or her State, irrespective of whether the overall conflict is just or unlawful.

---

[13] J. Becker and S. Shane, *"Secret "Kill List" Proves a Test of Obama's Principles and Will,"* THE NEW YORK TIMES, 29 May 2012, magazine section.

[14] M. WALZER, JUST AND UNJUST WARS 37 (1977).

The question still arises why soldiers and combatants could be killed as cannon fodder, given that they were humans with various rights including the right to life. Here Walzer again speaks for a long tradition, saying that soldiers have made themselves into dangerous people.[15] If soldiers take up arms and wear uniforms, they make themselves different from other humans and their moral or legal status changes in ways that are otherwise hard to fathom. For Walzer, and even for his most recent critics, soldiers forfeited their rights when they made themselves into soldiers who fought without just cause.[16] The case of conscripts is slightly more troublesome, and reminiscent of the problem of involuntary human shields discussed in Chapter 9. However, conscripted combatants who have lost their right to the full protection of their lives can regain that protection by voluntarily becoming prisoners of war (one thinks of the thousands of Iraqis that surrendered in whole divisions during the 1991 Gulf War, for example).

In a sense, it is the uniform that gives soldiers and combatants a different status from civilians who do not identify themselves in terms of their role in a group or their status.[17] In the terms of the Geneva Conventions, they are combatants simply by virtue of their status as members of the armed forces of a State at war. By identifying themselves primarily in terms of their military units, uniforms, and organizational command structures, soldiers (i.e., combatants) make a public statement about the primary basis of their rights and duties. This is a rather important, but often overlooked element of lawful combatant status because of the duty to distinguish oneself from the civilian population and the accompanying mandate to direct all activities only against combatants at all times. In other words, there is an element of expected conduct that underlies even status-based rights and duties of the combatants. The laws and customs of war determine both their rights as well as their obligations, i.e., their benefits and burdens. If the enemy State needed to give an explanation for why its soldiers were shooting at a particular individual, all that was necessary was to point out that that individual wore the uniform of the enemy State.

Another consideration has to do with the moral or legal equality of combatants. For the protection of soldiers and combatants, rules of war have emerged over the centuries—the rules of IHL—that were meant to make war more humane in the sense that noncombatants were shielded from its harshest effects wherever possible. These rules, epitomized in the Geneva Conventions, prohibited the cruel treatment of soldiers and also prohibited the intentional causing of superfluous or unnecessary

---

[15] *Id.*, at 145.

[16] *See especially* J. MCMAHAN, KILLING IN WAR (2009).

[17] *See* C. Kutz, "*The Difference Uniforms Make: Collective Violence in Criminal Law and War,*" 33 PHILOSOPHY & PUBLIC AFFAIRS 148–180 (2005).

suffering. The main way to enforce such rules was to make them applicable to all soldiers, regardless of whether they fought with just cause or not, and hence to hold all states responsible for waging war only according to these rules.[18] Their protected situation, *vis-à-vis* situations of rule-less mass slaughter, as well as their vulnerability, *vis-à-vis* those who were not marked as those who could be killed, was determined by their status as members of the armed forces. In other words, combatant status conveyed the full panoply of rights and duties drawn from the laws and customs of war, and thus created the sense of obligation and expectations that guided the actions of commanders for several centuries.

Status-based decisions about who can be killed and who is responsible for that killing are problematic in some respects, but can be defended. If war can be justified, then there must be moral and legal ways to fight it. And war necessarily involves the killing or risk of killing lots of people. So, there is a kind of "war convention" as Walzer calls it, in which all and only soldiers can be subject to be killed.[19] But there are nonetheless significant necessity and proportionality restraints on such killing, and this is especially the case if one takes human rights seriously. Killing, even during war, is restricted by the principle that causing unnecessary and superfluous suffering is disallowed. And as we have seen and will revisit again, various arguments, controversial though they be, are being offered today for the proposition that if a soldier can be disabled by non-lethal means, the soldier cannot be killed by an enemy soldier. And to make such determinations seems to involve us in a process of assessment in which the shortcut of merely referring to status is an insufficient basis for targeting.

In summary, status was the basis for why soldiers and combatants could be killed, but that same status protected soldiers and combatants from the worst of war's effects. War crimes could be committed, but mainly only for the egregious violation of the rules of war. Such egregious acts in effect make the soldier no longer just someone who followed the rules and the commands of his or her commander.[20] War crimes trials partially unmask the soldier, taking him or her out of the military unit and treating the person as a human being who has behaved wrongly. Nevertheless, even in that instance, we are judging wrongful behavior in the context of a military situation in which the soldier's role cannot be ignored.

---

[18] *See* M. WALZER, JUST AND UNJUST WARS 41 (1977).

[19] *See generally* M. WALZER, JUST AND UNJUST WARS part three (1977).

[20] On how post-Nuremberg courts viewed superior orders, see *United States v. William List* et al. *(The Hostage Case), reprinted in Trials of War Criminals*, vol. XI at 1236.

III. THE CONTROVERSY OVER PROTOCOL I

The 1977 Additional Protocol I to the Geneva Conventions (Protocol I) marked the most ambitious attempt to widen the swath of people covered by the protections of the rules of war. This treaty is now widely seen as largely, but not entirely, reflective of accepted customary international law. Thus, States such as the United States that have not formally accepted the treaty remain bound by its provisions insofar as a particular precept or provision reflects binding international custom and State practice. For our purposes, this subset of principles certainly includes the treaty's core articulations about distinction, military objectives, proportionality, commanders' duties, and the basic targeting rules.

In two of its most controversial and highly charged provisions, Protocol I expands the class of combatants as follows:

Art 43. Armed forces

1. The armed forces of a Party to a conflict consist of all organized armed forces, groups and units which are under a command responsible to that Party for the conduct of its subordinates, even if that Party is represented by a government or an authority not recognized by an adverse Party. Such armed forces shall be subject to an internal disciplinary system which, inter alia, shall enforce compliance with the rules of international law applicable in armed conflict.

2. Members of the armed forces of a Party to a conflict (other than medical personnel and chaplains covered by Article 33 of the Third Convention) are combatants, that is to say, they have the right to participate directly in hostilities.

3. Whenever a Party to a conflict incorporates a paramilitary or armed law enforcement agency into its armed forces it shall so notify the other Parties to the conflict.

Art 44. Combatants and prisoners of war

...2. While all combatants are obliged to comply with the rules of international law applicable in armed conflict, violations of these rules shall not deprive a combatant of his right to be a combatant or, if he falls into the power of an adverse Party, of his right to be a prisoner of war, except as provided in paragraphs 3 and 4.

3. In order to promote the protection of the civilian population from the effects of hostilities, combatants are obliged to distinguish themselves from the civilian population while they are engaged in an attack or in a military operation preparatory to an attack. Recognizing, however, that there are situations in armed conflicts where, owing to the nature of the hostilities an armed combatant cannot so distinguish himself, he shall retain his status as a combatant, provided that, in such situations, he carries his arms openly:

(a) during each military engagement, and

(b) during such time as he is visible to the adversary while he is engaged in a military deployment preceding the launching of an attack in which he is to participate.

Acts which comply with the requirements of this paragraph shall not be considered as perfidious within the meaning of Article 37, paragraph 1 (c).[21]

The second sentence of Article 44(3), which has been the subject of so much debate through the decades, has been described as a last-minute compromise that proves the truism that a treaty is "a disagreement reduced to writing."[22] The ICRC Commentary notes that the text of Article 44 "is a compromise, probably the best compromise that could have been achieved at the time....Whatever the text, one might still consider that, when all is said and done, the protection of the civilian population is not assured unless both Parties to the conflict are genuinely concerned about this."[23] Article 44(3) purports to convey combatant status to some members of militias who do not wear uniforms or otherwise identify themselves in the normal way, as long as they meet the more relaxed standards set out in Article 44 (3) (a) and (b).[24]

The ultimate US rejection of Protocol I was based largely on the conclusion that its expansive text could provide a pretext for terrorist acts and that the legal

---

[21] Protocol Additional to the Geneva Conventions of August 12, 1949, and Relating to the Protection of Victims of International Armed Conflicts (Protocol I), June 8, 1977, 1125 U.N.T.S. 3, Articles 43 and 44.

[22] CHRISTOPHER GREENWOOD, ESSAYS ON WAR IN INTERNATIONAL LAW 217 (2006).

[23] COMMENTARY ON THE ADDITIONAL PROTOCOLS OF 8 JUNE 1977 TO THE GENEVA CONVENTIONS OF 12 AUGUST 1949, Art. 44, at 522, ¶ 1685 (Sandoz et al, eds 1987), *available at* http://www.icrc.org/ihl.nsf/COM/470-750001?OpenDocument.

[24] The *Tadic* case also further refined and extended the idea of armed conflict and who is to be considered as participating in what was called "protracted armed conflict." *See* Prosecutor v Dusko Tadic, Case No. IT-94-1-A, Appeal Judgment (Int'l Crim. Trib. For the Former Yugoslavia July 115, 1999). *See also* Prosecutor v. Jean Paul Akayesu, Case No. ICTR-96-4-T, Judgment, ¶¶ 619-620 (Sept. 2,1998). On the issue of how to understand intensity of attack, see Prosecutor v. Ramush Hardadinaj, Case No. IT-04-84-T, Trial Judgment, ¶ 49 (Int'l Crim. Trib. For the Former Yugoslavia Apr. 3, 2008); Prosecutor v. Fatmir Limaj, Case No. IT-03-66-T, Judgment, ¶ 90 (Int'l Crim. Trib. For the former Yugoslavia, Nov. 30, 2005).

links of national reservations and understandings would be insufficient protection against the temptation of many States to protect terrorist acts under the rhetoric of lawful combatancy. The NATO allies of the United States shared a common sense of disappointment at the disingenuous manner that Protocol I purported to protect unlawful acts committed by non-State actors, but they also sought to preserve its genuinely progressive measures (such as the proportionality formulations that we have discussed so much). Despite a common abhorrence for terrorist acts, the NATO allies ultimately disagreed with the US decision to abstain from Protocol I, based on their common commitment to the multilateral instrument in its own right.

To that end, they issued authoritative diplomatic statements that comported with the humanitarian goals of Protocol I, but would serve to limit future interpretations of its most contentious provisions should disputes arise over their meaning and normative import. In the wake of extensive discussions with the United States, NATO allies Belgium, Canada, France, Germany, Ireland, Italy, The Netherlands, Spain, and the United Kingdom (UK) all ratified Protocol I subject to the following reservations (using the examplar of the UK reservation):

> It is the understanding of the United Kingdom that:
> - the situation in the second sentence of paragraph 3 can only exist in occupied territory or in armed conflicts covered by paragraph 4 of Article 1;
> - "deployment" in paragraph 3(b) means any movement towards a place from which an attack is to be launched.

This language sought to inhibit terrorist operations by making the duty to carry one's arms openly as broad as possible (deliberately paraphrasing the US definition of "deployment" from December 1977).

At the same time, the NATO allies sought to restrict the coverage of Article 44 to a very limited context (arguably no more extensive than the *levee en masse* provisions previously found in Article 4 of the 1949 Geneva Convention on Prisoners of War). This narrow construction would protect an authentic struggle for self-determination to reclaim sovereignty from an occupying power that temporarily displaced sovereignty. On the other hand, the subjective assessments of non-State actors who merely rebelled against the legitimate authorities of a sovereign state would be excluded from the umbrella of lawful combatancy on the basis of this interpretation.

The NATO allies sought to ensure that the provisions of Article 44 could not be extended by analogy to provide legal coverage that could otherwise serve to facilitate the commission of terrorist acts. Other major non-NATO allies, such as Australia,[25] Japan,[26] Korea,[27] and New Zealand,[28] reached substantively identical conclusions and made nearly identical statements at the time of ratification. The NATO allies and the US simply selected different pathways to manifest identical substantive concerns. To this day, no state has accepted that Article 44 in fact operates to create combatant status. It is rather a dead letter in practice.[29]

The point of this diplomatic and legal history is that it is critically important to crystallize the reality that any attempt by the Obama Administration to justify expanded targeted killings to a transnational non-State armed group based on status alone is simply unsupportable under international law. To be clear, status was the basis for why soldiers and combatants could be killed, but that same status protected soldiers and combatants from the worst of war's effects. War crimes could be prosecuted, but mainly only for egregious violation of the rules of war. Insofar as combatants comply with their obligations under the laws and customs of warfare, they are immune from prosecution for their conduct. Egregious departures from established

---

[25] It is the understanding of Australia that in relation to Article 44, the situation described in the second sentence of paragraph 3 can exist only in occupied territory or in armed conflicts covered by paragraph 4 of Article 1. Australia will interpret the word *deployment* in paragraph 3(b) of the Article as meaning any movement towards a place from which an attack is to be launched. It will interpret the words "visible to the adversary" in the same paragraph as including visible with the aid of binoculars, or by infrared or image intensification devices.

[26] The Government of Japan declares that it is its understanding that the situation described in the second sentence of paragraph 3 of Article 44 can exist only in occupied territory or in armed conflicts covered by paragraph 4 of Article 1. The Government of Japan also declares that the term *deployment* in paragraph 3 (b) of Article 44 is interpreted as meaning any movement towards a place from which an attack is to be launched.

[27] In relation to Article 44 of Protocol I, the situation described in the second sentence of paragraph 3 of the Article can exist only in occupied territory or in armed conflicts covered by paragraph 4 of Article 1, and the Government of the Republic of Korea will interpret the word deployment in paragraph 3 (b) of the Article as meaning any movement towards a place from which an attack is to be launched.

[28] New Zealand: It is the understanding of the Government of New Zealand that in relation to Article 44 of Protocol I, the situation described in the second sentence of paragraph 3 (b) of the Article as meaning any movement towards a place from which an attack is to be launched. It will interpret the words "visible to the adversary" in the same paragraph as including visible with the aid of any form of surveillance, electronic or otherwise, available to help keep a member of the armed forces of the adversary under observation

[29] *See* Michael A. Newton, *Exceptional Engagement: Protocol I and a World United Against Terror,* 42 TEX. INT'L L. J. 323 (2009)(discussing the rejection of protected status under Article 44 both in the context of Protocol I diplomacy and in the major multilateral terrorism treaties following 9/11). With the caveat that the Swiss government received a letter on June 21, 1989, to the effect that "the Executive Committee of the Palestine Liberation Organization, entrusted with the functions of the Government of the State of Palestine by decision of the Palestine National Council, decided, on May 4, 1989, to adhere to the Four Geneva Conventions of August 12, 1949, and the two Protocols additional thereto." On September 13, 1989, the Swiss Federal Council informed the States-Party to the Protocol that it was not in a position to decide whether the letter constituted an instrument of accession, "due to the uncertainty within the international community as to the existence or non-existence of a State of Palestine."

legal and moral duties in effect make the soldier no longer just someone who followed the rules and the commands of his or her commander.[30]

To be fair, neither the Bush nor Obama Administrations ever sought to fully justify extraterritorial drone strikes on the basis that any terrorist anywhere could be targeted based merely on an executive branch presumption of combatant status. This is, in part, a reflection of the unwillingness to concede that Al Qa'ida has a lawful prerogative to conduct operations on its own authority and an accompanying immunity under international law that might derive from combatant status. This in turn warrants further examination of the legal and moral rationale for killing during an armed conflict of a non-international character that might provide unquestionable legal grounds for targeted killings.

IV. BEHAVIOR AND DOMESTIC LAW ENFORCEMENT

In those cases in which status alone cannot determine whether someone can be justifiably killed during war, then some kind of process must be employed to make this determination rationally and reasonably. If the war fighter is treated according to how he or she has behaved, not merely according to his or her status, it is to move into a different domain in which a domestic law enforcement framework, not an IHL framework, is predominant. Domestic law enforcement looks to the specific acts of the person—not to that person's status. Rules of evidence in contemporary domestic legal systems, by and large, make it impossible for a person to be convicted merely because of who he or she is. Domestic criminal trials focus on the acts and behavior of the defendant to the exclusion of nearly all else.

Like the rules of IHL, the rules of domestic law enforcement can work to the benefit but also the detriment of the defendant. The exclusion of status in determining guilt means that the defendant cannot generally appeal to his or her good character or valued position in a social group. It violates the essence of fair trial standards to decide innocence or guilt based on the perpetrator's tribe or religion or sect or extended familial relations. But the domestic criminal law exclusion of status as the dispositive basis for punishment also means that the defendant must be treated according to what he or she did and not on the basis of being a gang member or homeless person, for instance.[31] The rules of domestic law enforcement are designed to place the greatest weight on the side of the rights of the defendant since on the

---

[30] On how post-Nuremberg courts viewed superior orders, see *United States v. William List* et al. *(The Hostage Case)*, reprinted in *Trials of War Criminals*, vol. XI at 1236.

[31] On the idea that status is not sufficient for criminal prosecution, see Palmer v. City of Euclid, Ohio, 402 U.S. 544 (1971).

opposite side of a criminal case is the representative of the State, the prosecutor, who is presumed to have much greater resources at his or her disposal including the extensive staff of a police force.

The IHL and domestic law enforcement frameworks are very different from each other in most respects. In war crimes trials, we often see on display the incongruities of mixing these frameworks. Soldiers are supposed to follow orders and are generally praised—not blamed—when they follow their commanders' orders. Such reasoning gave rise to the defense of superior orders, which historically protected soldiers from successful prosecution. But since the Nuremberg trial, the defense of superior orders cannot provide a sufficient rationale for rationalizing away criminal conduct, thus stripping the war fighter of a defense that was largely based on his or her status, as someone who was trained to follow orders scrupulously. In fact, in modern professionalized military forces, soldiers are taught that they have the express duty to disobey unlawful orders, i.e., those orders that purport to compel the commission of war crimes.

So, we can see that the rationales are different for the domestic law enforcement as opposed to the IHL framework. In war, soldiers and combatants are to be treated according to a moral and legal standard unlike the everyday standard. Soldiers can rightfully be killed, but only by those soldiers who were also being held to a higher moral and legal standard. Soldiers can rightfully kill, but only because they are soldiers (i.e., lawful combatants). And because they are soldiers, they can rightfully be killed as well, but again only insofar as they are soldiers. The status as a combatant is determinative.

It is interesting that the Obama Administration recognized that the targeted killing of an American citizen does raise due process issues, but did not recognize this problem concerning non-Americans.[32] But even for American citizens, the Obama Administration argued that any due process concerns are satisfied with internal deliberations in the executive branch. In this sense, we see recourse to a blurring of the law paradigms similar to that occasioned by the shifting standards applied to the treatment of so-called "unlawful enemy combatants" detained by the US at Guantanamo Bay post 9/11.[33] Enemy combatants were detained and transported to Guantanamo simply by reference to their status, as insurgent fighters. Evidence of their alleged actions in Afghanistan and Iraq was relevant only insofar as it helped

---

[32] J. Becker and S. Shane, *"Secret 'Kill List' Proves a Test of Obama's Principles and Will,"* THE NEW YORK TIMES, 29 May 2012, magazine section.

[33] *See* David Luban, *The War on Terrorism and the End of Human Rights*, 22 PHILOSOPHY & PUBLIC POLICY QUARTERLY 9–14 (2002).

to establish their status, hence providing the rationale for detaining them until the cessation of hostilities pursuant to the law of armed conflict.

However, as successive administrations defended the continuing rights to detain such "unlawful enemy combatants," the focus shifted to affirmative justifications grounded in examination of the evidence that they represented an ongoing threat to US interests—this was in practice a conduct based determination. The *habeas corpus* hearings in US federal courts have been evidence-based inquiries into the alleged conduct of the detainee accompanied by a judicial inquiry into the grounds for continued detention on the basis of the conduct and its relationship to an ongoing threat against US persons or interests. Our point is that due process simply cannot be disregarded even by repeated reference to status as the overarching determinative legal issue—and this has been consistent since September 11, 2001, despite efforts to oversimplify the rhetoric.

Indeed, in an important paper on our topic, Mark Maxwell argued that "the law of war must focus on the middle ground, looking at both the organized armed group and the conduct of the individual within that group to reach a reasoned conclusion that an individual to be targeted is a member of the group."[34] Yoram Dinstein has observed, "one cannot fight the enemy and remain a civilian."[35] Just as it is possible for the rights that attach to combatant status to change (by becoming a prisoner of war, for example), or to lose the immunity that goes with combatant status (by failure to comply with the law of war), the terrorist cannot properly be termed a civilian in the same sense as those innocents who huddle in their homes while combat rages round them. By choosing to participate in hostilities, particularly in a manner that defies the very notions of human decency and compassion, modern terrorists should not be protected by a shield of combatant immunity derived from the very body of law that they deliberately flout.

On the other hand, according to the domestic law enforcement model, people who are accused of criminal behavior are to be arrested and tried before an impartial tribunal with the full panoply of safeguards characteristic of the rule of law.[36] Criminals are innocent until proven guilty by reference to an impartial fact-finder. Enemy combatants are primarily identified by their status rather than their behavior, either by the uniforms they wear or by the role they play in armed conflict. They

---

[34] Mark Maxwell, *Rebutting the Civilian Presumption: Playing Whack-A-Mole Without a Mallet, in* Targeted Killings: Law and Morality in an Asymmetrical World 55 (C. Finkelstein, J.D. Ohlin, and A. Altman, eds 2012).

[35] Yoram Dinstein, *Unlawful Combatants*, 32 Isr. Y.B. Hum. Rts. 247, 248 (2002).

[36] Of course, there are certain cases in which some of these due process rights can be waived, such as an emergency situation in which the public safety requires acting very quickly against someone whose rights are then "balanced" against the immediacy of the security need. We return to this point later.

are presumed to be enemy combatants if they wear the uniform of the enemy or are otherwise identified as enemy combatants.[37] This is important because of the permissive nature of *jus in bello* described in Chapter 7. In normal circumstances, the combatant directing military efforts against a legitimate military target acts lawfully unless it is established that the weapons used or the degree of force was unnecessary to accomplish a military purpose (an assumption favoring the attacking party). Even with the permissive benefit of assumed legality, each and every military action must not be disproportionate in the overall context.

There is an exception to how defendants are treated in criminal trials as well, having to do with the penalty phase of the trial. Although guilt and innocence are only supposed to turn on the conduct or behavior of the defendant, status can re-emerge when punishment is considered. Here, the status of the defendant as a respectable member of her church or civic group can count in mitigation of the penalty.[38] But there is a proportionality requirement nonetheless: that the punishment fit the crime, that the penalty be somehow proportionate to the guilty act of conduct as we discussed in Chapter 3. Proportionality, as we will see, can be status based as well. And in the following sections, we will ask how proportionality should be understood in targeted killings, from a domestic law enforcement (conduct or behavior) framework as well as from an IHL (status) framework.

V. LAW ENFORCEMENT, PROPORTIONALITY, AND DUE PROCESS

Some targeted killings today seem to fit best under the status model derived from IHL, and will be investigated in the next section of this chapter. But other targeted killings seem to fit best under the domestic law enforcement's conduct model, or at least under a hybrid model. These latter cases of targeted killing will be taken up in the remainder of the current section of this chapter. This distinction is most pointed in those cases in which the killing is justified as a matter of serving the interests of justice rather than merely a killing during war, as was true of the way President Obama characterized the killing of Osama bin Laden.[39]

Indeed, the pursuit of justice was a key goal of US policy since September 11, 2001. Barely a week after the terrorist attacks, President Bush addressed a Joint Session of Congress, aware that the world—and perhaps the terrorist network—was listening.

---

[37] *Id.,* at 11.

[38] On the idea that evidence of the status of the defendant could be submitted for mitigation, see Payne v. Tennessee, 501 U.S. 808 (1990).

[39] *See* J. McMahan, *Targeted Killing: Murder, Combat, or Law Enforcement,* TARGETED KILLINGS: LAW AND MORALITY IN AN ASYMMETRICAL WORLD 135 (C. Finkelstein, J.D. Ohlin, and A. Altman, eds., 2012).

President Bush acknowledged the threat to the rule of law posed by unchecked private armies and declared that "we are a country awakened to danger and called to defend freedom. Our grief has turned to anger, and anger to resolution. Whether we bring our enemies to justice, or bring justice to our enemies, justice will be done." President Bush's declaration of this clear national goal was met by thunderous applause from the assembled US Congress and audience (which also included British Prime Minister Tony Blair).[40] If targeted killings are a matter of justice, then they should be understood in due process terms—and yet this has not happened and is unlikely to happen in the current use of drones for targeted killings in Pakistan and elsewhere in the war on terrorism.

We believe that, in some cases, an argument can be mounted for the restriction of targeted killing on due process grounds. Especially if the target of the killing is identified by what he or she allegedly has done, and if the rationale for killing him or her is one of retribution or deterrence, or some other version of a justice-based rationale, then due process concerns come to the fore. But to defend this view, we must think about why due process concerns have been seen to be such important constraints on punishment, especially lethal punishments as seem to be involved in targeted killings based on the behavior or conduct of the one targeted.[41]

Due process concerns, at least in the Anglo-American legal tradition, can be traced back to Magna Carta. The main concern with due process is to block arbitrary treatment on the part of government officials. In 1215, the government officials who were most worrisome were those who either were issuing decrees or who were in charge of the jails and prisons. Magna Carta was an agreement between the King and noblemen in England, which was reaffirmed by an act of Parliament in 1679, and at more than a dozen other occasions. In 1215, the king needed to levy taxes to support his various war efforts abroad and the nobles only agreed to such levies on the condition that the king agreed to certain restraints on his seemingly unbridled authority. One of the most significant of the restraints was that of habeas corpus, the right of persons who were incarcerated to petition for their temporary release from jail so that they could challenge the basis of the incarceration.[42] Such constraints

---

[40] President George W. Bush, Address to a Joint Session of Congress, Sept. 30, 2001, available at http://www.whitehouse.gov/news/releases/2001/09/20010920-8.html. Secretary of State Powell expressed a similar sentiment in his first public comments: "A terrible, terrible tragedy has befallen my nation, but ... you can be sure that America will deal with this tragedy in a way that brings those responsible to justice. You can be sure that as terrible a day as this is for us, we will get through it because we are a strong nation, a nation that believes in itself." BOB WOODWARD, BUSH AT WAR 10 (2002).

[41] Presidents Bush and Obama talked of seeing that justice was done to the terrorists who were targeted for assassination, thus seemingly invoking the domestic law enforcement model.

[42] *See* Larry May *Magna Carta and International Law*, American Bar Association volume on the 800th anniversary of Magna Carta, forthcoming in 2014.

against the possible abuse of power by government officials have been crucial for fairness as well as the appearance of fairness, which is so important for the rule of law.[43] Conduct-based targeting is evidence sensitive, and the worry has been that a government can manipulate that evidence unless serious restraints are in place.

One of the central concerns in cases involving those who are targeted because of their conduct or behavior involves how we regard the so-called war on terrorism. There may be a sense in which this is truly a war in that armed actions are taken by two sides that seem irreconcilably bent on killing each other. There may also be some sense in which the war on terrorism is a non-standard war, as the use of the term *asymmetrical* to describe it implies. As a result, the war on terrorism might require a kind of response on a hybrid status-plus-conduct model. If all of this is true, then perhaps the due process worries can be partially allayed.

The difficulty with the argument just advanced is that it is unclear why due process concerns can be allayed in this situation if they have not seemed to be allayed in somewhat similar cases over the centuries. Typically, due process constraints on government officials, such as habeas corpus, have been lifted only in the most extreme cases. The United States Constitution, for example, allows for the suspension of the right of habeas corpus only in times of emergency. Short of saying that the war on terrorism involves a permanent or long-term emergency situation, the targeting of a particular terrorist suspect does not automatically mean that due process concerns have been allayed simply by a showing that there is some reason to believe that the targeted individual is indeed a terrorist.[44] This hearkens back to the invocations of imminence made by Bush Administration officials. However, merely saying that imminence warrants targeted killings leaves an abundance of legal questions unanswered.

Even the designation of being a *terrorist* is ambiguous between the category of domestic law enforcement that is grounded in conduct or behavior, and the category of IHL that is grounded in status. Indeed, this is one reason why a hybrid model might be rightfully employed to confront terrorist suspects. Terrorists have been identified either by being members of certain organizations, such as Al Qa'ida, or by being someone thought to be responsible for a specific act of terrorism, such as the bombing of the USS Cole[45] or the Khobar Towers in Saudi Arabia. But in most

---

[43] *See* LARRY MAY, GLOBAL JUSTICE AND DUE PROCESS (2011).

[44] *See* Oren. Gross and F. Ni Aolain, Law in Times of Crisis: Emergency Powers in Theory and Practice (2006).

[45] At the time of this writing, Abd al-Rahim Hussein Muhammed Abdu Al-Nashiri, a Saudi national, is charged in a US Military Commission with perfidy, murder in violation of the law of war, attempted murder in violation of the law of war, terrorism, conspiracy, intentionally causing serious bodily injury, attacking civilians, attacking civilian objects, and hazarding a vessel. The charges arise out of an attempted attack on the USS THE SULLIVANS in January 2000, an attack on the USS COLE in October 2000, and an attack on the MV Limburg in October 2002. All of the trial motions, judicial rulings, and transcripts may be found at http://www.mc.mil/CASES/MilitaryCommissions.aspx.

cases, today, the identification of someone as a terrorist is made on the basis of both criteria. And for this reason, it may make sense to employ a hybrid model, drawing elements from both these legal frameworks.[46]

The question then is how such a hybrid framework should be constructed? Under the Bush Administration, enemy combatants were also treated by a hybrid model, but under that model, these combatants were effectively given fewer rights than they would have had under either the domestic law enforcement or IHL framework on their own. Of course, it is also possible to construct a hybrid framework that would provide more rights than enemy combatants would have under either framework on its own. A more reasonable framework than either of these two would be one tailored to the specific conditions that gave rise to the need for a hybrid approach that mixes elements from the status model and the conduct or behavior model. Mark Maxwell puts the point well in calling for a new approach to dealing with novel forms of warfare such as terrorism: "The test for status must be the threat posed by the group and the member's course of conduct which allows that threat to persist."[47]

We propose that, in cases in which enemy combatants or terrorists are identified on the basis of both status and behavior, they be granted protections that would be most consonant with the treatment they would receive in the prevailing paradigm at that time and place and in keeping with the best way to secure the greatest overall good. In this sense, the armed conflict threshold is dispositive for targets closely engaged in conflict zones because as we have already noted status is subordinated to other considerations in the law enforcement regime. Furthermore, short of having crossed the armed conflict threshold, it is not conceptually possible to implement a policy of immediate resort to lethal force.

At best, in a law enforcement context short of armed conflict, lethal force may be used only as a last resort (i.e., necessity on the basis of no feasible alternative), and only in proportion to the immediate threat posed by the target. In this setting, the individual actions of the target become far more relevant than the tangential linkage to an organization, even if that organization is conducting active hostilities elsewhere. To reach the decision to target, the decision-maker will have the luxury of time to assess available intelligence and evaluate the conditions necessary for a capture/kill decision. As we noted in Chapter 6, an affirmative duty to capture rather than kill combatants remains *lex ferenda* within the *jus in bello* regime. However, because decisions to launch drone strikes are not made in the heat of battle, in a

---

[46] Mark Maxwell, *Rebutting the Civilian Presumption: Playing Whack-A-Mole Without a Mallet, in* TARGETED KILLINGS: LAW AND MORALITY IN AN ASYMMETRICAL WORLD 55 (C. Finkelstein, J.D. Ohlin, and A. Altman, eds., 2012).
[47] *Id.*

perfect world the analysis should be vetted in some judicial or quasi-judicial proceeding to determine whether the alleged conduct or behavior of the enemy combatant or terrorist is indeed well substantiated.[48] In addition, though, the suspect can be
killed rather than captured if there is the likelihood that such capture would involve
unreasonable risk to public security or those attempting the capture. Self-defense
cases are different.

Our general position is that if the suspect to be targeted is primarily identified
by the alleged behavior in which he or she engaged, there is good reason to require
the full panoply of due process rights. From that perspective, the use of lethal
force would be severely constrained by the law enforcement, human-rights-based,
approach. As the widely accepted Basic Principles on the Use of Force and Firearms
by Law Enforcement Officials states:[49]

> Law enforcement officials shall not use firearms against persons except in
> self-defense or defense of others against the imminent threat of death or seri-
> ous injury, to prevent the perpetration of a particularly serious crime involving
> grave threat to life, to arrest a person presenting such a danger and resisting their
> authority, or to prevent his or her escape, and only when less extreme means
> are insufficient to achieve these objectives. In any event, intentional lethal use
> of firearms may only be made when strictly unavoidable in order to protect life.

---

[48] *See* Report of the Special Investigatory Commission on the Targeted Killing of Salah Shehadeh, 27 February
2011, *available at* http://www.pmo.gov.il/NR/rdonlyres/DA339745-7D9F-40C7-B20F-4481AAF1F4C7/0/
reportshchade.pdf (in Hebrew). The special investigatory commission published its final conclusions on the
targeted killing of Hamas military leader Salah Shehadeh in July 2002. At that time, an Israeli military aircraft
dropped a one-ton bomb on Shehadeh's house, killing him and at least 14 other people, including Shehadeh's
assistant, his wife, and his 15-year old daughter, and injuring 150 additional people. Applying the parameters
for lawful conduct under the Targeted Killing case, the Commission found that as commander of the Hamas
military wing in Gaza and second only to the spiritual leader of the Hamas, Shehada was correctly classified
as taking a direct part in hostilities. Alternative ways of neutralizing him, including detention, were impracti-
cal, since Shehadeh took shelter in a very dense refugee camp in Gaza and any operation to detain him would
have (overly) endangered the lives of many Israel Defence Force (IDF) soldiers. Therefore, it was reasonable
to decide to launch a targeted killing operation. Regarding harm to others, the commission concluded that
Shehadeh's assistant was himself a legitimate target, and that the death of Shehadeh's wife was a calculated and
legitimate incidental injury. However, the death of Shehadeh's 15 year-old daughter was not anticipated. Indeed,
the operation had previously been canceled twice due to a high probability that the daughter was present in
the house. The commission considered that the outcome of the operation, namely 13 civilian deaths and many
others injured, was disproportionate, in retrospect. This was also the retrospective assessment of the majority
of military authorities involved, who stated that had such an outcome been anticipated, the operation would
not have been carried out. The commission found that the gap between expectations and outcome resulted
from inadequate information gathering and analysis processes, which led to the belief that the incidental injury
would be less extensive than it was. It noted that various operational constraints led to an imbalance in considering the military necessity of targeting Shehadeh against the need to protect uninvolved civilians.

[49] Eighth United Nations Congress on the Prevention of Crime and the Treatment of Offenders, Havana, 27
August to 7 September 1990, U.N. Doc. A/CONF.144/28.Rev.1, at 118 (1990).

These principles reflect the concept of necessity in its more literal sense, and obviously set a far higher set of criteria than has been used to defend drone strikes to date. On the other hand, if the suspect is identified by both behavior and status, then it is probably acceptable to use a hybrid framework.

Some of the normal due process mechanisms may be suspended temporarily but a judicial or quasi-judicial proceeding should review the case under a domestic law template with an eye towards consistent and independent evaluative standards before the suspect can be subject to targeted killing. To reiterate what we said at the beginning of this chapter, targeted killings should be permitted under exceptional circumstances to defend against severe and imminent threats; political convenience, ego, or expediency do not meet this criteria as a matter of course. And here there is good reason to think that this process should be impartial, and not a mere consultation by members of the executive branch.

There is at least one other option, given the near certainty that the targeted killing would depend to a large extent on justifications provided by highly classified materials. This option would be for the executive branch to prepare an unclassified extract of the targeting folder and present it to an independent magistrate or independent commander for review, much like the procedures followed under the Classified Information Procedures Act in the US federal courts as well as under the Military Commissions Act of 2009. After all, if that process for handling classified information is sufficient for the trial of Khalid Sheik Mohammed, why would it not be suitable for the target killing of his Al Qa'ida associates? In the next section, we explore the case in which the suspect is only identified on the basis of status, for instance, as an enemy combatant.

VI. WAR AND THE SELF-DEFENSIVE KILLING OF COMBATANTS

The most obvious way to think of targeted killings is the model of other killings during war or armed conflict. If the United States is at war with a particular State or non-State actor, then targeted killings can be seen as simply one form of warfare. Jordan Paust treats targeted killing primarily as a form of self-defensive actions by States. Paust also spends time supporting the idea that targeted killings can also be justified as normal killing in armed conflict.[50] Paust sees these categories as separable even though they are often connected. We will begin this section by briefly explaining

---

[50] Jordan. Paust, *Self-Defense Targetings of Non-State Actors and Permissibility of US use of Drones in Pakistan*, 19 J. Transn'l L. & Pol'y (2010) 237–280.

why we do not separate these two considerations in thinking about how to justify targeted killings during war or armed conflict.

There are reasons to think that even in the pure IHL framework, targeted killing can only justifiably occur if the killing of a named target is *necessary* as a kind of self-defensive killing. We will readily grant that the idea of self-defensive killing by States is not an easy concept itself to justify in moral terms, as David Rodin and others have shown.[51] But leaving that issue aside, it should nonetheless be hard to justify killing rather than capturing a named terrorist within the IHL framework unless the terrorist's capture would cause an imminent risk to one's own troops or to the pursuit of the just cause, which is almost always understood in self-defense terms. Though this is controversial, we think that this is at least the way we should think of things as a matter of *lex ferenda*. After all, counterterrorism remains centered in the law enforcement regime for most nations.

Imminence is the key component in all self-defense killings. However, it is true that in the regime of IHL, imminence often takes on a broader meaning because the larger justifications of military necessity may not be geographically or temporally constrained to the precise place and time of the killing. And it seems to us that there are rarely killings directed against terrorist actors that can be justified without a showing of imminent threat.

In this context, we should consider again the ICRC's Interpretive Guidance on the Notion of Direct Participation in Hostilities under International Humanitarian Law (Interpretive Guidance).[52] Here is one of the most important parts of the ICRC findings for our purposes:

> In sum, while operating forces can hardly be required to take additional risks for themselves or the civilian population in order to capture an armed adversary alive, it would defy basic notions of humanity to kill an adversary or to refrain from giving him or her an opportunity to surrender where there manifestly is no necessity for the use of lethal force.[53]

This ICRC view builds on one interpretation of the diplomatic precedent[54] and presents an important perspective about how to view targeted killings even if they are to be understood not in the framework of domestic law enforcement.

---

[51] *See* DAVID RODIN, WAR AND SELF-DEFENSE (2002).

[52] *See* Jan Kleffner, *Section IX of the ICRC Interpretive Guidance on Direct Participation in Hostilities: The End of Jus in Bello Proportionality as We Know It?* 45 ISRAEL LAW REVIEW (2012) 35–52.

[53] ICRC, *Interpretive Guidance on the Notion of Direct Participation in Hostilities under International Humanitarian Law*, at 82.

[54] *See* Ryan Goodman, *The Power to Kill or Capture Enemy Combatants*, 24 EUROPEAN J. INT'L L., 26–41(2013).

The contrasting images of war are ones that see all killing in a war of self-defense as justified versus ones that see only necessary killing as justified. The latter claim is not that any killing that is necessary is justified since the principle of proportionality then must also be satisfied. We can see the application of proportionality in such cases in the following quotation from a famous case before the Israeli High court:

> if a terrorist taking a direct part in hostilities can be arrested, interrogated or tried, those are the means that should be employed.[55]

Here, as in the ICRC Interpretive Guidance, necessity and proportionality considerations are seen to bar targeted killing of terrorists unless this is necessary, and necessity is to be narrowly construed based on the immediate context. Elsewhere, we have considered the claim that human rights law is applicable in times of war or armed conflict, as is becoming recognized in some operational contexts.

On the other hand, the ICRC approach has been criticized with respect to terrorist actors because it would require specific information that the target is involved in a "continuous combat function" within the group that "involves the preparation, execution, or command of acts or operations amounting to their direct participation in hostilities."[56] This is problematic for two reasons. First, the ICRC approach seems to commingle targeting criteria based on status *and* conduct. Second, it would create one standard for actual combatants (targetable only based on status) and a differing standard for members of armed groups outside the armed forces by requiring assessments of conduct at the time of the strike and information on the linkage between that actor and the organization.[57]

In any event, a literal reading of the ICRC position in conjunction with Article 44(3) of Protocol I would lead one to suppose that a person could engage in hostilities, put down his or her weapons, hide among the innocent civilian populace, strike at will, and yet claim combatant status (with an accompanying combatant immunity from prosecution) for those warlike acts provided that a weapon is visible to an enemy at the precise moment it is used. This on-again-off-again combatant status would corrode the law of unlawful combatancy to its vanishing point and, in our view, seriously endanger the right to life of any truly innocent civilians endangered by the terrorist's presence.

---

[55] *Targeted Killings Decision*, ILDC 597 (IL 2006), para 40.
[56] ICRC, *Interpretive Guidance on the Notion of Direct Participation in Hostilities under International Humanitarian Law*, 34.
[57] *See* Michael N. Schmitt, *Deconstructing Direct Participation in Hostilities: The Constitutive Element*, 42 N.Y.U. J. INT'L: L. & POL'Y 697 (2010).

Most important, one needs to consider the human rights of combatants, even of enemy combatants, if human rights law is rendered applicable to the situation of war or armed conflict. In the case of targeted killings during war or armed conflict, considerations of humanity might well lead to the positions of the ICRC and the Israeli High Court if circumstances permit. At the same time, it would be intellectually consistent to demand some respect for human rights from all participants to a conflict, and the desire of the terrorist actor to deliberately deny other innocent civilians might well bolster the military advantage prong of the proportionality analysis if one takes human rights seriously. And the most significant way to view such situations is in terms of necessity and proportionality infused with the idea of basic respect for all persons, which is the hallmark of the human rights regime.

Proportionality in dealing with terrorists is increasingly being interpreted in human rights terms, even during war and armed conflict. In this sense, proportionality can be understood as putting restrictions on when combatants can be killed, especially if they could be captured instead. Such a position is directly relevant to the controversy about the use of targeted killing in the "war on terrorism."[58] In the IHL framework, there is no reason to rule out all targeted killings because it may very well turn out that the person targeted needs to be stopped now before many more people are killed by him or her. But there would need to be such a proportionality assessment, and even those who support targeted killings often admit that the best strategy would be to appeal to an impartial institution that could make such determinations.[59] We will not pursue the question of which institution would be best suited to assess proportionality in such cases, but will comment on the normative principles that should guide such an institution.

In targeted killing cases, understood in the IHL framework—as supplemented by human rights considerations, the difficulty is that, without a clear determination of the dangerousness of the person targeted, proportionality assessments are nearly impossible. Unlike the domestic law enforcement framework, the IHL framework does not require that the status of the person be determined beyond a reasonable doubt. But proportionality and necessity nonetheless require that it be reasonably certain that the person to be killed is a threat to the lives of others and that there is no non-lethal way to eliminate that threat.

Commanders can generally be trusted to make such an assessment, if the threat is one that is apparent on the ground, as it were. But many targeted killings concern

---

[58] See A. Altman and C.H. Wellman, *From Humanitarian Intervention to Assassination: Human Rights and Political Violence*, 118 ETHICS 228–257 (2008).
[59] *Id.,* at 257.

people who are believed to be the head of various terrorist groups, and the knowledge of such facts and the risk that such groups pose if their leaders are not killed now are very hard for a commander on the ground to ascertain. At the same time, the obligations flowing from *jus in bello* to take all feasible precautions to minimize or eliminate collateral damage are not transferrable from the commander to some intelligence functionary or some political official.

Proportionality intrudes itself in several important ways into the decision to engage in targeted killing. Most important, proportionality will not allow the decision to kill to be made solely on the status of the individual in question, even if we are not working within the domestic law enforcement framework. Considerations of status alone may allow for a determination that a person is indeed an enemy combatant or a leader of a terrorist group. But proportionality demands more than this if the individual is to be targeted for killing rather than for capture. The killing needs to be offset by the clear showing of greater harm to others if the target is not killed. And there must be clear evidence that the killing must take place now, rather than capture for instance, for the killing not to be disproportionate.

So we reach an interesting result. One might think that proportionality is easy to show in the case of targeted killing since only one person is targeted versus many others whose lives will be saved. But the loss of even this one life must be outweighed by the anticipated military advantages of the targeted killing; merely referring to the status of this person is not sufficient. One must show that the individual needs to be killed to save the lives of others, or to prevent great harm to others, and that capturing him or her will not have the same positive effect. In the next section, we will explore these issues in terms of international criminal law in which proportionality assessments also are key considerations.

VII. TARGETED KILLING AND PROPORTIONALITY IN THE INTERNATIONAL CRIMINAL COURT

The international criminal tribunals have partially followed the ICJ in how they have understood proportionality and necessity. The Rome Statute allows criminal punishment for disproportionate attacks during armed conflict. As we saw earlier, one of the violations of the laws of war—disproportionate attack—is defined as,

> Intentionally launching an attack in the knowledge that such attack will cause incidental loss of life or injury to civilians or damage to civilian objects or widespread, long-term and severe damage to the natural environment

which would be clearly excessive in relation to the direct overall military advantage anticipated.[60]

Proportionality here ranges over damages to civilian lives, to civilian objects, and even over the natural environment, but not over the lives of combatants.[61] As indicated above, the ICRC is at the forefront of challenging this view in that the ICRC opens the door for some consideration of the loss of combatant lives also to be a part of such proportionality assessments.

As we have noted, in the context of the ICC, the Rome Statute "definition of the offense of launching a disproportionate attack adds the word 'clearly' to the text of the provision as it appears in Additional Protocol I. This addition is intended to indicate to the Court that only obvious cases of disproportionate attacks should be punished."[62]

Consequently, if we are in the realm of international criminal punishment, only *clearly* disproportionate attacks are prosecutable.

It seems to follow that if one were to adopt the proportionality standard used in the Rome Statute, there will be few prosecutions for disproportionate attacks.[63] This is simply because few such attacks are clearly disproportionate. As a result, it may be that the ICC standard might require a more careful assessment than is typically made so as to determine what is clearly disproportionate and what is not. This again supports the idea advanced earlier that some kind of impartial showing must be made concerning proportionality if these issues are considered in a domestic law enforcement framework.

At a minimum, we would expect that the executive branch would prepare a single document that clearly articulated the analysis of overall military advantage anticipated, as well as foreseeable civilian casualties, etc. Such a document could be shared with the US Senate Intelligence Committee for example, and an unclassified extract might be given to an independent commander for review, if not to an independent magistrate or other judicial body modeled on the Foreign Intelligence Surveillance Court (FISC). Even if we are not focused on who can be prosecuted for disproportionate killing, there are useful insights that can be gleaned from the international tribunals, and the framing, "clearly excessive in relation the concrete and direct overall military advantage anticipated," provides the threshold for analysis that should be documented as a part of the *ex ante* decision-making process.

---

[60] Rome Statute Article 8(2)(b)(iv).
[61] The ICTY has reaffirmed the idea that proportionality must be observed in considering strategies in armed attack. See Review of the Indictment Pursuant to Rule 61, Prosecutor v. Milan Martic, ICTY Case No. IT-95-11-R61, ¶ 18 (Int. Trib. Former Yugoslavia 13 March 1996).
[62] JUDITH GARDHAM, NECESSITY, PROPORTIONALITY, AND THE USE OF FORCE BY STATES 134 (2004).
[63] And expanding the domain over which the proportionality assessment applies to those prosecutions of some combatants.

In some sense, the ICC has adopted what we earlier called a hybrid framework. The ICC, as an international court that prosecutes war crimes, is following a domestic law enforcement model to a certain extent in how evidence is processed and because its rulings are meant to further entrench the rule of law globally. But the ICC is also concerned with war crimes and hence also to a certain extent follows some of the most important provisions of the IHL model as well, although restricted by some human rights considerations. This is reflected in the Elements of Crimes document that specifies that "[t]he requirement of 'unlawfulness' found in the Statute or in other parts of international law, in particular international humanitarian law, is generally not specified in the elements of crimes." The elements thereby expressly rely on the settled body of law for their interpretation and application in the midst of criminal proceedings. Hence, the ICC can be seen as giving guidance about how a hybrid model might be understood, especially in cases of targeted killings.

The targeted killing, by drones and other means, of so-called terrorists can thus be approached from a variety of perspectives in terms of proportionality in law. If the targets are not combatants then on most conceptions of the principle of distinction or discrimination they cannot be targeted for killing at all. Indeed, the Appeals Judgment in the ICTY Blaškić case made it clear that neither necessity nor proportionality can help justify these killings if civilians are intentionally targeted because "there is an absolute ban on the targeting of civilians in customary international law."[64] It is important to note that military necessity cannot provide grounds for the direct targeting of civilians. As articulated by the US Department of Defense General Counsel, however, the lines with respect to the persons that may be targeted are blurred in practice:

> An "associated force" as we interpret the phrase has two characteristics to it: (1) an organized armed group that has entered the fight alongside al Qa'ida, and (2) is a co-belligerent with al Qa'ida in hostilities against the United States or its coalition partners. In other words, the group must not only be aligned with al Qa'ida. It must have also entered the fight against the United States or its coalition partners. Thus, an "associated force" is not any terrorist group in the world that merely embraces the al Qa'ida ideology.[65]

---

[64] Prosecutor v. Tihomir Blaškić, Case No. IT-95-14-A, Appeals Judgment, ¶ 109 (Int'l Crim. Trib. For the Former Yugoslavia July 29, 2004); Prosecutor v. Zoran Kupreskic, Case No. IT-95-16-T, Judgment, ¶¶ 524-525 (Int'l Crim. Trib. For the Former Yugoslavia Jan. 14, 2000).
[65] Jeh C. Johnson, Address at the Dean's Lecture at Yale Law School: National Security Law, Lawyers and Lawyering in the Obama Administration (Feb. 22, 2012).

Most terrorists can be seen as at least mixed cases in that they act as combatants in the sense that they engage or participate in military or paramilitary operations even though they also do not meet the legal criteria for being combatants in that they do not wear uniforms, carry arms openly, or display insignias. To reiterate, there is no foundation under international law for a status-based class of combatant during a non-international armed conflict. The concept of combatant immunity in the nontraditional, asymmetric struggle against terrorists is thus an oxymoron—a legal impossibility.

Assuming that the targeted terrorist is not clearly a civilian, one may be tempted to follow Protocol I, the ICRC Interpretive Guidance, and the Israeli *Targeted Killings* decision in thinking that terrorists have rights and cannot be killed if other avenues, such as capture, are open. Indeed, insofar as international law is moving in this human rights direction, a case can be made for the proposition that, if "a terrorist taking a direct part in hostilities can be arrested, interrogated or tried, those are the means that should be employed."[66]

It can be further argued that if human rights law applies to terrorist cases, then proportionality is also applicable in a way that the *Wall* case understood proportionality. Not only does proportionality concern the lives and property of civilians, as well as the natural environment, but also, it is our view that proportionality calculations must be made concerning the killing of the terrorist combatant. This means that there must be a calculation (almost surely by an impartial actor) that the killing of the terrorist is not disproportionate in light of the military objective to be achieved by this death. Targeted killings can be justified in some few cases using this analysis, provided that the identification of the target is primarily made on the basis of status and not conduct or behavior. Situations of immediate imminence to prevent an ongoing attack provide a somewhat different problem, and the narrowly framed proportionality analysis drawn from the human rights regime would be both more relevant and more attainable.

If the identification of the target is made solely or mainly on the basis of the alleged wrongful behavior of the one targeted, then due process concerns must be satisfied as well. And, in this respect, targeted killing will be very hard to justify without some form of hearing to determine whether, on the basis of the facts and the law, the terrorist deserves to be killed. In some few cases, it may be that the terrorist is seen as such an imminent danger that he or she can be killed with only a preliminary hearing. That hearing will have to establish the prima facie dangerousness of allowing the terrorist to live or be captured, as opposed to being killed

---

[66] *Targeted Killings Decision,* ILDC 597 (IL 2006), § 40.

along with a full justification of the urgent defensive need to launch lethal force as the first resort.[67] But these cases will be few indeed—restricted to cases in which the terrorist suspect is on the verge of committing an act of terrorism, or the capture of the terrorist would risk the lives of the law enforcement officers who have been dispatched to arrest the terrorist. One could see saving Washington or London in this manner from a devastating nuclear or an attack with weapons of mass destruction, but it is hard to imagine a consistently applied set of criteria that would permit lethal targeting with the frequency that it seems to have been applied over the past six years.

Targeted killing raises a host of problems in international law and Just War theory and is not a simple matter either to be banned or to be accepted in all cases. We have primarily applied proportionality criteria to try to shed some light on these controversial questions. In the majority of cases, some kind of judicial or quasi-judicial proceeding should precede the targeted killing. And only in the most exigent of circumstances can all due process considerations be dispensed with. In any event, arrest or capture should be contemplated if circumstances permit. Only if such strategies prove useless or overly risky should targeted killing be contemplated.

---

[67] On the issue of how dangerousness is to be assessed especially for proportionality see *Ewald K. Case,* Switzerland, *Prosecutor v. Markus Reinhardt,* Cantonal Court of the Grisons, February 28, 2002, §§ 12-13, as discussed in N. Melzer, *Targeted Killing in International Law* (Oxford: Oxford University Press, 2008). And on how the identification of combatants is to be made in difficult cases, see Judgment, *Prosecutor v. Ramush Haradinaj,* ICTY Trial Chamber, Case No. IT-04-84-T, 3 April 2008, § 60, and Judgment, *Prosecutor v. Ljube Boskoski and Johan Tarculovski,* ICTY Trial Chamber, Case No. IT-04-82-T, 10 July 2008, §§ 199–203.

11

THE NATURE OF WAR AND THE IDEA OF CYBERWAR

WAR IS MORALLY and legally problematic in that it is an institution that involves the intentional killing and disabling of humans. Rules or laws of war have been established over the millennia that are designed to restrict the activities of war to make war and its effects more humane while not making war impermissible. War is triggered if a State's territorial integrity or sovereign immunity are breached. Today, other forms of armed conflict are recognized, such as civil war, which lack these triggers. But the naming of a conflict as a *war* still is very important for determining which rules or laws are relevant. Against this background, we will consider various conceptual issues surrounding *cyberwar* and say something about how proportionality affects these deliberations.

We accept the premise found in the Obama Administration Cyberspace Policy Review that "international norms are critical to establishing a secure and thriving digital infrastructure."[1] International law touches cyberspace in far-reaching areas ranging from technical standards, technology sharing and export, data preservation and privacy, sovereign responsibilities, prosecution of cybercrimes, regulation of intellectual property, and, of course, the parameters for the use of force.

Section I, gives a brief historical survey of definitions of war. In Section II, we argue that cyber attacks, as now constituted, do not rise to the level of what has historically been called war, and this is equally true of contemporary accounts of armed conflict. In Section III, it is argued that a different paradigm is needed for cyber attacks today that is not premised on the idea that large numbers of people will

---

[1] The White House, Cyberspace Policy Review: Assuring a Trusted and Resilient Information and Communications Infrastructure (2009), *available at* www.whitehouse.gov/cybersecurity.

261

be permissibly killed or disabled. It is certainly true that the *lex lata* understanding of military objectives includes enemy property as well as persons, which of course could include computer networks or electronic facilities. In cyber attacks, the aim is to disable machines not humans, at least in the current time, and so the type of rules governing cyber attacks need not necessarily resemble those governing war or armed conflict. In Section IV, we consider problems with assimilating the cyber attacks of today to the war paradigm. And in Section V, we look especially at problems of proportionality that arise in discussing cyber attacks as war.

I. THE HISTORICAL DEFINITIONS OF WAR

Francisco Suarez, writing at the end of the sixteenth century, called attention to the various meanings of the word *war* but indicated that only one was proper:

> An external contest at arms which is incompatible with external peace is properly called war, when carried on between two sovereign princes or between two states. When however, it is a contest between a prince and his own state, or between citizens and their state, it is termed sedition. When it is between private individuals it is called a quarrel or duel. The difference between these various kinds of contest appears to be material rather than formal.[2]

So, although Suarez recognized that the term war is used for several different forms of contest, war is only used properly to refer to contests of arms between States.

Alberico Gentili, also writing at the end of the sixteenth century, employs a very similar definition to that offered by Suarez, but Gentili offers a few more thoughts on the nature of war that may help us understand the idea of cyberwar:

> War is a just and public contest of arms. In fact war is nothing if not a contest, and it is a contest of arms, because to wage war in one's mind and not with arms is surely cowardice, and not war...And although much is accomplished in war without the use of arms, yet there is never a war without the preparation of arms...Furthermore, the strife must be public; for war is not a broil, a fight, the hostility of individuals.[3]

---

[2] Francisco Suarez, *On War* (DISPUTATION XIII, DE TRIPLICI VIRTUE THEOLOGICA: CHARITATE), *in* SELECTIONS FROM THREE WORKS Disputation XIII, 800 (Gladys L. Williams, Ammi Brown, and John Waldron, trans., Oxford: Clarendon Press, 1944)(1610).

[3] ALBERICO GENTILI, THE LAW OF WAR (DE JURE BELLI) 12 (John C. Rolfe, trans., Oxford: At the Clarendon Press, 1933) (1588–1589).

For Gentili, even though much of war does not concern arms, there is no war without at least the preparation of arms.

To think of war as a contest of arms, or of weapons, seems to leave open the door for cyberwar since the use of cyber attacks can be characterized as a contest involving a certain kind of *weapon*, a destructive computer program placed clandestinely into a foreign computer system. What is less clear is whether it makes sense to think that there could be a *contest* involving the use of computer programs. The difficulty is that the use of computers to destroy property is not the sort of action that has been characterized by contests of arms. The contests of arms that Suarez, Gentili, and many others thought was characteristic of war, is the mutual use of arms that are directed not at property, but at the lives of opposing soldiers.

Hugo Grotius, writing at the beginning of the seventeenth century, can also be consulted on the topic of what constitutes arms. Here is how he understands the idea of arms that has been so important in the definition of war:

> Now, even as actions have their inception in our minds, so do they culminate in our bodies, a process that may be called "execution." But man has been given a body that is weak and infirm, wherefore extracorporeal instruments have also been provided for its service. We call these instruments "arms." They are used by the just man for defense and [lawful] acquisition, by the unjust man, for attack and seizure. Armed execution against an armed adversary is designated by the term "war."[4]

Writing in 1609, Grotius here gives the term *arms* a very broad definition that could seemingly encompass the use of computer programs, which after all are extensions of a person's body in some sense. And these programs certainly allow people to execute their decisions in the sense of putting these decisions into concrete action.

A bit later in his life, in 1625, Grotius came to a different conception of war that is worth considering. He tells us that "Cicero defined war as a contending by force. A usage gained currency, however, which designates by the word not a contest but a condition; thus war is the condition of those contending by force, viewed simply as such."[5] Here two things are worthy of note. Grotius expands the domain to take into account contests of force, not merely ones that employ arms. And Grotius also stresses that war is not merely a contest but a "condition." Grotius does not elaborate

---

[4] HUGO GROTIUS, ON THE LAW OF PRIZE AND BOOTY (DE JURE PRAEDAE) Ch. II, 30 (Gwladys L. Williams trans, Oxford: At the Clarendon Press, 1950)(1605).

[5] HUGO GROTIUS, THE LAW OF WAR AND PEACE Bk. I, Ch. 1, Sec. I (Francis W. Kelsey trans., Oxford Clarendon Press 1925) (1625).

but it seems relatively clear that he thinks of war as a state of affairs that continues for a time, not merely a single act of contesting as would be true in a duel or a jousting match, for instance.

To see war as a condition or state of affairs is to see war as perhaps a series of contests, or battles, isolatable from each other but bound together in that they are all in the service of a particular cause. In this sense, *cyberwar* would only be war if it involved more than merely a single attack spurred by a computer program. But of course there is nothing in principle to prevent there being a series of cyber attacks that collectively constituted a cyberwar. But war normally involves two parties, each States, employing arms in a continuing state of affairs.

In this respect, one needs to think about the implicit idea that war is a *public* condition—all of the views of war distinguish the public conflict, which is called war, from the private act of conflict, which goes by the name sabotage, sedition, or even duel. Part of what is involved here is that war is openly declared and the element of surprise is thereby limited. This gives the other side a fair chance to try to repel the attacking forces. Economic espionage, on the other hand, relies on secrecy as its *modus operandi*. Recall our earlier discussion of the Just War concept that resort to war requires an *ex ante* announcement of the conditions necessary to avoid resort to warfare in the first place. Yet, the best known examples of cyberwar have been clandestine, with nothing like a declaration of war or even, initially, an admission that the destructive computer program has come from a particular State. Indeed, the US and Israel, widely believed to be responsible for launching the 2010 program STUXNET against the computers at a nuclear facility in Iran, have as of this writing still not acknowledged the source of STUXNET.

Again, though, cyber attacks do not have to be clandestine. But until they are public acts, it is once again hard to see them as instances of war properly so called. And it is hard to imagine a computer virus or worm being successfully used against a foreign computer system if it is acknowledged in advance. So, the prohibitions on clandestine warfare that run throughout the Just War tradition seems not to sit well with the idea of cyberwar.

At the end of the seventeenth century, Pufendorf has yet another variation on the definition of war that brings our discussion much closer to contemporary usage.

some states expressly denote a relation toward other men than do others, since they signify distinctly the mode in which men mutually transact their business. The most outstanding of these are *peace* and *war*.... Now peace is that state in which men dwell together in quiet and without violent injuries, and render their mutual dues as of obligation and desire. War, however, is a state of men who are naturally inflicting or repelling injuries or are striving to extort by force what is due to them.[6]

By *state* here, Pufendorf means a condition in which persons find themselves in various moral relations. On the basis of the states that pertain to humans, there are obligations at play. War is a state of men, of persons in plural not singular. War is the state of men inflicting or repelling injuries, or attempting to do so. As a result, war creates obligations on the people who are in this state.

Pufendorf defines war in a way that makes the inflicting and repelling of injuries the key component. Cyberwar could merely be the type of war that involves injuring or attempting to injure someone by means of malicious computer programs. But there is a problem with this idea—cyberwar does not aim to inflict injury on persons but on other computers. And most importantly, cyber attacks are not aimed at inflicting or repelling injuries on common soldiers, who Pufendorf says are authorized by their States to inflict injuries on the common soldiers of the enemy State.[7] It may be true that nonphysical injury is what a cyber attack is aimed at, but then it is not clear that a physical response of the sort that war involves is justified as a response.

In our view, Pufendorf is right to say that the term *war* has been reserved for the recourse to violent force by one State against another State, in which the violence is primarily directed at the soldiers of the enemy State. The laws and customs of war that have been constructed since the seventeenth century have been designed to limit the horrors of war that mainly concern the killing of civilians and the suffering of soldiers. In the next section, we explain in more detail why we think that so-called cyberwar is not the kind of war that is primarily of interest to those who have written on the rules and laws of war.

II. THE RULES OF WAR AND CYBERWAR

War has historically focused on public contests that involve arms and especially those contests that involve the attempt to kill or wound soldiers of the opposing State. So-called cyberwar can be seen as a kind of contest of force and perhaps even of arms, but such attacks are rarely public and the point of cyber attacks is not typically to kill or wound soldiers but to destroy property. Of course, the destruction of property, such as the computer programs that control centrifuges in a nuclear power

---

[6] SAMUEL PUFENDORF, ON THE LAW OF NATURE AND NATIONS (DE JURE NATURAE ET GENTIUM) 9 (C.H. Oldfather and W.A. Oldfather trans., Oxford: At the Clarendon Press, 1934)(1672).

[7] *Id.*, at 11.

plant or the electric power grid that supplies power to military installations, certainly can have as their foreseeable secondary effects that civilians and perhaps also soldiers will suffer. But the primary aim of cyber attacks today is not publicly to kill or wound soldiers. In our estimation, this is an important difference between cyber attacks and warfare.

Henry Wheaton, writing in 1836, presents what is often thought to be the modern notion of war:

> A contest of force between independent sovereign States is called a public war. If it is declared in form, or duly commenced, it entitles both the belligerent parties to all the rights of war against each other. The voluntary or positive law of nations makes no distinction, in this respect, between a just and unjust war. A war in form, or duly commenced, is to be considered, as to its effects, as just on both sides. Whatever is permitted by the laws of war to one of the belligerent parties is equally permitted to the other.[8]

Recognizing a contest of force as a war means that various rights, not recognized in other situations, pertain. Most important, the rights of war allow, among other things, for the intentional killing and wounding of people (soldiers) and/or the destruction of property that would normally be forbidden.

A contest as a public war involves rules designed to minimize suffering but not completely to restrict intentional killing and wounding. This is because war is thought to be different from most other spheres of life. Before designating a contest or condition as one of war, care must be taken since such a designation carries with it significant permissions. War, especially the defensive war, is not outlawed but seen as at least a necessary evil. Once this is recognized, then the rules of war are framed so as to make war as humane as possible, given that killing and wounding will occur as a matter of right for the parties.

If an attack is raised to the level of being called a war, this means that that attack is treated according to the special rules governing war and armed conflict. And this means that the killing or wounding of people is not proscribed but is instead accepted, at least for the direct attacks on soldiers and even for many indirect attacks on civilians. The main task of the laws and customs of war, at least as understood today under international humanitarian law (IHL), is to contain the violence in the most humane way that still allows for large-scale killing and wounding. And the rationale is that if States resort to war as a means of national self-defense, the

---

[8] Henry Wheaton, Elements of International Law 295–296(George Grafton Wilson ed. 1936)(1836).

successful execution of the war requires permission for its soldiers to kill or wound enemy soldiers.

But the question is why, in cyberwar, we would want to allow for large-scale killing and wounding, settling instead only to contain some of the violence that results from cyber attacks rather than to treat the cyber attacks as non-war attacks that must conform to a stricter standard. It is not clear that cyber attack, to be successful as a matter of sovereign self-defense, needs to be granted the permission to kill or wound in order to effect a purposeful counterresponse purpose. Indeed, cyber attacks seem to be most successful if the main destruction is already limited to property and only incidentally harms soldiers or civilians. Since the intention to kill or wound enemy soldiers is not an essential component of cyber attacks, the war convention's equal permissions to kill and be killed would make for an awkward and often inappropriate basis for decision-making.

One reason that some theorists might equate cyber attacks to war is that the recent examples of cyber attacks seemingly violated the territorial integrity of a sovereign State. Such a violation typically triggers the categorizing of these attacks as an act of war. Acts of war are those that violate the territorial integrity or sovereign immunity of a State. The laws of war are in part aimed at protecting sovereign States from infringements on their sovereignty. The trigger for an act of aggression has been the crossing of a State's borders by uninvited foreign troops. In a sense, cyber attacks seem to follow this model because the computer worm or virus does cross the State's borders and is most certainly uninvited.

Yet, there are reasons to doubt that cyber attacks today are enough like uninvited border crossings by foreign troops automatically to count as acts of war. Three factors are important in creating the consensus over the centuries that the borders of sovereign States should not be crossed by uninvited foreign troops. First, there is a concern that crossing of borders by foreign troops will undermine the self-determination of citizens of the attacked State. Second, the uninvited foreign troops, as constituted by armed and dangerous soldiers, risk the killing of the soldiers of the attacked state. Third, uninvited foreign troops can cause great disruption of the normal workings of a State and also risk the physical well-being of the citizens of the attacked State. We will explain and apply these considerations in the following paragraphs.

First, cyber attacks do not cross borders in the way that foreign troops do. The main worry about territorial integrity concerns the threat to the self-determination of a State that follows upon a physical invasion by foreign troops. The attacks that involve computer programs today do not have the same kinds of worries normally associated with armed border crossings. Cyber attacks can be quite disruptive of the normal functioning of a State, and can certainly lead to deaths as a side effect of those attacks. But cyber attacks only cross borders in a sense of the term "cross."

Although there is some physical material that crosses borders in a cyber attack, no uninvited person traverses the border and sets foot in the State in question. In fact, by the standards of the International Court of Justice (ICJ) given that cyber attacks are rarely if ever directly attributable to another sovereign State, the concept of armed attack is inapposite.

Second, because in the launching of a cyber attack there is no intention directly to kill enemy soldiers there is another reason not to extend to cyber attacks the label of war with its corresponding rules allowing for killing and wounding but seeking only to render the killing and wounding more humane. The reciprocal permission to kill and wound on both sides of a public war does not need to be extended to cyber attacks that seek to undermine a State by non-lethal means. Cyber attacks can occur pretty much unhindered whether or not the permission to kill and be killed is extended to troops on either side. There are good reasons to see cyber attacks similarly to the use of economic sanctions rather than foreign troops.

Third, the kind of disruption of services that a cyber attack can achieve is insufficient to count as an act of war. Think about embargoes in this respect. Embargoes involve the attempt to stop trade between two or more States by the act of one State. Embargoes are not considered acts of war. But economic blockades are considered acts of war since they involve the physical intrusion into the territorial waters of a State by the uninvited military forces of a foreign State. As we will see in a later section, cyber attacks are more like embargoes than economic blockades. Like embargoes, cyber attacks can cause great disruption and result in deaths within the target State.

But if embargoes are contemplated, we do not treat them according to the standards of IHL, according to which we say that there is an equal right to kill combatants or that the only worry is about the collateral killing of civilians. Instead, embargoes are treated according to the standard moral and legal conceptions concerning human rights among other categories not the special moral and legal rules of war. Cyber attacks should be similarly treated in our view. Think of the coordinated crash of the banking and broadcast systems in South Korea that took place in early 2013. Even if they could be attributed to North Korean official action, it could hardly be argued that they were of sufficient nature, scope, duration, and intensity to constitute armed conflict in the traditional threshold. Like embargoes, there is no physical presence of foreign troops in the target State.

The rules or laws of war are somewhat different from the rules concerning everyday life. Except in the rare case of attacks that warrant a defensive response, people in everyday life do not make themselves liable to be attacked by others merely because they put on uniforms, carry arms openly, or follow a chain of command. The rules of war are exceptional rules for very exceptional circumstances. And whether one agrees with these rules being extended equally to soldiers who fight on the just as well as the unjust sides of a war, the rules of war are only justified because of the exceptional, and we would say emergency, circumstances of State aggression.

Cyberwar may very well call for its own special rules and laws, although we shall next give reasons to doubt this, but the use of the rules of war for this type of attack is simply not warranted. Cyber attacks may be so disruptive, as if they target the electrical grid of a State, that special rules for how morally and legally to deal with such attacks may have to be crafted. But we do not see why the rules and laws designed for war should be applied to cyber attacks, given how different from war cyber attacks seem to be. We next explore how these issues are viewed through the lens of *lex lata* international law, before proceeding to ask what kind of model of rules is best suited *lex ferenda* to cyber attacks.

III. CURRENT *JUS AD BELLUM* AND *JUS IN BELLO* PROPORTIONALITY AND CYBERSPACE

In this section, we compare the current and historical understandings of war and armed conflicts in international law, especially in the context of the Just War tradition. Two major conceptual questions are relevant to the *jus ad bellum* analysis in international law: (1) When does a cyber operation amount to a "use of force" that is prohibited by article 2(4) of the United Nations (UN) Charter?[9] and (2) When does a cyber-operation amount to an "armed attack" that would warrant the use of force in self-defense—or preemptive self-defense if the attack is imminent—under article 51 of the UN Charter?[10] Many experts have concluded that both terms, "use of force" and "armed attack," refer to "military attacks or armed violence" and would thus exclude all cyber operations.[11]

On the other hand, Michael Schmitt is surely correct in asserting that a cyber operation with a sufficient extent and gravity based on its effects would constitute a use of force in violation of the Article 2(4) threshold.[12] Such a consequences test nicely adapts formalistic notions of the terms "use of force" and "armed attack" to fit cyber operations. In turn, the *jus ad bellum* thresholds would be satisfied. From this perspective, it is indeed possible that an effect of coercion towards another state would be sufficient to constitute a cognizable use of force. Cyber operations could

---

[9] UN Charter art. 2, para. 4.

[10] UN Charter art. 51.

[11] Matthew C. Waxman, Cyber-attacks as "Force" Under UN Charter Article 2(4), INTERNATIONAL LAW & THE CHANGING CHARACTER OF WAR 43 (Naval War College Blue Book Series Vol. 87), *citing* Tom J. Farer, "Political and Economic Coercion in Contemporary International Law," 79 AM. J. INT'L L. (1985) 405, 408.

[12] Michael N. Schmitt, *Cyber Operations and the Jus in Bello: Key Issues*, in INTERNATIONAL LAW & THE CHANGING CHARACTER OF WAR 69, 94 (Naval War College Blue Book Series Vol. 87).

also generate a lawful right of response if they targeted another state's weapons systems, infrastructure such as dams or nuclear plants, or air traffic control systems. It is important to note that if the purpose of a cyber operation is to generate such effects, it is an attack even if the operation fails before the effects can take place.[13]

The *jus ad bellum* framing of proportionality requires that a lawful resort to force be proportional to the asserted *casus belli*.[14] This is proportionality in the narrowest sense, i.e., that which is necessary and limited to the means directly related to eliminating the threat presented. A provocation sufficient to trigger a right to use military force in self-defense[15] in turn warrants a cyber attack that is designed to eliminate the threat presented. In the words we have often quoted by Daniel Webster, the act "justified by the necessity of self-defense, must be limited by that necessity, and kept clearly within it."[16] Lawful self-defense is delimited by the desired diplomatic objective.

For illustrative purposes, recall the formulation from the human rights context, the European Court of Human Rights (ECHR) decided *Khatsiyeva and others v. Russia*[17] by holding that

> [t]he use of force which may result in the deprivation of life must be no more than "absolutely necessary"…[which] indicates that a stricter and more compelling test of necessity must be employed than that normally applicable when determining whether State action is "necessary in a democratic society."…Consequently, *the force used must be strictly proportionate to the achievement of the permitted aims*."[18] (emphasis added)

In the context of cyber attacks, such a stringent linkage between the asserted preventive purpose and the effects inflicted is obviously impossible. For example, a "sniffer" program[19] that is discovered on a Pentagon mainframe may well have

---

[13] *Id.*, at 94.

[14] Oscar Schachter, *In Defense of International Rules on the Use of Force,* 53 UNIVERSITY OF CHICAGO LAW REVIEW 113, 132 (1986)("[A]cts done in self-defense must not exceed in manner or aim the necessity provoking them.").

[15] Michael N. Schmitt, Asymmetrical Warfare and International Humanitarian Law, 62 AIR FORCE LAW REVIEW 1, 297 (2008).

[16] R.Y. Jennings, "The Caroline and McLeod Cases," 32 AM. J. INT'L L. 82, 89 (1938).

[17] http://cmiskp.echr.coe.int/tkp197/view.asp?item=1&portal=hbkm&action=html&highlight=Khatsiyeva&sessionid=91907041&skin=hudoc-en.

[18] *Id.* at ¶ 129 (emphasis added).

[19] Sniffers monitor network data. A sniffer can be a self-contained software program or a hardware device with the appropriate software or firmware programming. Sniffers usually act as network probes or "snoops." They examine network traffic, making a copy of the data without redirecting or altering it. Some sniffers work only with TCP/IP packets, but the more sophisticated tools can work with many other protocols and at lower

replicated in ways that cannot be determined and have transferred unknowable volumes of information. This is not a theoretical scenario. The US Department of Defense (DOD) confirmed in 2008 that its classified computer network was compromised, and had within it a "digital beachhead" for delivering plans to unknown sources.[20] In 2005, hackers traced to China, in an effort dubbed Titan Rain, accessed computers belonging to the DOD and the Departments of Energy, Homeland Security, and State.[21] In the same year, the US Pentagon identified 79,000 attempted intrusions, up from 54,000 in 2003.[22]

Both the source of a cyber attack and the true extent of the damage it has caused will generally be opaque. Thus, requiring a tight symmetry between a particular cyber operation and an assessment of the damage likely to be suffered at the hands of a purported enemy would provide a functional free pass to any adversary. This is not to suggest that there are no conceivable constraints on cyber attacks. On the contrary, because the *jus ad bellum* proportionality standards simply do not neatly fit with the cyber context, the *jus in bello* standards become the vital load bearing norm.

The current conceptions of *jus in bello* proportionality seem remarkably well adapted to the evolving practice of cyber operations. However, the situations in which cyber attacks are conducted as part of an ongoing armed conflict to which the laws and customs of war fully apply are today rare indeed. The standard is not one of absolute perfection or mechanistic implementation.

In a cyber attack, IHL permits a holistic assessment of the constituent elements in which the anticipated military advantage can be aggregated, and may well be deemed to be greater than the sum of the isolated dimensions. According to Herbert Lin, Chief Scientist of the Computer Science and Telecommunications Board, National Research Council of the National Academies, indirect effects are almost always more important than direct effects on the confidentiality, integrity, authenticity of source, and the availability of computers, data, or networks.[23] Malicious software can of course lead directly to fatal results that impact privileged civilians,[24] but reports of

---

levels including Ethernet frames. Years ago, sniffers were tools used exclusively by network engineers. Today, however, these utilities have become popular on the Internet with hackers and the merely curious. <http://compnetworking.about.com/od/networksecurityprivacy/g/bldef_sniffer.htm>

[20] Duncan Hollis, "An E-SOS for Cyberspace," 52 *Harv. Int'l L.J.* (2011) 373, 390. In 2009, the Pentagon announced that it spent $100 million in six months to repair damages from cyber attacks it suffered. *See* Pentagon Bill to Fix CyberAttacks: $100 M, C.B.S. NEWS, (7 April 2009). <http://www.cbsnews.com/stories/2009/04/07/tech/main4926071.shtml>

[21] Bradley Graham, "Hackers Attack Via Chinese Web Sites," *Wash. Post*, (Aug. 25, 2005) < http://www.washingtonpost.com/wp-dyn/content/article/2005/08/24/AR2005082402318.html>.

[22] *Ibid.*

[23] *See* Herbert S. Lin, "Offensive Cyber Operations and the Use of Force," 4 *J. Nat'l Sec. L. & Pol'y* (2010) 63, 68.

[24] *See* Leslie Meredith, "Malware Implicated in Fatal Spanair Plane Crash," *TechNews Daily*, (20 Aug. 20, 2010)< http://www.technewsdaily.com/malware-implicated-in-fatal-spanair-crash-1078/>

directly fatal cyber effects are exceptional and the indirect results of cyber attacks represent the main thrust of proportionality analysis.

For example, US officials discovered malicious programs placed within the American power grid in 2009 that would permit unknown adversaries to control the power production and delivery throughout the country.[25] In 2007, a Central Intelligence Agency (CIA) official revealed that cyber attacks had created a blackout in a country.[26] To be clear, cyber operations must be based on the best available technology, and tailored to be as discriminate as can reasonably be achieved. Nevertheless, a reasonably foreseeable aggregate military advantage arising from a cyber operation could still meet the threshold of legality provided that the military advantage anticipated (or sought to be achieved by precise technology) is not merely speculative or hypothetical (hence meeting the "concrete and direct" requirement.) The advantages that inhere from a particular cyber operation will seldom become immediately apparent, and can be expected fully to manifest themselves. This approach is precisely within the latitude of the *jus in bello* proportionality rule as it is currently configured.

Furthermore, the law is clear that a cyber operation may permissibly cause some degree of discomfort or inconvenience or even concrete harm to protected civilians or civilian objects, provided that such consequences are not clearly excessive. The inclusion of environmental concerns as an explicit dimension of the proportionality analysis is most welcomed. Hence a cyber operation designed to disable a power grid that in turn affects water supplies or agricultural operations would be subject to law of war review. However, only damage to civilian lives and property is relevant to the proportionality analysis. Though loss of functionality might rise to the level of legally cognizable damage, the inconvenience, annoyance, and stresses occasioned by cyber operations do not qualify as collateral damage.[27]

This is the genius of the STUXNET attacks. Rather than focusing on nuclear facilities or tests that could result in the release of radioactive materials, the STUXNET worm was designed to target a tiny, common type of computer equipment known as "programmable logic controllers." Such equipment was vital to the operations of the centrifuges in Iran's Bushehr power plant, which produces plutonium that may be used for weapons, as well as Iran's uranium-enrichment plant

[25] *See* Siobhan Gorman, *Electricity Grid in U.S. Penetrated by Spies*, WALL ST. J., (Apr. 8, 2009), http://online.wsj.com/article/SB123914805204099085.html.

[26] Ellen Nakashima & Steven Mufson,' Hackers Have Attacked Foreign Utilities, CIA Analyst Says,' *Wash. Post* (19 Jan. 2008) <http://www.washingtonpost.com/wp-dyn/content/article/2008/01/18/AR2008011803277.html>

[27] Tallinn Manual on the International Law Applicable to Cyber Warfare, Prepared by the International Group of Experts at the Invitation of the NATO Cooperative Cyber Defence Center of Excellence, 160 (Michael N. Schmitt ed. 2013).

at Natanz.[28] In retrospect, analysts have been able to confirm that STUXNET was designed to target and damage nuclear centrifuges by speeding them up, while sending false readings to computers to prevent technicians from realizing what was happening.[29] Even if reported consequences had been felt by the larger population, the "clearly excessive" standard is dispositive for a modern proportionality analysis.

We do recognize that there may well be some exceptional circumstances in which the law of countermeasures might be relevant to cyber attacks. Echoing the *jus in bello* standard, Judge Vereschetin's dissent in the Hungary/Slovakia case in the International Court of Justice[30] described proportionality as a "basic requirement for the lawfulness of a countermeasure," which is to be determined "in the circumstances of the case."[31] In his words, "reference to equivalence or proportionality in the narrow sense…is unusual in State practice…[which] is why in the literature and arbitral awards it is suggested that the lawfulness of countermeasures must be assessed by the application of such *negative criteria* as "not [being] manifestly disproportionate," or "clearly disproportionate" [or] "not out of proportion.""

Lastly, both the Rome Statute of the ICC and Protocol I subsumed the operational standard for practice into the criminal law norm. This is important, because it establishes quite a high threshold for prohibited (i.e., disproportionate) operations. The attack must be intentionally launched "in the knowledge" that its effects would foreseeably result in an impermissible scope of damage to civilian lives or property. The very nature of cyber operations lends itself to highly technical and sophisticated codes that are intended to have limited and often undiscovered effects.

The intentional design of narrowly tailored technological cyber operations seems to lend itself to categorization as a "feasible measure" taken by responsible officials to insulate the population at large from the effects of a particular attack. In fact, it may be technologically possible to respond in a fully automated, almost instantaneous manner precisely against the computer or IP address responsible for a particular network intrusion. Such a narrowly tailored response could even be categorized as a permissible reprisal, particularly in light of the fact that the textual prohibitions on

---

[28] Iran Confirms STUXNET Worm Halted Centrifuges, (*CBSNews*, 29 Nov.2010) < http://www.cbsnews.com/stories/2010/11/29/world/main7100197.shtml>.

[29] John Markoff, "Malware Aimed at Iran Hit Five Sites," (*The New York Times*, 11 February 2011)<http://www.nytimes.com/2011/02/13/science/13STUXNET.html>.

[30] *Case Concerning the Gabcikovo-Nagymaros Project (Hungary/Slovakia)* [1997] I.C.J. 7, [25 Sept. 1997] 5

[31] *Id.* at 223 (Vereschetin, J., dissenting)(emphasis added).

reprisals in international law are meant to protect people, not property.[32] Of course, it is entirely conceivable that some adversary would intentionally cause civilian damage, which would violate the established *jus in bello* and perhaps create a state of actual armed conflict between states. In general, however, it is difficult to envision narrowly crafted code designed to achieve a particular effect or result within a designated network intrusion that would also fail properly to calibrate the intended effect or result in a reasonably foreseeable degree of disproportionate harm

IV. A PARADIGM SHIFT FOR CONCEPTUALIZING CYBER ATTACKS

We need a paradigm shift from seeing cyber attacks as a form of warfare to seeing cyber attacks as similar to embargoes. The rules of war are, by design, meant to apply only to situations that are exceptional. In such situations, it is thought that the normal rules and laws of society need to be adjusted, in some cases quite radically. Specifically, situations of war involve the clash of armies almost always claiming to act in national self-defense, each aiming at inflicting massive destruction on the other side so as to incapacitate and render harmless the threat of enemy armies. It is true that some cyber attacks may have similar rationales, namely national self-defense. But the point of cyber attacks is not to incapacitate as many enemy soldiers as possible. And because of this significant difference, cyber attacks should not be assimilated to the war paradigm. We argued in Section II that there are also other dissimilarities between cyber attacks and war or armed conflict.

A better paradigm for most cyber attacks than the war paradigm is one closer to the rules of everyday life, in which killing is not seen as justified and even sometimes required. In everyday life, there is a near-absolute prohibition on intentional killing, even if the person targeted is an enemy soldier. Indeed, soldiers have not done anything to make them liable to be killed if a cyber attack is launched. Or if there are some soldiers that have the liability to be attacked, it will be the very few soldiers that it takes to create and install a computer worm or virus in a foreign computer system. Soldiers cannot kill other soldiers in everyday life since all killing is seen as the same, and subject to the same near-absolute prohibition that comes from seeing everyone as a bearer of human rights.

---

[32] This is the implicit application of the principle conceded in the official International Committee of the Red Cross (ICRC) commentary which recognizes that though the "prohibition of attacks by way of reprisals and other prohibitions of the same type contained in Protocol I and in the Geneva Conventions have considerably reduced the scope for reprisals in time of war. At most, such measures could now be envisaged in the choice of weapons and in methods of combat used against military objectives." COMMENTARY ON THE ADDITIONAL PROTOCOLS OF 8 JUNE 1977 TO THE GENEVA CONVENTIONS OF 12 AUGUST 1949, Art. 51, ¶ 1985 (Sandoz et al, eds 1987).

Some theorists have recently argued that war itself should be assimilated to the standards of everyday life, specifically to the standards of individual self-defense in the face of lethal attacks.[33] But even these theorists do not mean the moral and legal rules of everyday life but the moral and legal rules concerning emergencies if a person is attacked and can only save his or her own life by mounting a lethal attack. The kinds of attacks that cyber attacks constitute do not pose such stark choices about the retaliatory use of lethal violence. Indeed, the best way at the moment to confront a cyber attack is by counter cyber attacks rather than anything lethal at all. Indeed, calling these counter attacks cyber "attacks" at all seems itself inappropriate since the acts may be purely defensive in the sense that they merely put up a shield that blocks the computer virus or worm from entering computer systems in the target state. In addition, there is often not really any need for a counter attack, at least not in the way attacks are understood. Purely defensive action that risks no one's life or even property is the main way that cyber attacks are confronted and stymied.

The better paradigm for cyber attacks is based in the intentional infliction of harm on property and other aspects of the infrastructure of a State, including but not limited to the State's ability to engage in successful economic transactions with other States, both sending goods out for export sale as well as bringing goods into for import sales. Cyber attacks theoretically could risk life and limb of the citizens of the state that is attacked. But this is certainly also true of economic embargoes. In Iraq, after the first Gulf War the civilian population suffered more harm as a result of embargoes from the war itself but, at the least, the losses that involved loss of life were unintended effects.

Cyber attacks interfere with the ability of a State to maintain communication between humans in the State and the various modes of infrastructure that are run by computers. And cyber attacks also disrupt the ability of a State to communicate with people in other States for mutually beneficial matters. The inflow and outflow of information in a society is disrupted but such disruption is better seen in the paradigm of economic exports and imports rather than the model of troops attacking each other or engaging in lethal attacks against foreign troops that are aggressing against them.

Insofar as cyber attacks and embargoes interfere with the sovereign functioning of a State, they are certainly not to be taken lightly. But in the Just War tradition as well as contemporary international law, embargoes are treated very differently from war or armed conflict—and this seems completely right to us. In the nineteenth century, Wheaton distinguished between embargoes that affect a State's own output

---

[33] *See* Henry Shue, *Do We Need a "Morality of War"?* *in* David Rodin and Henry Shue, eds., JUST AND UNJUST WARRIORS: THE MORAL AND LEGAL STATUS OF SOLDIERS 87 (David Rodin and Henry Shue, eds. 2008).

commerce and embargoes that physically restrain goods delivered by ship as input. The seizure of ships as a means to enforce an embargo verges on an act of war insofar as the intention is to take property of a State. But embargoes that are enforced by civil authority alone are not counted as acts of war and are governed by different rules than acts of war.[34]

In contemporary international law, embargoes are generally considered acts short of war. But trade embargoes, for instance, are restricted in various ways. Today, international legal practice has recognized certain embargoes as illegal, namely those that affect the free access to medicines, medical supplies, and certain basic foods that are important for the prevention of unnecessary suffering by civilian populations. Some of the restrictions on embargoes resemble restrictions on acts of war, but the overall regime is different in that embargoes are not generally seen as able to inflict loss of life on soldiers and other combatants. The longstanding US embargo of goods to and from Cuba was condemned by a series of UN declarations—but this was because of the effects of the embargo, especially on medical care in Cuba, not because the embargo was seen as an act of war.

We believe that cyber attacks should be regarded similarly to embargoes with respect to most of the points just covered in the preceding paragraphs. Embargo regimes do not allow for the killing of soldiers and other combatants; indeed, killing caused by embargoes is generally condemned, just as would other more predictable types of killing outside of the context of war or armed conflict. So, since it is physical destruction rather than killing or disabling soldiers that is the point of cyber attacks, we should not assimilate cyber attacks to the paradigm of war or armed conflict.

One objection to our view could build on the analogy with embargoes to argue that cyber attacks are aggressive measures that, in embargoes, can constitute acts of war. Indeed, it is the physical intrusion into the territory of the targeted State that can turn embargoes from civil administrations into acts of war. One could argue that cyber attacks normally are aggressive in this twofold sense: There is invasion of the territory of the targeted State, and there is an attempt to harm significantly the physical property of the targeted State. So, just as aggressive acts of embargo are counted as moving into the war paradigm, cyber attacks could be similarly treated in the war paradigm as well.

Our response to this objection is first to point out that the main worry about aggressive embargoes is that they will indeed involve the killing of civilians as a directly anticipated point of the embargo—namely to make the civilian population suffer. Yet, cyber attacks do not have civilian suffering as a directly anticipated or

---

[34] HENRY WHEATON, ELEMENTS OF INTERNATIONAL LAW 312–313(George Grafton Wilson ed. 1936)(1836). Wheaton here refers favorably to Vattel.

intended effect. It is true that some cyber attacks—for instance, those that target the computers responsible for the water supply or electrical grid of a State—are likely to effect civilian death and suffering. And in such cases, calling cyber attacks acts of war may indeed be warranted. But this is different from seeing the regime of cyber attacks as generally best approached though a paradigm of war and armed conflict. Rather, if cyber attacks are closely linked with the civilian death and suffering sufficient to constitute an armed attack or in the context of an armed conflict, only then should we employ the war paradigm, and even then as an exception to the usual way that cyber attacks should be understood.

A second objection is that cyber attacks are more serious assaults on the sovereignty of a State than we have recognized. Increasingly, most of the major services that States provide for their citizens are controlled by computers that can be subjected to malicious worms and viruses. The disruption of basic services to a population is also a disruption to the sovereign ability of a State to maintain the peace and security of its population. The sovereignty of the State is challenged in much the same way that an invasion challenges the sovereignty of a State, and leads to the charge that an act of war has occurred.

Our response to the second objection is to admit that cyber attacks can have just the wide-ranging effects that have been indicated. But once again, we would point out that the necessary response to cyber attacks is not to kill enemy soldiers but rather to defend the cyber networks of the targeted state. This requires a broadly conceived and integrated national strategy that touches areas of commerce, technology, industry, telecommunications, among other areas. And we concede that, if the effects of cyber attacks do have an impact on the civilian population, it gives us a reason to shift the paradigm, then just as in cases of embargoes. We will next elaborate our reasons to worry about the wholesale assimilation of cyber attacks to the model of war and armed conflict.

V. THE PROBLEMS OF ASSIMILATING CYBER ATTACKS TO A WAR PARADIGM

One way to see some of the potential problems with assimilating cyber attacks to a war paradigm versus an economic embargo paradigm is in the different departments of the government in charge of each. In the US, wars are the primary purview of the DOD (which used to be called the War Department), whereas embargoes are primarily handled through the Department of State (in which matters of diplomacy are its prime purview). When consigned to the DOD, cyber attacks are under the direction of generals and complex bureaucratic staff structures integrated into a military culture that sees intentional killing and wounding as acceptable, indeed nearly required, parts of their mandate. In the Departments of Commerce, Treasury, State, and Justice by contrast, intentional killing and wounding is not acceptable behavior, just as is true in most of the rest of ordinary life.

If cyber attacks are put under the purview of generals in the US Pentagon, there will be less inclination to restrain the development of cyber attack technology, especially the development of a more lethal means of attack than is currently possible. If instead, cyber attacks are treated as we treat economic embargoes, there will be significant restraint on developing cyber weapons that are lethal. As part of the normal regime of how killing is viewed in ordinary life, cyber attacks would not be developed alongside other lethal means of attack. This is one of the main worries in assimilating cyber attacks to military attacks that are designed to effect maximal destruction of lives of soldiers and other combatants.

Policy concerning cyber attacks, if housed in the Department of State or Homeland Security, would then be linked to the diplomatic means available for pursuing State interest. Indeed, if we can state anything regarding the nature of cyberwar with confidence, it involves a wide cross-section of public and private actors, treaty obligations, moral and legal regimes (both domestic and international), and raises a host of interagency complexities. In fact, it may be time to contemplate reorganization of the executive branch by consolidating cyberspace policy into one national coordinator, in the same way that the National Intelligence Council has authority to reach into the various intelligence functions across the executive branch.

Framing cyber attacks as similar to economic embargoes, we can think of cyber attacks as acts short of war that States should contemplate prior to the stage in which States begin contemplating recourse to the violence of war. But if cyber attacks are assimilated into the war paradigm at the outset, there will not be the advantage of having a potent alternative to war and armed conflict that can be employed by negotiators and other officials who are focused on peaceful settlement of disputes.

Another problem with assimilating cyber attacks to military attacks is that the States against which they are used will be more likely to respond militarily rather than merely to try to block the attacks with countercyber means or organize diplomatic resistance in the world community. This is the scenario that has developed since it was widely made known, although not officially acknowledged, that the STUXNET virus used against the centrifuges in Iran were designed and launched by the United States and Israel. Iran has vowed to kill Americans and Israelis for what it regards as the act of war that was perpetrated by the use of the STUXNET virus. The response that surely would be best for world peace is either merely to build better cyber defenses or launch retaliatory cyber attacks but not immediately to escalate to the plane of killing and threats of killing that is the normal domain of armed conflict. In addition, as late as December 2012, more than two years after the

STUXNET attack, Iran is still using that supposed military attack as a reason to claim that it needs to defend its sovereignty by any means necessary.

Curtailing or cabining cyber attacks in the way that economic embargoes are controlled would alleviate the risks to world peace that are the effect of cyber attacks understood as just one of many military means to attack a State's sovereignty. How then, should we properly view such cyber attacks as that involving STUXNET, if not as a military attack on Iran's sovereign rights. We see cyber attacks as deterrents and means of pressuring States rather than offensive weapons, once again similar to the way that economic sanctions are employed.

Cyber attacks can be deterrents in the way they were used against Iranian centrifuges. Neither the US nor Israel launched the STUXNET virus so as to invade and conquer Iran, but only to set back Iran's nuclear missile capability. And from all accounts, the plan succeeded. In addition, there was the implicit message that other cyber attacks would be launched if Iran tried to rebuild its nuclear weapons capability. STUXNET also created diplomatic space for continued dialogue on the relations between Iran and the other States in the region on a host of issues. The cost of cyber attacks is so small compared to the damage that can be done, as is well known, that States would be well advised to accede to the pressure and simply stop the prohibited activity that has brought upon itself the cyber attack.

Cyber attacks can also be used as a means of pressuring States to act more peaceably or stop acting in threatening ways to their own citizens or to citizens of neighboring states. If cyber attacks are used against the banking industry of a bellicose or oppressive state, this could significantly increase the pressure on the target state to cease these illegal activities and rejoin the community of peaceable states. And the disruptions could be intensified until it became unpalatable for the target state to continue policies disfavored by the international community. The advantage of deterrence and pressure is muted, we believe, if cyber attacks are merely one form of military attack in a state's arsenal. The world will be a safer place also if States do not think of their cyber capabilities in military rather than in diplomatic terms. Cyber attacks should not be seen as a step in the cycle of conflict whereby states seek to impose their will on each other by force. And we will all be better off if we do not extend to cyber attacks the immunity from sanction if people are killed as a result of their being used, which would be the logical culmination of extending the war convention.

We have argued that cyberwar is badly named as a form of war. Rather, in our view, cyber attacks should be understood as a type of diplomatic strategy that is similar to the way that economic embargoes have been used over the centuries. This means that there is an alternative paradigm readily available for how cyber attacks are understood that does not force us to invent something out of whole cloth.

Our view of cyber attacks is that they are a form of lawful retorsion, i.e., lawful unfriendly acts made in response to a violation by another state. At best, they may represent a form of countermeasure, i.e., an unlawful act undertaken in response to a previous unlawful act attributable to another sovereign. Thus, lawful cyber attacks are those that are proportional to the injury suffered and narrowly tailored to restore the status quo ante. The Draft Articles on State Responsibility make it clear that a lawful countermeasure must be designed as a temporary response that can be terminated once normal relations are secured. In this way, cyber attacks can be limited in scope, duration, and effect and therefore predictably move us farther from the threshold of warfare. And although the parallel between embargoes and cyber attacks is not perfect, we have given reasons for thinking that the embargo paradigm is much better than the war paradigm for understanding cyber attacks.

VI. CONCLUDING THOUGHTS ON PROPORTIONALITY AND CYBERWAR

As we have seen in earlier chapters, and in Section III of this chapter, proportionality is understood quite differently if we are not operating in the context of war or armed conflict. Cyber attacks, in our view, fall into the category of attacks that are short of armed attacks. The main reason for this is that the cyber attacks are not aimed at the taking of lives, and so the counter-measures that involve taking, or risk of taking, lives should not be presumed to be justified. Outside of the context of war or armed conflict, proportionality basically is governed by human rights rather than humanitarian concerns. And this means that the use of armed force is completely restricted only to those situations of emergency.

Countermeasures short of armed conflict, especially those that do not respond to armed conflict, are strictly controlled in international law. It is not presumed that armed actions will be considered proportionate merely if collateral damage is minimized. The higher standard employed is the one we addressed in Chapter 6 in our discussion of human rights and proportionality. In this respect, the killing of soldiers as a countermeasure to a cyber attack that is not aimed at the killing of soldiers would normally be considered disproportionate.

If cyber attacks are taken out of the *war or armed conflict* category and instead considered *actions short of armed conflict,* the response to them is not drawn in terms of Article 51 actions. Article 51 of the UN Charter enshrined the idea that States had "an inherent right of self defense."

Nothing in the present Charter shall impair the inherent right of individual or collective self-defense if an armed attack occurs against a Member of the

United Nations, until the Security Council has taken measures necessary to maintain international peace and security.

If cyber attacks are not assimilated to the model of armed attack, then States are not regarded as having the right to take armed action as a countermeasure. Nearly all armed action taken as a countermeasure to a less armed or unarmed attack is very likely to be considered disproportionate.

As we argued earlier in this chapter, if the armed conflict threshold has not been crossed, the rules of humanitarian law, that are fairly permissive concerning counter-measures taken in response to armed attack, are replaced by rules of human rights law, and other regimes of rules concerning proportionality, that are much more restrictive. If cyber-attacks are considered more like embargoes than like armed attacks, there will be very serious consequences for what is considered proportionate and what disproportionate as a countermeasure.

Several judgments of the ICJ, most especially the *Oil Platforms Case* and the *Nicaragua Case*, set out very different standards of proportionality that must be met if a State is responding to an attack that falls short of an armed attack. We will explore this issue in much more detail in our final chapter, Chapter 12. Suffice it here to say that it will matter greatly if cyber attacks are seen as fitting into the category of attacks short of armed attacks. In such a case, we do not assume that proportion-ality restraints will justify killing as a countermeasure since the main issue will be to diminish cruelty and collateral damage. Instead, the main issue is to prohibit killing altogether, since the intentional taking of life not in response to a threat to life vio-lates the human rights of the persons attacked.

As a final point, it should be noted again that there could be cyber attacks that rise to the level of armed attacks, although this is neither the case nor even likely at the moment. Throughout this chapter, we have argued that cyber attacks, because they do not involve arms in a usual sense, are to be treated more like embargoes than like war or armed conflict. If it should turn out that cyber attacks risked especially innocent lives, then our assessments would have to change. But before cyber attacks are assimilated to the model of war, the intentional risk of killing would have to be shown as one of the main aims of that instance of cyber attack. It makes an enormous difference whether an attack is called an armed attack, or an act of war, as opposed to an act that falls short of the threshold conditions for war. Cyber attacks today gener-ally do not cross the armed conflict threshold and should not be afforded the more permissive understanding of what *jus in bello* proportionality requires.

12

THRESHOLDS OF *JUS IN BELLO* PROPORTIONALITY

OUR FINAL CHAPTER attempts to summarize and provide more detail for the major considerations that we have argued constitute proportionality in international law, especially for *jus in bello* proportionality. Proportionality is the overarching principle that helps strike the appropriate balance between ethical imperatives, tactical convenience, strategic manipulation, and undue emotionalism. Indeed, as the ICRC notes:

> The entire law of armed conflict is, of course, the result of an equitable balance between the necessities of war and humanitarian requirements. There is no implicit clause in the Conventions which would give priority to military requirements. The principles of the Conventions are precisely aimed at determining where the limits lie; the principle of proportionality contributes to this.[1]

We will be addressing two different audiences in this final chapter. First, we will address those soldiers and leaders who are making decisions on the ground and do not have time to make complex proportionality calculations. In this respect, our discussion of rules of thumb is most pertinent. In addition, we will address legal scholars as well as military and political leaders who need to decide what level of proportionality analysis is needed in a specific situation, given the levels of permissiveness of

---

[1] COMMENTARY ON THE ADDITIONAL PROTOCOLS OF JUNE 8, 1977 TO THE GENEVA CONVENTIONS OF AUGUST 12, 1949, at 683, ¶ 2206 (Sandoz et al, eds 1987), *available at* http://www.icrc.org/ihl.nsf/COM/470-750001?OpenDocument.

the laws of war. In this respect, our discussion of thresholds is most apt. Our vision of thresholds is that they help to prevent the conflation of ideas that has been our concern by giving a basis for freedom of action since the principle of proportionality functions as a default-governing constraint.

And so in this chapter we seek to achieve two goals. We will first provide some rules of thumb to guide practitioners in the field who must make decisions about determining proportionate and disproportionate responses to armed attacks or other hostile acts. The rules of thumb can guide decision-making across the thresholds we will discuss, and may well be the key to a rapid and reasonable proportionality determination. As one American Brigade Combat Team leader from Afghanistan told us:

> General Petraeus' tactical directive ensured we took proportionality into account where we believed non-combatants could be. This was imperative to achieve the strategic endstate of our COIN [counterinsurgency] fight in Afghanistan. We have the ability to adjust our tactical and operational approach based on endstate goals. We do not need to have an overly restrictive interpretation of proportionality preemptively constrain our ability to effectively engage the enemy without taking into account the actual conditions on the ground or our desired effects/endstate.

In essence, that tactical directive provided the rules of thumb, while the doctrinal context provided the intellectual scaffolding needed to determine the correct application of proportionality. In order to slice through the misconceptions and misperceptions that have operational consequences, we will offer an account of the five thresholds that need to be crossed, based on the context, in order for something to be considered disproportionate in *jus in bello* proportionality.

In this chapter, we devote short sections to each of the rules of thumb and threshold considerations. So, in Section I, we will consider four rules of thumb: (1) the common denominator principle, (2) the civilian precautionary principle, (3) the unobserved target principle, and (4) the respect for fellow humans principle. In Section II, we will develop our five thresholds: (1) the symmetric status threshold, (2) the imminence and self-defense threshold; (3) the extreme emergency threshold, (4) the preemption or hostile action threshold, and (5) the controlled area threshold. And then in Section III, we conclude this work by explaining and defending our orientation in the book, which has been explicitly from the perspective of the soldier or commander.

I. INITIAL RULES OF THUMB FOR *JUS IN BELLO* PROPORTIONALITY

In the first chapter, we mentioned two rules of thumb that we will now say some more about as we also add two more rules of thumb that have arisen in other chapters. These rules of thumb, as we said earlier, are principles that guide behavior in a class of common cases in which proportionality considerations arise. They provide cross-cutting guidance that may well recur in a variety of scenarios, and are intended to apply to all of the thresholds we will describe. These rules of thumb are designed to give guidance concerning the problems commonly faced by commanders and combatants who are trying to navigate the minefields of situations that involve decision making that concerns the lives of others, in particular civilians, comrades, and "enemies," confronted on a regular basis.

A. *The Common Denominator Principle*

A first rule of thumb responds to the problem of the nearly incommensurable values that need to be weighed for any proportionality assessment. This rule of thumb is the *common denominator principle*, namely: Try to find a common metric to translate both types of value. The key to making proportionality manageable is to have weighing that can be done between things that are similar not dissimilar whenever feasible. It is much easier if the value of the military objective can be couched in terms of lives to be protected or saved so that the costs of such an operation, also often drawn in stark terms of the risk of loss of noncombatant or combatant lives, can be assessed more straightforwardly.

In order to follow this rule of thumb, the commander or even the combatant needs to try to ascertain the goals of an operation, and even understand the goals of the wider war of which that the operation is a part. And once one is relatively clear about these goals and likely consequences, one must use this knowledge. To do so, the values need to be comparable and the easiest way is to find a common denominator of the values being weighed against each other.

Soldiers and commanders should not settle for what seems to be the insurmountable problem of near incommensurables. Often, it is relatively easy to think of the competing values in terms of lives lost versus lives likely to be saved, for instance. No one should be allowed to hide behind their lack of knowledge, for in this position of ignorance, they will simply not be able to know whether their acts are disproportionate, which blocks the most important restraint against abusive behavior by soldiers who wield tremendous power.

B. *The Civilian Precautionary Principle*

The second rule of thumb partially responds to the weighing problem. The weighing problem concerns the difficulty of figuring out how much weight to give to the various kinds of lives that are potentially risked by military operations. This rule of thumb is the *civilian precautionary principle*, namely: Whenever civilian lives are greatly risked incidental to a tactic, very clear weighty military objectives have to be discerned for the tactic to be prima facie proportionate.

There is already a similar principle of *jus in bello*, the discrimination or distinction principle. This principle says that civilians should not be *directly* targeted during armed conflict. The second of our proposed proportionality rules of thumb, the civilian precautionary principle, deals with situations in which civilians will be *indirectly* targeted, as a matter of possible collateral damage. The indirect killing of civilians is not necessarily disproportionate. At the same time, the principles of proportionality and distinction should not be conflated by jurists that presume intentional targeting from the indirect, but foreseeable effects of lawful targeting. But for such indirect killings to be justified, there must be very clear objectives that outweigh the risk of civilian casualties. This is particularly true in the context of involuntary human shields, as the reader will recall from our discussion in Chapter 9. In our view, civilian lives are most in need of protection, even as we have also argued that the lives of soldiers should not be dismissed from proportionality assessments. The key in our view is that practitioners clearly articulate the competing considerations and the basis for their proportionality assessments.

C. *The Unobserved Target Principle*

The third rule of thumb is the *unobserved target principle*, namely: Indirect artillery fire into built-up civilian areas should not be taken in the absence of express authority from a more senior level of command. This is related, but distinct from other prohibitions on indiscriminate fire. Taken to its logical conclusion, this rule of thumb stipulates that decision makers all the way up the chain of command should be consulted if the tactic or strategy is known to involve combat in an area with a high concentration of civilians. In practice though what is required is that soldiers and their immediate commanders seek approval from superiors whenever they contemplate attacking a target that is unobserved. The one exception to this would be an instance of immediate personal or unit self-defense from incoming fire, as we will discuss in our second threshold below.

The worry addressed by this rule of thumb is that if a target is not directly observed, it is very difficult to tell whether and how many civilians may be nearby and at risk, or even how many combatants, including possibly one's own fellow soldiers, may be at risk if the target is attacked. Indeed, it is very hard to make proportionality assessments at all if the surrounding area of the site of a projected attack is not observed. On the other hand, this principle is designed to protect persons, and the traditional law of armed conflict that permits indirect fire into unobserved terrain to achieve a definite military objective is unaffected. In rare cases of overwhelmingly important consequences, it might be proportionate to attack an unobserved target in the vicinity of civilian areas, but all available information needs to be secured. The best way to guarantee access to this knowledge is to require approval up the chain of command, where a greater font of knowledge is often lodged.

This rule of thumb also is clearly aimed at building counterinsurgency campaigns that have been very carefully thought through by various levels of decision-makers. One of the hallmarks of counterinsurgency is that it often involves attacking targets that the attacking soldiers have not themselves previously observed. Involving officers up the chain of command increases the likelihood of securing the best information, which will result in the most accurate proportionality assessment that is possible.

D. *The Respect for Fellow Humans Principle*

Finally, we offer a fourth rule of thumb, the *respect for fellow humans principle*. This rule of thumb holds that: Regardless of the circumstances, never forget that those who are one's enemy are fellow human beings who deserve at least minimal respect. This principle correlates with our overarching approach to proportionality: Make combatants more aware of the value of lives of all sorts involved in armed conflict and in response to hostile actions. And as we have stressed, this most definitely includes the human lives of soldiers, on both sides, one's own and the enemy's. Of course, what counts as showing sufficient respect for fellow humans can vary with the circumstances, but there is a core here that stays constant and has led us to argue that the human rights of soldiers should never be totally discounted.

This fourth rule of thumb is grounded in a strong moral principle that has been nearly unchallenged since the eighteenth-century philosopher Immanuel Kant's writings and is at the core of the Universal Declaration of Human Rights as well as the Preamble of the Charter of the United Nations. Respect for the dignity and value of all human lives is now acknowledged as the hallmark of modern civilized societies. War should not be seen as so outside of normal moral considerations that the principle of respect for persons is disregarded. The correlate of this rule of thumb is that one should never contemplate taking the life of a fellow human being, directly

288 Proportionality in International Law

or indirectly, unless the circumstances are truly exigent. And the classic formulation of *jus in bello* proportionality implicitly derives from this rule of thumb, in our view. We are merely making explicit what is already embedded in the rule.

II. THE THRESHOLDS OF *JUS IN BELLO* PROPORTIONALITY

The five thresholds that we will now catalogue are the core of our reformulation of the proportionality principle as applied, which we have set out in various ways and with numerous examples throughout this book. The thresholds to be discussed in more detail below can be briefly characterized as follows. The first threshold is the one that is most lenient, namely, if there is a symmetrical war between two States' professional soldiers. The second threshold is nearly as permissive as the first, even if the conflict is asymmetric, namely, if the self-defense of the soldiers or their unit is in serious jeopardy.

The third threshold is not as permissive as the first two, but not quite as restrictive as the human rights threshold, namely, if there is an emergency that provides a serious threat to a society, often from those who are terrorists. The fourth threshold is one of hostile action or preemption, in which attacks by non-State actors are occurring or very likely to occur. Here, the standard of proportionality is highly restrictive, although again not quite as high as that used in human rights law, in which the right to life for all humans is such that it can only be jeopardized if much greater loss of life on the side of the balance is at stake. And the fifth exemplifies something similar to the human rights regime, in situations in which the State has effective control over a civilian population or almost total authority over an area.

So we postulate a scale of threshold considerations. Once one crosses a given threshold, say that of self-defense, the correct rule of first resort for proportionality is determined by that threshold. What counts as a proportionate attack gets more and more permissive as one moves up the scale of thresholds from 5 to 1. Or, to put it another way, as one moves down the scale from 1 to 5, and it is clear that the other thresholds have not been crossed, then what counts as a proportionate attack gets more and more restrictive. The reason to discuss proportionality in terms of thresholds is that once it is clear that one does not cross one threshold, there is likely to be another threshold that one has crossed that is actually less permissive than might otherwise appear to be true. Our goal is to provide clarity of analysis.

We dissected the details of proportionality in its various usages throughout the book, yet it is striking that we still need the thresholds to simplify its application in the important context of armed conflict. To summarize the thresholds that implicate varying applications of proportionality, the five threshold markers are these: (1) an armed attack by troops of one State that attack so as to jeopardize the sovereign immunity or territorial integrity of another sovereign State; (2) an imminent threat to the self-defense of combatant or unit; (3) an extreme emergency that poses a serious threat to a society by the actions of non-State actors; (4) a hostile attack that requires a preemptive attack to avert risk to lives; and (5) a situation of a controlled area, such as occupied territory. Let us examine in more detail each of these thresholds before drawing out some overall conclusions.

A. *The Symmetric Status Threshold*

Historically, the rules governing proportionality were developed on the assumption that war would be fought by relatively large sovereign States, with armies that had similar professional training. The classic conception of combatancy and combatant immunity derived from this foundation. By extension, the strict principle that the principle of reciprocity by which the obligations of one State are not gauged by reference to the actions of the other State during the conflict flowed from this intellectual conception of armed conflict. We devoted the entirety of Chapter 5 to the development of the core *jus in bello* proportionality principle that developed against this backdrop. The rules of proportionality today must take account that most armed conflicts are not between sovereign States but among a diverse assortment of actors, and we cannot assume a common professionalization of the fighters involved. Most confrontations called wars are more likely to be conflicts or just hostile interactions. In each case, there are somewhat different proportionality considerations.

If we are in a situation in which the parties to the conflict are not both States in the traditional sense of this term, then the rules of proportionality are the default position of conforming to a higher bar set by virtue of customary international law. In other words, even if the historical rationale for fully imposing the demands of *jus in bello* on both parties. on the basis of reciprocal expectations. has changed, the same standards apply in asymmetric conflicts in which one side will almost certainly fail to comply with *jus in bello*. In fact, there are many asymmetric conflicts in which the non-State participants explicitly reject the application of *jus in bello*. Two considerations will also be important though, and will be the basis of the last two threshold considerations: First, is the danger of the non-armed conflict so extreme that it should be treated similarly to a full-fledged armed attack? Second, is the conflict nonetheless a hostile action that should have a proportionality level set between the standard humanitarian law understanding of proportionality and the human rights understanding?

For asymmetric armed conflicts, the proportionality bar is generally higher than for conflicts between two States; at least that is the current thinking in international law concerning the second threshold. During an asymmetric armed conflict, typically, there is some residual area in which the full body of human rights law applies, yet often operates alongside the application of broader principles drawn from the laws and customs of warfare. A great deal has been written on this middle-ground, asymmetric conflict and the precise circumstances in which the *lex specialis* of humanitarian law displaces the normal operation of the human rights regime. It is not our intent to fully resolve these debates in this concluding chapter. Yet it is worth asking, as matter of *lex ferenda* rather than *lex lata*, why and whether the character of the actors should matter for proportionality assessments. At least in part, the more permissive threshold for satisfying proportionality in symmetric wars has to do with the presumption of reciprocity—States generally recognize reciprocal restraints of various sorts, and the idea of proportionality is only one of those restraints.

In asymmetric conflicts, by contrast, the presumption of reciprocity has never been granted. As we have said, this has a lot to do with the lack of professional socialization that is quite important in restraining the actions of combatants. It also flows from the fact that asymmetric actors are, by definition, not affiliated with a particular State in the sense that their actions can be attributed to the authority of a particular State by the operation of established international law. Nevertheless, nonprofessionalized participants in armed conflict should not be merely treated as pirates or the highway robbers of old. But they should also not be glamorized as if they were soldiers with an esprit de corps. The incentive structures applicable to such participants in conflicts are by definition distinctive from those applicable to states. Here proportionality, or more specifically the charge of disproportionate attack, is one of the few restraints that is likely to have any teeth in restraining the fighters in these asymmetric conflicts.

What specifically is meant by saying that the threshold for satisfying proportionality in asymmetric conflicts is more restrictive? The most important thing at play here is that the killing of one noncombatant is hardly ever justified, even as a matter of collateral damage. Phrased another way, even in the conflicts in which a straightforward *jus in bello* application of proportionality is warranted, based on the context, the normal law enforcement paradigm operates on the margins. And it is equally important that it will take more to justify the killing of one combatant by another than in symmetric conflicts. We are not claiming that there should be a full-scale embrace of human rights norms in asymmetric conflicts. Rather, though, the norms are slightly more restrictive than in traditional symmetric conflict, hence force should be used in a more calibrated manner.

B. *The Imminence and Self-Defense Threshold*

The second threshold involves ascertaining if one is responding to an actual armed attack. In order to make this assessment, one must realize that in international humanitarian law (IHL), there is a clear threshold that has to be crossed for something to be considered an *armed attack* sufficient to justify lethal measures of self-defense that would not otherwise be considered to be permissible.

In some circumstances, even if the armed conflict threshold has not been crossed, a similar standard of proportionality may apply. For this to occur, the attack being responded to must cross a self-defense threshold, at which the lives of the soldiers or the coherence of the military unit of which the soldiers are part, is facing a very serious likelihood of being jeopardized. Mere speculative considerations concerning what possible losses there are to others are not sufficient to justify self-defensive action.

So, one important threshold is whether a conflict rises to the level of being a very serious attack of the sort that involves such serious issues of self-defense that there is a relatively low bar for what counts as proportionate countermeasures. It should also be said that one does not cross this threshold of what is similar to armed conflict merely with the appearance of threat to oneself or the unit. (Recall our discussion of cyber attacks.) In a sense, all military operations risk threat to self or unit. But what is significant is how best to understand the uniqueness of this particular situation in the context of other armed conflicts.

In the easiest cases, the threshold is crossed for persons acting under immediate personal and unit self-defense. Remember the account of the Australians in Chapter 8. If soldiers respond to an ambush with hasty fire and a covering base of fire, they operate under the immediate and adrenaline-driven need to preserve their lives and those of their comrades. It would often be inhumane to treat the soldiers being attacked in a way that would make any tactics that are necessary to save their lives disproportionate. In fact, in our view an overly restrictive view of proportionality, imposed after the fact from the comfort of a conference room or the cold of a courtroom, would be to undervalue the human right to life of those soldiers. The classic case involves an immediate threat as soldiers respond with immediate fire in an ambush or to repel an attack. The need for as much firepower as possible to suppress enemy action is obvious, and the opportunity to gain information on the possibility of collateral civilian casualties practically nonexistent. These are cases that are clear-cut based on the concrete rights of unit and individual self-defense, and no elaborate proportionality calculations are needed.

There are other cases that sit at the cusp of the threshold. Here necessity's relationship to proportionality is often crucial. The response may indeed be disproportionate, even in cases of self-defense, if taking lethal action was not necessary to avert the threat. And the cases at the cusp will be ones in which the response seems otherwise excessive, yet we grant those under attack a certain latitude; we allow them to put great weight on the fact that they reasonably believe their own lives to be at great risk. We seek to avoid the frustration expressed by one British soldier speaking of his experience in Afghanistan who said, "I agree with [the restrictions imposed by commanders on the basis of their understandings of proportionality and necessity during counterinsurgency operations] to the extent that previously too many civilians were killed but we have got people shooting at us and we are not allowed to shoot back."[2]

What we do not favor, though, is the view that the entirety of war or armed conflict should be understood on the model of self-defense. War is much more complicated than the simple analogy to personal self-defense cases can illuminate. Symmetrical armed conflict is a contest of States, and asymmetrical armed conflict is a contest of arms between States, typically very large non-State actors. In the midst of armed conflict. there are many occasions in which the self-defense of soldiers is not at issue at all and the default *jus in bello* considerations based on reasonableness and the feasibility of other courses of action may well predominate.

Nonetheless, for soldiers who have been placed into a certain context by others and find themselves under attack and fearing for their lives, our threshold approach grants them great latitude in terms of proportionality. It is much too much to ask of soldiers, who are already making enormous sacrifices for their countries, to also be forced to comply with rules of proportionality that deny them the right to use the force required for self-defense.

C. The Extreme Emergency Threshold

If it can be shown that the purpose of an act or a rule is to advance extremely important purposes for a society in an emergency, then proportionality constraints will be somewhat relaxed, even though the conflict is asymmetric and does not involve self-defense. The classic case is insurgents or terrorists that threaten widespread destruction in the target society. The attacks of 9/11/2001 were not launched by one State against another State. Indeed, the group that launched the attack did not represent even a significant political subsection of a State. And yet the attack

---

[2] Thomas Harding, *Curbs on Firing at Taliban Are Putting Us at Risk, Troops Warn*, THE TELEGRAPH, 14 (July 7, 2010).

caused great loss of civilian life, and had it been fully successful, would have disrupted the entire political system in the United States. So, lethal response could be proportionate even though the threshold of proportionality is still restrictive compared to the proportionality threshold of traditional symmetric war. This is another way of saying that the overall military advantage anticipated must be substantial, or even well-nigh imperative.

Distinguishing proportionate and disproportionate responses to terrorism is vexing in the extreme. One problem is that the sheer military power of a State like the United States, compared to that of Al Qa'ida on 9/11/2001, is nearly incalculable. Is this a reason to argue for especially strong restraint? In addition, the Al Qa'ida fighters were not then nor are they now, professional fighters who recognize reciprocal restraints; it is hard to ascertain the extent to which the Goliath of the US should be restrained toward the David of Al Qa'ida. As we have already indicated, we support more restraint in asymmetrical wars than in symmetric wars, but less so if grave societal purposes are not implicated. It is this latter claim that needs defense.

Our reasoning is based on the return of the analogy of personal self-defense transposed to the domain of societies. If the State or society's existence, or a sizeable section of its population, is threatened by the actions of a non-State actor, the State has the right to defend itself, and if necessary, to do so by lethal responses. One cannot forget that the protection of the fundamental right to life is one of the existential imperatives of the modern state. In other words, the state must defend the basic human rights of its constituents. But the right of State self-defense, especially against non-State actors, is much more limited than the right of self-defense for soldiers or units.

One reason for the disparity is that non-State actors are much less likely to conquer and subjugate a State than would lethal assaults taken by another State. In a commentary on a case concerning an act that criminalized those who provide material support for terrorists, the Canadian judge in *Khawaja*, made an important observation.

I add this. The breadth of the impugned provisions reflects Parliament's determination that "there is substantive harm inherent in all aspects of preparation for a terrorist act because of the great harm that flows from the completion of terrorist acts": *R. v. Ahmad* (2009), 257 C.C.C. (3d) 199 (Ont. S.C.J.), at para. 60. In the context of the present analysis, it is appropriate to exhibit due deference to this determination. The criminalization under s. 83.18 of a broad range of interactions that have the potential—and are intended to—materially enhance the abilities of terrorist groups is *not grossly disproportionate* nor *overbroad in relation to* the objective of prosecuting and, in particular, of preventing terrorism.(emphasis added)[3]

We would argue similarly that, in emergency situations, the threshold of what initially appears to be proportionate is somewhat relaxed, so that what would otherwise be considered a disproportionate response is allowed.

Yet, the fact of an emergency does not change or allow everything. Some courts, such as the European Court of Human Rights and the Israeli High Court, have said that the correct threshold for terrorists is always the human rights threshold of proportionality. We do not go that far, but accept that the human rights proportionality analysis should be the norm, absent exigent circumstances. The fact of an emergency for a State in terms of its self-defense does not have the same effect as if the emergency were for an individual in self-defense terms (i.e., the preceding thresholds are distinguishable—the second is primarily a *jus in bello* threshold while the third is primarily a *jus ad bellum* threshold).

Decision-makers should precisely articulate the basis for proportionate responses so that they may bear the burden imposed under the human rights model for supporting their actions, yet they should clearly document the need to shift that burden as the circumstances dictate. In this respect, the inherent right of self-defense under Article 51 of the UN Charter does not translate into a license to disregard or greatly undervalue proportionality restraints. The response must be minimized whenever possible, though we would stop short of imposing the human-rights-derived duty to arrest a person unless lethal force is imperatively required in the circumstances prevailing at the precise time and place. The point is not that we disregard human rights considerations, but that, in certain emergencies, self-defense cuts in regardless of normal human rights considerations.

D. *The Preemption or Hostile Action Threshold*

In cases in which imminence has not been satisfied, the appropriate threshold is one of preemption, as distinct from mere presumption of legality. If preemption can be ascertained, the standards of proportionality are less lenient than those for self-defense, but less strict than for human rights.

The preemption threshold is crossed if the impending attack to be countered is still sufficiently serious to make us think that it is reasonable to respond with lethal force. In addition, the impending attack must be one that is not merely speculative in the sense that one sees the need for some kind of preventive action. Preemption

---

[3] R. *v.* Khawaja, 2012 S.C.C. 69, para.63 (2012).

requires a showing of imminence and immediacy of threat, not mere speculative threats of a prevention model.

At the merits stage of the Oil Platforms Case (Islamic Republic of Iran v United States of America),[4] Judge Simma in his Separate Opinion[5] made reference to the work of the International Law Commission (ILC) in relation to countermeasures, specifically referring to Articles 49 to 54. This occurred in the context of his discussion of the question of whether measures involving the use of armed force were permissible reactions in response to a use of armed force stopping short of an armed attack:

> I am less satisfied with the argumentation used in the Judgment by which the Court arrives at the—correct—conclusion that, since the Iranian mine, gunboat or helicopter attacks on United States shipping did not amount to an "armed attack" within the meaning of Article 51 of the Charter, the United States actions cannot be justified as recourse to self-defense under that provision. The text of paragraph 51 of the Judgment might create the impression that, if offensive military actions remain below the—considerably high—threshold of Article 51 of the Charter, the victim of such actions does not have the right to resort to—strictly proportionate—defensive measures equally of a military nature. What the present Judgment follows at this point are some of the less fortunate statements in the Court's Nicaragua Judgment of 1986. In my view, the permissibility of strictly defensive military action taken against attacks of the type involving, for example, the Sea Isle City or the Samuel B. Roberts cannot be denied. What we see in such instances is an unlawful use of force "short of" an armed attack ("*agression armée*") within the meaning of Article 51, as indeed "the most grave form of the use of force." Against such smaller-scale use of force, defensive action—by force also "short of" Article 51—is to be regarded as lawful. In other words, I would suggest a distinction between (full-scale) self-defense within the meaning of Article 51 against an "armed attack" within the meaning of the same Charter provision on the one hand and, on the other, the case of hostile action, for instance against individual ships, below the level of Article 51, justifying proportionate defensive measures on the part of the victim, equally short of the quality and quantity of action in self-defense expressly reserved in the United Nations Charter.[6]

---

[4] Oil Platforms (Islamic Republic of Iran v United States of America), Merits, ICJ Reports 2003, p. 161.
[5] Oil Platforms (United States of America v Islamic Republic of Iran), Separate Opinion of Judge Simma, ICJ Reports 2003, p. 324.1214 *Id.*, at 331–332, para. 12.
[6] *Id.*

In our view, what is crucial is the distinction between "armed attack" and "hostile action," each having its own threshold of proportionate countermeasures.

Here we see one judge struggling with the standard of proportionality to adopt when the defensive action falls below the threshold of armed attack, as required by the text of Article 51. What is then called hostile action falls short of armed attack, but can still be understood as having a proportionate and armed countermeasure. So, although there is a threshold for what counts as an armed attack, having fallen below the threshold does not rule out proportionate and even armed countermeasures.

Having referred to a passage from the judgment of the ICJ in the Military and Paramilitary Activities case,[7] Judge Simma observed that the Court had there drawn:

> [...] a distinction between measures taken in legitimate self-defense on the basis of Article 51 of the Charter and lower-level, smaller-scale proportionate countermeasures which do not need to be based on that provision. In view of the context of the Court's above dictum, by such proportionate counter-measures the Court cannot have understood mere pacific reprisals, more recently, and also in the terminology used by the International Law Commission, called "countermeasures." Rather, in the circumstances of the Nicaragua case, the Court can only have meant what I have just referred to as defensive military action "short of" full-scale self-defense.[8]

In most cases, we agree with Judge Simma that in hostile action cases, proportionate responses will nearly always be defensive in nature (and, in this respect, the fourth threshold is close to the domestic law enforcement model we have discussed in Chapter 10).

---

[7] *Id.*, at 332, quoting Military and Paramilitary Activities in and against Nicaragua (Nicaragua v United States of America), Merits, ICJ Reports 1986, p. 14 at 127, para. 249.

[8] In the footnote accompanying the reference to the International Law Commission's use of the terminology of "countermeasures," Judge Simma made specific reference to the prohibition of countermeasures involving the threat or use of armed force contained in Article 0(1)(a): Cf. Articles 49-54 of the ILC's text on the Responsibility of States for Internationally Wrongful Acts, [...]. The Commission strictly excluded from its concept of "counter-measures" any such measures amounting to a threat or use of force; cf. Article 50, para. 1 (a).1243, 1241 Ibid., at p. 332, quoting Military and Paramilitary Activities in and against Nicaragua (Nicaragua v United States of America), Merits, ICJ Reports 1986, p. 14 at 127, para. 249. 1242 Oil Platforms (United States of America v Islamic Republic of Iran), Separate Opinion of Judge Simma, ICJ Reports 2003, p. 324, at p. 332, para. 12. 1243 *Id.*, p. 332, note 19.

E. *The Controlled Area Threshold*

The most restrictive application of *jus in bello* is in areas that are highly controlled by a State. The obvious modern instance is the law of occupation during which military necessity is so attenuated that the effect is to disfavor military action with lethal consequences in almost every instance short of absolutely imperative individual self-defense. We term this the controlled area threshold because we conceive it to be broader than simply periods of occupation in the context of armed conflicts between States. This same threshold may well apply during periods of counterinsurgency operations in which an armed conflict not of an international character continues to simmer intermittently.

The relationship of a subjugated civilian population to a foreign power temporarily exercising *de facto* sovereignty is regulated by the extensive development of the law of occupation.[9] And in recent years, a steady stream of cases has imposed human-rights-based treaty obligations onto occupying States as we described earlier. In those contexts, the State obligations assumed, for instance, by virtue of the European Convention of Human Rights and Fundamental Freedoms, supersede the application of *jus in bello* derived law of occupation (specifically Part IV of the Fourth Geneva Convention). Thus, the normal presumptions about necessity and proportionality have shifted from the law of war requirements into the far more constrained human rights framework.

During periods of occupation, lethal force is uncontroverted if it is based on absolute necessity and no other lesser alternative is reasonably available. This of course contrasts with the normally predominant *jus in bello* principle during conflict (threshold one), with its presumption that lethal force is deemed to be authorized whenever reasonably necessary to advance a particular military goal. In other words, lethal force during wartime may be used to subjugate the enemy or destroy lawful military objectives with the minimum expenditure of time, ammunition, and loss of life. The whole point of occupation is that active hostilities are no longer necessary. Hence, it is completely appropriate to shift the conceptual foundation of proportionality toward the human rights or law enforcement model.

The classic context of occupation law does not expressly constrain *jus in bello* proportionality but obliquely restrains its utility in a variety of ways. In terms of legal rights and duties, a nation is considered occupied territory if it is "actually placed

---

[9] Regulations annexed to Hague Convention IV of 1907 respecting the Laws and Customs of War on Land (hereinafter 1907 Hague Regulations), entered into force 26 Jan. 1910, *reprinted in* A. Roberts & R. Guelff (eds.), DOCUMENTS ON THE LAWS OF WAR, 3rd edition, Oxford University Press, Oxford, 2000, p. 73; Fourth Geneva Convention, Arts. 47–78.

under the authority of the hostile army."[10] This legal criterion is fulfilled if the following circumstances prevail on the ground: First, the existing government structures have been rendered incapable of exercising their normal authority. Second, the occupying power is in a position to carry out the normal functions of government over the affected area.[11] For the purposes of United States policy, occupation is the legal status occasioned by "invasion plus taking firm possession of enemy territory for the purpose of holding it."[12] Although a state of occupation does not "affect the legal status of the territory in question,"[13] the assumption of authority over the occupied territory implicitly means that the existing institutions of society have been swept aside.

Because the foreign power has displaced the normal domestic offices, the cornerstone of the law of occupation is the broad obligation that the foreign power—the occupant—must "take *all* the measures in his power to restore, and ensure, as far as possible, public order and safety."[14] In the authoritative French, the occupier must preserve "l'ordre et la vie publics" (i.e., the public order and life).[15] In our view, there may well be some areas of counterinsurgency operation or humanitarian relief following natural disasters for which these principles can be extrapolated to mean that the dominant principle derives from human rights. Lethal force would therefore be very restricted in these transitory zones between the law of peace and the law of warfare. In these settings, the burden of proof should shift towards the party applying lethal force.

To be clear, we do not favor a complete conflation of human rights law with *jus in bello* in these controlled area settings that would result in a radical change in how proportionality is viewed. We do, however, note that the very hallmarks of firm

---

[10] 1907 Hague Regulations, Art.42. *See also* THE LAW OF LAND WARFARE, DEPARTMENT OF THE ARMY FIELD MANUAL 27-10, WASHINGTON, 1956, ¶ 351 [FM 27–10].

[11] THE MANUAL OF THE LAW OF ARMED CONFLICT, UK MINISTRY OF DEFENCE 275, ¶ 11.3 (2004), P. 275.

[12] US *ARMY FIELD MANUAL 27-10*, ¶ 352.

[13] PROTOCOL I (NOTE 15) ART.4. The United States policy in this regard is clear that occupation confers only the "means of exercising control for the period of occupation. It does not transfer the sovereignty to the occupant, but simply the authority or power to exercise some of the rights of sovereignty." US ARMY FIELD MANUAL 27-10, ¶ 358.

[14] 1907 HAGUE REGULATIONS, OP. CIT. (NOTE 84), ART.43 (EMPHASIS ADDED).

[15] *Id.* The conceptual limitations of foreign occupation also warranted a temporal limitation built into the 1949 Geneva Conventions that the general application of the law of occupation "shall cease one year after the general close of military operations"; Fourth Geneva Convention (note 14), Art. 6. Based on pure pragmatism, Article 6 of the Fourth Geneva Convention does permit the application of a broader range of specific treaty provisions "for the duration of the occupation, to the extent that such Power exercises the functions of government in such territory." The 1977 Protocols eliminated the patchwork approach to treaty protections with the simple declaration that "the application of the Conventions and of this Protocol shall cease, in the territory of Parties to the conflict, on the general close of military operations and, in the case of occupied territories, on the termination of the occupation"; Protocol I (note 15), Art. 3(b).

control over an area mitigate for an understanding of proportionality that is similar to the restrictive human rights application. Military necessity is generally subordinated to the need for order and maintenance of peace in areas of the occupied territory. Conflict is not the norm.

In particular, enemy threats can be isolated and the presumption is thus that the need to use lethal force is the exceptional case that becomes far less necessary as control over the area becomes more firmly established. In other words, the use of lethal force must have an affirmative legal authority and should be narrowly tailored to what is absolutely needed to accomplish that lawful purpose. Proportionality in these situations, as in the law enforcement and human rights domains, is limited to consideration of the degree of force needed in the immediate area for the immediate purpose, unlike the broader considerations in *jus in bello* that operate with no per se geographic or temporal limits. To reiterate, in these situations, the spectrum of proportionality is skewed toward the human rights model but there is no perfect overlay.

III. CONCLUSIONS

Throughout this book, we have addressed a myriad of issues related to the modern law and practice of proportionality. We have had two primary goals. First, we hope to prompt clarity of debate regarding the correct formulation of *lex lata* proportionality in its various contexts. As we have already observed, the very concept of proportionality provides a template for reaching a balanced approach that can be applied to assess inherently complex and subjective decision-making processes. There is a danger, however, that the very familiarity with the term makes its use formulaic and often unreflective.

Lt. Gen. Sir Ian Hamilton, summarized the problem of battle history in the Preface to his own observer's diary of the Russo-Japanese War, entitled *A Staff Officer's Scrap Book*. His thought is often quoted out of context, but the longer text of his 1905 comment is more than apropos to our discussion of proportionality:

> If facts are hurriedly issued, fresh from the mint of battle, they cannot be expected to supply an account which is either well balanced or exhaustive. On the other hand, it is equally certain that, when once the fight has been fairly lost or won, it is the tendency of all ranks to combine and recast the story of their achievement into a shape which shall satisfy the susceptibilities of national and regimental vain-glory. It is then already too late for the painstaking historian to set to work. He may record the orders given and the movements which ensued,

and he may build hopes and fears which dictated those orders, and to the spirit and method in which those movements were executed, he has for ever lost the clue. On the actual day of battle naked truths may be picked up for the asking; by the following morning they have already begun to get into their uniform.

Proportionality is not an infinitely malleable notion that can become a self-justifying norm. It does have a fixed and accepted form in each of its diverse usages, but the correct application of the principle depends entirely on the facts available, the reasonable perceptions of participants, and the overall motivations of the decision-makers, that is, on subjective assessments. As we have shown, proportionality cannot simply be cut and pasted into the thinking of practitioners and lawyers across contexts with monolithic meaning. We think it vitally important to be clear about the correct standard of proportionality to be followed so that it functions as intended to achieve its laudatory goals—balance, symmetry, effectiveness, humanity. In this respect, we have also raised questions about the prevailing standard from the perspective of *lex ferenda*. We have not been satisfied with merely describing the current state of international law.

Second, our overarching goal has been to address these issues from the perspective of a soldier or commander who has to make decisions, often in the heat of battle. They are asked to accomplish difficult missions based on a good-faith application of the legal and moral norms in the context of seemingly overwhelming obstacles. It is for this reason that we have often asked how a commander or soldier can be expected to know something if the context in which he or she is acting makes it very hard to gain this knowledge—and this is another place where subjectivity enters into proportionality assessments, although here there is quasi-objective component in that the consideration should be what a reasonable person would know or expect.

Proportionality assessments should not be so hard to make that people on the ground give up trying to make them. For the law to atrophy to such a state of esoteric obsolescence would surely mean greater loss of life among the civilian population and would endanger the very professional foundations of the military art. And proportionality assessments should not be so simple that they amount to what people are doing anyway, pretty much regardless of what that is or its effects. Instead, proportionality assessments should make the commander or soldier aware of the immense power they wield and of the relevant range of consequences involved in wielding that power. In most cases, proportionality imposes a stringent requirement, even if it does not completely restrain lethal force in practice.

In addition, and controversially, we have strongly argued that the lives of soldiers should not be completely irrelevant in proportionality assessments. One of our reasons has been because soldiers have human rights. And another of our reasons has also been because we wish to have proportionality considerations instill in soldiers the idea that they are agents who must make decisions for themselves, and not merely to see themselves as automatons being directed by someone else's design. In most of the legal and moral discussions of proportionality today, the main consideration to be weighed against pursuing a military objective is the likelihood of collateral damage (i.e., killing) of noncombatants. We have argued that we also need to take some account of other lives, especially those of the soldiers involved in the conflict.

We believe that one of the key considerations in any attempt to professionalize, or increase professionalization, is for the individuals involved to take a critical stand toward what they are doing in their professional roles.[16] And it is vitally important that they then take this critical approach with them into their day-to-day lives as professional warriors. One way to encourage such an attitude is to acknowledge the often severe moral dilemmas and paradoxes that are faced by most professionals. Any attempt to provide rules to aid the professional decision-makers, must be made in light of how hard it is to make decisions on the ground, and with an understanding of the unhappiness of professionals who feel that their compliance includes being second-guessed by people who have no experience of the life of a professional soldier.

In the context of war, armed conflict, and hostile operations, it is vitally important to have soldiers and other combatants take themselves seriously. They are not pawns in an elaborate chess game, nor are the people they are shooting at cardboard cutouts on a firing range. What we ask soldiers to do during war and other conflicts is to shoot and sometimes kill other humans. We want these soldiers to realize that the enemy they are fighting includes fellow humans who are also mainly professionals trying to do a good job in their assigned roles.

And most important, if we want soldiers and other combatants to take seriously the humanity of the enemy, not merely the enemy civilians but all of the humans who make up the enemy population, we will have to take seriously the human status of our own soldiers. As we have said, we hope that it is clearly arcane and obsolete today to refer to our own soldiers as cannon fodder. At the same time, soldiers should not be infantilized by proportionality assessments that seem only to consider the likely collateral damage to civilians—which could overlook that soldiers' actions have the direct consequences of causing or making more likely the death of fellow soldiers–on both their own side and the enemy side.

---

[16] *See* LARRY MAY, THE SOCIALLY RESPONSIVE SELF (1996).

So we have chosen to address proportionality from the perspective of a humanely trained soldier, and we believe that this means taking seriously the lives of soldiers in proportionality calculations. This does not mean that the value of the lives of soldiers should always outweigh other values, especially if compared to the lives of innocent civilians. We assume, in this book, that some wars are, or at least could be just, and there is sometimes good reason to assign our soldiers the task of disabling or even killing other soldiers. As we have indicated, there is a scale of proportionality thresholds, from more restrictive to more permissive. But at all points along the scale, the lives of soldiers should be considered to have value and not dismissed in proportionality assessments.

As has been known historically, as long as there have been lethal contests of arms, it is easier to get our soldiers to kill by demonizing the enemy. But it is also quite clear that such demonization has significantly contributed to the perpetration of atrocities and war crimes. In addition, the difficulties of getting soldiers at the end of conflict to return to peaceable conduct, especially toward those who were enemies, remains difficult. To diminish this difficulty, soldiers should consider all soldiers' lives, their own and those of the enemy, as valuable and important to to the calculations of whether a contemplated tactic or action is disproportionate.

The critics of our approach might accuse us of human rights imperialism designed to undermine the effectiveness of war fighters. The north star for our work has been to strive toward a consistent articulation of proportionality that is correct in its context and therefore more capable of achieving its purposes. As Judge Bonello wrote in his concurring opinion in *Al-Skeini,*

> I confess to be quite unimpressed by the pleadings of the United Kingdom Government to the effect that exporting the European Convention on Human Rights to Iraq would have amounted to "human rights imperialism."...I believe that those who export war ought to see to the parallel export of guarantees against the atrocities of war. And then, if necessary, bear with some fortitude the opprobrium of being labeled human rights imperialists.... being branded in perpetuity a human rights imperialist, I acknowledge sounds to me particularly seductive.

We have similarly been attracted to the idea that human life matters, even during war and other conflicts of arms, and have been worried by the charge that we have been excessively concerned about human rights, especially those of soldiers. We might thus be criticized for taking seriously the human rights of soldiers that are often neglected in discussions of proportionality and other aspects of the rules of modern warfare. Throughout this book, we have worked towards an intellectually consistent synthesis of conceptions of proportionality in modern international law. It seems to us that modern human rights law and *jus in bello* can best be balanced by taking seriously the rights of soldiers.

Soldiers are professionals whose societies demand very dangerous and morally unappealing acts. Proportionality restrains their freedom of action, but it is also important to recognize that the lives of these soldiers are often endangered and that proportionality restraints should not dehumanize soldiers put into tragic choice situations not of their own making. In the end, we can do no better than to say that we have approached proportionality from the standpoint of the soldier and the commander—seeing them as people of dignity and good faith. We can bear the opprobrium of being labeled supporters of soldiers even as we take a very different position about being labeled supporters of war.

Bibliography

Acer, Y. (2003), THE AEGEAN MARITIME DISPUTES AND INTERNATIONAL LAW (Farnham: Ashgate Publishing).

Addendum—Eighth Report on State Responsibility, U.N. Doc. A/CN.4/318/Adds.5-7 (1980), *available at* http://legal.un.org/ilc/documentation/english/a_cn4_318_add5-7.pdf .

Adenas, M., and S. Zleptnig (2007), *Proportionality: WTO Law: in Comparative Perspective*, 42 TEXAS INTERNATIONAL LAW JOURNAL 371.

Afton Chemical Limited v. Secretary of State for Transport, Case C-343/09, E.C.R. I-07027 (2010).

Agreement on Subsidies and Countervailing Measures, Arts. 4.10, 7.9, Annex 1A, Marrakesh Agreement Establishing the World Trade Organization, 1869 UNTS 401 (1999), *available at* http://www.wto.org/english/docs_e/legal_e/24-scm.pdf (visited on August 2, 2013).

Akande, D. (2010), *Clearing the Fog of War? The ICRC's Interpretive Guidance on Direct Participation in Hostilities*, 59 INTERNATIONAL & COMPARATIVE LAW QUARTERLY 180.

Al-Bihani v. Obama (Al-Bihani III), 619 F.3d 1, 4 (D.C. Cir. 2010).

Allen, J. (November 30, 2011), COMISAF'S Tactical Directive, available at http://lgdata. s3-website-us-east-1.amazonaws.com/docs/905/474743/ISAF__General_Allen__Tactical_ Directive_of_Nov_2011.pdf (visited on October 10, 2013).

Altman, A., and C.H. Wellman (2008), *From Humanitarian Intervention to Assassination: Human Rights and Political Violence*, 118 ETHICS 228.

Anscombe, E., (2006) *War and Murder, reprinted in* THE MORALITY OF WAR (New York: Prentice-Hall, Inc., Larry May, Erik Rovie, and Steve Viner, eds.).

Application of the Convention on the Prevention and Punishment of the Crime of Genocide (Bosnia and Herzegovina v. Serbia and Montenegro)(February 26, 2007), Judgment, 2007 I.C.J. REPORTS 43, *available at* http://www.icj-cij.org/docket/files/91/13685.pdf (visited on August 18, 2013).

Aquinas, SUMMA THEOLOGICA (1265–1273)(London: Catholic Way Publishing, Fathers of the English Dominican Province, trans. 1936).

Aristotle (2d. ed. 1999), THE NICOMACHEAN ETHICS (Cambridge, MA: Hackett Publishing, Terence Irwin, trans.).

Association Kokopelli v. Graines Baumaux SAS, Case C-59/11, E.C.R. (2012).

Augustine, THE CITY OF GOD (c. 420)(New York: Penguin Books, Henry Bettenson, trans.).

Azurix v. Argentina, (July 14, 2006), Award.

Bainton, R. (1960), CHRISTIAN ATTITUDES TOWARDS WAR AND PEACE: A HISTORICAL SURVEY AND CRITICAL REEXAMINATION (Nashville: Abingdon Press).

Bankovic and Others v. Belgium, (2001), XII Eur. Ct. H.R. 333, *reprinted in* 123 I.L.R. 94.

Barak, A. (2012), PROPORTIONALITY: CONSTITUTIONAL RIGHTS AND THEIR LIMITATIONS (New York: Cambridge University Press).

Address at the Jim Shasha Center of Strategic Studies of the Federmann School for Public Policy and Government of the Hebrew University of Jerusalem (Dec. 18, 2007).

Bargewell, E. (June 15, 2006), Article 15-6 Investigation, "Simple Failures" and "Disastrous Results" (Washington: US Department of the Army).

Bassiouni, M.C. (2d. ed. 1999), CRIMES AGAINST HUMANITY IN INTERNATIONAL CRIMINAL LAW (Ardsley, New York: Transnational Publishers).

The New Wars and the Crisis of Compliance with the Law of Armed Conflict by Non-State Actors, 98 JOURNAL OF CRIMINAL LAW & CRIMINOLOGY 761 (2008).

Beatty, D. (2004), THE ULTIMATE RULE OF LAW (New York: Oxford University Press).

Becker, J., and S. Shane (May 29, 2012), *Secret "Kill List" Proves a Test of Obama's Principles and Will,* THE NEW YORK TIMES MAGAZINE.

Beit Sourak Village Council v. the Government of Israel, (2004) HCJ 2056/04, *available at* http:elyon1.court.gov.il/files_eng/04/560/020/A28/04020560.a28.htm .

Bellinger, J., and W. Haynes (June 2007), *A US government response to the International Committee of the Red Cross Study on Customary International Humanitarian Law,* 89 INTERNATIONAL REVIEW OF THE RED CROSS, No. 866, 443.

Bentham, J. (1996), INTRODUCTION TO THE PRINCIPLES OF LAW AND MORALS (Oxford: Oxford University Press, J.H. Burns and H.L.A. Hart, eds.).

Berger, J. (February 21, 2010), *U.S. Commander Describes Marja Battle as First Salvo in Campaign,* N.Y. TIMES.

Best, G. (1994), WAR AND LAW SINCE 1945 (Oxford: Clarendon Press).

Bothe, M., K.J. Partsch, A. Waldemar, and W. Solf (1982), NEW RULES FOR VICTIMS OF ARMED CONFLICTS: COMMENTARY ON THE TWO 1977 PROTOCOLS ADDITIONAL TO THE GENEVA CONVENTIONS OF 1949 (Leiden: Martinus Nijhoff).

Bouchie de Belle, S. (No. 2, 2008), *Chained to Canons or Wearing Targets on their T-shirts: Human Shields in International Humanitarian Law,* 90 International Review of the Red Cross 883.

Brennan, J. (September 16, 2011), *Strengthening Our Security by Adhering to Our Values and Laws,* Address at Harvard Law School.

Brussels Project of an International Declaration Concerning the Laws and Customs of War (August 27, 1874), *reprinted in* THE LAWS OF ARMED CONFLICTS: A COLLECTION OF CONVENTIONS, RESOLUTIONS, AND OTHER DOCUMENTS (Leiden: Martinus Nijhoff, Dietrich Schindler and Jiri Toman, eds., 1988).

Bush, G.W., Address to a Joint Session of Congress, Sept. 30, 2001.

Byers, M. and S. Chesterman (2003), *Changing the Rules About Rules? Unilateral Humanitarian Intervention and the Future of International Law, in* HUMANITARIAN INTERVENTION: ETHICAL, LEGAL, AND POLICY DILEMMAS (Cambridge: Cambridge University Press, J.L. Holzgrefe and Robert Keohane, eds.).

C. v. Australia, Comm. 900/1999, U.N. Doc. A/58/40, Vol. II, at 188, 4.28 (HRC 2002).

Case Concerning Armed Activities in the Territory of the Congo (Democratic Republic of the Congo v. Uganda), 2005 I.C.J. Reports 168, available at http://www.icj-cij.org/docket/files/116/10455. pdf (visited on September 4, 2013).

Case Concerning the Continental Shelf (Libyan Arab Jamahiriya/Malta) (June 3, 1985), Judgment, 1985 I.C.J. REPORTS 49, *available at* http://www.icj-cij.org/docket/index.php?sum=353&cod e=lm&p1=3&p2=3&case=68&k=a8&p3=5 (visited on October 7, 2013).

Case Concerning the Gabčikov-Najymaros Project (Hungary/Slovenia)(September 25, 1997), 1997 I.C.J. REPORTS 7, *available at* http://www.icj-cij.org/docket/files/92/7375.pdf .

Case of Al-Skeini and Others v. United Kingdom, (July 7, 2011), Application no. 55721/07, (ECtHR Grand Chamber), *available at* http://hudoc.echr.coe.int/sites/eng/pages/search. aspx?i=001-105606 (October 5, 2013).

Case of Giuliani and Gaggio v. Italy, (March 24, 2011), Application no. 23458/02, (EctHR Grand Chamber), *available at* http://hudoc.echr.coe.int/sites/eng/pages/search.aspx?i= 001-104098 (visited on October 10, 2013).

Case of Khatsiyeva and Others v. Russia, (January 17, 2008), Application No. 5108/02, *available at* http://hudoc.echr.coe.int/sites/eng/pages/search.aspx?i=001-84450 (visited on October 8, 2013).

Cassese, A. (2000), *The Martens Clauses: Half a Loaf or Pie in the Sky*, 11 EUROPEAN JOURNAL OF INTERNATIONAL LAW 187.

CBS News (November 29, 2010), Iran Confirms STUXNET Worm Halted Centrifuges, *available at* http://www.cbsnews.com/stories/2010/11/29/world/main7100197.shtml (visited on October 12, 2013).

Center for Law and Military Operations (2001), LAW AND MILITARY OPERATIONS IN KOSOVO, 1999–2001: LESSONS LEARNED FOR JUDGE ADVOCATES (Charlottesville: The Judge Advocate General's Center and School).

Center for Law and Military Operations (2000), RULES OF ENGAGEMENT (ROE) HANDBOOK FOR JUDGE ADVOCATES (Charlottesville: The Judge Advocate General's Center and School).

Chandrasekaran, R. (September 6, 2009), *Sole Informant Guided Decision on Afghan Strike*, WASHINGTON POST.

Ciampi, A. (2011), *Invalidity and Termination of Treaties and Rules of Procedure, in* THE LAW OF TREATIES BEYOND THE VIENNA CONVENTION (Oxford: Oxford University Press, Enzo Cannizaro, ed.).

Cianciardo, J. (2010), *The Principle of Proportionality: The Challenge of Human Rights*, 3 JOURNAL OF CIVIL STUDIES 177.

Clausewitz, C. (1833), ON WAR (Princeton: Princeton University Press, Michael Howard and Peter Paret, eds., trans., 1976).

Clinton, W.J. (December 31, 2000), *Statement on the Rome Treaty on the International Criminal Court*, 37 WEEKLY COMPILATION OF PRESIDENTIAL DOCUMENTS 4 (January 8, 2001), *reprinted in* DIGEST OF UNITED STATES PRACTICE IN INTERNATIONAL LAW, 2000

(Washington: International Law Institute, S. Cummins and D. Stewart, eds.), *available at* http://www.state.gov/documents/organization/139599.pdf (visited on October 3, 2013).

Coates, A.J. (1997), THE ETHICS OF WAR (Manchester: Manchester University Press).

Cohn, M. (2010), *Legal Chronicles: The Evolution of Unreasonableness and Proportionality Review of the Administration in the United Kingdom*, 58 AMERICAN JOURNAL OF COMPARATIVE LAW 583.

Coker v. Georgia, 433 U.S. 584, 592, 97 S.Ct. 2861, 53 L.Ed.2d 982 (1977).

Crawford, E. (2010), THE TREATMENT OF COMBATANTS AND INSURGENTS UNDER THE LAW OF ARMED CONFLICT (New York: Oxford University Press).

Crawford, J. (2002), THE INTERNATIONAL LAW COMMISSION'S ARTICLES ON STATE RESPONSIBILITY: INTRODUCTION, TEXT, AND COMMENTARIES (Cambridge: Cambridge University Press).

Criddle, E.J. (2012), *Proportionality in Counterinsurgency: A Relational Theory*, 87 NOTRE DAME L. REV. 1073.

Czech, M. (May 6, 2008), *Gentlemen, Do Not Play With the Army*, GAZETA WYBORCZA.

Davis, G. (1907), *Doctor Francis Lieber's Instructions for the Government of Armies in the Field*, 1 AMERICAN JOURNAL OF INTERNATIONAL LAW 13.

Decision by the Arbitrators, Brazil—Export Financing Programme for Aircraft—Recourse to Arbitration by Brazil under Article 22.6 of the DSU and Article 4.11 of the SCM Agreement, (August 28, 2000), WT/46/ARB.

Decision by the Arbitrator, Canada—Export Credits and Loan Guarantees for Regional Aircraft, Recourse to Arbitration by Canada under Article 22.6 of the DSU and Article 4.11 of the SCM Agreement, (February 17, 2003), WT/DS70/AB/R.

Declaration of St. Petersburg (November 29, 1868), *reprinted in* DOCUMENTS ON THE LAWS OF WAR (Oxford: Oxford University Press, Adam Roberts and Richard Guelff, eds 3d ed., 2000).

Defense Legal Policy Board (May 30 2013) REPORT OF THE SUBCOMMITTEE ON MILITARY JUSTICE IN COMBAT ZONES (Arlington: US Department of Defense), *available at* http://www.caaflog.com/wp-content/uploads/20130531-Subcommittee-Report-REPORT-OF-THE-SUBCOMMITTEE-ON-MILITARY-JUSTICE-IN-COMBAT-ZONES-31-May-13-2.pdf (visited on October 1, 2013).

Dennis, M., (2005), *Application of Human Rights Treaties Extraterritorially in Times of Armed Conflict and Military Occupation*, 99 AMERICAN JOURNAL OF INTERNATIONAL LAW 119.

Dennis, M., and M. Surena (2008), *Application of the International Covenant on Civil and Political Rights in Times of Armed Conflict and Military Occupation: The Gap between Legal Theory and State Practice*, 13 EUROPEAN HUMAN RIGHTS LAW REVIEW 714.

Department of the Army (2007), FIELD MANUAL NO. 3-24, MARINE CORPS WARFIGHTING PUBLICATION NO. 3-33.5, COUNTERINSURGENCY (Washington: Department of the Army).

Desmedt, A. (2001), *Proportionality in WTO Law*, 4 JOURNAL OF INTERNATIONAL ECONOMIC LAW 441–480 (2001).

DIGEST OF UNITED STATES PRACTICE IN INTERNATIONAL LAW, 1976 (Washington: International Law Institute, Eleanor C. McDowell, ed.).

Dill, J., and H. Shue (2012), *Limiting the Killing in War: Military Necessity and the St. Petersburg Assumption*, 26 ETHICS & INTERNATIONAL AFFAIRS 311–333.

Dinstein, Y. (3d ed. 2001), WAR, AGGRESSION, AND SELF-DEFENSE (Cambridge: Cambridge University Press).

Legitimate Military Objectives Under the Current Jus in Bello in LEGAL AND ETHICAL LESSONS OF NATO'S KOSOVO CAMPAIGN, 78 NAVAL WAR COLLEGE INTERNATIONAL. LEGAL STUDIES (Newport: U.S. Naval War College, Andru Wall ed., 2002).

Unlawful Combatants, 32 ISRAEL YEARBOOK OF HUMAN RIGHTS 247 (2002).

"Dispute Concering Delimitation of the Maritime Boundary Between Bangladesh and Myanmar in the Bay of Bengal (Bangladesh/Myanmar)" (March 14, 2002), Case No. 16, Judgment (International Tribunal for the Law of the Sea), *available at* http://www.itlos.org/fileadmin/itlos/documents/cases/case_no_16/1-C16_Judgment_14_02_2012.pdf (visited on October 7, 2013).

Dörmann, K. (2003), ELEMENTS OF WAR CRIMES UNDER THE ROME STATUTE OF THE INTERNATIONAL CRIMINAL COURT (Cambridge: Cambridge University Press).

Doswald-Beck, L. (February 28, 1997), *International Humanitarian Law and the Advisory Opinion of the International Court of Justice on the Legality of the Threat or Use of Nuclear Weapons*, 316, INTERNATIONAL REVIEW OF THE RED CROSS.

Doty, G. (1998), *The United States and the Development of the Laws of Land Warfare*, 156 MILITARY LAW REVIEW 224.

Draper, G.I.A.D. (1956), *The Interaction of Christianity and Chivalry in the Historical Development of the Law of War*, X INTERNATIONAL REVIEW OF THE RED CROSS 3.

Eberheart v. Georgia, 433 U.S. 917, 97 S. Ct. 2994, 53 L. Ed. 2d 1104 (1977).

Eddings v. Oklahoma, 455 U.S. 104, 111–112, 102 S.Ct. 869, 71 L.Ed.2d 1 (1982).

Edenberg, E., and L. Larry May (2013), *Introduction, in* JUS POST BELLUM AND TRANSITIONAL JUSTICE (Cambridge: Cambridge University Press, Larry May and Elizabeth Edenberg, eds.).

Eighth United Nations Congress on the Prevention of Crime and the Treatment of Offenders, Havana, August 27 to September 7, 1990, U.N. Doc. A/CONF.144/28.Rev.1, at 118 (1990).

El-Shifa Pharm. Indus. Co. v. United States, 607 F.3d 836 (D.C. Cir. 2010) (en banc).

Elderfield, J. (2013), *Introductory Note to the International Criminal Tribunal for the Former Yugoslavia: The Prosecutor v. Gotovina et. al.* 52 I.L.M. 72 (2013).

Elliott, J. (June 23, 2012 ProPublica), *Washington's Silence Creates doubts on deaths*, SYDNEY MORNING HERALD.

Engle, E. (Winter 2012), *History of the General Principle of Proportionality: An Overview*, X DARTMOUTH LAW JOURNAL 1.

Entous, A. (May 18, 2010), *Special Report: How the White House Learned to Love the Drone*, REUTERS.

Enmund v. Florida, 458 U.S. 782, 801, 102 S.Ct. 3368, 73 L.Ed.2d 1140 (1982).

Ergi v. Turkey, App. No. 2388/94, (July 28, 1988), Judgment, 232 Eur. H.R. Rep. 388, *available at* http://www.unhcr.org/refworld/topic,4565c225b,459e72b12,3ae6b6291c,0,,,TUR.html

Feinberg, J. (1977), *Voluntary Euthanasia and the Inalienable Right to Life*, The Tanner Lectures on Human Values.

Feldmann, A., and M. Perala (July 2004), *Reassessing the Causes of Nongovernmental Terrorism in Latin America*, 46 LATIN AMERICAN POLITICS AND SOCIETY 101, *available at* http://onlinelibrary.wiley.com/doi/10.1111/j.1548-2456.2004.tb00277.x/abstract (visited on October 10, 2013).

Fenrick, W. (No. 3 2001), *Targeting and Proportionality During the NATO Bombing Campaign Against Yugoslavia*, 12 EUROPEAN JOURNAL OF INTERNATIONAL LAW 489.

Final Report to the Prosecutor by the Committee Established to Review the NATO Bombing Campaign Against the Federal Republic of Yugoslavia (June 13 2000), *reprinted in* 39 I.L.M. 1258 (2000).

Finnegan, P. (2004), *The Study of Law as a Foundation of Leadership and Command: The History of Law Instruction at the United States Military Academy at West Point*, 181 MILITARY LAW REVIEW 112 (2004).

Forsythe, D. (1978), *Legal Management of Internal War: The 1977 Protocol on Non-International Armed Conflicts*, 72 AMERICAN JOURNAL OF INTERNATIONAL LAW 272.

Franck, T. (2008), *On Proportionality of Countermeasures in International Law*, 102 AMERICAN JOURNAL OF INTERNATIONAL LAW 715.

Fuller, L. (1965), THE MORALITY OF LAW (New Haven: Yale University Press).

Furman v. Georgia, 408 U.S. 238, 311 (1972).

Galula, D. (1963), PACIFICATION IN ALGERIA 1956–1958 9 (RAND Corporation 2006).

Gardham, J. (2004), NECESSITY, PROPORTIONALITY, AND THE USE OF FORCE BY STATES (Cambridge: Cambridge University Press).

Gazzini, T. (2005), THE CHANGING RULES ON THE USE OF FORCE IN INTERNATIONAL LAW (Manchester: Manchester University Press).

General Comment No. 31 (May 26, 2004), Nature of the General Legal Obligation Imposed on States Parties to the Covenant, Doc. No. CCPR/C/21/Rev.1/Add.13.

Geneva Convention for the Amelioration of the Condition of the Wounded and Sick in Armed Forces in the Field, *opened for signature* Aug. 12, 1949, 75 U.N.T.S. 31, 6 U.S.T. 3114.

Geneva Convention for the Amelioration of the Condition of Wounded, Sick, and Shipwrecked Members of Armed Forces at Sea, *opened for signature* Aug. 12, 1949, 75 U.N.T.S. 85, 6 U.S.T. 3217.

Geneva Convention Relative to the Treatment of Prisoners of War, *opened for signature* Aug. 12, 1949, 75 U.N.T.S. 287, 6 U.S.T. 3316.

Geneva Convention Relative to the Protection of Civilians in Time of War, *opened for signature* Aug. 12, 1949, 75 U.N.T.S. 287, 6 U.S.T. 3516.

Gentili, A. (1598), DE JURE BELLI (Oxford: Clarendon Press, John C. Rolfe, trans., 1933).

Goodman, R. (2013), *The Power to Kill or Capture Enemy Combatants*, 24 EUROPEAN JOURNAL OF INTERNATIONAL LAW 26.

Gorka, M., and A. Zadworny (April 28, 2008), *Afraid to Shoot*, GAZETA WYBORCZA.

Gorman, S. (August 8, 2009), *Electricity Grid in U.S. Penetrated by Spies*, WALL STREET JOURNAL.

Graham, B. (August 25, 2005), *Hackers Attack Via Chinese Web Sites*, WASHINGTON POST, *available at* http://www.washingtonpost.com/wp-dyn/content/article/2005/08/24/AR2005082402318.html (visited on October 12, 2013).

Green, L. (2d. ed. 1999), *What is—Why is There—The Law of War? in* ESSAYS ON THE MODERN LAW OF WAR (Ardsley, New York: Transnational Publishers).

THE CONTEMPORARY LAW OF ARMED CONFLICT (3d. ed., 2008).

Greenwood, C. (2006), ESSAYS ON WAR IN INTERNATIONAL LAW (Nottingham: Cameron May).

Gross, M. (2010), MORAL DILEMMAS OF MODERN WAR: TORTURE, ASSASSINATION, AND BLACKMAIL IN AN AGE OF ASYMMETRIC CONFLICT (New York: Cambridge University Press).

Gross, O., and F. Ni Aolain (2006), LAW IN TIMES OF CRISIS: EMERGENCY POWERS IN THEORY AND PRACTICE (Cambridge: Cambridge University Press).

Grossman, D. (1995), ON KILLING: THE PSYCHOLOGICAL COST OF LEARNING TO KILL IN WAR AND SOCIETY (New York: Back Bay Books).

Grotius, H. (1625), THE LAW OF WAR AND PEACE (Oxford: Clarendon Press, Francis W. Kelsey trans., 1925).

ON THE LAW OF PRIZE AND BOOTY (DE JURE PRAEDAE)(1605), (Oxford: At the Clarendon Press, Gwladys L. Williams, trans., 1950).

Guerrero, (1996), LA CINVULACIÓN NEGATIVA DEL LESISLADOR A LOS DERECHOS FUNDAMENTALES (MCGRAW HILL/INTERAMERICANADE ESPANA).

Gulec v. Turkey (1998), Judgment, 28 EUR. H.R. REP. 121, *available at* http://www.unhcr.org/refworld/publisher,ECHR,,TUR,3ae6b6a918,0.html

Gunn, J. (2005), *Deconstructing Proportionality in Limitations Analysis*, 19 EMORY INTERNATIONAL LAW REVIEW 465.

Hague Convention IV Respecting the Laws and Customs of War on Land (October 18, 1907), *reprinted in reprinted in* DOCUMENTS ON THE LAWS OF WAR (Oxford: Oxford University Press, Adam Roberts and Richard Guelff, eds., 3d ed., 2000).

Haley, J.O. (2011), *Introduction—Beyond Retribution: An Integrated Approach to Restorative Justiproce*, 36 WASHINGTON UNIVERSITY JOURNAL OF LAW AND POLICY 1.

Hamdan v. Rumsfeld, 548 U.S. 557, 662–631 (2006).

Hampson, F. (2009), *Is Human Rights Law of Any Relevance to the War in Afghanistan? in* THE WAR IN AFGHANISTAN: A LEGAL ANALYSIS, 85 NAVAL WAR COL. INTERNATIONAL LAW STUDIES 485 (Newport: U.S. Naval War College, Michael Schmitt, ed.).

Harding, T. (July 7, 2010), *Curbs on Firing at Taliban Are Putting Us at Risk, Troops Warn*, THE TELEGRAPH.

Harmelin v. Michigan, 501 U.S. 957, 111 S. Ct. 2680, 115 L. Ed. 2d 836 (1991).

Hart, H.L.A. (1960), THE CONCEPT OF LAW (Oxford: Oxford University Press).

Hartigan, R. (1983), FRANCIS LIEBER, LIEBER'S CODE AND THE LAW OF WAR (Edison, N.J.: Transaction Publishers).

Headley (2004), *Proportionality Between Crimes, Offenses, and Punishments*, 17 ST. THOMAS LAW REVIEW 247.

Henckaerts, J.-M., and Louise Doswald-Beck (2005), CUSTOMARY INTERNATIONAL HUMANITARIAN LAW VOLUME I: RULES (2005)(Cambridge, Cambridge University Press).

Her Majesty the Queen v. Mohammed Momin Khawaja (2008), Ontario Superior Court of Justice, Court File 04-G30282, *reprinted in*, 1 Terrorism International Case Law Reporter 319 (New York: Oxford University Press, Michael Newton, ed. 2008).

Hersh, S.M. (October 22, 2001), *King's Ransom: How Vulnerable Are the Saudi Royals*, NEW YORKER, *available at* http://www.freerepublic.com/focus/fr/549600/posts (visited on October 2, 2013).

Hoelzel v. Chicago, 85 S.W.2d 126, 133 (Mo. 1935).

Hollis, D. (2011), *An E-SOS for Cyberspace*, 52 HARVARD INTERNATIONAL LAW JOURNAL 373.

Human Rights Council (September 15, 2009), *Human Rights in Palestine and Other Occupied Arab Territories, Report of the United Nations Fact Finding Mission on the Gaza Conflict*, U.N. Doc. A/HRC/12/48.

Human Rights Situation in Palestine and Other Occupied Arab Territories, Report of the Special Rapporteur on the situation of human rights in the Palestinian territories occupied since 1967 (February 11, 2009), U.N. Doc. A/HRC/10/20.

ICSID case no. ARB(AF)/00/2, Award (May 29, 2003), *reprinted in* 43 I.L.M. 134 (2004) [Arbitrators: Horacio A. Grigera Nao´n (Argentine), President; Jose´ Carlos Fernández Rozas (Spanish) and Carlos Bernal Verea (Mexican)], *available at* http://www.worldbank.org/icsid/cases/laudo-051903%20-English.pdf (visited on March 12, 2012).

Ilaşcu and others v. Russia and Moldova, Application No. 48787/99, Reports 2004–VII, *In re Yamashita*, 327 U.S. 1, 15 (1946).

In the case of James and Others (February 21, 1986), Application Number 8793/79, Judgment (ECtHR).

International Committee of the Red Cross (ICRC), COMMENTARY ON THE ADDITIONAL PROTOCOLS OF JUNE 8, 1977 TO THE GENEVA CONVENTIONS OF AUGUST 12, 1949 (Leiden: Martinus Nijohff, Yves Sandoz, Christopher Swinarski and Bruno Zimmerman, eds.), *available at* http://www.icrc.org/ihl.nsf/COM/470-750001?OpenDocument (visited on October 9, 2013).

ICRC (2012), EXPERTS REPORT, OCCUPATION AND OTHER FORMS OF ADMINISTRATION OF FOREIGN TERRITORY, *available at* http://lgdata.s3-website-us-east-1.amazonaws.com/docs/905/474159/ICRC_expert_meeting_-_occupation.pdf (visited on August 15, 2013).

ICRC (1999), HOW DOES LAW PROTECT IN WAR? (Geneva: Marco Sassoli and Antoine Bouvier, eds.).

ICRC (1978), 14 OFFICIAL RECORDS OF THE DIPLOMATIC CONFERENCE ON THE REAFFIRMATION AND DEVELOPMENT OF INTERNATIONAL HUMANITARIAN LAW APPLICABLE IN ARMED CONFLICTS, GENEVA (1974–1977).

International Transport Workers' Federation and Finnish Seamen's Union v. Viking Line ABP and OÜ Viking Line Eesti, (December 11, 2007), Judgment of the Court (Grand Chamber), Case C-438/05, 2007 E.C.R. I-10779, *available at* http://eur-lex.europa.eu/LexUriServ/LexUriServ.do?uri=CELEX:62005J0438:EN:HTML (visited on September 15, 2013).

Jennings, R.Y. (1938), *The Caroline and McLeod Cases*, 32 AMERICAN JOURNAL OF INTERNATIONAL LAW 82.

Johnson, J. (Feb. 22, 2012), *National Security Law, Lawyers and Lawyering in the Obama Administration*, Address at the Dean's Lecture at Yale Law School.

Joseph, S., J. Schultz, and M. Castan, (2d ed. 2005), THE INTERNATIONAL COVENANT ON CIVIL AND POLITICAL RIGHTS: CASES, MATERIALS, AND COMMENTARY (Oxford: Oxford University Press).

Keegan, J. (1983), THE FACE OF BATTLE: A STUDY OF AGINCOURT, WATERLOO, AND THE SOMME (New York: Penguin Books).

Kingdom of the Netherlands v. High Authority of the European Coal and Steel Community (1955), Case 6/54, ECR 103.

Kingsbury, B., and Stephan Schill (2009), *Investor-State Arbitration as Governance: Fair and Equitable Treatment, Proportionality and the Emerging Global Administrative Law*, *in* Albert Jan van den Berg, 50 Years of the New York Convention 5 (2009), *available at* http://papers.ssrn.com/sol3/papers.cfm?abstract_id=1466980 .

Kirgis, F. (August 17, 2006), *Some Proportionality Issues Raised by Israel's Use of Armed Force in Lebanon*, ASIL INSIGHTS, *available at* http://www.asil.org/insights060817.cfm .

Klaidman, D. (2012), KILL OR CAPTURE: THE WAR ON TERROR AND THE SOUL OF THE OBAMA PRESIDENCY (New York: Houghton Mifflin Harcourt).

Kleffner, J. (2012), *Section IX of the ICRC Interpretive Guidance on Direct Participation in Hostilities: The End of Jus in Bello Proportionality as We Know It?*, 45 ISRAEL LAW REVIEW 35.

Knoblock, J. (1988), XUNZI: A TRANSLATION AND STUDY OF THE COMPLETE WORKS (Stanford: Stanford University Press).

Köchler, H. (2001), *Humanitarian Intervention in the Context of Modern Power Politics*, 4 Interntional Progress Org., Studies in Int'l Relations XXVI, *available at* http://i-p-o.org/koechler-humanitarian-intervention.pdf .

Krauss, C. (January 18, 2013), *At Algerian Oil and Gas Fields Once Thought Safe, New Fears and Precautions*, N.Y. TIMES.

Kulish, N. (November 29, 2007), *An Afghanistan War-Crimes Case Tests Poland's Commitment to Foreign Missions*, N.Y. Times.

Kumm, M. (2003), *Constitutional Rights as Principles: On the Structure and Domain of Constitutional Justice*, 2 INTERNATIONAL JOURNAL OF CONSTITUTIONAL LAW (I-CON).

Kutz, C. (2005), *The Difference Uniforms Make: Collective Violence in Criminal Law and War*, 33 PHILOSOPHY & PUBLIC AFFAIRS 148.

Labonte, M. (2009), *Jus Post Bellum, Peacebuilding, and Non-State Actors: Lessons from Afghanistan*, *in* ETHICS, AUTHORITY, AND WAR: NON-STATE ACTORS AND THE JUST WAR TRADITION 221–225 (Eric A. Heinze and Brent J. Steele, eds., 2009)(Palgrave Macmillan).

Lackey, D. (1989), THE ETHICS OF WAR AND PEACE (Upper Saddle River, NJ: Prentice-Hall).

Landau-Tasseron, E. (2006), *"Non-Combatants" in Muslim Legal Thought* (Washington: Hudson Institute, Center on Islam, Democracy, and the Future of the Muslim World), *available at* http://www.hudson.org/files/pdf_upload/NonCombatants.pdf (visited on October 4, 2013).

Laval un Partneri Ltd v. Svenska Byggnadsarbetareförbundet and Others, (December 18, 2007), Case C-341/05, Judgment of the Court (Grand Chamber), 2007 E.C.R. I-11767, *available at* http://eur-lex.europa.eu/Notice.do?val=461500:cs&lang=en&list=465487:cs,461500:cs,449132:cs,417170:cs,398955:cs,397342:cs,395464:cs,395463:cs,395460:cs,395459:cs,&pos=2&page=1&nbl=16&pgs=10&hwords=laval~&checktexte=checkbox&visu= (visited on July 31, 2013).

Legal Consequences of the Construction of a Wall in the Occupied Palestinian Territory (July 9, 2004), Advisory Opinion, 2004 I.C.J. REPORTS 136 (International Court of Justice), *reprinted in* 43 I.L.M. 1009 (2004), *available at* http://www.icj-cij.org/docket/files/131/1671.pdf (visited on August 18, 2013).

Legality of the Threat or Use of Nuclear Weapons (July 8, 1996), Advisory Opinion, 1996 I.C.J. REPORTS 66 (International Court of Justice), *available at* http://www.icj-cij.org/docket/files/93/7407.pdf .

Legault, L., and B. Hankey (1993), *Method, Oppositeness and Adjacency, and Proportionality in Maritime Boundary Delimitation*, *in* I INTERNATIONAL MARITIME BOUNDARIES (Leiden: Martinus Nijhoff and Jonathan I. Charney, eds.).

LG&E v. Argentina (United States/Argentina BIT), (October 3, 2006), Case No. Arb/02/1, Decision on Liability, *available at* http://arbitrationlaw.com/files/free_pdfs/LG%26E%20v%20Argentina%20-%20Decision%20on%20Liability.pdf (visited at October 7, 2013).

Lin, H. (2010), *Offensive Cyber Operations and the Use of Force*, 4 JOURNAL OF NATIONAL SECURITY L. & POLICY 63.

Luban, D. (2002), *The War on Terrorism and the End of Human Rights*, 22 PHILOSOPHY & PUBLIC POLICY QUARTERLY 9.

Malvesti, M. (Winter-Spring 2002), *Bombing bin Laden: Assessing the Effectiveness of Air Strikes as a Counter-Terrorism Strategy*, 26/1 FLETCHER FORUM WORLD AFFAIRS 17–29.

Markoff, J. (February 11, 2011), *Malware Aimed at Iran Hit Five Sites*, THE NEW YORK TIMES, *available at* http://www.nytimes.com/2011/02/13/science/13STUXNET.html .

Marlantes, K. (2011), WHAT IT IS LIKE TO GO TO WAR (New York: Atlantic Monthly Press).

Marshall, S.L.A. (1966), THE OFFICER AS LEADER (Mechanicsburg, PA: Stackpole Books).

Mastroianni, G., and Wilbur J. Scott (Summer 2011), *Reframing Suicide in the Military*, PARAMETERS.

Mathieu-Mohin and Clerfayt v. Belgium, App. No. 9267/81, 10 EUR. H.R. REP. (1987).

Maxwell, M. (2012), *Rebutting the Civilian Presumption: Playing Whack-A-Mole Without a Mallet, in* TARGETED KILLINGS: LAW AND MORALITY IN AN ASYMMETRICAL WORLD 55 (Oxford: Oxford University Press, C. Finkelstein, J.D. Ohlin, and A. Altman, eds.).

May, L. (2012), AFTER WAR ENDS: A PHILOSOPHICAL PERSPECTIVE (Cambridge: Cambridge University Press).

AGGRESSION AND CRIMES AGAINST PEACE (2008) (CAMBRIDGE UNIVERSITY PRESS).

Contingent Pacifism and the Moral Risks of Participating in War, 25 PUBLIC AFFAIRS QUARTERLY 95 (No. 2, 2011).

Contingent Pacifism and Selective Refusal, 43 JOURNAL OF SOCIAL PHILOSOPHY 1 (No. 3, Spring 2012).

Grotius and Contingent Pacifism, JOURNAL OF THE HISTORY OF ETHICS, on-line journal.

A Hobbesian Account of Cruelty and the Rules of War, 26 LEIDEN JOURNAL OF INTERNATIONAL LAW 1.

LIMITING LEVIATHAN: HOBBES ON LAW AND INTERNATIONAL AFFAIRS (2013) (Oxford: Oxford University Press).

WAR CRIMES AND JUST WAR (2007)(Cambridge: Cambridge University Press).

The UN Charter, Human Rights Law, and Contingent Pacifism, in 23 FLORIDA STATE UNIVERSITY JOURNAL INTERNATIONAL LAW (2014).

THE SOCIALLY RESPONSIVE SELF (1996)(Chicago: the University of Chicago Press).

McCann v. United Kingdom, App. No. 18984/91, 21 Eur. H.R. Rep. 97 (1995).

McChrystal, S. (July 6, 2009), COMISAF TACTICAL DIRECTIVE.

McGonigle-Leyh, B. (2011), PROCEDURAL JUSTICE? VICTIM PARTICIPATION IN INTERNATIONAL CRIMINAL PROCEEDINGS (Cambridge: Intersentia Press).

McMahan, J. (2009), KILLING IN WAR (Oxford: Oxford University Press).

(2012), *Targeted Killing: Murder, Combat, or Law Enforcement, in* TARGETED KILLINGS: LAW AND MORALITY IN AN ASYMMETRICAL WORLD 135 (Oxford: Oxford University Press, C. Finkelstein, J.D. Ohlin, and A. Altman, eds.) 135–155.

Meltzer, N. (2009), ICRC, INTERPRETIVE GUIDANCE ON THE NOTION OF DIRECT PARTICIPATION IN HOSTILITIES UNDER INTERNATIONAL HUMANITARIAN LAW, *available at* http://www.icrc.org/eng/assets/files/other/icrc-002-0990.pdf .

Targeted Killing or Less Harmful Means?—Israel's High Court Judgment on Targeted Killing and the Restricive Function of Military Necessity (2006), 9 YEARBOOK OF INTERNATIONAL HUMANITARIAN L. 109.

TARGETED KILLING IN INTERNATIONAL LAW (Oxford: Oxford University Press, 2008).

Meredith, L. (August 20, 2010), *Malware Implicated in Fatal Spanair Plane Crash*, TECHNEWS DAILY, *available at* http://www.technewsdaily.com/malware-implicated-in-fatal-spanair-crash-1078/ (visited on October 12, 2013).

Meron, T. (2006), THE HUMANIZATION OF INTERNATIONAL LAW (Leiden: Martinus Nijhoff).

Milanovic, M. (2011), *Norm Conflicts, International Humanitarian Law, and Human Rights*, *in* INTERNATIONAL HUMANITARIAN LAW AND INTERNATIONAL HUMAN RIGHTS LAW (OXFORD: OXFORD UNIVERSITY PRESS).

Military and Paramilitary Activities in and against Nicaragua (*Nicarauga v. U.S.*)(June 27, 1986), Judgment, Dissenting Opinion of Judge Schwebel, 1986 I.C.J. 14, *available at* http://www. icj-cij.org/docket/files/70/6523.pdf (visited on October 10, 2013).

Miller, J.L. (December 3, 2001), *Sly Sly: A Journalist's Latest Tricks*, NATIONAL REVIEW.

Mitchell, A. (2006), *Proportionality and Remedies in WTO Disputes*, 17 EUROPEAN JOURNAL OF INTERNATIONAL LAW 985.

THE MANUAL OF THE LAW OF ARMED CONFLICT (2004), UK Ministry of Defence (Oxford: Oxford University Press).

Morar v. IDF Commander in Judaea and Samaria (2006), HCJ 9593/04, 2 ISRAEL L. REP. 56.

Mulrine, A. (June 27, 2011), *How Afghanistan Civilian Deaths have Changed the Way the US Military Fights*, THE CHRISTIAN SCIENCE MONITOR, *available at* http://www.csmonitor.com/USA/Military/2011/0727/How-Afghanistan-civilian-deaths-have-changed-the-way-the-US-milita ry-fights (visited on July 31, 2013).

Murphy, C. (2010), A MORAL THEORY OF POLITICAL RECONCILIATION (Cambridge: Cambridge University Press).

Nakashima, E., and S. Mufson (January 19 2008), *Hackers Have Attacked Foreign Utilities, CIA Analyst Says*, WASHINGTON POST.

Neuman, N. (2004), *Applying the Rule of Proportionality: Force Protection and Cumulative Assessment in International Law and Morality*, 7 YEARBOOK OF INTERNATIONAL HUMANITARIAN LAW 79.

NEW YORK POST, Editorial page (September 14, 2006), *Insanity*.

Newton, M.A. (2013), *A Synthesis of Community Based Justice and Complementarity*, *in* INTERNATIONAL CRIMINAL JUSTICE AND LOCAL OWNERSHIP: ASSESSING THE IMPACT OF THE JUSTICE INTERVENTION (Cambridge: Cambridge University Press, Carsten Stahn, ed.).

Exceptional Engagement: Protocol I and a World United Against Terror, 42 TEXAS INTERNATIONAL LAW JOURNAL 323–375 (2009).

Inadvertent Implications of the War Powers Resolution, 45 CASE WESTERN RESERVE JOURNAL OF INTERNATIONAL LAW 173 (2012).

Humanitarian Protection in Future Wars, *in* 8 INTERNATIONAL PEACEKEEPING: THE YEARBOOK OF INTERNATIONAL PEACE OPERATIONS 349 (Harvey Langholtz *et al.*, eds., 2004).

Modern Military Necessity: The Role and Relevance of Military Lawyers, 12 ROGER WILLIAMS UNIVERSITY LAW REVIEW 877 (2007). *The International Criminal Court Preparatory Commission: The Way It Is & The Way Ahead*, 41 VIRGINIA JOURNAL OF INTERNATIONAL LAW 204 (2000).

Nissenbaum, D. (January 26–27, 2012), *In Former Taliban Sanctuary, An Eerie Silence Takes Over*, WALL STREET JOURNAL 1,7.

Nossiter, A., and S. Sayare (January 17, 2013), *Americans Held Hostage In Algeria Gas-Field Raid*, N.Y. TIMES.

Ochoa-Ruiz, N., and E. Salamanca-Aguado (2005), *Exploring the Limits of International Law relating to the Use of Force in Self-defence*, 16 EUROPEAN JOURNAL OF INTERNATIONAL L. 499.

O'Donovan, O. (2003), THE JUST WAR REVISITED (Cambridge: Cambridge University Press).

One-on-One with General David Petraeus: One of Our Most Powerful Military Leaders Talks About Iraq and Afghanistan, VU Cast Vanderbilt University's News Network (Mar. 5, 2010), *available at* http://www.youtube.com/watch?v=mgake-R32YE/ (visited on October 9, 2013).

OFFICIAL RECORDS OF THE DIPLOMATIC CONFERENCE ON THE REAFFIRMATION AND DEVELOPMENT OF INTERNATIONAL HUMANITARIAN LAW APPLICABLE IN ARMED CONFLICTS, GENEVA (1974–1977)(1978), (Bern: ICRC).

Ofrer v. Austria, App. No. 524/59, Judgment (ECtHR), 6 YEARBOOK OF THE EUROPEAN CONVENTION ON HUMAN RIGHTS 680.

Oil Platforms (Islamic Republic of Iran v. United States of America), Merits, 2003 ICJ REPORTS 161.

Oil Platforms case (Islamic Republic of Iran v. United States of America), Counter-memorial and counter-claim submitted by the United States of America (June 23, 1997), *available at* http://www.icj-cij.org/docket/index.php?p1=3&p2=3&k=0a&case=90&code=op&p3=1 .

Oil Platforms case (Islamic Republic of Iran v. United States of America), Reply and Defence to Counter-claim submitted by the Islamic Republic of Iran, (March 10, 1999), *available at* http://www.icj-cij.org/docket/index.php?p1=3&p2=3&k=0a&case=90&code=op&p3=1.

Orakhelashvili, A. (2006), PEREMPTORY NORMS IN INTERNATIONAL LAW (Oxford: Oxford University Press).

Orend, B. (2008), *Jus Post Bellum: A Just War Theory Perspective* in JUS POST BELLUM: TOWARDS A LAW OF TRANSITION FROM CONFLICT TO PEACE 31(The Hague: T.M.C. Asser Press, Carsten Stahn and Jan K. Kleffner, eds.).

Osiel, M. (1999), OBEYING ORDERS: ATROCITY, MILITARY DISCIPLINE, AND THE LAW OF WAR (Edison, NJ: Transaction Publishers).

Owen, M., and K. Maurer (2012), NO EASY DAY: THE FIRSTHAND ACCOUNT OF THE MISSION THAT KILLED OSAMA BIN LADEN (New York: Dutton books).

Palmer v. City of Euclid, Ohio, 402 U.S. 544 (1971).

Parks, H. (2010), *Part IX of the ICRC "Direct Participation in Hostilities" Study: No Mandate, No Expertise, and Legally Incorrect*, 42 N.Y.U. J. INTERNATIONAL L. & POLICY 769.

Parra, A. R. (2012), THE HISTORY OF ICSID (Oxford: Oxford University Press).

Paust, J. (2010), *Self-Defense Targetings of Non-State Actors and Permissibility of US use of Drones in Pakistan*, 19 JOURNAL OF TRANSNATIONAL LAW & POLICY 237.

Payne v. Tennessee, 501 U.S. 808 (1990).

Peers, W.R. (1979), THE MY LAI INQUIRY 230 (New York: W.W. Norton).

Petraeus, D.H. (May 10, 2007), Letter from the Commanding Officer of Multi-National Force-Iraq, to Multi-National Force-Iraq *available at* http://smallwarsjournal.com/blog/7-september-general-petraeus-letter-to-troops-of-mnf-i (visted on October 9, 2013).

PHILO (1890), THE SPECIAL LAWS (London: H.G. Bohm and C.D. Yonge, trans.).

Pincova and Pinc v. the Czech Republic, (November 5, 2002), Application no. 36548/97, Judgment (ECtHR), *available at* http://echr.ketse.com/doc/36548.97-en-20021105/view/ (visited on October 7, 2013).

Poland v. European Commission (March 7, 2013), Case No. Case T-370/11, Judgment of the General Court (Seventh Chamber), *available at* http://curia.europa.eu/juris/document/document.jsf?text=&docid=134563&pageIndex=0&doclang=EN&mode=req&dir=&occ=first&part=1&cid=1002171 .

Powell v. Alabama, 287 U.S. 45, 68–69 (1932).

Prosecutor v. Jean Paul Akayesu, Case No. ICTR-96-4-T, Judgment (Int'l Crim. Trib for Rwanda, September 2,1998).

Prosecutor v. Tihomir Blaškić, Case No. IT-95-14-T, Judgment (ICTY, March 3, 2000).

Prosecutor v. Tihomir Blaškić, Case No. IT-95-14-A, Appeals Judgment (ICTY, July 29, 2004).

Prosecutor v. Ljube Boskoski and Johan Tarculovski, Case No. IT-04-82-T, Judgment (ICTY, July 10, 2008).

Prosecutor v. Galić, Case No. IT-98-29-A, Appeal Judgment (ICTY, Nov. 30, 2006).

Prosecutor v. Gotovina et al., Case No. IT-06-90-A, Appeal Judgment (ICTY, Nov. 16, 2012).

Prosecutor v. Milan Martic, Case No. IT-95-11-R61, Review of the Indictment Pursuant to Rule 61 (ICTY, September 13, 1996).

Prosecutor v. Miroslav Deronjic, Case No. IT-02-61-S, Judgment on Sentencing Appeal (ICTY, March 30, 2004), *available at* http://www.unhcr.org/refworld/docid/4146efc94.html (visited on January 30, 2013).

Prosecutor v. Stanislav Galić, Case No. IT-98-29, Judgment, (ICTY, Dec. 5, 2003).

Prosecutor v. Ramush Haradinaj, Case No. IT-04-84-T, Judgment (ICTY, April 3, 2008).

Prosecutor v. Kupreškić, Case No. IT-95-16, Judgment (ICTY, Jan. 14, 2000).

Prosecutor v. Fatmir Limaj, Case No. IT-03-66-T, Judgment (ICTY, Nov. 30, 2005).

Prosecutor v. Momir Nikolić, Case No. IT-02-60/1-A, Judgment on Sentencing Appeal (ICTY, Mar. 8, 2006).

Prosecutor v. Dusko Tadic, Case No. IT-03-66-T, Decision on the Defense Motion for an Interlocutory Appeal on Jurisdiction (ICTY, Oct. 2, 1995).

Prosecutor v. Dusko Tadic, Case No. IT-94-1-A, Appeal Judgment (ICTY, July 11, 1999).

Protocol Additional to the Geneva Conventions of August 12, 1949, and relating to the Protection of Victims of International Armed Conflicts (Protocol I), 1125 U.N.T.S. 3 (June 8, 1977).

Prugh, G.S. (1975), LAW AT WAR: VIETNAM 1964-1973 74 (Washington: Department of the Army).

Public Committee against Torture in Israel and Palestinian Society for the Protection of Human Rights and the Environment v. Israel and Others, Case No. HCJ 769/02, Judgment, Volume 2 2006 ISRAEL LAW REPORTS 459 (the Supreme Court Sitting as the High Court of Justice, December 14, 2005), *available at* http://elyon1.court.gov.il/Files_ENG/02/690/007/A34/02007690.A34.pdf (visited on October 12, 2013).

Pufendorf, S. (1672), ON THE LAW OF NATURE AND NATIONS (DE JURE NATURAE ET GENTIUM, (Oxford: Clarendon Press, C.H. Oldfather and W.A. Oldfather, trans., 1934).

Questore di Verona v. Diego Zenatti (October 21, 1999), Case C-67/98, Judgment of the Court, ECR I-07289, *available at* http://eur-lex.europa.eu/LexUriServ/LexUriServ.do?uri=CELEX:61998J0067:EN:HTML (visited on October 7, 2013).

R. v. Arkell, 2 S.C.R. 695 (1990).

R. v. Khawaja (December 14, 2012), 2012 SCC 69.

Rawls, (1971), A THEORY OF JUSTICE (Cambridge, Massachusetts: The Belknap Press of Harvard University Press).

Regulation (EU) No. 513/2011 of the European Parliament and of the Council of May 11, 2011 amending Regulation (EC) No. 1060/2009 on credit rating agencies, para. 25, Official Journal of the European Union, L 145/30 (May 31, 2011), *available at* http://eur-lex.europa.eu/ LexUriServ/LexUriServ.do?uri=OJ:L:2011:145:0030:0056:EN:PDF .

Reisman, M., and W.K. Leitzau (1991), *Moving International Law from Theory to Practice: The Role of Military Manuals in Effectuating the Laws of Armed Conflict, in* THE LAW OF NAVAL OPERATIONS, 64 NAVAL WAR COL. INTERNATIONAL LAW (Newport: U.S. Naval War College, Horace B. Robertson, Jr., ed.).

Report of the High-level Panel on Threats, Challenges and Change (2004), *A more secure world: our shared responsibility*, U.N. Doc. A/59/565, *available at:* http://www2.ohchr.org/ English/bodies/hrcouncil/docs/gaA.59.565_En.pdf.

Report of the International Law Commission Covering its Second Session, June 5–July 29, 1950, U.N. GAOR, 5th Sess., Supp. No. 12, U.N. Doc. A/1316, *reprinted in* THE LAWS OF ARMED CONFLICTS: A COLLECTION OF CONVENTIONS, RESOLUTIONS, AND OTHER DOCUMENTS (Leiden: Martinus Nijhoff, Dietrich Schindler and Jiri Toman, eds., 1988).

Report of the Special Investigatory Commission on the Targeted Killing of Salah Shehadeh, February 27, 2011, *available at* http://www.pmo.gov.il/NR/rdonlyres/DA339745-7D9F-4 0C7-B20F-4481AAF1F4C7/0/reportshchade.pdf (in Hebrew).

Resnik, J. (1988), *On the Bias: Feminist Reconsiderations of the Aspirations for Our Judges*, 61 SOUTHERN CALIFORNIA LAW REVIEW 1877.

Reynolds, J. (2005), *Collateral Damage on the 21st Century Battlefield: Enemy Exploitation of the Law of Armed Conflict, and the Struggle for a Moral High Ground*, 56 AIR FORCE LAW REVIEW 1.

Ristroph, A. (2005), *Proportionality as a Principle of Limited Government*, 55 DUKE LAW JOURNAL 263.

Rodin, D. (2002), WAR AND SELF-DEFENSE (Oxford: Oxford University Press).

Rodley, N. (2009), *The Extraterritorial Reach and Applicability in Armed Conflict of the International Covenant on Civil and Political Rights: A Rejoinder to Dennis and Surena*, 14 EUROPEAN HUMAN RIGHTS LAW REVIEW 628.

Rogers, A.P.V. (2009), *Direct Participation in Hostilities: Some Personal Reflections*, 48 MILITARY LAW & LAW OF WAR REVIEW 143.

Rome Statute of the International Criminal Court (July 17, 1998), U.N. Doc. A/CONF.183/9, 2187 U.N.T.S. 90, *entered into force* July 1, 2002, *reprinted in* 37 I.L.M. 999, *available at* http:// untreaty.un.org/cod/icc/statute/99_corr/cstatute.htm .

Roper v. Simmons, 543 U.S. 551, 125 S.Ct. 1183 (2005).

Rose, G. (August 26, 2011), *Irregular warfare blows hole in Geneva rules*, THE AUSTRALIAN 33.

Rubin, A. (1988), THE LAW OF PIRACY, 63 NAVAL WAR COLLEGE INTERNATIONAL LAW STUDIES (Newport: U.S. Naval War College), *available at* https://www.usnwc.edu/ getattachment/4fab43dc-2cd2-4595-8420-4038d7bc1426/The-United-States-of-America-and-the-Law-of-Piracy.aspx .

Rubinstein, A., and Y. Roznai (2011), *Human Shields in Modern Armed Conflicts: the Need for Proportionate Proportionality*, 93 STANFORD LAW AND POLICY REVIEW 94.

Ruichi Shimoda et. al. v. The State, 355 Hanrei Jiho 17 (1963), 32 I.L.R. 626, *translated in* 8 Jap. Ann. Int'l L. 231 (1964), *available at* http://www.icrc.org/ihl-nat .

Ryan, C. (April 1983), *Self-Defense, Pacifism, and the Possibility of Killing,* 93 ETHICS 508.

Safire, W. (August 13, 2006), *On Language: Proportionality* N.Y. TIMES.

Sanchez, R.S. (2008), WISER IN BATTLE (New York: Harper Perennial).

Schabas, W. (No. 2 2007), *Lex Specialis? Belt and Suspenders? The Parallel Operation of Human Rights Law and the Law of Armed Conflict, and the Conundrum of Jus Ad Bellum,* 40 ISRAEL LAW REVIEW 592.

THE INTERNATIONAL CRIMINAL COURT: A COMMENTARY ON THE ROME STATUTE (2010) (Oxford: Oxford University Press)

Schachter, O. (1986), *In Defense of International Rules on the Use of Force,* 53 UNIVERSITY OF CHICAGO LAW REVIEW 113.

Scharf, M.P. (2013), CUSTOMARY INTERNATIONAL LAW IN TIMES OF FUNDAMENTAL CHANGE: RECOGNIZING GROTIAN MOMENTS (Cambridge: Cambridge University Press).

Scheffer, D.J. (1999), *The United States and the International Criminal Court,* 93 AMERICAN JOURNAL OF INTERNATIONAL LAW 14.

Schmitt, M. (2008), *Asymmetrical Warfare and International Humanitarian Law,* 62 AIR FORCE LAW REVIEW 1.

Cyber Operations and the Jus in Bello: Key Issues, in INTERNATIONAL LAW AND THE CHANGING CHARACTER OF WAR 69, 87 NAVAL WAR COLLEGE INTERNATIONAL L. STUDIES 215 (Raul A. "Pete" Pedrozo and Daria P. Wollschlaeger, eds.).

Deconstructing Direct Participation in Hostilities: The Constitutive Element, 42 N.Y.U. JOURNAL OF INTERNATIONAL LAW & POLICY 697 (2010).

Fault Lines in the Law of Attack, in TESTING THE BOUNDARIES OF INTERNATIONAL HUMANITARIAN LAW 277 (Susan C. Breau and Agnieszka Jachec-Neale, eds. 2006).

Precision Attack and International Humanitarian Law, 87 INTERNATIONAL REVIEW OF THE RED CROSS 445 (2005).

Human Shields in International Humanitarian Law, 38 ISRAEL YEARBOOK ON HUMAN RIGHTS 17 (2008).

Seneca, *On Anger, in* SENECA: MORAL AND POLITICAL ESSAYS (Cambridge: Cambridge University Press, John M. Cooper and J.F. Procope, eds., trans. 1995).

On Mercy, in SENECA: MORAL AND POLITICAL ESSAYS (Cambridge: Cambridge University Press, John M. Cooper and J.F. Procope, eds., trans. 1995).

Shakespeare, KING LEAR, Act I, Scene IV, spoken by the Duke of Albany.

Sherman, N. (2005), STOIC WARRIORS: THE ANCIENT PHILOSOPHY BEHIND THE MILITARY MIND (Oxford: Oxford University Press).

Sherman, W.T. (1875), MEMOIRS OF GENERAL W.T. SHERMAN (Des Moines: The Library of America 1990).

Short, *Operation Allied Force From the Perspective of the NATO Air Commander, in* LEGAL AND ETHICAL LESSONS OF NATO'S KOSOVO CAMPAIGN, 78 NAVAL WAR COLLEGE. INTERNATIONAL LAW STUDIES 215 (Andru Wall, ed., 2002).

Shue, H. (2008), *Do We Need a "Morality of War"? in* JUST AND UNJUST WARRIORS: THE MORAL AND LEGAL STATUS OF SOLDIERS 87 (New York: Oxford University Press, David Rodin and Henry Shue, eds.).

Sloane, R. (2009), *The Cost of Conflation: Preserving the Dualism of Jus ad Bellum and Jus in Bello in the Contemporary Law of War*, 34 YALE JOURNAL OF INTERNATIONAL LAW 47.

Solem v. Helm, 463 U.S. 277, 284 (1983).

Schmidt, M.A. (December 14, 2011), *Junkyard Gives up Secret Accounts of Massacre in Iraq*, N.Y. TIMES.

Schill, S. (Nov. 2006), *Revisiting a Landmark: Indirect Expropriation and Fair and Equitable Treatment in the ICSID Case Tecmed*, 3 TRANSNATIONAL DISPUTE MANAGEMENT 1.

Schwartkopf, N., with Petre, P. (1992), IT DOESN'T TAKE A HERO (New York: Bantam Books).

Solis, G. (2010), THE LAW OF ARMED CONFLICT: INTERNATIONAL HUMANITARIAN LAW IN WAR (Cambridge: Cambridge University Press).

Sosa v. Alvarez-Machain, 542 U.S. 692, 750 (2004).

Spyridon Roussalis (Claimant) v. Romania (Respondent), ICSID Case No. ARB/06/1 (Award), (December 7, 2011), *available at* https://icsid.worldbank.org/ICSID/FrontServlet?requestTy pe=CasesRH&actionVal=showDoc&docId=DC2431_En&caseId=C70.

State Farm Mutual Auto. Ins. Co. v. Campbell, 538 U.S. 408 (2003).

Statute of the International Court of Justice (June 26, 1945), 59 Stat. 1055, 3 Bevans 1179.

Steinhardt, R. (1994), *Book Review, European Administrative Law*, 28 GEO. WASHINGTON JOURNAL OF INTERNATIONAL LAW & ECONOMICS 225.

Stoke-on-Trent v. B&Q, (1992) Case C-169/91,1992 E.C.R. I-6625.

Stone, J. (1954), LEGAL CONTROLS ON INTERNATIONAL CONFLICT .

Suarez, F. (1610), *On War* (DISPUTATION XIII, DE TRIPLICI VIRTUE THEOLOGICA: CHARITATE), *in* SELECTIONS FROM THREE WORKS Disputation XIII (Oxford: Clarendon Press, Gladys L. Williams, Ammi Brown, and John Waldron, trans., 1944).

Sweet, A., and Mathews, J. (2008), *Proportionality Balancing and Global Constitutionalism*, 47 COLUMBIA JOURNAL OF TRANSNATIONAL LAW 72.

Taber, R. (2002), WAR OF THE FLEA: THE CLASSIC STUDY OF GUERILLA WARFARE (Dulles VA: Potomac Books).

TALLINN MANUAL ON THE INTERNATIONAL LAW APPLICABLE TO CYBER WARFARE (2013), Prepared by the International Group of Experts at the Invitation of the NATO Cooperative Cyber Defence Center of Excellence (Cambridge: Cambridge University Press, Michael N. Schmitt, ed.).

Taylor, R. (June 2011), *The Capture Versus Kill Debate: Is the Principle of Humanity Now Part of the Targeting Analysis When Attacking Civilians Who Are Directly Participating in Hostilities?*, THE ARMY LAWYER.

Territorial and Maritime Dispute (Nicarauga v. Colombia)(November 19, 2012), Judgment, (International Court of Justice), *available at* http://www.icj-cij.org/docket/files/124/17164. pdf (visited on March 18, 2013).

Tempelman v. Directeur van de Rijksdienst(2005), Joined Cases C-963 & C-97/03E.C.R. I-1895.

The "Honsinmaru" Case (Japan v. Russian Federation) Application for Prompt Release (August 6, 2007), Case No. 14, Judgment (International Tribunal for the Law of the Sea), *available at* http://www.itlos.org/fileadmin/itlos/documents/cases/case_no_14/Judgment_ Honshinmaru_No._14_E.pdf (visited on October 7, 2013).

The "Juno Trader Case" (Saint Vincent and the Grenadines v. Guinea-Bissau) Application for Prompt Release, (December 18, 2004), Case No. 13, Judgment (International Tribunal for the Law of the Sea), *available at* http://www.itlos.org/fileadmin/itlos/documents/cases/case_no_13/judgment_181204_eng.pdf (visited on September 9, 2013).

THE STATUTE OF THE INTERNATIONAL COURT OF JUSTICE: A COMMENTARY (2006) (Andreas Zimmerman, Christian Tomushat, Karin Oellers-Frahm, eds. 2006).

Tison v. Arizona, 481 U.S. 137, 149, 107 S.Ct. 1676, 95 L.Ed.2d 127 (1987).

Treaty of Lisbon, Amendments to the Treaty on European Union and to the Treaty Establishing the European Community, Doc. No. C 306/10 (December 17, 2007), OFFICIAL JOURNAL OF THE EUROPEAN UNION.

Tridimas, T. (1996), *The Principle of Proportionality in Community Law: From the Rule of Law to Market Integration*, 31 IRISH JURIST 83.

UNITED NATIONS CHARTER

United Nations Conference on Trade and Development, (2012), EXPROPRIATION: UNCTAD SERIES ON ISSUES IN INTERNATIONAL INVESTMENT AGREEMENTS, A SEQUEL, *available at* http://unctad.org/en/Docs/unctaddiaeia2011d7_en.pdf (visited on October 7, 2013).

United Nations Convention on the Law of the Sea (December 10, 1982), 1833 U.N.T.S. 397, *available at* http://www.un.org/depts/los/convention_agreements/texts/unclos/UNCLOS-TOC.htm (visited on October 2, 2013).

United Nations Convention on Prohibitions or Restrictions on the Use of Certain Conventional Weapons Which May Be Deemed to Be Excessively Injurious or to have Indiscriminate Effects, Protocol I (October 27, 1980), U.N. Doc. A/Conf.95/15, 19 I.L.M. 1523.

United Nations General Assembly, General Assembly Resolution 56/83 (December 12, 2001), and corrected by document A/56/49(Vol. I)/Corr.4. International Law Commission, *Draft Articles on Responsibility of States for Internationally Wrongful Acts, available at* http://untreaty.un.org/ilc/texts/instruments/english/draft%20articles/9_6_2001.pdf.

United Nations Human Rights Committee, *General Comment No. 29*, U.N. Doc. CCPR/C/21/Rev.1/Add.11 on Art. 4 ICCPR, ¶ 16 (2001).

United Nations Human Rights Committee, *General Comment No. 31 [80], The Nature of the General Legal Obligation Imposed on States Parties to the Covenant,* Adopted on March 29, 2004 (2187th meeting), U.N. Doc. CCPR/C/21/Rev.1/Add. 13.

Doc. CCPR/C/GC/34, *available at* http://www2.ohchr.org/english/bodies/hrc/comments.htm (visited on August 18, 2013).

United Nations, Report of the Secretary-General, (1970), *Respect for Human Rights in Armed Conflict.*, U.N. Doc. A/8052.

United Nations, *Report of the Secretary General pursuant to paragraph 2 of Security Council Resolution 808*, (May 29, 1993), U.N. Doc. S/2-5704.

United Nations Security Council Resolution 664 (August 18, 1990), U.N. Doc. S/RES/664, *available at* http://unscr.com/en/resolutions/664 (visited on October 11, 2013).

United States—Definitive Safeguard Measures on Imports of Circular Welded Carbon Quality Line Pipe from Korea, (February 15, 2002), Report of the Appellate Body, WTO doc. WT/DS202/AB/R. (WTO Appellate Body).

United States—Tax Treatment for "Foreign Sales Corporations" Recourse to Arbitration by the United States under Article 22.6 of the DSU and Article 4.11 of the SCM Agreement, (August 30, 2002), Case No. WT DS/108/ARB, *reprinted in* 41 I.L.M. 1400 (2002).

UNITED STATES CONSTITUTION, AMEND X

United States v. Krupp (1950), 9 TRIALS OF WAR CRIMINALS BEFORE THE NUREMBERG MILITARY TRIBUNALS UNDER CONTROL COUNCIL LAW NO. 10, 1436.

United States v. Wilhelm von Leeb, et al.(The High Command Case)(1949), US Military Tribunal, Nuremberg, Judgment of October 27, 1948, XII LAW REPORTS OF TRIALS OF WAR CRIMINALS (London: United Nations War Crimes Commission), available at http://www.ess.uwe.ac.uk/wcc/ghctrial1.htm (visited on October 11, 2013).

US Department of the Army (1956), THE LAW OF LAND WARFARE, DEPARTMENT OF THE ARMY FIELD MANUAL 27-10 (Washington: Government Printing Office).

US Department of Justice, *White Paper: Lawfulness of a Lethal Operation Directed Against a U.S. Citizen Who Is a Senior Operational Leader of Al-Qa'ida or An Associated Force, available at* http://msnbcmedia.msn.com/i/msnbc/sections/news/020413_DOJ_White_Paper.pdf .

Uthman al-Mukhtar, (December 26, 2010), *Local Sunnis Haunted by the Ghosts of Abu Ghraib*, SUNDAY HERALD.

Vattel, E. (1758), LE DROIT DES GENS, OU PRINCIPES DE LA LOI NATURELLE, APPLIQUÉ À LA CONDUITE ET AUX AFFAIRES DES NATIONS ET DES SOUVERAINS (THE LAW OF NATIONS, OR PRINCIPLES OF THE LAW OF NATURE, APPLIED TO THE CONDUCT AND AFFAIRS OF NATIONS AND SOVEREIGNS)(Washington: Carnegie Institution, Charles G. Fenwick, trans. 1916).

Vernon, A. (June 23, 2006), Editorial, *The Road From My Lai*, N.Y. TIMES.

Vitoria, F. (1557), DE INDUS ET DE IVRE BELLI REFLECTIONES, (REFLECTIONS ON INDIANS AND ON THE LAWS OF WAR)(Washington DC: The Carnegie Institution, John Pawley Bate trans., 1917).

Waldron, J. (Winter 2009), *Post Bellum Aspects of the Laws of Armed Conflict*, 31 LOYOLA L.A. INTERNATIONAL LAW & COMPARATIVE LAW REVIEW 31.

Walzer, M. (1977), JUST AND UNJUST WARS (New York: Basic Books).

Wasiński, M. *Odpowiedść Prawna Polki za incydent w Nangar Khel* a stwo i prawo miesie c ni organ r es enia prawni w pols ich 26 nós.

Waxman, M. (2011), *Cyber-attacks as "Force" Under UN Charter Article 2(4), in* INTERNATIONAL LAW AND THE CHANGING CHARACTER OF WAR, 87 NAVAL WAR COLLEGE INTERNATIONAL LAW STUDIES 43 (Raul A. "Pete" Pedrozo and Daria P. Wollschlaeger, eds.).

Wheaton, H. (1836), ELEMENTS OF INTERNATIONAL LAW (George Grafton Wilson ed., 1936).

Will, G. (JUNE 20, 2010), *Futility in Afghanistan: An NCO Fires off a Round of Illumination*, WASHINGTON POST.

Witt, J.R. (2012), LINCOLN'S CODE: THE LAWS OF WAR IN AMERICAN HISTORY (New York: Free Press).

Womack, B. (2003), *The Development and Recent Application of the Doctrine of Command Responsibility: With Particular Reference to the Mens Rea Requirement, in* 1 INTERNATIONAL CRIME AND PUNISHMENT: SELECTED ISSUES (University Press of America, Sienho Yee, ed., 2003).

Wright, L. (Nov. 9, 2009), *Letter From Gaza: CAPTIVES—What really happened during the Israeli attacks*, THE NEW YORKER 47.

Xiuli, H. (2007), *The Application of the Principle of Proportionality in Tecmed v. Mexico*, 6 CHINESE JOURNAL OF INTERNATIONAL LAW 635.

Yesh Din v. Commander of IDF Forces in Judaea and Samaria, et. al, (December 26, 2011), HCJ 2164/09.

Ziegler, R., and S. Otzari (No. 1, 2012), Do Soldiers' Lives Matter?, 45 ISRAEL LAW REVIEW 53.

Zwaan-de Vries v. the Netherlands, Comm. No. 182/1984, U.N. Doc. CCPR/C/29/D/182/1984 (1987).

Index